STATISTICAL PROCESS CONTROL AND QUALITY IMPROVEMENT

Gerald Smith
Cayuga Community College

Merrill, an imprint of
Macmillan Publishing Company
New York

Collier Macmillan Canada, Inc.
Toronto

Maxwell Macmillan International Publishing Group
New York | *Oxford* | *Singapore* | *Sydney*

Editor: Stephen Helba
Production Editor: Constantina Geldis
Cover Designer: Brian Deep

This book was set in Times Roman.

Macmillan Publishing Company
866 Third Avenue, New York, New York 10022

Collier Macmillan Canada, Inc.

Library of Congress Cataloging-in-Publication Data

Smith, Gerald, 1939–
    Statistical process control and quality improvement / Gerald
Smith.
        p.   cm.
    Includes index.
    ISBN 0-675-21160-3
    1. Process control—Statistical methods.   2. Production
management—Quality control.   I. Title.
TS156.8.S618   1991
658.5′62—dc20   90-41213
                                                                    CIP

Printing: 1 2 3 4 5 6 7 8 9   Year: 1 2 3 4

To Julie

MERRILL'S INTERNATIONAL SERIES
IN ENGINEERING TECHNOLOGY

PREFACE

NEED

Statistical process control (SPC) is not a new topic in industry: It has been used off and on since its development in the 1920s. However, since the 1970s it has become an extremely important tool. A new economic age is developing in which the demand for quality is rapidly increasing, with a resulting global competition of companies striving to provide that quality. The detection system of final inspection, a costly method of quality control, is giving way to a prevention system that uses in-process inspection and SPC to build quality into a process. This change requires extensive training in SPC. Also, for the most effective application of SPC, management must coordinate a team effort in which everyone in the work force can contribute meaningfully to the quality effort.

PURPOSE

This book was written with the following goals:

- To give the student a solid foundation on control charts: setting scales, charting, interpreting, and analyzing process capability.
- To teach the student the quality concepts and problem-solving techniques associated with statistical process control.
- To present a management philosophy for successful application of statistical process control.
- To provide a readable source of SPC topics that the student can refer to as the on-the-job need arises.

FLEXIBILITY

This book is designed for use in two-year and four-year colleges, as well as industry. The order of the chapters features a low-level mathematics approach so that anyone with a basic mathematics background can learn the control chart concepts in Chapters 1 through 8, the problem-solving concepts in Chapter 10, and the case studies in Chapter 13.

This books is mathematics-friendly:

- Only the needed mathematics is presented.
- The mathematics knowledge that is required for each topic is reviewed at the introduction of the topic.
- All the mathematics for the entire book is logically developed in Appendix A.

The entire book contains enough material for a three-credit-hour course. The mathematics prerequisite for someone studying the entire book should be Elementary Algebra.

The recommended sequence for college is Chapters 1 through 4, Appendix A, and then Chapters 5 through 13. This covers the goals, philosophy, and basic control chart concepts first; all the mathematics second; and the control charting and other related topics third. The needed math is then reinforced because it is covered again with the specific SPC topics.

The recommended sequence for industry is Chapters 1 through 10 and 13. Chapters 11 and 12 are more job-specific and may be taught to particular groups. Appendix A can be taught at any time if a more thorough understanding of the probability concepts in chart interpretation or sampling is desired. Appendix A can also be taught piecemeal to provide more depth or additional work to accompany the mathematics topics that are presented as needed in the text.

EXAMPLES AND ILLUSTRATIONS

The examples have been carefully chosen to provide a thorough understanding of the concepts involved. A detailed, step-by-step format has been used throughout the book to provide a pattern that can be used effectively, both for the immediate problems and for future reference. The examples feature worksheets and control charts to be filled in by the student and completed worksheets and charts for checking results.

ACKNOWLEDGMENTS

I thank the following reviewers for their comments and suggestions: Thomas Lavender, Catawba Valley Community College; Clarence Fauber, Indiana State University; George MacRitchie, Owens Technical College; Gary Winek, Southwest Texas State University; Steven Redmer, Lakeshore Technical College; Robert Walder, Clark State Community College; Michael Bowman, Indiana University–Purdue University; and Donna Summers, University of Dayton.

CONTENTS

5
The Normal Probability Distribution   69

6
Variables Control Charts   95

7
Precontrol Charts and Individuals and Moving Range (x and MR) Charts   157

8
Attributes Control Charts 189

9
Interpreting Control Charts 215

10
Problem Solving 265

13
Case Studies

385

A
Mathematics and Statistics

393

B
Charts and Tables 469

C
Glossary of Symbols   480

Index   483

1

INTRODUCTION TO STATISTICAL PROCESS CONTROL

OBJECTIVES

- Know the statistical signals that are used to improve a manufacturing process.
- Differentiate between the detection model and the prevention model for quality control.
- Identify the goals for using statistical process control (SPC).
- Learn the techniques that utilize SPC.
- Identify several positive effects of SPC.
- Learn the problem-solving model that utilizes SPC for process improvement.
- Describe four important aspects of quality.

Dedication to constant improvement in quality and productivity is needed to prosper in today's economic climate. Yesterday's standards are not good enough in the world-class competition that is becoming the norm for more and more businesses. Today one company's product competes with similar ones produced in other countries. The "Made in America" label is no longer enough to sell a product; the consumer looks for the best value in a product. If U.S. companies want to succeed in a world market, their products must be competitive.

Today each company employee must be committed to the use of effective methods to achieve optimum efficiency, productivity, and quality to produce competitive goods. Statistical process control (SPC), in its broad sense, is a collection of production methods and management concepts and practices that can be used throughout the organization. SPC involves the use of statistical signals to improve performance and to maintain control of production at higher quality levels. It can be applied to any area where work is done. The statistical concepts that are applied in SPC are very basic and can be learned by everyone in the organization. Production workers must know how SPC applies to their specific jobs and how it can be used to improve their output. Supervisors must be aware of the ways SPC can be used in their sections, be prepared to help their production workers utilize SPC, and be receptive to suggestions for improvements from the workers who are effectively using SPC. Managers must know how SPC can be used to improve quality and productivity simultaneously. They must create and maintain a management style that emphasizes communication and cooperation between levels and between departments. Their goal must be to develop a working atmosphere that maximizes everyone's contribution to the production of competitive products.

1.1 PREVENTION VERSUS DETECTION

One of the major problems in manufacturing today is that some companies' version of quality control is simply to find defective items after they are made. This is referred to as the *detection* system of quality; however, this system doesn't really achieve quality, even though it does weed out some products of excessively poor quality. SPC, on the other hand, leads to a system of *prevention*, which will replace the existing system of detection. Statistical signals are used to improve a process systematically so that the production of substandard materials is prevented.

Detection models, as Figure 1.1 illustrates, usually rely on a corps of inspectors to check the product at various stages of production and catch errors. This quality control method is extremely inadequate and wasteful. Money, time, and materials are invested in products or services that are not always usable or satisfactory. After-the-fact inspection is uneconomical and unreliable. Inspection without analysis and subsequent action on the process neither improves nor maintains product quality. Inspection plans cannot find all the defective items, and the waste is appalling! The company pays an employee to make the defective item and then pays an inspector to try to find it. If the inspector finds it, the company pays another employee to fix it. Also, defective products that aren't found lead to warranty costs, reputation damage, and cancelled orders. Unless action is taken to correct a faulty process, the percent of the output that is defective will remain constant.

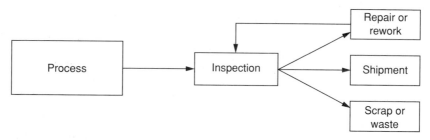

FIGURE 1.1
The detection model.

EXAMPLE 1.1 How good are your inspection skills? In the following paragraph, treat the letter *f*, whether capitalized or lowercased, as a defective item. Inspect the paragraph and count the number of defective items.

The study of SPC can be both fun and rewarding for everyone. When you find out that the fundamental ideas of statistics are fairly easy to learn, you will discover that your efforts result in a great deal of satisfaction. If you treat a production problem as a puzzle, the application of SPC provides clues for its solution, and when the puzzle is finally solved the feeling of satisfaction is very fulfilling. Puzzles can be frustrating, but their final solution is fun.

Solution

There are twenty-three defective items. Did you find them all the first time? The second time? This example illustrates one of the problems with inspection: It is easy to miss defective items. The results can actually be worse when two inspectors are used, because the first inspector expects the second inspector to find the missed defectives and the second inspector assumes that the first inspector found all the defective items. Shared responsibility can mean that no one takes responsibility.

One of the statistics lessons taught later in this text emphasizes that unless improvements are made on the manufacturing process, the percent of defective products that are produced now, next week, and next year will remain substantially the same. That is why it makes sense to avoid producing the defective item in the first place! This is the basis for the prevention model.

The prevention model uses statistical signals at appropriate points in the process to improve the procedure and to maintain control at the improved level. Statistical signals provide an efficient method for analyzing a process to indicate where improvements can both prevent the manufacture of defective items and improve the quality of the items produced. This is illustrated in Figure 1.2.

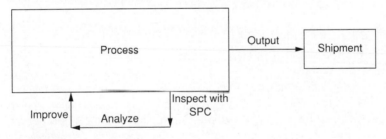

FIGURE 1.2
The prevention model.

Prevention avoids waste! If the product isn't flawless the first time, fix the process so the products will be right the next time. Monitor the process so that needed adjustments can be made before quality suffers.

Statistical process control is becoming the core around which businesses are run. Important decisions from optimum adjustment time decisions made at the shop-floor level to process change decisions made by management involve SPC. Statistical methods and techniques, such as control chart analysis of a process or its output, are now being used extensively to make economically sound decisions. The process analysis leads to appropriate actions for achieving and maintaining a state of statistical control and for reducing process variability.

A major obstacle to achieving high quality is product variability. Design quality may differ between products—for example, the Lincoln Towncar has design quality superior to that of the Ford Escort—but the demand for quality exists within each design category. All cars should have consistently high quality regardless of their competition, and that quality can only be achieved by decreasing the variability of all component parts.

SPC can improve quality by reducing product variability and production efficiency by decreasing scrap and rework. It can be used to monitor a process to determine when substandard items are about to be produced so that adjustments can be made to prevent the production of defective items.

1.2 SPC GOALS

The following are the primary goals of SPC:

- Minimize production costs. This is accomplished with a "make it right the first time" program. This type of program can eliminate costs associated with making, finding, and repairing or scrapping substandard products.
- Attain a consistency of products and services that will meet production specifications and customer expectations. Reduce product variability to a level that is well within specifications so the process output will match the desired design quality. This consistency leads to process predictability, which benefits the company by helping management meet quantity targets.
- Create opportunities for all members of the organization to contribute to quality improvement.
- Help management and production employees make economically sound decisions about actions affecting the process.

SPC can be used by both management and production people because it includes statistical methods that utilize the expertise of all employees of the company for problem solving. Management can use SPC as an effective tool for reducing operating costs and improving quality by using its methods for organizing and implementing the quality effort. The entire process becomes predictable so managers can achieve better planning for quantity targets. SPC creates a new management philosophy: Lines of communication are opened among all employee levels for the betterment of the company and the product.

Statistical process control also works for production employees. These employees can use it to develop effective tools to work more efficiently (not necessarily harder). When employees learn SPC they work more intelligently. They know from their control charts when they're doing a good job. SPC gives them the opportunity to influence work operations and be responsible for their jobs. It can help increase employees' pride in their work by allowing them input into the production process. Production workers are often the most qualified employees to determine what is right or wrong with their particular step in the process: as contributing members of a process control team, they can help with quality improvement.

1.3 STATISTICAL QUALITY CONTROL

Quality control has historically featured an inspection plan, gauge control, scrap and salvage control to handle substandard products, and acceptance procedures for incoming materials.

Statistical quality control uses statistical techniques for each of the four categories:

1. For inspection, Pareto charts (bar graphs used to prioritize problems), process control charts (charts of sample measurements over time), and process flow charts (charts of individual product measurements over time) are used to decide what should be inspected. The inspection data are charted to maintain statistical control and to aid in the reduction of process variability.
2. Gauge control involves statistical analysis that accounts for an instrument's stability over time, accuracy ("true" value versus measured value), repeatability (repeated use by the same person), reproducibility (repeated use by different people), and overall accuracy (combined effect).
3. Scrap and salvage is phased out as improvements are made in personnel training and in the process. Deming's 14 Points,[1] a list of management responsibilities outlined in Chapter 2, can be used as the basis of a management plan that can be a guide for companywide improvement.
4. Acceptance sampling plans involving inspection charts and operating curves are being phased out in favor of self-certified quality plans. Vendors are now asked to provide proof of quality.

Statistical process control must be adopted as an integral part of a long-term policy for continuous improvement in product quality and productivity. If SPC is limited to the use of control charts only, positive results will be rather limited. There is no quick fix for quality problems. SPC charts and techniques will show where problems exist and provide hints of the problem cause. Management must establish a responsive action process. SPC can be applied in any area where work is done: It is used to solve problems in engineering, production, inspection, management, service, and accounting. To be truly effective, however, SPC must become an important segment of corporate life as part of a total quality control program. It is an integral part of a new philosophy for doing business. Management has to change its traditional top-down approach and create, through proper training, a structure that is fully intralevel cooperative. New lines of communication must be formed, responsibility must be realistically assigned where the work is done, and a spirit of full cooperation for the good of the company must prevail.

1.4 STATISTICAL PROCESS CONTROL TECHNIQUES

Essential techniques in SPC include the use of

1. Process control charts to achieve and maintain statistical control at each phase of the process.

---

[1] W. Edwards Deming, *Quality, Productivity, and Competitive Position* (Cambridge, MA: Massachusetts Institute of Technology, 1982).

2. Process capability studies that use control charts to assess process capability in relation to product specifications and customer demands.
3. Statistical sampling as part of a self-certification plan for vendors.
4. Gauge capability studies.

SPC is an important tool and leads to many process improvements and positive process results such as

- Uniformity of output
- Reduced rework
- Fewer defective products
- Increased output
- Increased profit
- Lower average cost
- Fewer errors
- Higher quality output
- Less scrap
- Less machine downtime
- Less waste in production labor-hours
- Increased job satisfaction
- Improved competitive position
- More jobs

The preceding list is interactive: When SPC helps create a product that is low in variability and well within specifications, the output is more uniform and of higher quality. That automatically means that there are fewer defects to rework and less scrap, so output and profit increase. The use of SPC by production personnel can show the way toward refining the process and ironing out mistakes. More work time and machine time can be geared toward making good products instead of repairing faulty ones, so costs decrease. This leads to a lower average cost, an improved competitive position, and more jobs because demand for the company's product will increase.

1.5 THE PROBLEM-SOLVING MODEL

Step 1

The initial step toward applying SPC is diagramming and analyzing the process to decide where control charts may best be applied. Brainstorming sessions with representatives from all levels—from the shop floor to management—can be effectively used to create a thorough picture of the process. Useful tools for this procedure include flow charts (the step-by-step process flow), cause and effect diagrams (an organized list of potential problem causes), and storyboards (another way of picturing process flow). Quality is a companywide effort; cooperation and teamwork are needed to achieve it.

Step 2

After the process has been diagrammed, the second step is to find the best areas to concentrate the control chart efforts. Pareto charts, which graph the types of defects in a process, are very useful for showing the problems according to priority.

Step 3

The third step in this quality effort is variable identification. Critical measurements and other important characteristics such as surface condition need to be identified.

Step 4

The fourth step involves statistically testing the gauges using a gauge capability study. This must be done before measurements are taken for control charting. The variation that shows up on the control charts must reflect the process variation that needs to be reduced. If gauge variation is present in excessive amounts (there will always be some gauge variation), causes of the process variation cannot be isolated.

Step 5

The fifth step dictates the use of control charts to get the process in statistical control. There are two main sources of variation: One is embedded in the system and is referred to as common cause variation, and the other, which should be eliminated at this step, is called special cause, or assignable cause, variation and can be eliminated by the process control team. The team uses the control chart to find an out-of-control situation, evaluates what happened at that specific time to cause it, and then works to prevent that cause. This procedure continues until the control chart indicates that there are no more special cause variation problems. By this time the process is running as well as it possibly can without process modifications and is said to be in statistical control.

Step 6

The sixth step is to put the operator in charge. This step and step five actually occur simultaneously because the operator should be doing the control charting and attaining statistical control with the help of the process control team. The operator must know what this step entails:

- The operator must be taught what is "right."
- The operator needs the means for determining if that phase of the process is right.
- The operator must be able to change what is wrong in order to achieve statistical control.
- The operator is *responsible* for that specific phase in the process.

Step 7

The seventh step is applied once the process is in statistical control following steps five and six. This step is used to determine how capable the process is according to product specifications and customer expectations. A process capability study will measure the extent of common cause variation, or the inherent variability in the process, for comparison with the allowable variation given in the product specifications.

Step 8

The eighth step is designed to improve the process. Eighty-five percent or more of the process problems are handled at this stage, according to quality consultant W. Edwards Deming.[2] Changes in the process require management action. Teamwork and brainstorming sessions involving representatives from all levels of the operation can determine probable causes of excessive variation in the process. Process changes can be analyzed on control charts either singly or in variable interaction studies for signs of process improvement. When improvements are found, management must follow through and see that the appropriate changes are incorporated in the process *without backsliding*.

Step 9

The ninth and final step calls for a switch to precontrol, a monitoring technique that compares a measurement with target and warning measurements, when the process is in control and capable. This is a much simpler system and is quite effective for monitoring a process. An occasional return to control charts can provide a check on process capability. Another alternative at this step is to continue using control charts but increase the time interval between samples.

The Absolutes of Quality

The use of SPC has many positive side effects that were listed previously, but the main purpose in using it is to assist in improving quality and to control the desired level of quality when it is attained. There are four *absolutes of quality,* according to consultant Philip Crosby.[3]

1. "The definition of quality is conformance to requirements." All parts are well within design specification and the finished product conforms to design specifications.
2. "The system of quality is prevention," not detection. Prevention methods require a cost of only 3 to 4 percent of the sales dollar, whereas detection methods eat up 18 to 22 percent of the sales dollar.
3. "The performance standard is *zero defects*" for products bought and sold, the company goal should be no defects.

---

[2] Deming, *Quality, Productivity, and Competitive Position*.
[3] Philip B. Crosby, *Quality Without Tears* (New York: McGraw-Hill Book Company, 1984), 59, 68, 74, 85.

4. "The measure of quality is the price of nonconformance." That price consists of direct costs for doing things wrong or poorly and indirect costs that are related to customer satisfaction with cost, quality, service, and on-time delivery.

The goals, techniques, and results of SPC have been discussed briefly in this introduction along with a general outline of a problem-solving model. The various tools mentioned, such as diagrams and charts, are explained in detail in the following chapters.

EXERCISES

1. What is the detection model for quality control?
2. What is the prevention model for quality control?
3. What are the primary goals of SPC?
4. What techniques does SPC involve?
5. What are some of the improvements that can result from using SPC?
6. What are the nine steps in the problem-solving model?
7. What are the four absolutes of quality?

2

STRIVING FOR QUALITY: MANAGEMENT'S PROBLEM AND MANAGEMENT'S SOLUTION

OBJECTIVES

- Discuss the historical background to management's problem.
- Know Deming's 14 points for management.
- Learn Crosby's symptoms of trouble.
- Define Crosby's absolutes of quality.
- Discuss Crosby's 14 steps to quality improvement.
- Identify the major changes needed to institute a quality process.
- Know the major pitfalls that must be avoided when starting the quality process.

Technical literature abounds with SPC success stories in U.S. industry, but it also hints at many unmentioned failures. The Japanese have cornered the market for some products and have become the benchmark for quality with others; their industries are using SPC. Their remarkable success has been attributed to their widespread use of statistical signals. In an attempt to catch up, some U.S. companies have tried crash courses in statistics and SPC training but have accomplished nothing. If a statistics method works for the Japanese, why doesn't it work for *all* the U.S. companies that try it? Comparisons have been made between Japanese and U.S. schools, families, workers, and management techniques to try to pinpoint critical differences and discover the secret to Japanese success.

The answer that has slowly emerged is that SPC and other basic applications of statistics are absolutely necessary to achieve top quality but that they must also be combined with the appropriate management methods.

2.1 MANAGEMENT'S DILEMMA

American management techniques have been developed by 40 years of minor competition, quantity pressures to meet a seemingly unquenchable, worldwide demand, and a secondary regard to quality. Companies took a "weed out the bad ones, but keep that production rolling" attitude.

Management-employee relationships have been primarily adversarial in the United States. This relationship stems from a history of big business exploitation of workers and the reactionary pressures of the unions. Many companies have become accustomed to a constant power struggle between union and management. There is so much distrust that confrontations over contracts have led to plant closings and lost jobs.

An additional attitude problem hinders labor-management relations. Artisan skills long ago gave way to repetitive assembly line work. Workers were given relatively little training to do a very specific job. They were not credited with much knowledge of the process in which they were involved. The difference in education levels of management and the work force, combined with this process of deskilling jobs, has brought about a general underestimation of employees' intelligence and abilities. In many companies the worker has become the quality scapegoat. Management is convinced that poor quality stems from the faults of inadequate workers.

The educational lines that lead to management positions include primarily business and engineering. Neither curriculum, in all its variations, has traditionally included coursework on quality achievement or quality control (QC). Quality and QC were always relegated to checkers and inspectors to identify the bad products, both incoming and outgoing. Quality and productivity were conceived as opposing attributes. Slow careful work was thought to lead to high quality and low productivity, whereas fast work was associated with high productivity and low quality. The concept that high quality may be accompanied by high productivity and low production costs is completely foreign to many Chief Executive Officers (CEOs).

U.S. managers, with their heritage of disregard for quality, their noncommittal attitudes toward employees, and their adversarial management techniques, are now in a quandary. They are being economically defeated by companies that have a sense of fairness in their management style, respect and admiration for the abilities of their employees, and a firm commitment to competitive quality. Changes must be made in order for U.S. companies to claim their share of the top in an emerging global economy.

2.2 LEADERSHIP BY MANAGEMENT

Management can no longer pass the buck and blame poor quality on the workers. According to W. Edwards Deming, only about 15 percent of the quality problem can be attributed to the worker.[1] The other 85 percent of the problem is embedded in the manufacturing process, and nothing can be changed with the process unless it is management-directed.

---

[1] W. Edwards Deming, *Quality, Productivity, and Competitive Position* (Cambridge, MA: Massachusetts Institute of Technology, 1982).

Another favorite management dodge is the claim that U.S. companies can't compete with foreign companies because the U.S. wage scale is too high. The wage discrepancy between the U.S. industries and their foreign competitiors can often be counterbalanced by a combination of better technology, a better educated work force, and better management methods all focused on producing a top quality product. There are some U.S. companies that have already turned things around. Their quality has improved, and they have beaten the competition. There have also been cases in which U.S.-run plants have been closed, bought by Japanese firms, and reopened successfully with Japanese top management and the same American workers. Sharp Electronics of Japan did that with a company in Tennessee, and that plant has produced well over a million TV sets and microwave ovens since the change. A turn-around can be accomplished in U.S. industry, but management must lead the way.

One initial step that management must take toward making top quality products is to hire a quality consultant. The quality consultant will direct changes and provide the necessary training. Each consultant or consulting firm will have a specific plan, but all of the quality plans will have a pattern similar to the plans recommended by top consultants W. Edwards Deming and Philip Crosby. The basic recommendations of these two experts are presented in the following sections.

2.3 DEMING'S WAY

W. Edwards Deming is perhaps the consultant most responsible for awakening U.S. industry to the need for higher quality. Deming developed many of his management concepts during World War II. The control charts, developed by Walter Shewhart at Bell Laboratories in the 1920s, were used by many U.S. industries during the war. After the war, however, the emphasis in most U.S. companies evolved toward quantity. The demand for U.S. goods was high, and Deming's emphasis on top quality fell on deaf ears. He and another quality consultant, Joseph Juran, are credited with teaching management concepts, Statistical Process Control, and ways to implement the various SPC techniques to the Japanese. Deming was invited to Japan in 1950 as a quality consultant and convinced the Japanese that their only chance to succeed as a producing nation was to make top quality products. Those old enough to remember the shoddy goods produced by the Japanese, both before World War II and after, will realize what a dramatic change their quest for quality has brought about in the value of their products.

Deming returned to the United States in the late 1970s dedicated to changing the U.S. way of doing business. He knew that the Japanese businesses he had helped were dominating world markets with their products and that the competing U.S. companies were being forced out of business. He was featured on national television in an NBC documentary titled "If Japan Can . . . Why Can't We?" in 1980. Since that time he has been working steadily with many of America's major industries.

Deming's message is that quality starts at the top of the corporate structure and pervades every phase and level all the way to the shop floor. Without top management's unequivocal commitment and constant pressure for higher quality, a company's efforts will usually be wasted.

Management style has to change too. Companies must work strategically to beat the competition: Each employee in the company must be a contributing member of the company team, dedicated to making top quality products. Many companies have an operation structure in which supervisors and engineers are responsible for making production improvements. However, these workers are usually so involved in solving the company's never-ending sequence of daily problems that they can devote very little of their time to improvements. Companies that initially thrived because of technological improvements in a product are stalled when it comes to new innovations and advancement in technology. Instead of falling behind the competition, these companies should get more people involved in process improvements. In fact, *everyone* involved in a process should take part in process improvements. Companies need a new teamwork structure that will actively involve all employees. This *is* possible, and it has already happened in some companies, but management has to lead the way. Management must organize and orchestrate the company team. Deming has outlined a 14-point management plan to coordinate a company-team approach to top quality and high productivity.

2.4 DEMING'S 14 POINTS FOR MANAGEMENT[2]

1. "Create a constancy of purpose to improve quality and service, to become competitive, and to stay in business."

Many companies become trapped in a constant sequence of short-term solutions and become overinvolved in immediate problems. It is very important to budget for the future. Long-term planning is a necessity and must be based on an unshakable policy of high quality. Continually investigate the possibility for new products, new markets, and new ways to compete efficiently in the present markets. Plan carefully for the necessary training, equipment, and production. Allocate funds for ongoing education, design improvements, and equipment maintenance. Both management and production workers should constantly seek technological improvements of processes. Major technological breakthroughs do occur, but a continuous sequence of small gains in efficiency and minor improvements over a period of two or three years can often be the best path toward beating the competition.

2. "Adopt the new philosophy."

There is a new economic age of competition in a global economy. Previously accepted delays, mistakes, poor quality, and poor workmanship are no longer tolerated because other companies are always trying to do better. Every company should be striving to eliminate substandard products. Defects and defective items are not free: The total cost of producing, finding, and disposing of or repairing a defective item exceeds the cost of producing a good one.

---

[2]Reprinted from *Quality, Productivity, and Competitive Position* by W. Edwards Deming by permission of MIT and W. Edwards Deming. Published by MIT, Center for Advanced Engineering Study, Cambridge, MA 02139. Copyright 1982 by W. Edwards Deming.

3. "Cease dependence on mass inspection."

Inspection, by itself, is too late and too costly. Scrap, downgrading, and rework do not correct the process: The process will keep producing the same proportion of defective items until process improvements are made. Basic applications of statistics are needed at every phase of a process in order to make necessary improvements or to maintain an acceptable level of quality and production. Inspection must be built in as an integral part of the improvement-maintenance procedure, not as the single control of quality.

4. "End the practice of awarding business on the basis of price tag alone."

Learn to use meaningful measures of quality as well as price when deciding on purchases. Eliminate suppliers who cannot provide statistical evidence of quality. Both government and industry are being cheated when they follow rules that award business to the lowest bidder without considering quality. A large fraction of the problems that lead to poor quality and low productivity are due to poor quality incoming parts and materials and low quality machines and tools.

Purchasing managers should be trained to judge quality based on appropriate statistical evidence. Specifications have to be thorough so that incoming parts and material will blend properly in production assembly. The critical measurements on all incoming parts and material must be known. In some situations it may be necessary to follow a sample of incoming material through the whole production process to be sure that it blends adequately.

In order to qualify for the contract, suppliers should meet the following standards.

- Their management should be actively involved in the 14-point program.
- There should be evidence of sustained use of SPC. Any vendor who cannot provide evidence of quality will either have higher costs or will be sacrificing quality.
- The aim of suppliers should be to improve quality and decrease costs to the point at which customers search them out.
- A dependable source, responsive to needs on a long-term arrangement, is more important than initial price. Economies should result. If two or more suppliers are used on an item, a cutback to one who satisfies these criteria will reduce costs. Quality will improve, too, because variation owing to different suppliers will be eliminated.

5. "Constantly and forever improve the system of production and service."

Continually search for problems, reduce waste, and improve quality in every phase of the process. Statistical leadership will be required to separate special cause and common cause variation and to design and analyze tests for reducing variation.

Quality must be built in from the design stage. Teamwork among the designers, manufacturers, and customers is necessary to ensure that the final product does what it was intended to do. Quality control teams should be formed to utilize the expertise from all phases of management and production associated with the process. The combined team effort can be very effective in increasing both quality and production.

6. "Institute modern training methods on the job."

One of the greatest wastes in the United States is the failure to use the full abilities of the work force. Training must include a thorough understanding of the entire process and an individual's part in it. Every worker should know who the customer is and what the customer requires. The customer is often the next person in the production process, and it is just as important to satisfy that customer as it is to satisfy the customer that eventually receives the final product.

Statistical methods must be used to determine when training is completed. A variable standard for acceptable work is a big problem in training and supervision that must be overcome.

7. "Institute modern methods of supervision."

Modern supervisors must be regarded as leaders and facilitators, not as overseers. They must emphasize quality first and look for improvements in production quantity within the quality framework. The improvement in quality will automatically result in some improved productivity.

Supervisors must report to management on all conditions that are barriers to quality and need correction, and management must be prepared to respond. Supervisors should help the workers perform quality work.

8. "Drive out fear."

The economic loss due to fear is appalling. Fear of asking questions, expressing ideas, and reporting trouble can lead to problems with quality and lagging improvements. Employees must develop confidence in management in order to participate fully in the company's quality process.

Workers cannot perform their best unless they feel secure. Fear of change, of new knowledge, and of new responsibilities has to be confronted.

9. "Break down barriers between staff areas."

People in research, design, purchasing, production, and sales must work as a team to anticipate production problems. A rush into production can often cause costly delays that could have been avoided by a team approach. Process problems can best be solved by quality control teams that have members in all areas associated with the process.

10. "Eliminate numerical goals for the work force."

Eliminate targets, slogans, posters, and unrealistic goals such as zero defects. That approach makes management appear to be dumping their responsibilities on the work force. It implies that properly motivated production workers can accomplish zero defects, higher quality, and higher productivity and ignores the fact that the bulk of the problem lies with management. Instead, offer a plan that has realistic goals.

11. "Eliminate work standards and numerical quotas."

These guarantee inefficiency and high cost. Quotas encourage sporadic work habits such as working fast until the quota is almost met and then easing off for the remainder of the shift, which is detrimental to the quality effort. Piecework is even worse. People are either paid to make defective items or penalized for something that could be the system's fault if defect penalties are involved. What really caused the defect, the worker or the process? There is no piecework in Japan!

A quota is a fortress against improvements in quality and productivity. Work standards, rates, incentive pay, and piecework are manifestations of an inability to understand and provide appropriate supervision.

12. "Remove barriers that hinder the hourly worker."

Nothing should interfere with the worker's ability to do a good job. Job instructions should be thorough, concise, and understandable, and problems with inspection or gauges should not reflect unfairly on the worker. The supervisor should listen to the worker's observations regarding process problems and report back on action taken.

13. "Institute a vigorous program of education and training."

An organization needs not only good people, but also people who are improving themselves with education. Encourage education: Eliminate the fear of layoffs. As quality and productivity increase, fewer people will be needed on some jobs, but education and retraining can move displaced workers to another department. Education in simple but powerful statistical techniques is required of all people in management, engineering, production, design, quality control, finance, purchasing, and sales.

14. "Create a structure in top management that will push every day on the above 13 points."

Agree on the direction you want to take. Have the courage to break with tradition and explain to employees via seminars and other means such as newsletters and meetings why the change is necessary and why everyone must be involved. Management will require guidance from an experienced consultant who can teach statistical methods and develop in-house teachers.

Methods for improvement of quality are transferable to different problems and circumstances. Problem-solving principles are universal in nature. There is no quick fix, however. Sufficient education, effort, and time are needed for the 14-point program to pervade and be followed by all levels of management.

In Deming's commentary on point 13, he emphasizes that the fear of layoffs should be eliminated. That's one of the big differences in management style between Japanese and U.S. companies. In lean times, when product demand drops, U.S. companies lay off workers. In Japan, there is a set pattern for lean times:

1. Corporate dividends are cut.
2. Salaries and bonuses of top management are cut.

3. Salaries for middle management are cut.
4. Workers salaries' are cut. Any work force reduction occurs naturally through attrition or voluntary discharge.

Japanese companies also take advantage of low production periods to build for the future. They place more emphasis on long-term projects. For example, when steel production dropped drastically worldwide, the Kawasaki steel plant had the work force build a new-generation blast furnace that would give them an edge when the lean times were over.

Deming's 14-point program has not been widely adopted by U.S. industry. Top managers in many companies simply do not believe it. No more piecework? Eliminate quotas? "We've got production schedules to meet!" Quality? "If the workers would do their jobs right, we wouldn't have that problem!" The trouble is really with management and the production process? "Don't be ridiculous!"

The 14 points are definitely idealistic, and even Deming agrees that to get a company to follow the program effectively can take years. U.S. executives have relied on short-term goals and solutions for so long that they can barely conceive of a ten-year plan that will gradually and fully adapt the 14 points to their company. Too often, companies in economic trouble will shake up their top management structures or institute new programs and then eagerly look for results in the next quarterly report.

How should a specific company adapt the 14 points? Every company has its existing management style and track record of improvement changes. The 14-point program requires such a drastic change in attitudes and interpersonal relationships that many companies are stymied at the very start. The plan calls for the development of communication skills: people dealing with people. Within-level communication, between-level communication, and inter-departmental communication all have to develop in order for the 14 points to work. Group dynamics and teamwork are needed for planning instead of the "decree from above."

Deming and all the other quality consultants insist that changes have to start at the top management level. Real improvement can't happen any other way. If major changes were initiated at any intermediate level, they would eventually meet with disapproval at some higher management level. Training starts at the top as well; all managers need to understand the concepts and reasons for the recommended changes that will be made when the work force is trained. Top management also has to initiate and promote the new management style and ensure that it is adopted at all levels.

2.5 CROSBY'S APPROACH

Philip Crosby is probably the most commercially successful quality consultant in the United States. He was the vice president in charge of quality operations for 14 years at ITT before leaving to form his own corporate consulting firm, Philip Crosby Associates. As an integral part of his consulting service, he and his associates run a quality college in Winter Park, Florida, for seminars on various quality topics. Crosby's concepts agree for the most part with Deming's 14 points, but there are a few notable exceptions. The main thrust of the Crosby method is that it provides more of a step-by-step plan for management to follow.

Symptoms of Trouble[3]

How does a company tell if it is heading for trouble? It may surprise some managers that what Crosby lists as a trouble indicator is standard operating procedure in many companies. The following are symptoms of organizational trouble:

1. "The outgoing product or service normally contains deviations from the published, announced, or agreed-upon requirements." There always seems to be another crisis or problem cropping up. Brush fire management and off-specification waivers are common.
2. "The company has an extensive field service or dealer network skilled in rework and resourceful corrective action to keep the customers satisfied." The company has a large rework department, a customer relations department, or both. Customer engineers may "customize" the product to customer requirements, but that may be an admission of on-site finishing and debugging. Service organizations also have hot lines and other trouble-handling procedures for system failures.
3. "Management does not provide a clear performance or definition of standard quality, so the employees each develop their own." The traditional routine follows a pattern that emphasizes a schedule first, cost second, and quality third. Sloppy definitions of quality allow for regular exceptions and a "close enough" attitude.
4. "Management does not know the price of nonconformance." Generally nonconformance with standards amounts to 20 percent or more of the sales dollar in production industries and 35 percent or more of the operating cost in service industries. When the costs of appropriate education and training, with the subsequent savings that always accompany doing things right, are compared with the losses, it's always astounding that action was not taken sooner.
5. "Management denies that it is the cause of the problem." Executives fail to realize that inadequate attention to quality is the main problem in their company and that quality improvement will eliminate what they currently perceive as the problem.

Crosby believes that U.S. businesses have had problems with quality because they don't take quality seriously. They have to be as concerned with quality as they are with profit. When management respects the rights of customers as much as they do the rights of owners, banks, and stockholders, then consistent quality will be achieved. Management must believe that there is absolutely no reason to deliver a nonconforming product or service. The chief executive officer must be dedicated to customer satisfaction, and that satisfaction has to be measured in a way that can lead to corrective action. Management should establish a companywide emphasis on defect prevention and use that as a basis for continuous improvement. Few managers understand how the SPC techniques work, so it is a top priority that they learn the concepts involved. Statistical signals are used throughout the operation, and in order for managers to provide the necessary leadership, they have to know the potential applications and reasons that these applications are so important to the quality effort.

---

[3]Reprinted from Philip B. Crosby, *Quality Without Tears* (New York: McGraw-Hill Book Company, 1984), 1–5.

Crosby's Four Absolutes of Quality[4]

1. "The definition of quality is conformance to requirements."

Be sure the requirements are clear, understandable, and when necessary, accepted. Emphasize a "do it right the first time" attitude. Management must insist that there is absolutely no reason for selling a faulty product to a customer.

2. "The system of quality is prevention."

The prevention method features corrective changes in the process when problems occur with the product. SPC is used as an integral part of the prevention system. Think ahead. Look for opportunities for error and take preventative action.

3. "The performance standard is zero defects."

If you do not insist on zero defects from your suppliers, you are telling them in effect that it is acceptable for them to send nonconforming parts and materials. If you do not insist on zero defects from your workers, you're also telling them that it is all right to produce nonconforming products. People are conditioned to accept the concept that to err is human and therefore believe that all humans will err, which is faulty logic. Errors occur in some situations, but not in others; it really becomes a function of importance. Crosby claims, "Mistakes are caused by two factors: lack of knowledge and lack of attention." Education and training can eliminate the first cause, and a personal commitment to excellence (zero defects) and attention to detail will cure the second.

Nebulous standards, such as the Acceptable Quality Level (AQL) for incoming products, have a detrimental effect on concepts of excellence and high quality, but specific standards like zero defects or "do it right the first time" will lead the way to problem prevention.

4. "The measure of quality is the price of nonconformance."

Quality, as a management concern, is not taught in management schools. Quality is considered a technical function, not a management function, because it is never evaluated in financial terms. Crosby states that "the cost of quality is divided into two areas—the price of nonconformance (PONC) and the price of conformance (POC)." *PONC* is the total cost of doing things wrong: It is the sum of all the costs that are unnecessary when the product is made correctly the first time. By Crosby's estimate, PONC is approximately 20 percent of the sales dollar in a product industry and 35 percent in a service industry. *POC*, alternatively, is the sum of the costs associated with the quality effort: prevention measures and education costs. POC is about 3 to 4 percent of the sales dollar.

---

[4]Crosby, *Quality Without Tears*, 1–5.

Crosby's 14 Steps to Quality Improvement[5]

1. Management commitment.

Senior management holds the key. It has the mission of changing the culture of the company. It has to initiate a hassle-free management style and insist on an attitude of strict conformance to requirements. Management's credibility is usually low at first because of its history of short-term, short-lived solutions. There are several ways to change that attitude. First, a firm, clear statement that emphasizes the company policy on quality should be issued. Second, quality should be the first item on all meeting agendas. Third, top management officials should compose clear messages on quality and deliver them to everyone. The basic policy message should make these points:

- "We will deliver defect-free products to our customers, on time."
- Our company policy is conformance to requirements, and "do it right the first time" is our method.
- Complete customer satisfaction is the goal.

2. The "quality improvement team."

The team needs a clear direction and a good leader. Form the team to guide, coordinate, and support the quality process. Its members should consist of people who are good at clearing roadblocks and who represent all parts of the operation.

A committee consisting of a full-time quality coordinator, the team chair, top management official(s), and a quality consultant sets the overall strategy for the team. The team members all need the same educational base in quality improvement. The team functions include the following:

- Setting up appropriate educational activities for all involved.
- Methodically creating procedures and actions.
- Learning more about quality improvements through continued work with the improvement process.

3. "Measurement."

Measure your progress. The team needs to know how it is doing as the quality process evolves. The team is continuously involved in sequences of input, process, and output; these aspects of the quality process can be measured.

4. "The cost of quality."

Maintain an ongoing cost of quality. The company comptroller can work out a cost analysis of the quality effort. The initial PONC should be determined before the quality effort begins so that POC and savings can be realistically reflected.

---

[5]Crosby, *Quality Without Tears*, 1–5.

5. "Quality awareness."

Create a total quality awareness. If a communication device such as a regular newsletter exists, use a part of it to keep all employees aware of the effort and successes associated with the quality process. Start a quality newsletter if there isn't one initially. Emphasize management's commitment, the quality policy, and PONC.

6. "Corrective action."

Use SPC and problem-solving techniques to identify problems, find their root cause, and eliminate them. If suppliers have quality problems, meet with them and discuss requirements and ways of reducing nonconformities. Crosby emphasizes that "the real purpose of corrective action is to identify and eliminate problems forever."

7. "Zero defects (ZD) planning."

"A zero defects commitment is a major step forward in the thrust and longevity of the quality management process." Start planning for ZD day early. Invite speakers from government, customer companies, management, and unions. The quality team should carefully plan this first public commitment of the company's new quality process.

8. "Employee education."

See that everyone receives the same education on the quality process.

9. "ZD day."

This is the day when management makes its official commitment to quality in front of everyone. The public commitment ensures that management is serious about quality. ZD day is important because it is a deterrent to management backsliding on the quality process.

10. "Goal setting."

Set goals for the quality team. "Major goals should be chosen by the team and put on a chart for all to see." The chart should show a progress indicator.

11. "Error-cause removal."

Ask people to submit statements about problems that they are aware of so that solutions can be developed. The response to this request is usually overwhelming, so be sure to set the error-response procedure ahead of time:

- Decide upon an initial response to the submitting person.
- Choose a method of analysis and action for each response.
- Make a concluding response to the submitting person.

12. "Recognition" of good work in the quality process.

The creation of a recognition program for both management and employees is an important part of the quality effort. Don't rush into it, though; make sure it's meaningful and well deserved. The program should do the following:

■ Recognize hard-working people that are valuable to the quality effort.
■ Ensure that those recognized are chosen by their peers.
■ Provide a clear picture of what quality work is.
■ Provide living "beacons of quality" for others to emulate on a daily basis.

13. "Quality councils."

"Bring the quality professionals together and let them learn from each other."

14. Repetition.

"Do it all over again." Quality improvement is an ongoing process. Choose a new team with perhaps a one-member carry-over from a previous team. The new team approach provides a fresh look at the quality process and the quality problems.

2.6   A COMPARISON OF DEMING'S 14 POINTS AND CROSBY'S 14 STEPS

Both Deming and Crosby emphasize a total commitment to the quality process by top management, and both strongly promote the prevention system. They both stress education and the concept that striving for quality is a never-ending process. Deming is more explicit with his 14 points, but Crosby gives more direction by providing specific steps to take. Crosby urges a hassle-free management style, and Deming encourages managers to drive out fear and remove barriers that come between the workers and their ability to do a good job. The language may differ, but the message is similar.

The two do differ on some concepts. Some of Deming's points, such as the need for eliminating quotas and work standards and using modern methods of training and supervision, aren't in Crosby's approach at all. Crosby believes that it is important to know PONC, keep an ongoing POC, maintain an awareness of the quality effort, and have a recognition program. Deming opposes slogans, posters, and "unrealistic" goals such as zero defects. He believes that they are a management responsibility dodge that implies that quality problems are due to poor work by the work force. Crosby, on the other hand, likes the slogans and posters as part of a quality campaign and strongly believes in the zero defect concept.

2.7   WHICH WAY TO TOP QUALITY?

The preceding comparison of the approaches to high quality by two of the best quality consultants in the country shows enough difference in style and content to raise the question, "Is there a best way?" Recent literature on quality seems to emphasize that a melding of statistical and management methods is needed to bring U.S. industries into world-class competition. The use of statistical methods by everyone involved in the manufacturing process is really the third phase of the industrial revolution, following mechanization and mass production. All of a company's employees need some knowledge of statistical methods for SPC and problem solving. Statistics courses are often the most feared courses in any curriculum of study, but by focusing on practical statistics and applying the procedures to in-house data, employees can learn the important concepts in a meaningful way. People who have been life-long math dodgers can deal effectively with on-the-job data when they're shown the basic techniques and given a calculator. Deming emphasizes the belief that simple statistical concepts form a powerful tool for industrial applications.

Management methods must improve! Management's major goal should be to maximize the quality effort of the entire company work force. This can be realistically achieved only by fostering a dedication to quality that permeates every level, and the generating power has to be at the top level. Furthermore, the management method has to be hassle-free, as Crosby calls it. People don't work in a dedicated manner when they are hassled. Deming refers to this as removal of fear and barriers. This ideal, positive approach promotes teamwork:

- All channels of communication are kept open.
- Everyone is treated with respect.
- All employees are well trained.
- Everyone has a clear concept of the goals, both broad and specific, and of their potential contribution toward achieving those goals.
- All workers and managers pursue those goals in a coordinated manner.

2.8 AVOID THE PITFALLS IN THE QUEST FOR QUALITY[6]

Companies should avoid the following situations as they introduce their new strategies:

1. "Instant results."

Quality consultants emphasize that there is no quick fix to the quality problem. Remember, the Japanese were first introduced to the concepts of applying statistical methods in 1950, and their dominating influence on world markets wasn't really felt until the late 1970s. Fortunately, U.S. industry doesn't have as far to go as Japanese industry did following World War II.

2. "Lack of commitment by management."

Do not dump the burden on the work force by providing SPC training and nothing else. The quality effort is a coordinated process that involves everyone, and management has to lead the way.

---

[6]Richard McKee, "The ABC's for Process Control," *Quality* (August 1985).

3. "Lack of long-term planning."

Too often management is looking for results in time for the next quarterly report. Short-term impatience leads to a waste of time, effort, and money. A haphazard approach involves no meaningful change in the system.

4. "Limited application."

If only one part of a process uses SPC, no improvement in quality will be realized. GIGO: Garbage In, Garbage Out! When SPC is started in an industry in a limited way, it should be applied to a complete process, not just a part of a process, from start to finish. Then it should be established in another complete process, and another, until the entire company uses SPC.

5. "Overdependence on computerized QC."

Thorough training with the hand-held calculator on the basic concepts is necessary for complete understanding of the concepts. Computerized outputs can then be analyzed properly by those at the workstation and by the process control team when necessary.

6. "No market research."

The customer is the most important part of the process. Management must know the level of quality that is expected by customers.

7. "Lack of funds committed to the quality process."

Do not "pinch pennies." The initial monetary outlay in education costs and in production time lost for on-the-job training may seem extensive, but keep that long-term plan in mind. Remember, PONC is about 20 percent or more of sales, and POC is about 3 to 4 percent of sales.

8. "Underestimating the work force."

The best competitive effort can occur only when everyone in the organization is actively contributing to the quality process. Keep avenues of communication open and make sure that all employees are aware that their input is important, is wanted, and is expected. Utilize the knowledge and skills of everyone associated with the process.

9. "Failure to acquire a statistician/consultant."

Hire a consultant to train the work force. After people learn the statistical concepts and techniques, they have to be trained to apply them.

10. "Failure to involve the suppliers."

The quality of incoming goods must equal the quality of your products. Garbage in, garbage out (GIGO)!

EXERCISES

1. Name three management problems that are causing some U.S. companies to fall behind their competitors.
2. List Deming's 14 points for management.
3. What new philosophy does Deming mention?
4. Why is mass inspection a poor approach to quality?
5. What quality criteria should be expected of a supplier?
6. Who should be involved in the quality process?
7. What is meant by modern methods of supervision?
8. Why does fear cause a company economic loss?
9. Why is it important to eliminate departmental barriers?
10. Why do you suppose work quotas have been used? Why should they be eliminated?
11. What are some of the barriers that prevent a worker from doing a good job?
12. Why is it necessary to eliminate the fear of layoffs when starting the quality process?
13. Why does the quality process have to start at the top management level?
14. List Crosby's symptoms of trouble.
15. What are Crosby's 14 steps to quality improvement?
16. What are POC and PONC?
17. What are the five criteria for promoting teamwork?
18. What are the main pitfalls in the quality process?

3

INTRODUCTION TO VARIATION AND STATISTICS

OBJECTIVES

- Understand that variation occurs in all measurements and that quality control translates to control of variation.
- Know the round-off rules.
- Distinguish between two types of variation: special cause and common cause.
- Know what distributions are and how they are used with SPC.
- Use the basic algebra concepts that are needed for the study of SPC.
- Calculate the mean, median, mode, range, and standard deviation for a set of numbers.
- Draw a histogram for a set of numbers.

The concept of measurement variation is introduced in this chapter, as are some statistical methods for measuring and describing that variation. Any large set of measurements will form a graphical pattern when the frequency of each measurement is charted; that pattern is called a *distribution*. The concept of distributions is very important because all the statistical process control techniques use the distribution of a limited number of measurements to imply the "true" distribution of all measurements.

3.1 VARIATION CONCEPTS

It is important to understand that no two products or characteristics are exactly the same. Their differences may be large or imperceptibly small, but they are always present. Any measurement is only as good as the measuring device and the person's reading of the measuring device.

Measurement Error

The concept of error in a measurement is the same whether the device is a ruler or a micrometer. The maximum error involved is always half the accuracy. The accuracy is the smallest unit of measurement. A measurement of 2.34 centimeters, for example, is accurate to the nearest hundredth of a centimeter, and the maximum error is .005 centimeters. If the width of a table top is measured to the nearest inch, any width between 41.5 inches and 42.499 inches will be called 42 inches. Likewise, if a bearing is measured to the nearest thousandth of an inch, a bearing measuring between .7475 inches and .748499 inches will be given the dimension .748 inches. If two bearings are thought to measure "exactly" .748 inches, a measuring device accurate to the nearest ten thousandth or hundred thousandth may be needed to show a difference, but the difference will be there.

A measurement is an approximate number because it has been *rounded off* to the accuracy implied in the measurement. Calculations with measurements must be properly rounded off so that the correct accuracy is implied in the calculated values.

EXAMPLE 3.1

A bar has been marked into two sections and each length measured. A meter stick marked to the nearest centimeter was used to measure the first part, and a ruler marked to the nearest millimeter was used to measure the second part. The two measurements were 96 centimeters and 15.3 centimeters. What is the length of the bar?

Solution

The answer is *not* 111.3 centimeters because that measurement implies that the true length of the bar lies between 111.251 centimeters and 111.349 centimeters.

Minimum possible measurements	Maximum possible measurements
95.5 cm	96.499 cm
+ 15.251 cm	+ 15.349 cm
110.751 cm	111.848 cm

The simple sum, 111.3, implies more accuracy in the true length of the bar than is warranted. The calculations with the minimum and maximum possible true measurements show the actual possible range in the true length of the bar.

The correct calculation method is to add the measurements, then round off the answer to match the accuracy of the least accurate number used in the calculations. The simple sum of 111.3 centimeters should be rounded off to 111 centimeters. This measurement has an implied accuracy of 110.51 centimeters to 111.49 centimeters, which more closely reflects the actual range of measurements determined by using the minimum and maximum values.

Round-off Rules

If the number to the right of the desired place value is more than half of that place value, round *up* to the next digit.

23.472 to the nearest tenth is 23.5.

4.1456 to the nearest thousandth is 4.146.

5692 to the nearest hundred is 5700.

If the number to the right of the desired place value is less than half of that place value, *truncate* to that place value.

23.414 to the nearest tenth is 23.4.

4.1454 to the nearest thousandth is 4.145.

5648 to the nearest hundred is 5600.

If the number to the right of the desired place value is exactly half of that place value, round to the nearest *even* number.

23.45 to the nearest tenth is 23.4.

4.1455 to the nearest thousandth is 4.146.

5650 to the nearest hundred is 5600.

17.295 to the nearest hundredth is 17.30.

Tolerance is an acceptable range of measurements on a specific dimension. The tolerance is usually set at the design stage of the product, but it may be changed at a later time, depending on how critical the measurement is. The tolerance is given as a target measurement plus or minus ($\pm$) the variation that is acceptable. The target measurement is usually centered in the tolerable range, as is implied by the plus or minus, but the tolerable range may occasionally be unsymmetric, such as $2.450^{+.001}_{-.003}$ inches. Any product that has its measurement beyond the tolerable range is said to be unacceptable or defective.

Suppose that ball bearings were to measure .745 $\pm$ .002 inches and that a large number of them were produced, measured to the nearest .0005 inches, and stacked according to size. The slots at each measurement between .743 inches and .747 inches would fill in a random manner, but as more were measured and stacked, the bearings would form a pattern that is called a *distribution*. This process is shown in Figures 3.1 to 3.4 (see page 30 for Figures 3.2, 3.3, and 3.4). The shape of the distribution can be described by a mathematical curve and the percentages in each section predicted using the branch of mathematics called statistics. Normally, most of the bearings will fall in the slots closest to the target measurement with the numbers per slot decreasing as the slots approach the tolerance limit. However, other distribution shapes are possible as well.

FIGURE 3.1
The first few bearings.

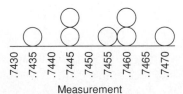

.7430 .7435 .7440 .7445 .7450 .7455 .7460 .7465 .7470

Measurement

FIGURE 3.2
More bearings accumulate.

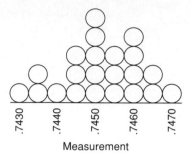

FIGURE 3.3
The day's accumulation forms a pattern shown by the curve.

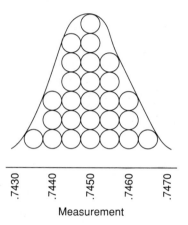

FIGURE 3.4
The pattern, or distribution, by itself.

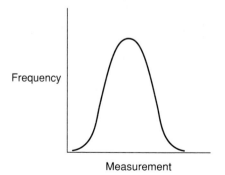

3.2 SPECIAL CAUSE AND COMMON CAUSE VARIATION

Two types of variation must be dealt with in SPC. The first is called special cause, or assignable cause, variation. It affects the process in unpredictable ways and can be detected by simple statistical techniques. It can be eliminated from the process by the worker or process control team in charge of that particular segment of the process; this is referred to as local action. Approximately 15 percent of all process problems can be handled by local action. When all the special cause variation is eliminated, the process is said to be in statistical control.

The second type of variation, called common cause variation, is inherent in the process. When the special cause variation has been eliminated, the process is working as well as it possibly can without modifications. Approximately 85 percent of all process problems are due to common cause variation. The only way to decrease common cause variation is to make improvements in the manufacturing process. The extent of common cause variation can be measured statistically and compared to specifications; if improvements are needed, action on the process is necessary. Management action is needed for any process changes.

Production quality is directly linked to the amount of variation in the product measurements. For example, quality is a factor in the closeness of fit of the various parts of an automobile, and quality is visible in large parts such as doors, hoods, and finish. The hidden quality lies in the moving parts of the engine and drive train, where top quality means years of trouble-free driving. In the manufacture of all products, there are critical measurements for which adherence to the right tolerances is necessary for high quality.

3.3 THE VARIATION CONCEPTS

Individual measurements are different, but as a group, they form a predictable pattern called a distribution. The distribution can be pictured as a statistical curve. The curve may be easier to conceptualize if imagined as stacks of like measurements within it. For example, if the curve in Figure 3.5 represents the distribution of a day's production of some specific product (dimension), how can it be interpreted? The horizontal scale in Figure 3.6 on page 32 is marked off in measurements. The columns above each measurement represent the stacked height, or frequency, of each specific measurement (the column of X's).

FIGURE 3.5
The distribution of a day's production.

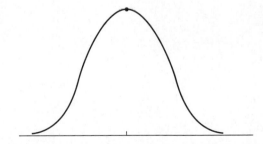

The distribution has the following measurable characteristics:

- Location: the middle, or average, value may differ for different samples. Figure 3.7 (page 32) shows three curves that differ only in their middle, or average, value.

FIGURE 3.6
The day's distribution curve with tallied measurements.

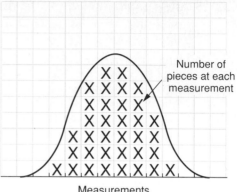

Measurements

FIGURE 3.7
Distributions in different locations.

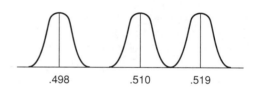

.498   .510   .519

■ Spread: the width of the curve is a measure of the extent of variation from one extreme to the other. Figure 3.8 shows three curves that differ in their spread, or range.

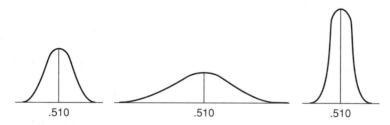

.510   .510   .510

FIGURE 3.8
Distributions with different amounts of spread.

■ Shape: the way the measurements stack up can cause different-shaped curves. Figure 3.9 shows three curves of different shape.

FIGURE 3.9
Distributions with different shapes.

3.4 DISTRIBUTIONS AND SPC GOALS

Figure 3.10 illustrates day-to-day production when special causes of variation are present. The special cause variation generally affects the process in unpredictable ways. What will tomorrow's output be? No one knows because of the erratic behavior of special cause variation! Most processes fit this pattern before a company introduces SPC because most processes have some degree of special cause variation.

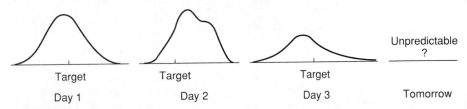

FIGURE 3.10
Special cause variation is present. The product distribution is therefore unpredictable.

Special cause variation has been eliminated in the distributions shown in Figure 3.11. The process is now predictable, so tomorrow's product distribution is known as well as next year's. Only common cause variation is present.

FIGURE 3.11
The process is in statistical control, so only common cause variation is present. Production is predictable.

The next step is to compare the distribution of the individual measurements with the specification limits. The specification limits along the measurement scale are shown in Figure 3.12 (see page 34). The lower specification limit (LSL) and the upper specification limit (USL) are determined by applying the tolerance to the target measurement. The goal is to tighten up the extent of variation so the product is well within specification.

Once the process is predictable, the distribution of individual measurements is statistically compared to the specification limits. The distribution curves in Figure 3.12 show that day after day, a constant percent of product is out of specification. The area under the curve corresponds to percentage of product, so the area in the shaded sections represents the percent of product that is out of tolerance, or out of specification. It shows that unless the process is improved to decrease common cause variation, the manufacturer will have to accept this constant percent of defective products.

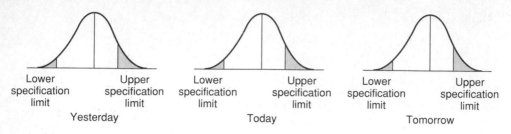

FIGURE 3.12
The process is predictable, but not capable. The shaded area represents a constant percent of product that exceeds specifications. The common cause variation is excessive.

The application of statistical process control methods can achieve the goal illustrated in Figure 3.13. The spread, or range, of the product's distribution pattern narrows when the amount of common cause variation in the process decreases so that the range of measurements is well within the specification limits and virtually no out-of-specification products are produced.

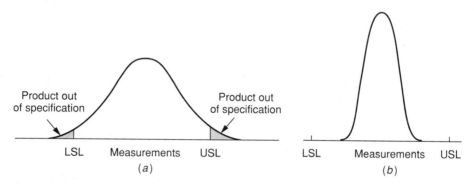

FIGURE 3.13
The goal of SPC is to change each day's production pattern from (a) to (b) by reducing product variability.

3.5 BASIC ALGEBRA CONCEPTS

To be effective, statistical process control must be used by virtually everyone involved in production and management, from materials acceptance to packing and delivery. SPC provides important information for management decision making. Part of the hands-on SPC procedure that is used by production people involves charting measurements and then using formulas to interpret the charts. Therefore, employees will have to learn (or relearn) a few algebraic concepts in order to use the statistical formulas.

A *variable* is a letter used to represent a number or measurement. Variables will be used in the various statistical formulas. *Formulas* are mathematical shorthand used to describe what operation (adding, subtracting, multiplying, dividing, or finding the square root) must be performed on numbers that the variables represent. Different numbers can be represented by variables in two ways:

1. Let x be one number and y be another.
2. Let x_1 be one number and x_2 be the other.

The first example uses a different letter for each measurement, and the second uses a subscripted variable with a different subscript for each number.

The operations are indicated as follows:

$x + y$ Add the two numbers that the variables represent.

If several numbers have to be added, a special symbol, $\sum$, can be used. $\sum x$, read "sum x," means that all the numbers represented by x should be added. For example, if there are 20 numbers, $\sum x$ is the sum of all 20. The addition can also be shown with the subscripted variables.

$x_1 + x_2 + x_3 + \cdots + x_{20}$ Add all 20 values.

The three dots indicate that the sequence of additions continues until the twentieth number is added. When the number of values is indefinite but all values must be added together, the subscripted form would be $x_1 + x_2 + x_3 + \cdots + x_n$ where the last subscript, n, stands for the number of values added.

$x_1 - x_2$	Subtract the second value from the first.
xy	Multiply the x value by the y value. Two variables together indicate multiplication.
$3y$	Multiply the y measurement by 3. A number next to a variable also indicates multiplication.
$\dfrac{x}{y}$	Divide the x value by the y value. A fraction line is used to indicate division.
$3(x + y)$	Add the x to the y value first, then multiply the sum by 3. The parentheses are grouping symbols and the operation within the grouping symbols must be done first. A number next to a grouping symbol indicates multiplication.

Formulas usually show more than one operation, and it's important to know which one to do first. Some operations take precedence over others, so the solution may be wrong if the operations are simply done in left-to-right order. The rule governing the mixture of operations is called the order of operations.

Order of Operations

1. Do all operations contained within grouping symbols (parentheses, fraction lines).
2. Do all powers and roots.

3. Do all the multiplications and divisions as they occur from left to right.
4. Do all the additions and subtractions as they occur from left to right.

When applying the order of operations, proceed in order from step 1 to step 4. If the step doesn't apply, skip to the next step.

$x + 3y$ The multiplication of 3 times the y value must be done first, and the addition of the x value to the product comes second. Notice that steps 1 and 2 did not apply; there are no grouping symbols, powers, or roots.

For example, if $x = 7$ and $y = 2$

$$x + 3y = 7 + 3(2) \quad \text{multiply first, then add.}$$
$$= 7 + 6$$
$$= 13$$

$\dfrac{x + x + x + \cdots + x_n}{n}$ Add the n values first because the fraction line is a grouping symbol. Then divide the sum by n, the number of values. The fraction line is both a grouping symbol and a division indicator.

To *square* a number means to multiply it by itself. A raised 2 is the algebraic indicator of this operation.

x^2 Multiply the value x by x.
7^2 Multiply 7 by 7, so $7^2 = 49$.
$8^2 = 64$ Multiply 8 by itself to get 64.

Squaring a number means raising it to the second power. In general, a *power* indicates a repeated multiplication of the base number.

$$5^3 = 5 \times 5 \times 5 = 125$$
$$3^4 = 3 \times 3 \times 3 \times 3 = 81$$

The *square root* is the opposite of the square. The root is the number that, when squared, gives the number under the radical sign (the $\sqrt{\ }$).

$\sqrt{9} = 3$ The square root of 9 is 3.
$\sqrt{36} = 6$ Squaring the root, in this case the 6, gives 36.
$\sqrt{16} = ?$ What number squared gives 16? $4^2 = 16$, so $\sqrt{16} = 4$.

Most of the time the number under the radical does not have a root that can be easily found by mental arithmetic. For those numbers, a calculator can be used.

$\sqrt{7} = ?$ Press 7 and then the $\sqrt{\ }$ button; the result is 2.6457513.

Roots other than square roots are indicated by a number wedged into the radical symbol. That number is called the *root index*. The fourth root of 81 is $\sqrt[4]{81}$. A root is the opposite of power, so the fourth root of 81 is the number that when raised to the fourth power gives 81.

$$\sqrt[4]{81} = 3 \quad \text{because} \quad 3^4 = 81.$$

Signed Numbers

Occasionally *signed numbers* occur in gauging or in statistical calculations. These numbers can be *positive* or *negative*. A positive number will either have no sign in front of it or "+" in front of it. A negative number will have "−" in front of it. For example, the following are classified as positive or negative.

3.4	Positive
−2.5	Negative
+4.8	Positive
0	Neither. Zero is the only number that is neither positive nor negative. It's the boundary number that separates the positives from the negatives on a gauge or scale (see Figure 3.14).

FIGURE 3.14
Signed numbers on gauges.

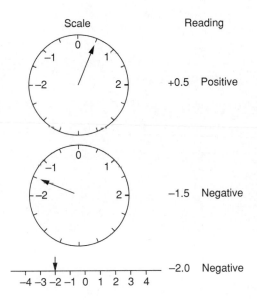

The signed number is the directed distance from the 0. The positive direction on a gauge or scale is right, clockwise, or up. The negative direction is left, counterclockwise, or down.

The *absolute value* of a number is the value without the direction. Two vertical bars represent the mathematical symbol for absolute value. For example, the absolute value of 2, represented by $|\,2\,|$, is 2. The absolute value of -5.3, which is written $|\,-5.3\,|$, is 5.3.

$$|-1.5| = 1.5 \qquad \text{The absolute value of } -1.5 \text{ is } 1.5.$$
$$|\,0\,| = 0 \qquad \text{The absolute value of } 0 \text{ is } 0.$$
$$|\,6.8\,| = 6.8 \qquad \text{The absolute value of } 6.8 \text{ is } 6.8.$$

Operations with Signed Numbers

There are two rules for addition with signed numbers. Rule 1: When the signs of the two numbers are the same, *add* their absolute values and *keep* the sign.

$$2.3 + 3.1 = 5.4 \qquad \text{The sum is the same sign as the addends.}$$
$$-4.1 + (-3.8) = -7.9 \qquad \text{Add 4.1 and 3.8 (the absolute values)}$$
$$\text{and keep the ``} - \text{'' sign.}$$

Rule 2: When the signs of the two numbers are different, *subtract* the smaller absolute value from the larger and *keep* the sign of the one with the larger absolute value.

$$4.8 + (-2.3) = 2.5 \qquad \text{Subtract 2.3 from 4.8 and keep the ``} + \text{''.}$$
$$(2.5 \text{ is the same as } +2.5.)$$
$$3.6 + (-5.4) = -1.8 \qquad \text{Subtract 3.6 from 5.4 and keep the ``} - \text{'' sign.}$$
$$-2.9 + 4.8 = 1.9 \qquad \text{Subtract 2.9 from 4.8 and keep the ``} + \text{''.}$$
$$-8.3 + 5.7 = -2.6 \qquad \text{Subtract 5.7 from 8.3 and keep the ``} - \text{''.}$$

There is also a rule for subtraction. Rule: *Change* the subtraction to addition and *change* the sign of the number on the right. Then use the addition rules.

$$1.43 - 2.6 \qquad \text{Make the two changes.}$$
$$\downarrow \searrow$$
$$1.43 + (-2.6) \qquad \text{Use addition rule 2.}$$
$$-1.17$$

$$-2.5 - 5.1 \qquad \text{Make the two changes.}$$
$$\downarrow \searrow$$
$$-2.5 + (-5.1) \qquad \text{Use addition rule 1.}$$
$$-7.6$$

$$-3.52 - (-4.21) \qquad \text{Make the two changes.}$$
$$\downarrow \swarrow$$
$$-3.52 + 4.21 \qquad \text{Use addition rule 2.}$$
$$.69$$

The following two rules apply for multiplication and division. Rule 1: If the two numbers being multiplied or divided have the *same* sign, the answer is *positive*.

$$-2 \times (-8) = 16$$

$$\frac{-24}{-3} = 8$$

$(-4.3)(-6.0) = 25.8$ Two sets of parentheses next to each other indicate multiplication.

$(-30.15) \div (-1.5) = 20.1$

$-5.2(-4.8) = 24.96$ A number next to a value in parentheses also indicates multiplication.

Rule 2: If the two numbers being multiplied or divided have *different* signs, the answer is *negative*.

$$3(-12.4) = -37.2$$

$$-4.5(2.3) = -10.35$$

$$\frac{-8.4}{2.1} = -4.0$$

$$\frac{6.3}{-1.5} = -4.2$$

When operating with signed numbers on a calculator, use the $\pm$ button to change the sign of the number in the display. For example:

Calculation	Calculator sequence	Answer
$4 - (-7.3)$	$4 - 7.3\pm =$	11.3
$-2.6(7.8)$	$2.6\pm \times 7.8 =$	-20.28
$\dfrac{5.43}{-2.8}$	$5.43 \div 2.8\pm =$	-1.939
$-4.3 - (2.4)(-5.1)$	$2.4 \times 5.1\pm = M$ $4.3\pm - MR =$ (Put the product in memory and then subtract using the memory recall.)	7.94

3.6   BASIC STATISTICAL CONCEPTS

A *population* is the set of all possible numbers or elements that could be considered for a situation (for example, all the measurements for a specific dimension on a part being produced). A *sample* is a set of numbers or elements taken from a population.

The concepts of inferential statistics have been developed to predict population values from the information gained by sampling the population. The samples must represent a true picture of the population in order to accurately predict the population values. A *random sample* is one in which every element in the population has an equal chance of being chosen for the sample.

All the statistical theories and formulas that use samples to estimate population values require random samples. An extensive amount of work has been done on sampling methods. These methods all deal with different ways to draw a random sample from the population. Any sample in which some elements of the population are more likely to be chosen for the sample than others is called a *biased* sample and should not be used.

Each piece produced in a manufacturing process has a specific number of dimensions, and each dimension has its own population of measurements. If all the measurements of a dimension are stacked up according to size, the distribution will usually take on a *normal* shape. In a normal distribution, which will be discussed more thoroughly in Chapter 5, most of the data clusters close to a central or middle value. The height of the stacks diminishes rapidly as the measurements get further from the central value. The shape of the normal distribution is a bell-shaped curve. This is shown in Figure 3.15.

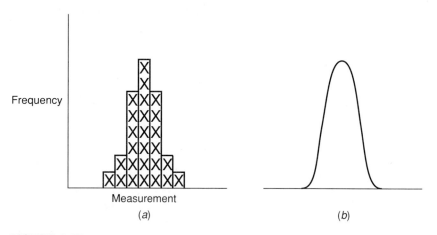

FIGURE 3.15
(*a*) A normal distribution of elements; (*b*) a normal (bell-shaped) distribution curve.

When a random sample is taken from a population and the pieces stacked according to size, the shape of the developing distribution can take almost any form. However, as more pieces are added, the shape of the sampled distribution will closely resemble that of the population's distribution. This concept was shown in Figures 3.1 to 3.4, and in that case, the population distribution will nearly match Figure 3.4. A large sample, usually defined as a sample with about 100 pieces, is needed for this to occur. The larger the sample, the more closely the sample distribution will resemble the population distribution.

Measures of the Center of a Distribution

The three characteristics of a distribution were presented in Figures 3.7 to 3.9. The first, location, is described using measures of the distribution's center. Mean, median, and mode are three measures used to determine the center.

Mean. The *mean* is the average value. Given a set of numbers, to find the average, or mean, add all the values and divide by the number of values that you added. The symbol for the mean is $\bar{x}$. The statistical notation or formula is $\bar{x} = (\sum x)/n$. It's read, "x bar equals the sum of the x values divided by the number of values, n." The formula can also be written

$$\bar{x} = \frac{x_1 + x_2 + x_3 + \cdots + x_n}{n}$$

where subscripts are used to indicate the different x values that are being averaged.

EXAMPLE 3.2

Given the measurements 8, 15, 12, 9, and 6, we find the mean and demonstrate the different formulas.

Solution

$$\bar{x} = \frac{\sum x}{n}$$

$$\bar{x} = \frac{8 + 15 + 12 + 9 + 6}{5}$$

$$\bar{x} = \frac{50}{5}$$

$$\bar{x} = 10$$

Following the directions of the formula, the five measurements are added first. Their sum, 50, is then divided by the number of measurements, 5. The mean, $\bar{x}$, is 10.

Also, if we designate $x_1 = 8, x_2 = 15, x_3 = 12, x_4 = 9$, and $x_5 = 6$, then

$$\bar{x} = \frac{x_1 + x_2 + x_3 + x_4 + x_5}{5}$$

$$\bar{x} = \frac{8 + 15 + 12 + 9 + 6}{5}$$

$$\bar{x} = \frac{50}{5}$$

$$\bar{x} = 10$$

Add the five measurements and then divide by 5. The mean, x, is 10.

A bar over a variable indicates an average for all the values of that variable. For example, R is the variable we use for the range. $\bar{R}$ is the average for all the R values. $\bar{R} = (\sum R)/N$ for N range values.

Median. The *median* is the middle value when all the numbers are put in order from smallest to largest. The middle value occurs in two ways: For an odd number of values, there will be just one value in the middle, but for an even number of values, there will be two values in the middle. In the first case, the median is the value in the center. In the second case, the median is the average of the two middle values. The symbol for the median is $\tilde{x}$.

EXAMPLE 3.3   Find the median, first for values 8, 15, 12, 9, and 6, and then for values 26, 20, 24, and 29.

Solution

In the first case we are given the values 8, 15, 12, 9, and 6.

6, 8, 9, 12, 15	Step 1. Order them.
$\tilde{x} = 9$	Step 2. There is an odd number of values, so the median is the one in the middle.

In the second case we are given the values 26, 20, 24, and 29.

20, 24, 26, 29	Step 1. Order them.
24, 26	Step 2. There's an even number of values, so the median is the average of the two middle numbers.
$\tilde{x} = \dfrac{24 + 26}{2}$	To find the average of the two middle numbers, add them and then divide by 2.
$\tilde{x} = \dfrac{50}{2}$	
$\tilde{x} = 25$	

There are two major control charts for variables that can be used in process control. One features the mean, and the other uses the median. The mean is the more traditional middle value in statistics; most of the statistical formulas use it. The median has more appeal in process control for some companies because it is easier to find in a set of measurements.

The median is a more stable measurement than the mean because it is unaffected by extreme data values. The two groups of numbers, 10, 13, 14, 17, and 21 and 10, 13, 14, 17, and 36, have the same median, 14, but different means. The mean of the second group increased from 15 to 18, which doesn't seem to represent the middle. For symmetrical distributions, the mean and the median will have virtually the same value.

Mode. The *mode* is the value that occurs the most in a group, or has the largest frequency. Given the data 1, 2, 4, 4, 5, 5, 6, 7, 8, 8, 9, 10, 10, 10, 12, 12, the mode is 10 because 10 occurs with the highest frequency. The mode is also used to describe distributions. The normal distribution has a single mode. The distribution shown in

Figure 3.16 is *bimodal* because it has two distinct high points. It doesn't matter that the frequency of the first peak is higher than that of the second; bimodal refers to the basic shape.

FIGURE 3.16
A bimodal distribution.

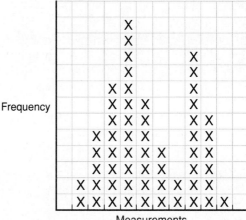

Measures of the Spread

The second characteristic of a distribution, the spread, was pictured in Figure 3.8. The spread of a distribution of measurements illustrates the extent of variability in those measurements.

Range. The *range, R*, is an easily calculated measure of the spread and is used extensively in process control. R is the difference between the largest and smallest data values.

$$\text{Range} = \text{largest value} - \text{smallest value}$$

EXAMPLE 3.4   Given the measurements 8, 15, 12, 9, and 6, find the range.

Solution

$$R = 15 - 6$$
$$= 9$$

Standard Deviation. The standard deviation is the more traditional measure of the spread in statistics and is generally reported with the mean. It can be approximated from the set of sample ranges when working with control charts. The data for some of the control charts that are discussed in Chapters 4 through 7 consist of small groups of measurements called samples, and each sample has a range value. There is an easy two-step procedure for calculating the standard deviation for the data on a control chart.

Step 1: Calculate the average sample range $\overline{R}$. The formula is $\overline{R} = (\sum R)/k$ for k values.

$$\overline{R} = \frac{R_1 + R_2 + R_3 + \cdots + R_k}{k}$$

Step 2: The symbol for standard deviation is σ (called *sigma*). Calculate σ.

$$\sigma = \frac{\overline{R}}{d_2}$$

The value of d_2, a control chart factor, depends on the sample size. Table 1.1 in Appendix B contains d_2 values.

EXAMPLE 3.5

Twelve samples of five measurements each have the following range values. Calculate the standard deviation of the measurements. 2.7, 3.2, 1.1, 2.5, 2.7, 0.4, 3.0, 2.2, 1.8, 2.6, 1.3, and 1.6.

Solution
Calculate $\overline{R}$.

$$\overline{R} = \frac{\sum R}{k}$$

$$= \frac{25.1}{12}$$

$$= 2.092$$

From Table 1.1 in Appendix B, $n = 5$, so $d_2 = 2.326$.
    Second, calculate σ.

$$\sigma = \frac{\overline{R}}{d_2}$$

$$= \frac{2.092}{2.326}$$

$$= .899$$

The defining formula for the standard deviation of a population of data is

$$\sigma = \sqrt{\frac{\sum(x - \overline{x})^2}{n}}$$

Usually the population of data is either too large or too inaccessible to utilize the defining formula for calculating σ. For this situation the population standard deviation is best estimated by the sample standard deviation, s.

$$s = \sqrt{\frac{\sum(x - \bar{x})^2}{n - 1}}$$

When the sample size, n, is large ($n > 30$), both formulas will give approximately the same value.

In the 1920s when Walter Shewhart developed his control chart concepts at Bell Laboratories, the calculation of σ for 100 or more sample values was a very tedious calculation. To make the calculations easier for the average worker, he developed a simpler formula,

$$\sigma = \frac{\bar{R}}{d_2}$$

based on the average of the sample ranges, $\bar{R}$. Shewhart's control charts were designed to give good information about a population of measurements based on 20 to 25 small samples. The sample sizes were usually $n = 3$ to $n = 5$, and the sample averages, $\bar{x}$, were charted along with the sample ranges, R. The range is the simplest measure of variability, and Shewhart's formula, $\sigma = \bar{R}/d_2$, gives a good estimate of the population standard deviation. However, the sample range is very sensitive to the sample size. The range values for larger samples will generally be larger than those for small samples. For example, the R values for $n = 5$ will be larger than the R values for $n = 3$. The d_2 constants, dependent on n, are designed to give consistent values of σ regardless of the sample size.

Calculation of σ can be easily done on a statistical calculator, but Shewhart's formula is still used with control charts because it is faster to calculate $\bar{R}$ for 25 samples than to calculate σ directly from 125 data values.

EXAMPLE 3.6

Given the measurements 8, 15, 12, 9, and 16, calculate the standard deviation with the formula

$$\sigma = \sqrt{\frac{\sum(x - \bar{x})^2}{n}}$$

The mean is $\bar{x} = (\sum x)/n = 60/5 = 12$. These steps simply follow the order of operations for the formula.

Solution
Step 1: Find the differences between the data values and the mean to calculate $(x - \bar{x})$.

$$8 - 12 = -4$$
$$15 - 12 = 3$$
$$12 - 12 = 0$$
$$9 - 12 = -3$$
$$16 - 12 = 4$$

Step 2: Square the differences to find $(x - \bar{x})^2$.

$$(-4)^2 = 16$$
$$(3)^2 = 9$$
$$(0)^2 = 0$$
$$(-3)^2 = 9$$
$$(4)^2 = 16$$

Step 3: Add the squared differences.

$$\sum(x - \bar{x})^2 = 16 + 9 + 0 + 9 + 16 = 50$$

Step 4: Divide by n, the number of values.

$$\frac{\sum(x - \bar{x})^2}{n} = \frac{50}{5} = 10$$

Step 5: Find the square root (use the $\sqrt{}$ button on the calculator).

$$\sqrt{\frac{\sum(x - \bar{x})^2}{n}} = \sqrt{10} = 3.162$$

$$\sigma = 3.162$$

The standard deviation in the preceding square root form is the most complicated statistical calculation we have encountered thus far. The simpler range method, $\sigma = \bar{R}/d_2$, is the one used in SPC. The square root method is included to illustrate the idea that conceptually, the standard deviation is something like an average difference between the data values and the mean.

EXAMPLE 3.7 Given the data 2.71, 2.92, 2.67, 2.78, 2.84, and 2.82, calculate the mean, median, range, and standard deviation, σ. Put the data in a column format in order (for the median) in column x and calculate $\sum x$.

x	$x - \bar{x}$	$(x - \bar{x})^2$
2.67	$2.67 - 2.79 = -.12$	.0144
2.71	$2.71 - 2.79 = -.08$	.0064
2.78	$2.78 - 2.79 = -.01$	.0001
2.82	$2.82 - 2.79 = .03$	.0009
2.84	$2.84 - 2.79 = .05$	.0025
2.92	$2.92 - 2.79 = .13$	.0169
$\sum x = 16.74$		.0412

Solution
Calculate the mean.

$$\bar{x} = \frac{\sum x}{n}$$

$$= \frac{16.74}{6}$$

$$= 2.79$$

The 2.79 value is used to calculate $x - \bar{x}$.

The data are ordered in the first column for the median. There is an even number of values, so the median is the average of the middle two:

$$\tilde{x} = \frac{2.78 + 2.82}{2}$$

$$= \frac{5.60}{2}$$

$$= 2.80$$

Calculate the range.

$$R = \text{largest value} - \text{smallest value}$$
$$= 2.92 - 2.67$$
$$= .25$$

For the standard deviation, σ: The x values were put in a column format and the mean was calculated to be 2.79. Calculate the differences $x - \bar{x}$ in column 2. Square the differences in column 3. Add the squared values in column 3 for $\sum(x - \bar{x})^2 = .0412$. Substitute the values found in the preceding steps into the formula and calculate the final answer. Divide first, then calculate the square root.

$$\sigma = \sqrt{\frac{\sum(x - \bar{x})^2}{n}}$$

$$= \sqrt{\frac{.0142}{6}}$$

$$= \sqrt{.00687}$$

$$= .083$$

The Histogram

A *histogram* is a picture of the data that shows the comparative frequency of the measurements. Figure 3.17 on page 48 is a histogram drawn from the following measurements:

12	11	6	17	10	14	11	12
11	7	9	11	12	9	10	16
11	13	12	7	13	15	14	10
10	12	15	8	10	11	9	11

The measurements range from 6 to 17, so the horizontal axis is marked off with these values. The initial histogram is in tally form. As we go through the set of data, we put an "X" above the appropriate value on the horizontal axis. The frequency naturally builds. The frequency value can be read from the vertical scale for each column.

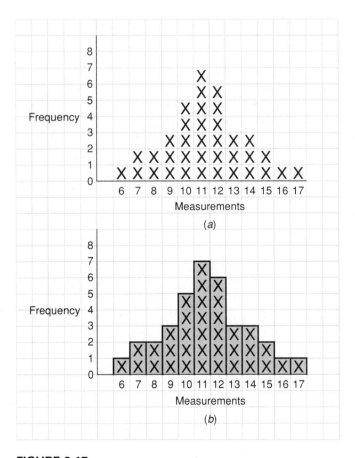

FIGURE 3.17
(*a*) The tally form; (*b*) the histogram.

The tally histogram is formalized to form the official histogram in bar graph form. Make a bar over each data value. The bars should touch, so the vertical sides will be at 5.5, 6.5, 7.5, 8.5, and so on up to 17.5 on the horizontal scale.

In many situations there are too many different individual values for this type of histogram to be meaningful. The histogram should have a distinct shape similar to

Figure 3.15 because it implies the shape of the population distribution. For example, if the 32 data values given for the histogram in Figure 3.17 ranged from 6 to 17 and were accurate to the nearest tenth with values like 7.2, 12.3, and 13.1, there would be too many different values to chart individually. There would be more than 100 values on the horizontal axis, if it was marked off in tenths, and the chart would consist of many columns with heights of 0, 1, or 2. Grouped data should be used when this occurs. See Figure 3.18. Groups of 6 to 8, 9 to 11, 12 to 14, and 15 to 17 can be formed and all the variates totaled in each to create a histogram for grouped data. It is important that all the group widths be the same. Chapter 5 provides a more detailed approach to the grouped data histogram.

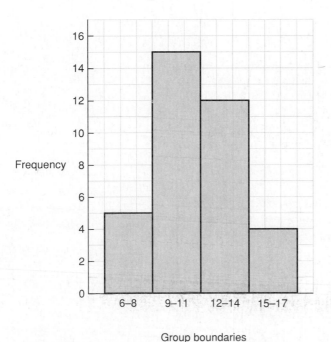

FIGURE 3.18
A histogram for grouped data.

EXERCISES

1. Round-off exercises.
   (a) Round off to the nearest thousandth.

   2.41349
   2.4157
   2.4198
   2.4173

(b) Round-off to the nearest hundredth.

$$4.245$$
$$4.246$$
$$4.242$$
$$4.2476$$
$$4.235$$
$$4.2451$$
$$4.2349$$

2. What are the two types of variation in SPC?
3. If the curve in Figure 3.4 represents the distribution of a day's production, how can it be interpreted in terms of frequency?
4. What are the three basic ways that distributions can differ?
5. If special cause variation is present, can a future distribution of product measurements be predicted?
6. If common cause variation is the only variation present, can a future distribution of product measurements be predicted?
7. Evaluate the following algebra expressions using the given values: $x_1 = 4, x_2 = 8, x_3 = 10, y = 9$.

(a) $\sum x$

(b) yx_2

(c) $x_3 - x_1$

(d) $7y$

(e) $\dfrac{x_3}{x_1}$

(f) $x_2 + 5x_1$

(g) y^2

(h) $\sqrt{x_1}$

(i) $\sqrt{x_2}$

(j) $\dfrac{x_1 + x_3}{3}$

8. For the following statistical calculations, complete the table.

x	$x - \bar{x}$	$(x - \bar{x})^2$
2.4		
1.6		
.8		
1.2		

(a) What is the symbol for the mean?
(b) What is the symbol for the range?
(c) What is the symbol for the median?
(d) What is the population standard deviation symbol?
(e) Calculate $\tilde{x}$.
(f) Calculate R.
(g) Calculate $\bar{x}$.
(h) Calculate σ using $\sigma = \sqrt{\sum (x - \bar{x})^2/n}$.

9. Given the table of measurements

24	26	30	28	29	28	29
29	25	30	26	29	27	31
32	28	28	27	27	26	27
25	29	27	30	28	27	28

    (a) Make a tally histogram.

    (b) Make a histogram for the individual measurements.

10. Evaluate:

    (a) $2 + (-9.4)$ **(f)** $-8.7 - 3.4$

    (b) $-6.5 + (-4.1)$ **(g)** $(2.4)(-3.6)$

    (c) $(9.2) + (-2.8)$ **(h)** $4.6 - (-3.8)$

    (d) $-3.4(-5.1)$ **(i)** $\dfrac{8.4}{-1.4}$

    (e) $\dfrac{-6.5}{-5}$ **(j)** $(-2.3)^2$

4

INTRODUCTION TO THE CONTROL CHART CONCEPT

OBJECTIVES

- Describe the two basic categories of control charts and the four types of control charts in each category.
- Plan random sample times.
- Describe the general preparations for control charting.
- Construct a median and range chart.
- Analyze a median and range control chart.

Control charts are the tools for statistical process control. Their use can provide more information about a process than a production worker with years of experience can. A powerful combination is formed when experienced workers use the control chart techniques, however, a combination that is instrumental in the production of quality products. Several types of control charts will be explained thoroughly later in the text, but the control charting concepts will be discussed informally here in order to present an overview of the topic.

4.1 VARIABLES AND ATTRIBUTES

There are two basic types of control charts: variables and attributes. *Variables* control charts use the actual measurements for charting. The types of variables control charts include the following.

1. Average and range charts ($\overline{x}$ and R). The average and range chart, commonly called the x-bar and R chart, consists of two separate charts on the same sheet of chart paper. One graph tracks the sample mean, $\overline{x}$, and the other tracks the sample range, R. Small samples of consecutive pieces are taken. The sample size

must be the same for all samples and usually consists of three to seven pieces. The dimension of interest is measured, and the measurements are recorded on the chart for each sample. The mean and range for each sample are calculated, recorded, and charted. The chart is analyzed as it develops for indications of special cause variation, and after about 25 samples, it is analyzed again to determine the location, spread, and shape of the distribution of measurements. The x-bar and R chart is the most commonly used control chart for variables.

2. Median and range charts ($\tilde{x}$ and R). The median and range chart is exactly like the x-bar and R chart, with one exception: The median is calculated and charted instead of the mean. The $\tilde{x}$ and R chart analysis also shows indications of special cause variation and the location, spread, and shape of the distribution of measurements. Some companies prefer the $\tilde{x}$ and R charts because the calculation of the median is easier and faster than the calculation of the mean. The Saginaw division of General Motors, for one, uses the $\tilde{x}$ and R charts extensively. One reason that the x-bar and R chart is usually preferred over the $\tilde{x}$ and R chart is that the x-bar and R chart is more sensitive to variation analysis.

3. Average and standard deviation charts ($\bar{x}$ and s). The $\bar{x}$ and s chart tracks x-bar on one part of the chart and the sample standard deviation, s, on the other. The $\bar{x}$ and s chart does everything that the x-bar and R chart does and is used in the same way. Although it is preferred to the R chart because the standard deviation is a better measure of variation than the range, $\bar{x}$ and s charts are not used as much as the other variables charts because the standard deviation is more difficult to calculate than the range. When production workers are provided with statistical calculators or when the sample measurements are taken automatically and computerized, however, the sample standard deviation is calculated automatically and found at the touch of a button. For this reason, the $\bar{x}$ and s charts will be used more extensively in the future and may eventually become the standard control chart in use.

4. Individual and moving range charts (x and MR). The x and MR chart is actually a single chart of individual measurements. Variability is estimated from the piece-to-piece variation, which is referred to as the *moving range*. This chart is much more limited in its use and application than the other variables charts because fewer data values are used to make the chart; consequently, the chart analysis is less reliable.

Attributes control charts use pass-fail information for charting. An item passes inspection when it conforms to the standards; a nonconforming item fails inspection. The types of attributes control charts include the following:

1. p charts. The p chart is a single chart that tracks the percent of nonconforming items in each sample. The sample sizes are large, usually 100 or more, and the sample sizes may vary on a single chart. Time is often the controlling factor on sample size because the sample may consist of all the pieces produced in an hour or a day.

2. np charts. The np chart tracks the number of nonconforming items in each sample. It is easier to use than the p chart because the percent of defective

items doesn't have to be calculated, but it has one restriction: All the samples must be the same size.

3. c charts. The c chart graphs the total number of nonconformances found in each piece or unit that is inspected.

4. u charts. Samples are taken and the total number of nonconformances in the sample is determined. The u chart then tracks the average number of nonconformances per unit.

Control charts for variables are more useful than charts for attributes, but attributes charts work best in some situations, such as when tracking paint flaws or surface smoothness. Most processes have measurable characteristics, however, and the measurement contains more information than a pass-fail or go–no go judgment. Small samples of three to seven are used in variables charts, whereas large samples of 100 or more are used with attribute data. Also, although measured data are more expensive (time-consuming) on individual pieces than go–no go gauges, fewer pieces need to be checked when using variables charts, so the time lapse for corrective action is less for variables charts than for attributes charts. Ongoing process analysis is also better with variables charts because the location (the middle value) is charted along with the piece-to-piece variability (the range); the shape of the distribution of measurements can be determined as well.

4.2 PREPARATION FOR CONTROL CHARTING

Management Direction

Management must establish an environment suitable for action and be totally committed to the use of control charts as an integral part of the move toward higher quality and productivity. People in every phase of the process have to be trained in basic statistical skills and be convinced of their importance. The application of statistics will direct the move toward better quality, higher productivity, and lower costs. Everyone's contribution is needed, so everyone must be involved.

Planning

The total process, from start to finish, should be outlined. Everything that can affect quality should be detailed: the machines, the materials, the methods, and the labor resources involved. The process can be charted in various ways. A process flow chart is a good start because it can evolve into a more complete storyboard that includes details to be considered for process improvement.

A process control team approach should be used. The size and complexity of the process determine whether one team will work for the entire process or subgroups should be formed for different phases.

The points in the process that are most promising for quality improvement must be determined by the process control team. Pareto charts and customer needs assessment can be important here. Where are the obvious trouble areas in the process? Look for evidence such as scrap, rework, or excessive overtime in specific areas. Chapter 10 gives more details on the planning process.

Minimize any unnecessary variation and obvious trouble before the control charting begins. Let the charts concentrate on the harder, more subtle problems; do not complicate the process by allowing known trouble spots to remain until they are "officially" uncovered by the control chart indicators.

Chart Commentary

Operators should keep a process log. They should note all relevant events that may somehow affect the process, such as tool changes, adjustments, new material lots, breaks in the work schedule, and power downs. Each time a sample is taken, the date, time, and other details must be noted on the chart, the log, or both.

Gauge Capability

Before measurements for charting are taken, the gauges must undergo a gauge capability study to determine the extent of gauge variation. If the study shows too much variability in the gauge, the gauge should be repaired or replaced with a better one; excessive gauge variation can "muddy the water" and confuse interpretation of the control charts. The control charts should primarily reflect process variation, not gauge variation.

Sampling Plan Preparation

A sampling plan must be carefully devised. The samples should fairly represent the population of measurements from which they are taken, so every effort must be made to ensure that *random samples* are attained. Decisions regarding the process at each charting situation rely on information gained from the samples. Each sample consists of a set of consecutive pieces in order to measure piece-to-piece variation. The number of pieces per sample is kept constant for each charting situation. These randomly chosen samples measure variation over time. At least 25 samples should be taken before the process can be analyzed for statistical control and process capability.

The sample size that is chosen is always a compromise between cost and reliability. In general, larger samples give more reliable results but cost more in worker time. Samples of three, four, or five are most common, but the situation may dictate the optimum sample size. For example, a sample of six is best from a machine with six spindles. In that case, if the samples are kept in order so that the first piece in the sample is always from the first spindle, the second piece is always from the second spindle, and so forth, individual spindle problems may be spotted as well as variation within the general control chart for the specific dimension being charted.

Sampling frequency also varies with the specific situation. The time it takes to produce one piece is a factor as well as the length of the production period. When control charts are first used at a specific point in a process, frequent samples will help to bring it into statistical control. When statistical control is attained, sampling frequency can be decreased. If the process is in statistical control but has too much variability so that it is not capable, more frequent samples are needed to assess process changes. There are several ways to organize a random sample, as the following examples illustrate.

EXAMPLE 4.1

Prepare a plan for 10 samples drawn during a shift that begins at 8:00 A.M.

Solution

Number a set of cards 0 through 7 and put the cards in a box marked "hour." Be sure that all the cards are the same size and shape. Mark a second set of cards 00 through 59 and put the cards in a box marked "minute." Again, be sure they are all the same size and shape.

    Decide on the number of samples to be taken on each shift; for this example we'll use 10. Draw and replace a card from the "hour" box 10 times. Be sure to mix the cards thoroughly before each draw. Record the numbers as shift hours. Simultaneously, draw and replace a card from the "minute" box and record the number with the corresponding "hour" draw. Add the hour and minute combinations to the starting time for the shift. If the shift begins at 8:00 A.M., the draw proceeds as follows:

hour	minute	sample times
0	22	8:22 A.M.
3	37	11:37 A.M.
4	36	12:36 P.M.
5	22	1:22 P.M.
1	45	9:45 A.M.
4	42	12:42 P.M.
5	53	1:53 P.M.
6	32	2:32 P.M.
6	21	2:21 P.M.
2	39	10:39 A.M.

If any sample times overlap, take two consecutive samples beginning with the first of the overlapping times.

EXAMPLE 4.2

The procedure shown in Example 4.1 can also be done using a random number table or a random number generator on a statistical calculator. Using three digits, decide which digit will correspond to the hour and which two will correspond to the minutes. If any random number value isn't in the appropriate domain (0 through 7 for the hour number and 00 through 59 for the minute number), skip it and go on to the next random number.

Solution

To illustrate, the three-digit random number on a statistical calculator will be used. The first digit will be the hour and the second two will be the minutes. The shift begins at 7:00 A.M. Random numbers that don't apply are crossed out.

Random number(s)	Procedure	Sample time
969, 617	7:00 A.M. + 6 hours, 17 minutes	1:17 P.M.
863, 430	7:00 A.M. + 4 hours, 30 minutes	11:30 A.M.
476, 758	7:00 A.M. + 7 hours, 58 minutes	2:58 P.M.
509	7:00 A.M. + 5 hours, 9 minutes	12:09 P.M.
151	7:00 A.M. + 1 hour, 51 minutes	8:51 A.M.
939, 075, 398, 592, 204	7:00 A.M. + 2 hours, 4 minutes	9:04 A.M.
292, 489, 932, 541	7:00 A.M. + 5 hours, 41 minutes	12:41 P.M.
735	7:00 A.M. + 7 hours, 35 minutes	2:35 P.M.
780, 864, 555	7:00 A.M. + 5 hours, 55 minutes	12:55 P.M.
143	7:00 A.M. + 1 hour, 43 minutes	8:43 A.M.

If one sample time runs into or overlaps another, depending on how long it takes to gather a sample, then consecutive samples are taken.

4.3 THE GENERAL PROCEDURE FOR AN $\tilde{x}$ AND R CHART

The detailed procedure for variables control charts will be given in Chapter 6. An overview of the control chart procedure is presented here using the median and range chart as an example. This overview will introduce the control chart concept and provide an application for the statistical concepts in Chapter 5.

EXAMPLE 4.3

Make an $\tilde{x}$ and R chart. A blank chart containing just the sample values is provided in Figure 4.3 on page 60. Do the charting in Figure 4.3 after each step in the procedure and check your results with the completed chart given in Figure 4.5(see page 61).

Solution

Step 1 As each sample is taken, record the sample measurements on the control chart. This is shown in Figure 4.1.

Sample Number	1	2	3	4	5	6	7	8	9	10
Record Sample Measurements	933	911	889	882	903	890	892	908	895	916
	897	898	915	913	930	940	912	920	920	890
	885	900	905	930	890	895	895	896	922	891
	900	905	902	900	890	909	896	894	928	920
	879	862	873	871	900	915	902	906	926	915
Median	897	900	902	900	900	909	896	906	922	915
Range	54	49	42	59	40	50	20	26	33	30

Step 1 (Record Sample Measurements)

Step 2 Calculate (Median, Range)

FIGURE 4.1
Measurements, medians, and ranges on the $\tilde{x}$ and R chart.

Step 2 Calculate the median and the range for each sample and record them on the control chart. In Figure 4.1, each sample column has the median and range value shown.

Step 3 Directly in line with the column of sample data, plot a point for the median and the range on their respective charts and connect them to the previous point with a straight line. This produces two *broken line* graphs on the control chart. This is illustrated in Figure 4.2.

Sample Number	1	2	3	4	5	6	7	8	9	10
Sample measurements	933	911	889	882	903	890	892	908	895	916
	897	898	915	913	930	940	912	920	920	890
	885	900	905	930	890	895	895	896	922	891
	900	905	902	900	890	909	896	894	928	920
	879	862	873	871	900	915	902	906	926	915
Median	897	900	902	900	900	909	896	906	922	915
Range	54	49	42	59	40	50	20	26	33	30

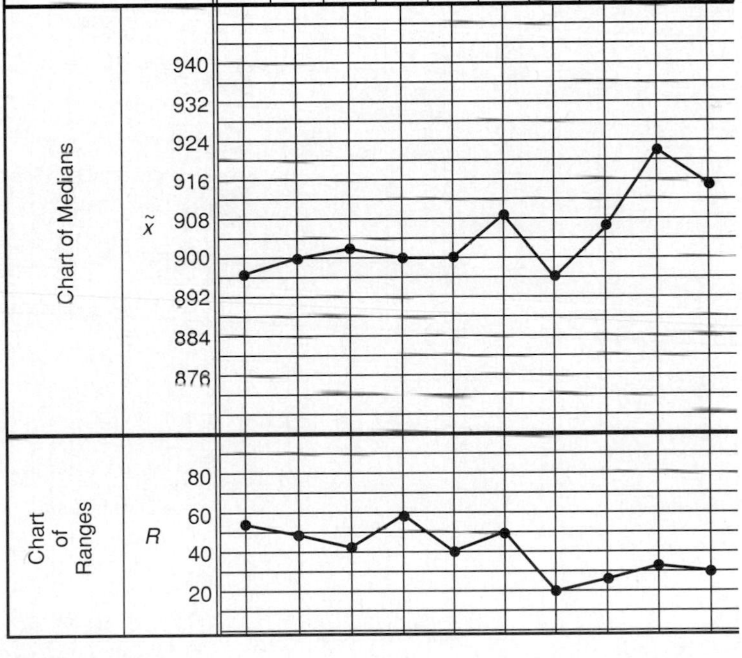

FIGURE 4.2
Plotting on the $\tilde{x}$ and R chart.

At this point you should be able to make the control chart in Figure 4.3 on page 60. It should look like Figure 4.4 (see page 61) when you finish.

Specification: 850 to 950

Sample Number	1	2	3	4	5	6	7	8	9	10	11	12	13	14	15	16	17	18	19	20	21	22	23	24	25
Sample measurements	933	911	889	882	903	890	892	908	895	916	901	908	909	895	893	909	885	897	912	882	896	912	926	917	884
	897	898	915	913	930	940	912	920	920	890	892	895	904	902	906	907	892	904	896	894	912	909	903	917	889
	885	900	905	930	890	895	895	896	922	891	892	896	906	902	917	904	942	916	932	941	907	913	908	918	912
	900	905	902	900	890	909	896	894	928	920	895	925	872	932	910	923	911	912	936	934	928	915	910	914	919
	879	862	873	871	900	915	902	906	926	915	898	933	927	932	925	888	916	920	913	917	926	928	885	925	898
Median	897	900	902	900																					
Range	54	49	42	59																					

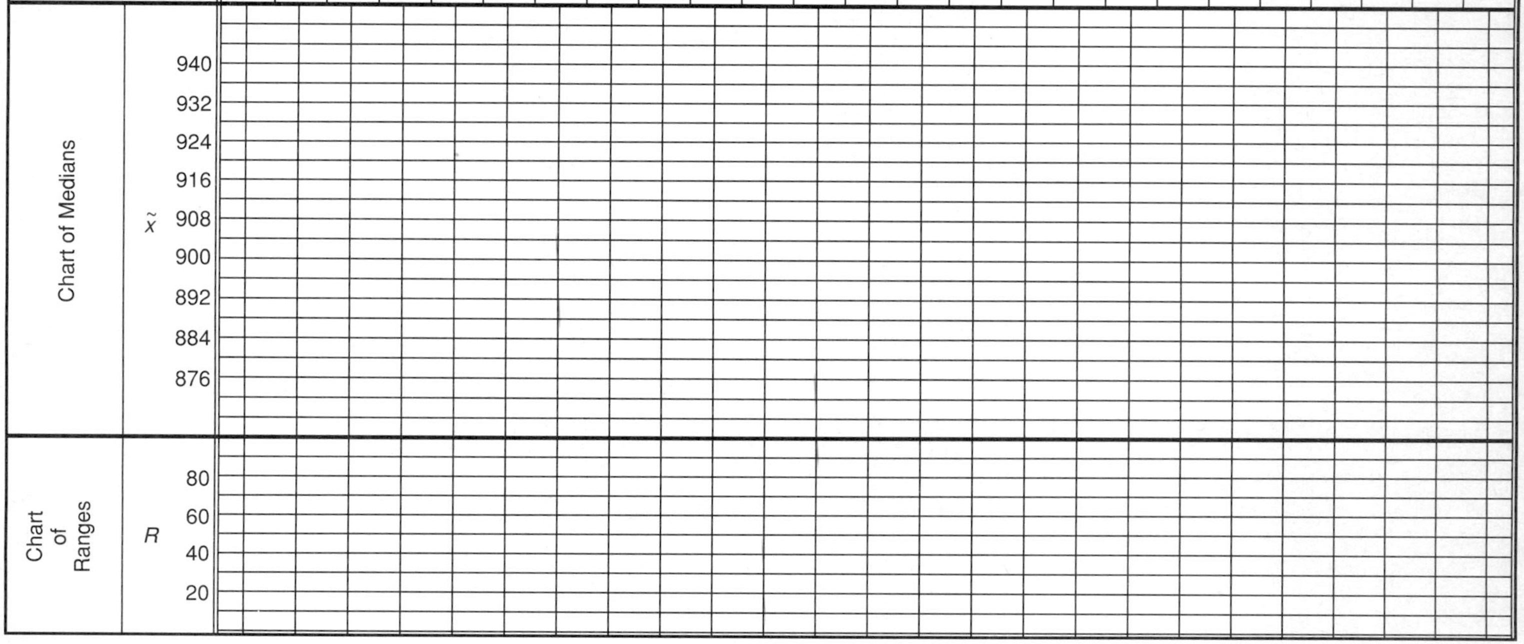

Chart of Medians

x̃: 940, 932, 924, 916, 908, 900, 892, 884, 876

Chart of Ranges

R: 80, 60, 40, 20

FIGURE 4.3
Calculate x̃ and R and make the x̃ and R chart.

60

Specification: 850 to 950

Sample Number	1	2	3	4	5	6	7	8	9	10	11	12	13	14	15	16	17	18	19	20	21	22	23	24	25
Sample measurements	933	911	889	882	903	890	892	908	895	916	901	908	909	895	893	909	885	897	912	882	896	912	926	917	884
	897	898	915	913	930	940	912	920	920	890	892	895	904	902	906	907	892	904	896	894	912	909	903	917	889
	885	900	905	930	890	895	895	896	922	891	892	896	906	902	917	904	942	916	932	941	907	913	908	918	912
	900	905	902	900	890	909	896	894	928	920	895	925	872	932	910	923	911	912	936	934	928	915	910	914	919
	879	862	873	871	900	915	902	906	926	915	898	933	927	932	925	888	916	920	913	917	926	928	885	925	898
Median	897	900	902	900	900	909	896	906	922	915	895	908	906	902	910	907	911	912	913	917	912	913	908	917	898
Range	54	49	42	59	40	50	20	26	33	30	9	38	55	37	32	35	57	23	40	59	32	19	41	11	35

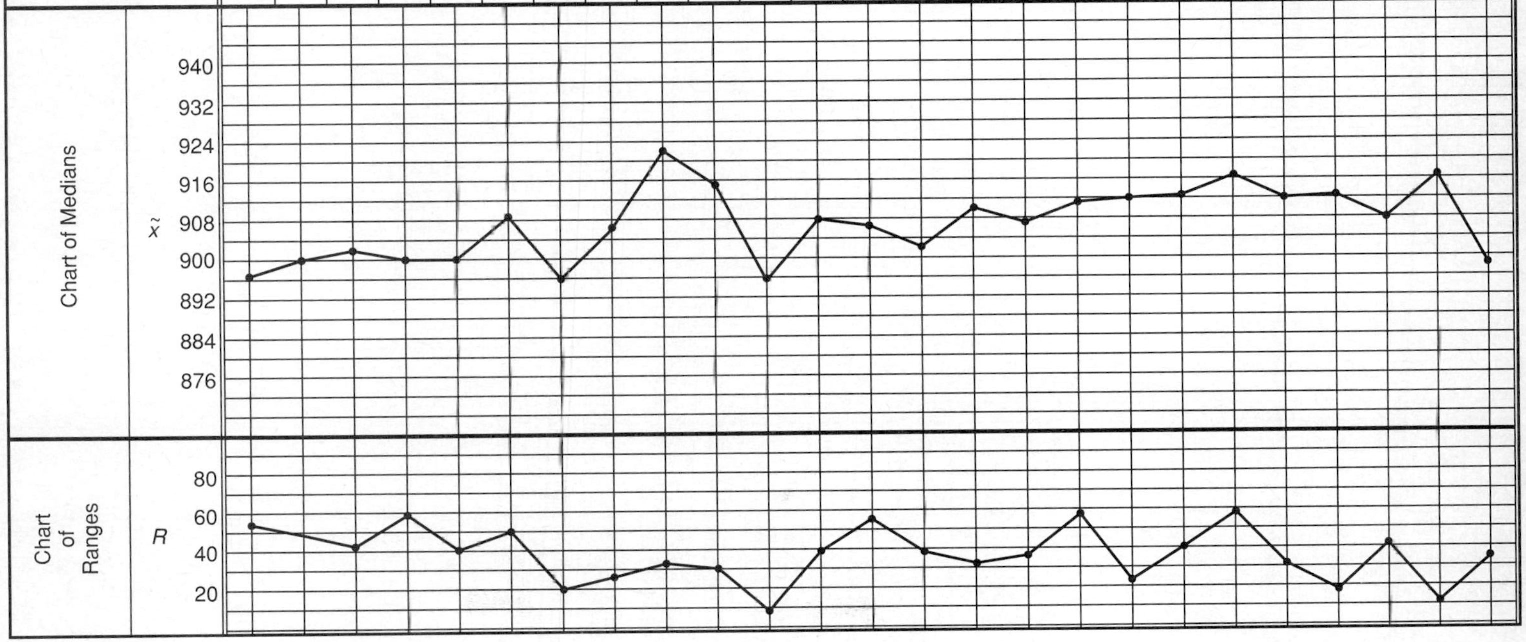

Chart of Medians

$\tilde{x}$

940
932
924
916
908
900
892
884
876

Chart of Ranges

R

80
60
40
20

FIGURE 4.4

The median and range values are charted and connected with straight line segments.

61

Sample Number	1	2	3	4	5	6	7	8	9	10	11	12	13	14	15	16	17	18	19	20	21	22	23	24	25
Sample measurements	933	911	889	882	903	890	892	908	895	916	901	908	909	895	893	909	885	897	912	882	896	912	926	917	884
	897	898	915	913	930	940	912	920	920	890	892	895	904	902	906	907	892	904	896	894	912	909	903	917	889
	885	900	905	930	890	895	895	896	922	891	892	896	906	902	917	904	942	916	932	941	907	913	908	918	912
	900	905	902	900	890	909	896	894	928	920	895	925	872	932	910	923	911	912	936	934	928	915	910	914	919
	879	862	873	871	900	915	902	906	926	915	898	933	927	932	925	888	916	920	913	917	926	928	885	925	898
Median	897	900	902	900	900	909	896	906	922	915	895	908	906	902	910	907	911	912	913	917	912	913	908	917	898
Range	54	49	42	59	40	50	20	26	33	30	9	38	55	37	32	35	57	23	40	59	32	19	41	11	35

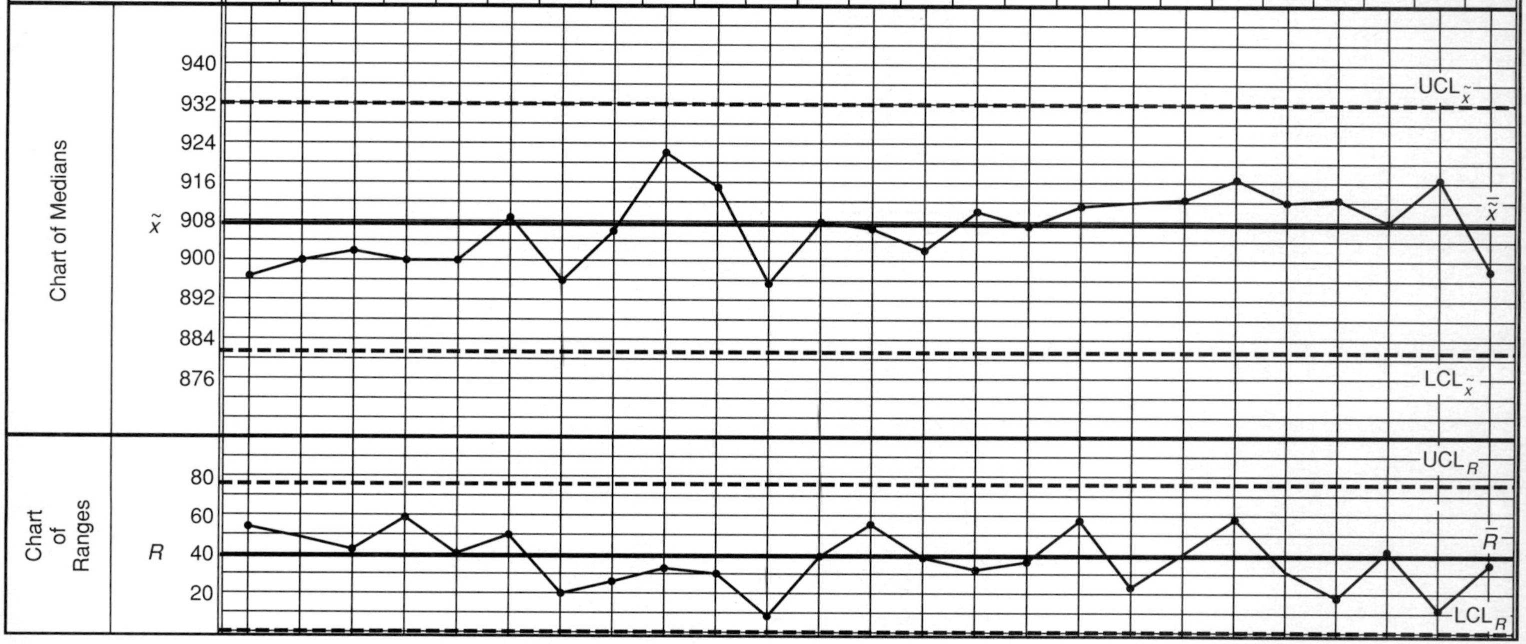

FIGURE 4.5

The $\tilde{x}$ and R chart with center lines and control limits.

62

Step 4   Calculate the averages and control limit values using the appropriate statistical formulas. Average the medians. Median values are recorded on the chart in Figure 4.5 (page 62). The symbol for the average of the medians is $\overline{\tilde{x}}$.

$$\overline{\tilde{x}} = \frac{897 + 900 + 902 + \cdots + 898}{25}$$

$$= \frac{22676}{25}$$

$$= 907.04$$

Next average the ranges. Range values are also recorded in Figure 4.5.

$$\overline{R} = \frac{54 + 49 + 42 + \cdots + 35}{25}$$

$$= \frac{926}{25}$$

$$= 37.04$$

Calculate the upper control limit for the $\tilde{x}$ chart ($\text{UCL}_{\tilde{x}}$). The formula is

$$\text{UCL}_{\tilde{x}} = \overline{\tilde{x}} + (\tilde{A}_2 \cdot R)$$

$\tilde{A}_2$ is a numerical constant that corresponds to the sample size. The table of constants is given in Appendix B, Table 1.2. The sample size is given in column n. Find 5 in the n column, go straight across to the $\tilde{A}_2$ column, and read the value. $\tilde{A}_2 = .691$.

$$\text{UCL}_{\tilde{x}} = \overline{\tilde{x}} + (\tilde{A}_2\overline{R})$$
$$= 907.04 + (.691 \times 37.04)$$
$$= 907.04 + 25.59464$$
$$= 932.63464$$

Calculate the lower control limit for the $\tilde{x}$ chart ($\text{LCL}_{\tilde{x}}$). The formula is

$$\text{LCL}_{\tilde{x}} = \overline{\tilde{x}} - (\tilde{A}_2 \cdot \overline{R})$$

The product in the parentheses is the same as that used in the $\text{UCL}_{\tilde{x}}$ calculation.

$$\text{LCL}_{\tilde{x}} = \overline{\tilde{x}} - (\tilde{A}_2\overline{R})$$
$$= 907.04 - 25.59464$$
$$= 881.44536$$

Calculate the upper control limit for the R chart (UCL_R). The formula is

$$\text{UCL}_R = D_4 \cdot \overline{R}$$

The value for the numerical constant D_4 is found in Table 1.2 of Appendix B. Locate the n value, 5, and go straight across to the D_4 column. $D_4 = 2.114$.

$$UCL_R = D_4\overline{R}$$
$$= 2.114 \times 37.04$$
$$= 78.30256$$

Calculate the lower control limit for the R chart (LCL_R). The formula is

$$LCL_R = D_3 \cdot \overline{R}$$

but the value of the numerical constant, D_3, is 0 for sample sizes less than 7. Therefore, $LCL_R = 0$.

Draw a solid line at the average values, $\overline{\overline{x}}$ and $\overline{R}$, and a dashed line at the control limits, $UCL_{\overline{x}}$, $LCL_{\overline{x}}$, UCL_R, and LCL_R. When you draw these lines on your chart in Figure 4.3, your completed chart should look like the chart in Figure 4.5.

Step 5 Interpret the pattern on the charts formed by the points and their broken-line graph for signs of special cause variation. If there is no obvious pattern, the points will be randomly scattered, with about two-thirds of them close to the average line and the other third spread out closer to the control limit lines. Figure 4.6 illustrates a control chart with a random pattern. Nonrandom patterns will be discussed thoroughly in Chapter 9, but a few of the basic ones are presented here in Figures 4.7, 4.8, and 4.9 (page 65).

One example of the ways the pattern on a control chart can lead to improved quality and decreased costs involves Figures 4.8 and 4.9. Companies that do not use SPC deal with tool sharpening and adjustments in three basic ways:

1. Sharpen or adjust tools when product measurements are beyond the specification limits. This rule is costly because some pieces of unacceptable quality must be made to indicate the need for tool adjustment.
2. Sharpen or adjust according to some specified time period. This rule leads to unnecessary downtime when the time period is too short and to poor or unacceptable quality when the time period is too long.

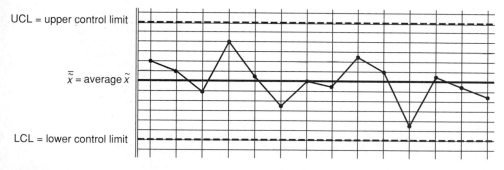

FIGURE 4.6
A random pattern of points.

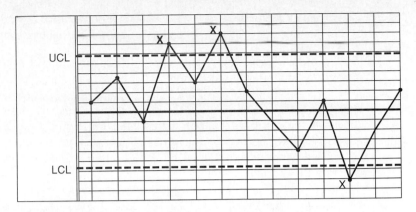

FIGURE 4.7
Points beyond the control limits, marked X, indicate special cause variation.

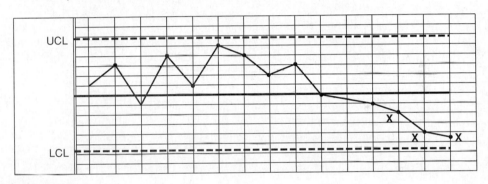

FIGURE 4.8
A trend or a run.

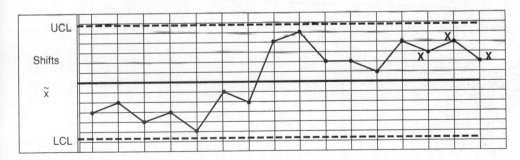

FIGURE 4.9
A shift.

3. Rely on the operator's experience. This rule can lead to either overadjustment or underadjustment. The overadjustment not only increases downtime but also decreases quality because "chasing" the target measurement increases overall variability. Every time the operator shuts down and adjusts the machine, a new distribution results. If this is done excessively the overall distribution of mea-

surements flattens out with several modes and a wider pattern. Underadjustment results in the production of some pieces of unacceptable quality.

When SPC is used, a *trend* or *run* on a control chart can show a need for sharpening or adjusting before poor quality items are made. Shifts can also indicate the same problem.

When these or other patterns show up, the process control team analyzes the chart commentary and other process information to determine what caused the out-of-control situation on the chart. When the cause is found, it's eliminated from the process and the out-of-control data are removed from the charts. The average and control limit values are recalculated with the remaining set of "good" data.

This analysis procedure continues until all the special cause problems have been eliminated. The process is then said to be in statistical control. Statistical control indicates that the process is currently working as well as it possibly can without process changes. The next question is, "Is that good enough?"

Step 6 Calculate the process capability. When statistical control is achieved, the distribution of the individual measurements may be analyzed statistically using the concepts in Chapter 5. The application of statistics will indicate what percent of the product is out of specification, or, if the output is entirely within specification, how much leeway or margin for error exists.

If the process is not capable, that is if it has too much variation embedded in the process, management action is necessary to make any improvements. The process must be changed somehow, and management must direct that change.

Step 7 Monitor the process. When a particular phase of a process is both in statistical control and capable, that part of the process should be monitored to ensure that it stays that way. The precontrol method, explained in Chapter 7, is a good monitoring technique. It is much easier than control charting and is quite effective. Another monitoring technique that can be used is to continue with the same control chart but decrease the sampling frequency.

As a post-script to Example 4.4, an analysis of the control chart reveals that the R chart appears to be in statistical control. There are no points beyond the control limits, and the pattern of the points within the control limits does not match any of the trouble patterns that were illustrated. The $\bar{x}$ chart doesn't have any points beyond the control limits, but a shift pattern is evident for samples 17 through 24. The process is not in statistical control, and the cause for the out-of-control situation should be determined.

EXERCISES

1. What are the two basic types of control charts, and how do they differ?
2. Name three types of variables control charts.
3. Name four types of attributes control charts.
4. Prepare a random sampling plan like Example 4.2 that tells the specific times that each sample should be taken. Ten samples are to be taken in an eight-hour shift that begins at 3:00 P.M. Each

sample consists of five pieces that take 15 minutes to produce. Use the following sequence of random numbers (in order columnwise) generated by a statistical calculator.

838	676	816	853	305
918	203	358	745	508
470	533	694	961	941
422	410	928	657	104
007	641	645	828	090
287	733	753	058	754
956	357	699	022	163
143	404	079	190	636

5. Seven samples of five measurements are recorded on the control chart in Figure 4.10.
   (a) Calculate $\tilde{x}$ and R for each sample; record them on the chart.
   (b) Chart the $\tilde{x}$ and R values and draw the broken-line graph.

Sample Numbers	1	2	3	4	5	6	7
Data Values	.732	.746	.748	.729	.739	.727	.729
	.741	.742	.726	.734	.741	.742	.734
	.740	.725	.717	.742	.745	.745	.734
	.728	.735	.734	.736	.737	.746	.738
	.735	.741	.736	.738	.742	.741	.729
Median							
Range							

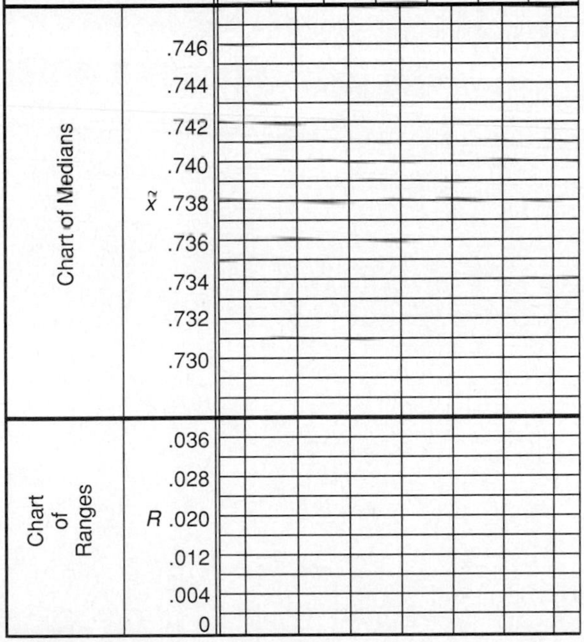

Chart of Medians

.746
.744
.742
.740
$\tilde{x}$ .738
.736
.734
.732
.730

Chart of Ranges

.036
.028
R .020
.012
.004
0

FIGURE 4.10
Exercise 5.

6. Which of the charts in Figures 4.11, 4.12, and 4.13 appears out of control and why?

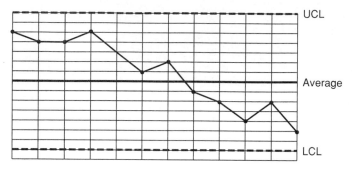

FIGURE 4.11
Exercise 6(a).

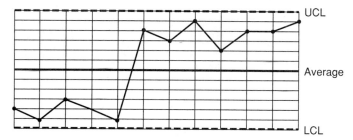

FIGURE 4.12
Exercise 6(b).

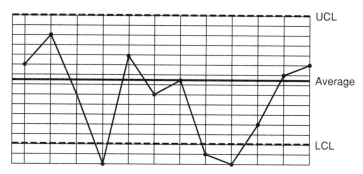

FIGURE 4.13
Exercise 6(c).

5

THE NORMAL PROBABILITY DISTRIBUTION

OBJECTIVES

- Make a frequency distribution.
- Construct histograms.
- Analyze histograms.
- Know the relationship between area under the normal distribution curve and the percentage of product measurements that it represents.
- Use the normal distribution tables.
- Calculate the percent of product that is out of specification.

Control charts, such as the median and range chart introduced in Chapter 4, will indicate when a specific point in a process is in statistical control. Further analysis is then necessary to determine how capable the process is at that point, or how the measurements compare with the specifications. Most distributions of measurements will have a pattern that closely matches the normal distribution after statistical control is achieved. The statistical analysis of the normal distribution is then applied to the product distribution using the data from the control chart, and the extent of variability from the target measurement is determined.

5.1 THE FREQUENCY DISTRIBUTION

A frequency distribution, in its simplest form, is a table that indicates all the different values from a set of data and the frequency with which each different value occurred. When the number of different values is so large that many of the values have a frequency of 0, 1, or 2, the values should be grouped; the frequency distribution will then list the groups and the number of data items in them (the frequency of each group).

Information on a population of measurements comes from the data in a sample. The sample data can be organized in many ways, depending on the number of groups, or classes, used, and each way provides a picture of the population distributionwith various degrees of accuracy. For every sample size, there is a preferred choice for the number of classes that will make the sample distribution most accurately mirror the population distribution. The G chart, which is given in Appendix B, Table 2, shows the recommended number of groups or classes that correspond to specific sample sizes.

The histogram, a picture of a frequency distribution, provides a logical lead into the concept of the normal distribution. In Chapter 3 the histogram was introduced as a picture of the shape of the distribution of measurements. However, with a large number of different values, measurements have to be grouped in a frequency distribution in order to picture the product distribution from the sample distribution. The more formal procedure for setting up a frequency distribution will be demonstrated here using the data from Table 5.1.

EXAMPLE 5.1

Construct a frequency distribution for the data in Table 5.1.

TABLE 5.1

Sample						Sample				
1	933	897	885	900	879	2	911	898	900	905	862
3	889	915	905	902	873	4	882	913	930	900	871
5	903	930	890	890	900	6	890	940	895	909	915
7	892	912	895	896	902	8	908	920	896	894	906
9	895	920	922	928	926	10	916	890	891	920	915
11	901	892	892	895	898	12	908	895	896	925	933
13	909	904	906	892	927	14	895	902	902	932	932
15	893	906	917	910	925	16	909	907	904	923	888
17	885	892	942	911	916	18	897	904	916	912	920
19	912	896	932	936	913	20	882	894	941	934	917
21	896	912	907	928	926	22	912	909	913	915	928
23	926	903	908	910	885	24	917	917	918	914	925
25	884	889	912	919	898						

Solution

Step 1   Scan the data for the range.

$$R = \text{largest} - \text{smallest}$$
$$= 942 - 862$$
$$= 80$$

Step 2   Should we use individual values or grouped values in the frequency distribution? Groups should be used in this case because there are so many different individual values. How many groups? The G chart shown in Appendix B, Table 2 indicates the optimum number of groups for the size of the set of data. For the 125 data values, 11 groups should be used.

Step 3   Find the group range, R_G, and set up the group endpoints. Divide the number of groups into the range and round up to determine the range of each group. *The group ranges must all be the same.*

$$80 \div 11 = 7.\overline{27} \qquad \text{Round } up \text{ to 7.3, or 7.4, or ..., or 8.0.}$$

The minimum group range is 7.3. Round up to 8 to make the group range easier to work with.

Step 4   Check to see how much the group boundaries will overlap the set of data. Add the product of the group range and the number of groups, $R_G \times G$, to the smallest data value, S.

$$(R_G \times G) + S = (8 \times 11) + 862 = 950$$

Subtract the largest data value from the result. The difference is the amount of overlap. If that difference is negative, check your round-up for the R_G value.

$$950 - 942 = 8 \qquad \text{The overlap is 8 units.}$$

If the frequency distribution starts at the smallest data value, 862, it will end at 950, which is 8 units larger than the largest data value, 942. When the overlap exceeds half of the group range, center the data by "backing up" half the number of overlap units. The overlap in this case, 8, is more than half of the R_G value, 8, so divide the overlap number in half and back up four units. The frequency distribution, then, begins at 858 (the lowest value, 862, minus four units). See Table 5.2.

TABLE 5.2
Group endpoints for the frequency distribution

858 to 866
866 to 874
874 to 882
882 to 890
890 to 898
898 to 906
906 to 914
914 to 922
922 to 930
930 to 938
938 to 946

Step 5 Complete the frequency distribution by determining the number of data values that fall in each group (the frequency). The completed frequency distribution consists of a column of group endpoints and a column of frequency values.

A histogram is usually drawn to "picture" the frequency distribution. Because a tally system is usually used to determine the frequency values, both can be done simultaneously by making a tally histogram.

Assign the group endpoints to the horizontal axis of the histogram and put an x in the appropriate column for each data value. Resort to double columns of x's in each group if the single columns reach the top of the chart. Balance the doubled, individual columns in each group when this is done to maintain the correct shape of the distribution of data. *If a data value coincides with a group endpoint, assign it to the higher class.* For example, 882 would be assigned to the fourth class and 890 would go in the fifth class. The tally histogram is shown in Figure 5.1. See also Table 5.3 on page 73.

FIGURE 5.1
Tally histogram.

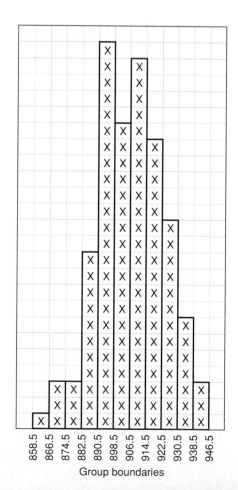

TABLE 5.3
The frequency distribution for
Example 5.1

Group boundaries	Frequency
858 to 866	1
866 to 874	3
874 to 882	3
882 to 890	11
890 to 898	24
898 to 906	19
906 to 914	23
914 to 922	18
922 to 930	13
930 to 938	7
938 to 946	3

5.2 HISTOGRAMS

The histogram is a bar graph with no space between the adjacent bars (see Figure 5.2). The following steps are used to make a histogram.

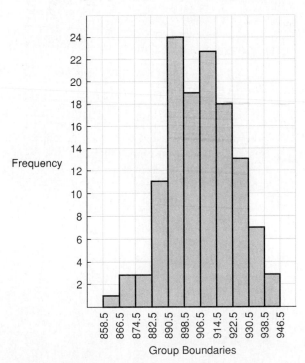

FIGURE 5.2
The histogram.

- Set the scale for the horizontal axis using the group endpoints from the frequency distribution. If the tally histogram was made initially, the same horizontal scale will be used.
- Set an appropriate scale for the vertical frequency axis.
- Make a bar of the proper height for each group. The adjacent bars should touch.

EXAMPLE 5.2

A set of data is given in Table 5.4.

1. Find the recommended number of groups on the G chart in Appendix B, Table 2.
2. Calculate the group range and set up the group boundaries.
3. Tally the data in a tally histogram with the group boundaries.
4. Make the frequency distribution.
5. Make the histogram.

TABLE 5.4
Data for Example 5.2

4.522	4.510	4.556	4.534	4.550	4.528	4.538
4.544	4.535	4.539	4.517	4.553	4.548	4.518
4.536	4.526	4.546	4.542	4.525	4.537	4.525
4.526	4.536	4.530	4.540	4.531	4.532	4.524
4.529	4.538	4.535	4.533	4.520	4.543	4.535

Solution

There are 35 data values, so either six or seven groups will be appropriate. We will use seven groups in this example. Following the preceding list of steps, we will next calculate the group range, check for overlap, and set boundaries.

$$R = 4.556 - 4.510$$
$$= .046$$
$$R_G = .046 \div 7$$
$$= .0065714$$
$$\cong .007$$
$$(R_G \times G) + S = (.007 \times 7) + 4.510$$
$$= 4.559$$
$$4.559 - 4.556 = .003$$

The overlap of .003 is less than half of R_G, so centering the data isn't necessary.

TABLE 5.5
Group boundaries

4.510 to 4.517
4.517 to 4.524
4.524 to 4.531
4.531 to 4.538
4.538 to 4.545
4.545 to 4.552
4.552 to 4.559

Check your arithmetic here in Table 5.5. The last boundary value should coincide with the $(R_G \times G) + S$ value. The tally histogram is shown in Figure 5.3, and the frequency distribution in Table 5.6. Figure 5.4 on page 76 illustrates the histogram.

4.510 to 4.516	X									
4.517 to 4.523	X	X	X	X						
4.524 to 4.530	X	X	X	X	X	X	X	X		
4.531 to 4.537	X	X	X	X	X	X	X	X	X	X
4.538 to 4.544	X	X	X	X	X	X	X			
4.545 to 4.551	X	X	X							
4.552 to 4.558	X	X								

FIGURE 5.3
The completed tally for Example 5.2.

TABLE 5.6
The frequency distribution
for Example 5.2

Group Boundaries	Frequency
4.510 to 4.517	1
4.517 to 4.524	4
4.524 to 4.531	8
4.531 to 4.538	10
4.538 to 4.545	7
4.545 to 4.552	3
4.552 to 4.559	2

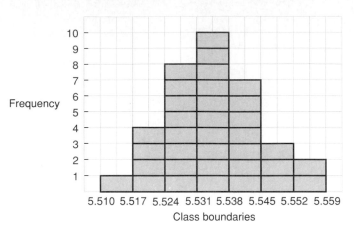

FIGURE 5.4
The completed histogram for Example 5.2.

Histograms are very important in SPC because all the usual statistical formulas that are used apply to a *normal probability distribution*. The normal distribution has the bell shape that was illustrated on some previous charts such as Figures 3.11 and 3.12. The histogram indicates when the distribution of data is normal or nearly so. A normal pattern is necessary for the application of the process capability formulas to give meaningful results.

If a histogram doesn't have the expected bell shape, then either something in the process is out of control and must be fixed or the shape of the distribution naturally follows some other basic pattern. If a different pattern is evident, the appropriate statistical distribution must then be matched to the shape of the histogram; the statistical formulas that accompany that distribution will then give the most meaningful results.

Histogram Analysis Examples

Production samples were organized into histograms for analysis. Figures 5.5 through 5.11 illustrate different trouble patterns and the possible causes for those patterns.

The two peaks shown in Figure 5.5 on page 77 may indicate that the variable of interest has not been isolated. Two or more process streams may be feeding into the process point being analyzed. The histogram in Figure 5.2 indicates that this type of problem occurred with the data from Example 4.3. The shift that was noted on the $\bar{x}$ chart coincides with the higher mode on the histogram. The result was an increase in overall variability.

The histogram in Figure 5.6 (page 77) may indicate a 100 percent inspection occurring with the low, out-of-specification product removed. Its pattern is almost normal, but the left tail section is missing.

Figure 5.7, shown on page 77, may indicate inspector flinching on the low, out-of-specification limit. The normal pattern is interrupted by a missing left tail section and an unusually high stack of measurements at the lower specification value. This is a strong indication that some out-of-specification pieces have been deemed "close enough."

FIGURE 5.5
A bimodal distribution: a mix of two or more distributions.

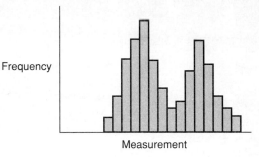

FIGURE 5.6
A distribution with the smaller measurements removed.

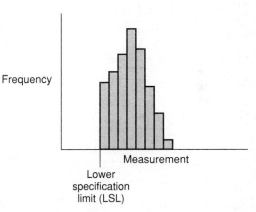

FIGURE 5.7
Inspector flinching at the lower specification limit.

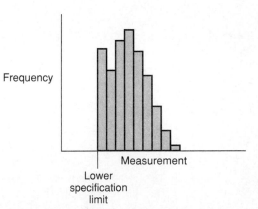

The histogram in Figure 5.8 shows inspector flinching on both out-of-specification limits. Both tail sections are missing and a high stack of measurements occurs at both specification limits.

FIGURE 5.8
Inspector flinching at both limits.

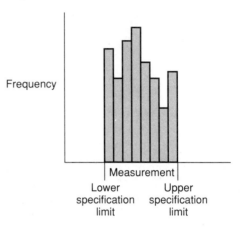

The inspector may have favorite readings, according to Figure 5.9, or the gauge may be faulty. Another possibility is that the distribution has several modes that are due to different spindles, shifts, operators, or machines.

FIGURE 5.9
A faulty gauge or poor training.

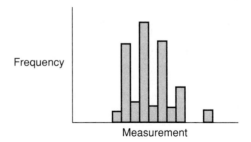

The histogram in Figure 5.10 on page 79 may be skewed because of excessive tool wear. The shape shows a different statistical distribution, such as the Poisson or the chi-square distribution; a statistical goodness-of-fit test would determine which fits best. If the tool cannot be normalized for a specified product run, a set of histograms from that process point will have to be matched to the statistical distribution that best describes that product distribution. The formulas from that distribution will be used in any capability analysis.

FIGURE 5.10
A skewed distribution.

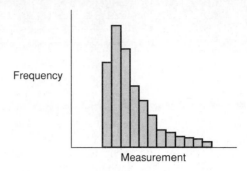

Frequency

Measurement

5.3 THE NORMAL DISTRIBUTION

Statistical curves and distributions are used to establish control limits for the process. The control limits are the outer boundaries for the values being charted, such as $\bar{x}$, $\tilde{x}$, or R. The control limits are the dashed lines drawn on the control chart in Chapter 4, Figure 4.5. The analysis of the process at the point being charted relies on the statistical properties of the normal curve. First of all, the *Central Limit Theorem* of statistics states that even though a population of measurements may not be normally distributed, the distribution of $\bar{x}$, the sample means from that population, will be. Also, the behavior of the $\bar{x}$ values is predictable to a certain extent; when a set of $\bar{x}$'s does not behave normally, something in the process must have caused that different behavior and subsequent out-of-control situation. For example, approximately 99.7 percent of all ($\bar{x}$) values should fall between control limit boundaries. When they do not, the process is out of control and must be corrected. Other out-of-control point patterns, such as those illustrated in Figures 4.8 and 4.9, also rely on properties of the normal distribution along with some rules of probability, or chance. In a capability analysis, which is done after the process is in statistical control, the individual measurements are statistically compared with the product specification limits to show what percent of the product, if any, is out of specification.

This type of analysis can be done with other statistical distributions, but is most often done with the *normal probability distribution*. If another distribution is deemed more appropriate, the concepts involved will be the same as those described in our normal curve discussion, but the charts and formulas will differ.

The normal distribution applies in a great many situations in which information concerning a population of measurements (from a particular phase or step in a process) is determined from information gathered in samples. The normal distribution is often the closest match to the actual frequency distribution of many measurements and outputs such as weights, times, yields, and heights. Distributions' tendency to fit the normal distribution was pictured in Figures 3.1 to 3.4.

There are several important characteristics of the normal distribution.

1. The curve has a single peak and is bell-shaped.
2. The curve is symmetrical about the center line: The shape on one side of the center appears to mirror the image on the other side.

3. The mean and median are at the center.
4. The "tails" of the curve flatten out and extend indefinitely along the horizontal axis, always approaching the line but never touching or crossing it.
5. The area under the curve represents the percent of product in various categories, or the probability (chance) that the product will be in a specific category.

There is no single normal curve, but a whole family of curves that are described by two measurements from the data.

- The mean locates the center of the curve.
- The standard deviation measures the spread of the curve.

The standard normal probability distribution table, or simply the normal curve table, can be used to find areas or probabilities associated with specific values of the variable or measurement. The normal distribution table is Table 3 in Appendix B.

A *z score* is the number of standard deviations from the center of the distribution. The areas given in the normal curve table correspond to *z* scores. Individual values or measurements are translated to *z* scores using the formula

$$z = \frac{x - \bar{x}}{\sigma} \qquad \text{or} \qquad z = \frac{x - \bar{\bar{x}}}{\sigma}$$

The $\bar{x}$ and σ values are determined from the entire set of data using formulas presented in Chapter 3. The second version of the *z* formula uses $\bar{\bar{x}}$ as the mean value. When the *z* formula is used for a capability analysis with the $\bar{x}$ and R control charts, $\bar{\bar{x}}$ is the mean of all the sample means, which equals the mean of all the *x* values. With both $\bar{x}$ (or $\bar{\bar{x}}$) and σ known, each *x* measurement will correspond to a specific *z* value.

The *z* value is 0 at the center of the curve because $x - \bar{x}$ is zero there. The *z* values are positive to the right of center, where *x* is larger than $\bar{x}$, and are negative to the left of the center, where *x* is less than $\bar{x}$. A negative *z* value calculated for a given *x* value indicates that the area of interest lies to the left of center. The same table values are used for both positive and negative *z* values because of the symmetry property of the normal curve.

The normal curve can be analyzed with either *x* values (the individual measurements) or *z* values in standard deviations. The horizontal scale on the normal curve can also be set up using either the *x* or *z* scores. Both horizontal scales are shown in Example 5.3. The *z* values are determined by using the measurement value, *x*, in the *z* formula.

EXAMPLE 5.3

Given the mean and standard deviation for a set of data, find the *z*-scale values that correspond to *x*.

$$\bar{x} = 35$$
$$\sigma = 4$$

Solution

The *z* scale can be determined from the *x* values with the *z* formula. Calculate *z* for $x = 43$.

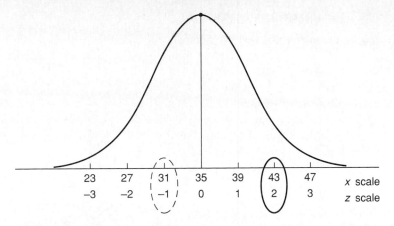

FIGURE 5.11
The normal curve with the scale of measurements (x) matched with the z scale.

$$z = \frac{x - \bar{x}}{\sigma}$$ Substitute values.

$$= \frac{43 - 35}{4}$$ Subtract first because the fraction line is a grouping symbol.

$$= \frac{8}{4}$$ Divide by 4.

$$= 2$$ The z value 2 corresponds to the x value 43 on the normal curve shown in Figure 5.11.

Calculate the other z values in the same manner using the x values from Figure 5.11. If $x = 31$, substitute $x = 31, \bar{x} = 35$, and $\sigma = 4$. Subtract first, then divide by 4.

$$z = \frac{x - \bar{x}}{\sigma}$$

$$= \frac{31 - 35}{4}$$

$$= \frac{-4}{4}$$

$$= -1$$

Because $z = 0$ at the center, the negative z value simply indicates that z is left of center. Here a z value of -1 matches an x value of 31 (see Figure 5.11).

The other z values shown in Figure 5.11 are calculated as follows:

$x = 23$	$x = 27$	$x = 35$	$x = 39$	$x = 47$
$z = \dfrac{23 - 35}{4}$	$z = \dfrac{27 - 35}{4}$	$z = \dfrac{35 - 35}{4}$	$z = \dfrac{39 - 35}{4}$	$z = \dfrac{47 - 35}{4}$
$z = -3$	$z = -2$	$z = 0$	$z = 1$	$z = 3$

Area under a Normal Curve

The area under the curve indicates a proportion, or percent, of the product or measurements; the area of various sections can be found using a statistical table. The complete table is Table 3 in Appendix B. You should find the area value in this table with each illustration.

The normal distribution table gives the *area* in the *tail section* of the curve that corresponds to a specific z value. A positive z value indicates that the area is in the right tail section; a negative z value indicates that the area is in the left tail section. The z values for the table range from 0.00 to 4.00.

To use the table, put the z value into a three-digit format (for example, .86 is changed to 0.86 and 1.4 becomes 1.40).

1. Find the first two digits of z in the z column on the left.
2. Match the third z digit with the appropriate column number on the right.
3. The *area* value is at the intersection of the *row* and the *column*.

The following display shows the area values that correspond to given z values. They are found in the normal distribution table (Table 3, Appendix B).

If $z = 1.52$	Row 1.5	Column 2	Area = .0643
If $z = -1.46$	Row 1.4	Column 6	Area = .0721
If $z = .7\ (0.70)$	Row 0.7	Column 0	Area = .2420
If $z = -2.03$	Row 2.0	Column 3	Area = .0212
If $z = 3\ (3.00)$	Row 3.0	Column 0	Area = .00135
If $z = 2.43$	Row 2.4	Column 3	Area = .0075
If $z = -1.86$	Row 1.8	Column 6	Area = .0314

In Example 5.3, the x values were given as 43 and 31, and the corresponding z values were calculated to be 2 and −1. The tail area for each is found in the normal distribution table as demonstrated in Example 5.4.

EXAMPLE 5.4 Find the area under the curve associated with $x = 43$ and $x = 31$ from Example 5.3 and interpret the results.

Solution

From the previous calculations, when $x = 43, z = 2$ and when $x = 31, z = -1$. For $z = 2$ (or 2.00), row 2.0 and column 0 give a tail area of .0228. Therefore, 2.28 percent of the area under the curve is to the *right* of $x = 43$, and 2.28 percent of the product has a value larger than 43. This is illustrated in Figure 5.12 on page 83.

For $z = -1$ (or –1.00), row 1.0 and column 0 give a tail area of .1587. This means that 15.87 percent of the area under the curve is to the *left* of $x = 31$, and that 15.87 percent of the product has a value less than 31. This is illustrated in Figure 5.13 (on page 83).

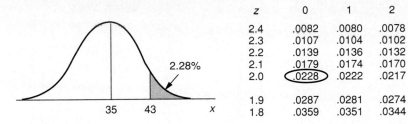

z	0	1	2
2.4	.0082	.0080	.0078
2.3	.0107	.0104	.0102
2.2	.0139	.0136	.0132
2.1	.0179	.0174	.0170
2.0	.0228	.0222	.0217
1.9	.0287	.0281	.0274
1.8	.0359	.0351	.0344

FIGURE 5.12
In Example 5.4, 2.28 percent of the measurements are larger than 43.

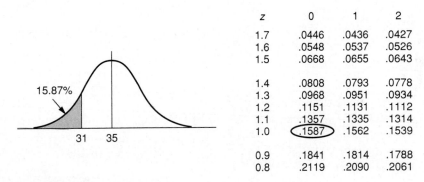

z	0	1	2
1.7	.0446	.0436	.0427
1.6	.0548	.0537	.0526
1.5	.0668	.0655	.0643
1.4	.0808	.0793	.0778
1.3	.0968	.0951	.0934
1.2	.1151	.1131	.1112
1.1	.1357	.1335	.1314
1.0	.1587	.1562	.1539
0.9	.1841	.1814	.1788
0.8	.2119	.2090	.2061

FIGURE 5.13
In Example 5.4, 15.87 percent of the measurements are less than 31.

EXAMPLE 5.5

Another example relates more directly to SPC: Suppose the product mean is .917 with a standard deviation of .014. Find the percent of product that is within one standard deviation of the mean, two standard deviations from the mean, and three standard deviations from the mean.

Solution
Add and subtract .014 to and from the mean to provide measurements that are one standard deviation from the mean. Add and subtract .028, or 2 × .014 to and from the mean to attain measurements that are two standard deviations from the mean. Adding and subtracting .042, or 3 × .014, will give measurements three standard deviations from the mean.

.917	.917	.917	.917	.917	.917
+.014	−.014	+.028	−.028	+.042	−.042
$x = .931$	$x = .903$	$x = .945$	$x = .889$	$x = .959$	$x = .875$

The z values for measurements $x = .931$ and $x = .903$ are $z = 1$ and $z = -1$, respectively, corresponding to one standard deviation from the mean:

$$z = \frac{x - \bar{x}}{\sigma} \qquad z = \frac{x - \bar{x}}{\sigma}$$

$$= \frac{.931 - .917}{.014} \qquad = \frac{.903 - .917}{.014}$$

$$= 1 \qquad = -1$$

The z values for measurements $x = .945$ and $x = .889$ are $z = 2$ and $z = -2$, respectively, corresponding to two standard deviations from the mean:

$$z = \frac{x - \bar{x}}{\sigma} \qquad z = \frac{x - \bar{x}}{\sigma}$$

$$= \frac{.945 - .917}{.014} \qquad = \frac{.889 - .917}{.014}$$

$$= 2 \qquad = -2$$

The z values for measurements $x = .959$ and $x = .875$ are $z = 3$ and $z = -3$, respectively, corresponding to three standard deviations from the mean:

$$z = \frac{x - \bar{x}}{\sigma} \qquad z = \frac{x - \bar{x}}{\sigma}$$

$$= \frac{.959 - .917}{.014} \qquad = \frac{.875 - .917}{.014}$$

$$= 3 \qquad = -3$$

Using Table 3 in Appendix B,

$$z = 1 \qquad \text{area} = .1587$$
$$z = 2 \qquad \text{area} = .0228$$
$$z = 3 \qquad \text{area} = .00135$$

The tail area is given in each case. This must be translated to the area in question, which is measured from the center. The total area under the curve is 1.00, which corresponds to 100 percent of all the measurements. The area under the curve on one side of the mean is .5 (half of the total area under the curve). Subtracting the tail area from .5 gives the area from the center (the mean) to the measurement. This is illustrated in Figure 5.14 (page 85).

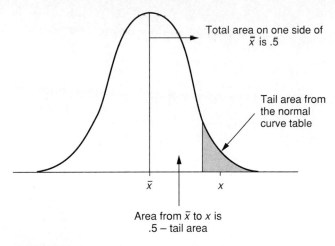

FIGURE 5.14
The area from $\bar{x}$ to x.

Using the symmetry property of the normal curve, double the center area to get the total area within one, two, or three standard deviations from the mean. The results are shown in Figures 5.15 and 5.16 (page 86).

$$z = 1, \text{tail area} = .1587$$
$$.5 - .1587 = .3413$$
$$2 \times .3413 = .6826$$

The mean, .917, is at the center. Approximately 68 percent, or .6826, of the product measures between .903 and .931, which are each one standard deviation from the mean.

$$z = 2, \text{tail area} = .0228$$
$$.5 - .0228 = .4772$$
$$2 \times .4772 = .9544$$

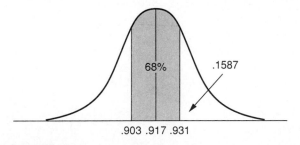

FIGURE 5.15
Sixty-eight percent (.6826) of the measurements are within one standard deviation of the mean.

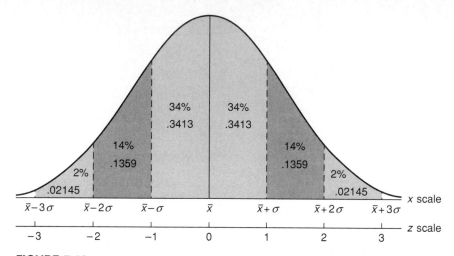

FIGURE 5.16
The normal curve with areas and percents associated with specific z values.

Approximately 95 percent (.9544) of the product measures between .889 and .945, which are two standard deviations from the mean. About 99.7 percent of the product is three standard deviations from the mean, between .875 and .959.

$$z = 3, \text{tail area} = .00135$$

$$.5 - .00135 = .49865$$

$$2 \times .49865 = .9973$$

The results of Example 5.5 maybe generalized for any application of the normal curve. Sixty-eight percent of the values will always be within one standard deviation of the mean, 95 percent of the values will always be within two standard deviations of the mean, and 99.7 percent of the values will always be within three standard deviations of the mean. This is illustrated in Figure 5.17 (see page 87).

If the histogram of the product measurements is bell-shaped, indicating a normal distribution, the normal curve analysis can provide much useful information about the true distribution of the measurements. More specifically, a normal curve analysis will show how the measurements compare with the target value and with the product specifications. This is illustrated in Example 5.6.

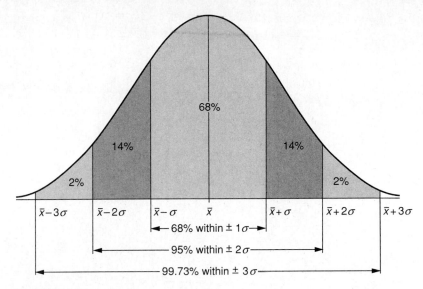

FIGURE 5.17
The standard deviation zones on the normal curve.

EXAMPLE 5.6

Continuing the work from Example 5.5, in which the product mean was .917 and the standard deviation was .014, suppose the product specifications are .880 to .930. Find the percent of the product that is out of specification.

Solution
Any area (or percent) evaluation with the normal curve involves the formula

$$z = \frac{x - \bar{x}}{\sigma}$$

The z gives the number of standard deviations from the center for each specific x value. Find the z value for each specification limit.

Using $x = .930$, the upper specification limit, make substitutions and calculate z.

$$z = \frac{x - \bar{x}}{\sigma}$$

$$= \frac{.930 - .917}{.014}$$

$$= \frac{.013}{.014}$$

$$= .93$$

$$= 0.93$$

Row 0.9 and column 3 give the area .1762 for $z = .93$. Next sketch the normal curve and put $x = .917$ at the center and $x = .930$ to the right. The z scale can be matched below the x scale: Place $z = 0$ at the center and $z = .93$ under the x value of .930. Shade the area to the right of $x = .930$. The shaded section illustrates the percent of out-of-specification product on the high side. This sketch is shown in Figure 5.18. Row 0.9 and column 3 give the tail area .1762, which means that 17.62 percent of the product is out of specification on the high side.

FIGURE 5.18
The total percent of out-of-specification measurements, with both USL and LSL in the z formula.

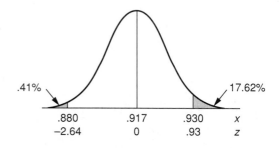

.41%   17.62%

| .880 | .917 | .930 | x |
| −2.64 | 0 | .93 | z |

Now use $x = .880$, the lower specification limit. Substitute the .880 for x, .917 for $\bar{x}$, and .014 for σ and calculate z.

$$z = \frac{x - \bar{x}}{\sigma}$$
$$= \frac{.880 - .917}{.014}$$
$$= \frac{-.037}{.014}$$
$$= -2.64$$

The negative z value indicates that the value is to the left of the center.

Using the same sketch of the normal curve, put $x = .880$ to the left of the center and $z = -2.64$ under the $x = .880$. Shade the area to the left of the .880. This represents the percent out of specification on the low side, as shown in Figure 5.18. Row 2.6 and column 4 give the area .0041, so .41 percent of the product is out of specification on the low side. The total percent out of specification (.41 percent + 17.62 percent) is 18.03 percent.

Excessive variation is the major battle manufacturers have today in achieving high quality products. When variation decreases, product quality increases.

EXAMPLE 5.7 Suppose improvement is made in the process from Example 5.6 that decreases the standard deviation, the measure of variation, from .014 to .005. Find the percent of product that is now out of specification.

Solution
Substitute $x = .930, \bar{x} = .917,$ and $\sigma = .005$ into the equation and calculate z.

$$z = \frac{x - \bar{x}}{\sigma}$$

$$= \frac{.930 - .917}{.005}$$

$$= \frac{.013}{.005}$$

$$= 2.60$$

The value $\bar{x} = .917$ is at the center, and the x value of .930 is at the right. The corresponding z scale is shown below the x scale, 0 at the center and the 2.60 under the .930. Row 2.6 and column 0 lead to a tail area of .0047, which indicates that .47 percent of the product is out of specification on the high side.
  For the low side, substitute $x = .880, \bar{x} = .917,$ and $\sigma = .005$ into the equation.

$$z = \frac{x - \bar{x}}{\sigma}$$

$$= \frac{.880 - .917}{.005}$$

$$= -7.4$$

Again, the negative z value indicates that the area is left of the center. The z value of 7.4 is not in the table, which means that the area to the left of -7.4 is 0.00000. There is area under the curve to the left of -7.4, but it is so small that this table, with accuracy to only five places, can't measure it.
  In the sketch of the normal curve, $x = .917$ is at the center, $x = .880$ is to the left, and $x = .930$ is to the right. The z scale can be shown below the x scale, with 0 under the center, 2.6 below the .930, and -7.4 below the .880. Shade the area to left of the .880 and to the right of the .930. This shaded area represents the percent that is out of specification and is shown in Figure 5.19.

FIGURE 5.19
The percent that is out of specification in
Example 5.7, in which the standard devia-
tion is reduced.

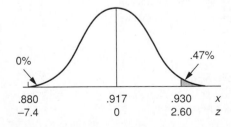

By decreasing the variation, the percent of out-of-specification product dropped from 18.03 percent to .47 percent. If the process could be readjusted so the mean was at the mid-specification value of .905, virtually all of the product would be in specification. This is shown in Example 5.8.

EXAMPLE 5.8

The process from Example 5.8 has been readjusted so the average measurement is $\bar{x} = .905$. Find the percent of product that is out of specification.

Solution

Substitute $x = .930, \bar{x} = .905$ and $\sigma = .005$. Subtract first, then divide.

$$z = \frac{x - \bar{x}}{\sigma}$$

$$= \frac{.930 - .905}{.005}$$

$$= 5.0$$

Sketch the curve, put $\bar{x} = .905$ at the center and $x = .930$ to the right, and match the z scale below it. Shade the area to the right, the out-of-specification section. The z value of 5.0 is not in the table, which means the tail area to the right is .00000 (not measurable with this table). The result is 0 percent out-of-specification product on the high end. Next, check the low side.

Substitute $x = .880, \bar{x} = .905$, and $\sigma = .005$.

$$z = \frac{x - \bar{x}}{\sigma}$$

$$= \frac{.880 - .905}{.005}$$

$$= \frac{-.025}{.005}$$

$$= -5.0$$

On the same sketch of the normal curve, mark $x = .880$ to the left and match the z scale below it. Shade the area to the left of .880 to represent the percent out of specification as shown in Figure 5.20. As before, $z = 5.0$ is not in the table, so the area to the left is .00000. We therefore have 0 percent out of specification on the low end, too.

FIGURE 5.20
USL and LSL analysis of Example 5.8: Tail area is 0 percent.

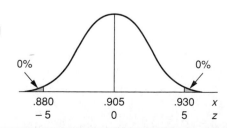

The following is the general procedure for finding the area or percent in a section using the normal curve:

1. The measurements must be normally distributed; the histogram of the measurements should be bell-shaped.
2. Determine the mean and standard deviation for the measurements. The formulas associated with the specific control chart will do this.
3. Sketch the normal curve, locate the $\bar{x}$ value at the center, label the x value(s) accordingly, and shade the area of interest.
4. Find the z scores for the x values that border the area of interest using $z = (x - \bar{x})/\sigma$ and show the z scale.
5. Convert the z scores to area values using the normal curve table.
6. Transform the table area to the area of interest.
7. Convert area to percent by multiplying by 100.

All the work in this text will use the tail area table, Table 3 in Appendix B. Other available versions of the normal curve table will be discussed briefly in Appendix A.

EXAMPLE 5.9

The process mean is $\bar{x} = 1.747$, and the standard deviation is $\sigma = .006$. If the specification limits are 1.740 to 1.760, what percent of the product is out of specification?

Solution
To sketch the process, draw a normal curve and locate $\bar{x}$ at the center. Set points 1.760 to the right and 1.740 to the left. Shade the tail areas to represent the percent of out-of-specification product, as shown in Figure 5.21. Calculate the z value for each specification limit.

FIGURE 5.21
The curve, LSL, USL, and $\bar{x}$ for Example 5.9.

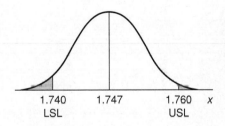

| 1.740 | 1.747 | 1.760 | x |
| LSL | | USL | |

$$z_1 = \frac{x_1 - \bar{x}}{\sigma} \qquad z_2 = \frac{x_2 - \bar{x}}{\sigma}$$

$$= \frac{1.740 - 1.747}{.006} \qquad = \frac{1.760 - 1.747}{.006}$$

$$= \frac{-.007}{.006} \qquad = \frac{.013}{.006}$$

$$= -1.17 \qquad = 2.17$$

$$\text{Area}_1 = .1210 \qquad \text{Area}_2 = .0150$$

$$12.1\% \text{ out (low)} \qquad 1.5\% \text{ out (high)}$$

The total product out of specification (12.1 percent + 1.5 percent) is 13.6 percent.

EXAMPLE 5.10 Suppose an improvement in the preceding process reduced the standard deviation from .006 to .003. What percent of the product is out of specification now?

Solution

The drawing will be the same as the one in Figure 5.21. Calculate the new z values.

$$z_1 = \frac{x_1 - \overline{x}}{\sigma} \qquad\qquad z_2 = \frac{x_2 - \overline{x}}{\sigma}$$

$$= \frac{1.740 - 1.747}{.003} \qquad\qquad = \frac{1.760 - 1.747}{.003}$$

$$= \frac{-.007}{.003} \qquad\qquad = \frac{.013}{.003}$$

$$= -2.33 \qquad\qquad = 4.33$$

$$\text{Area}_1 = .0099 \qquad\qquad \text{Area}_2 = .00000$$

$$.99\% \text{ out (low)} \qquad\qquad 0\% \text{ out (high)}$$

If the process mean could be adjusted to the mid-specification position of 1.750, both z calculations would be

$$z = \frac{.010}{.003}$$

$$= 3.33$$

$$\text{Area} = .00043$$

Both the high and the low side have .043 percent out of specification for a total of .086 percent out of specification.

The Value of Normal Curve Analysis

The examples illustrate that a sample of measurements can be analyzed to give extensive knowledge about the population of measurements from which they were drawn. The shape of the distribution (histogram) can serve as a trouble indicator, as shown in the section on histogram analysis. The normal curve analysis can indicate the percent of product that is out of specification as well as the percent of product between specific measurements. The decrease in product variability, as measured by the standard deviation, has a direct effect on the percent of product that is out of specification. The capability analysis that is discussed in Chapter 6 is an application of this latter concept.

The median and range chart that was introduced in Chapter 4 uses an important property of the normal curve that was demonstrated in Example 5.5 of this chapter. When the process is behaving normally (when it is in statistical control), virtually all the points, specifically 99.7 percent of them, should be within three standard deviations of the mean. Further, as the chart analysis work in Chapter 9 will elaborate, about two-thirds of the points, technically 68 percent, should be within one standard deviation of the mean.

When the points on the control chart do not behave in this way—when there are points beyond the control limits or unusual clusters of points within the control limits— the process is considered out of control. The cause or causes of the problem must then be determined and eliminated in order to bring the process into statistical control. After charting the 25 points on the $\tilde{x}$ and R chart in Chapter 4, statistical formulas were used to calculate the middle lines for $\overline{x}$ and $\overline{R}$, and the dashed lines which were called control limits. The middle lines were the average values for the variables $\tilde{x}$ and R, and the control limits corresponded to three standard deviations from those mean or average values. Once the control limit lines and average value lines were drawn, the chart could be analyzed.

The table of constants in Appendix B, Table 1 and the formulas used to calculate the control limits were developed by Walter Shewhart of the Bell Telephone Laboratories. The control limit formulas provide a quick and easy approximation of the 3σ lines using $\overline{R}$ and a special constant. Similar formulas accompany other control charts that are introduced in Chapters 6 and 7.

EXERCISES

1. Refer to the G Chart in Appendix B, Table 2. How many groups should be used for making a histogram if there are
   (a) 150 data values?
   (b) 70 data values?
   (c) 300 data values?
2. If your data ranges from a low of 2.824 to a high of 2.852 and you're making eight groups, what are the group boundaries?
3. (a) Make a tally histogram for the given data. Use the group boundaries 1.725 to 1.765, 1.765 to 1.805, 1.805 to 1.845, and so on.

1.81	1.86	1.87	1.85	1.87	1.81	1.85
1.76	1.79	1.82	1.89	1.83	1.79	1.83
1.84	1.93	1.85	1.87	1.86	1.78	1.87
1.73	1.81	1.81	1.98	1.95	1.81	1.86
1.77	1.94	1.74	1.90	1.84	1.86	1.87
1.87	1.74	1.73	1.81	1.74	1.73	1.90

   (b) How could the histogram be interpreted?
4. Use the normal distribution Table 3 in Appendix B to find the tail area associated with the following z values.
   (a) $z = 2.07$
   (b) $z = -1.53$
   (c) $z = -.64$
   (d) $z = 4.73$
   (e) $z = .5$
5. Calculate z, given the following sets of values.
   (a) $x = 9.2$, $\overline{x} = 8.3$, $\sigma = .48$
   (b) $x = 5.3$, $\overline{x} = 7.9$, $\sigma = 1.41$
   (c) $x = 3.475$, $\overline{x} = 3.494$, $\sigma = .0051$
   (d) $x = 6.924$, $\overline{x} = 6.910$, $\sigma = .0092$

6. If $\bar{x} = 1.832$ and $\sigma = .009$, find the percent of measurements that are
   (a) larger than 1.850.
   (b) smaller then 1.81.
   (c) between 1.81 and 1.82.
   (d) smaller than 1.825.
   (e) between 1.825 and 1.845.

7. If the specification limits are 2.230 to 2.250, $\bar{x} = 2.238$, and $\sigma = .0065$, what percent of the measurements would be out of specification?

8. If the standard deviation in Exercise 7 is decreased to .0025, what percent of the product is out of specification?

9. If the process in Exercise 7 is adjusted so that the mean is at the mid-specification value and the standard deviation is .0020, what percent of the product is out of specification?

6

VARIABLES CONTROL CHARTS

OBJECTIVES

- Make an $\bar{x}$ and R chart, an $\tilde{x}$ and R chart, and an $\bar{x}$ and s chart.
- Recognize basic out-of-control situations such as points beyond the control limits, shifts, and trends.
- Calculate and interpret process capability.

Control charts are the basic tools of SPC, and variables control charts are the best charts to use in many situations. They can quickly indicate if a process is in statistical control at specific process points, and their analysis can suggest causes of any out-of-control occurrence. They provide the basis for a capability study by indicating when a study can be made and by providing the data needed for the study. Incoming inspection is giving way to demands for proof of quality from a supplier, and variables control charts are used to supply that proof.

The first control chart we will discuss is the current industry standard, the $\bar{x}$ and R chart. The x-bar chart is favored over the median chart because the sample mean is considered more sensitive to analysis than the median. The mean is also the more traditional measure of central tendency. The R chart is currently favored over the s chart as a measure of piece-to-piece variability because it is much simpler to calculate. For smaller samples both R and s give adequate measures of variability. When the sample size is larger than 7, however, s gives the best measure of variability.

6.1 $\bar{x}$ AND R CHARTS

This variables control chart consists of two separate, broken-line graphs. One tracks the averages, $\bar{x}$, and the other tracks the range, R, of small samples of consecutive pieces. The sample size is usually three to seven, most commonly with samples of four or five. Consecutive pieces are used in each sample so that a measure of piece-to-piece variability can be attained as well as the overall variability that is determined by using all the data on the chart. The goals for using the chart were illustrated in Figures 3.10 to 3.13. *First*, the chart shows the presence of any out-of-control situations. The elimination of those problems will bring the process into statistical control. *Second*, the extent of embedded process problems can be measured in a process capability study. The measure of quality can be seen in a comparison of the $\bar{\bar{x}} \pm 3\sigma$ measurement spread with the design specifications. *Third*, if the process is not capable (if it has too much product variation and poor product quality), the chart is used to measure the amount of improvement that results when the process is changed. *Fourth*, the $\bar{x}$ and R chart provides the evidence when the process is both in control and capable. Within that goal structure there are four main functions of the chart.

First, the extent of piece-to-piece variation may be measured using the range values for the samples taken. The individual sample ranges may then be compared with the average of all the Range values and the $\bar{R} \pm 3\sigma_R$ values (the control limits) using the statistical concepts from Chapter 4. Product variability is in statistical control when no R values exceed the upper control limit and no trouble (nonrandom) patterns crop up between the control limits.

Second, the overall process variation may be measured by statistical calculations with the sample range values. The process variation will be used to determine the process capability with respect to the tolerance or specification limits once statistical control is achieved.

Third, the average measurement from the $\bar{x}$ chart may be found for comparison with the mid-specification or target value. The sample means are also analyzed with respect to the expected, normal spread of the $\bar{x}$ values indicated by the control limits, which are the $\bar{\bar{x}} \pm 3\sigma_{\bar{x}}$ boundaries. The product measurements are in statistical control when all the $\bar{x}$ values are between the control limits and no trouble patterns are apparent.

Finally, a histogram made from the measurements on the chart may determine if the measurements are normally distributed. Other process problems may show up on the histogram as well; histogram analysis was discussed in Chapter 5 using Figures 5.5 to 5.10.

Two types of variation show up on the control charts:

- *Special cause variation* shows up as out-of-control points and can be eliminated by either the operator in charge or the process control team.
- *Common cause variation*, the inherent process variation, shows up on the control charts as the variation in the points after the process is in statistical control and can be decreased only by management-directed action on the process.

The $\bar{x}$ and R Chart Procedure

1. Select a process measurement.

Choose a critical process measurement to chart. There may be obvious measurements for which process control is important, but in some cases, process analysis (as discussed in Chapter 10) may be necessary to determine the critical measurements. For initial efforts measurements should have good potential for process improvement or should be important in the self-certification plan. Self-certification includes the use of control charts and histograms as proof of good quality for the customer. Considerations could include the following:

- There *may be* a trouble spot in the process that the chart can detect.
- There *is* a trouble spot determined by evidence from scrap analysis or customer (or downstream) complaints that the chart will help resolve.
- The process capability must be known at this point in the process for the self-certification quality plan.

2. Decrease variability.

Eliminate any obvious sources of variation before starting the chart. Chart interpretation should concentrate on the less conspicuous problems.

3. Check the gauges.

Be sure the gauges are working properly and that gauge variation is at an acceptable minimum. Variation that shows up on the chart should primarily reflect process variation. Excessive gauge variation makes the interpretation of process variability more difficult and sometimes impossible. Gauge capability methods are discussed in Chapter 11. The *rule of 10* for gauges states that the gauge should be *10 times* more accurate than the measurement accuracy. For example, if a measurement is needed to the nearest thousandth, the gauge should measure to the nearest ten-thousandth. The rule of 10 is absolutely necessary to measure and control variability realistically.

4. Make a sample plan.

Devise a sampling plan that consists of two parts. First, choose the sample size. Larger samples of six or seven can lead to more reliable estimates of variation and average value but are more costly. The extra time involved to take the larger sample of measurements could be a factor. The cost of samples of four or five may be more reasonable. Small samples of two or three are appropriate for monitoring a process that is in statistical control, but if the product output is small, small samples used with an $\bar{x}$ and R chart can give more reliable process information than an individuals and moving range chart (discussed in Chapter 7). Second, determine the sampling frequency. The number of samples per shift depends on the product output, operator time available for measuring and charting, and the time pressure for statistical control. Methods for determining sampling times were discussed in Chapter 4.

5. Set up the charts and process log.

Choose the scale for the $\bar{x}$ chart and for the R chart. For a continuous charting situation, the chart scales will have been established on the previous chart. For a new chart, use an educated guess to set up the scales. When establishing scales, avoid the two extremes if possible: Keep scales from being too large or too small.

If the scale (or units per line) is too large, the points end up close together, vertically, and the broken-line graph looks almost straight. The middle line and the control limit lines will be close together and the chart will be hard to interpret. On the other hand, if the scale (or units per line) is too small, points end up off the chart and the broken-line graph looks like a very steep zig-zag. The control limit lines will end up off the chart or at the very top and bottom of the chart. Interpretation becomes too confusing.

Several educated guess routines are built around the fact that the graph needs room for the mid-line and the control limit lines *plus* a little more room above and below in case there are out-of-control points beyond the limits. The control limit lines lie three standard deviations away from the line of averages, which will hopefully be very close to the mid-specification value.

Take several samples and find the range of ranges, R_R:

$$R_{\text{largest}} - R_{\text{smallest}} = R_R$$

and the range of $\bar{x}$'s, $R_{\bar{x}}$:

$$\bar{x}_{\text{largest}} - \bar{x}_{\text{smallest}} = R_{\bar{x}}$$

A conservative estimate of the standard deviation of a statistic (a sample measurement such as $\bar{x}$ or R) is found by dividing the range of that statistic by 4. The symbol "$\approx$" means "approximately equal to." The standard deviation for ranges is

$$\frac{R_R}{4} \approx \sigma_R$$

The standard deviation for $\bar{x}$ is

$$\frac{R_{\bar{x}}}{4} \approx \sigma_{\bar{x}}$$

Three standard deviations, plus a little more, is approximately 4 standard deviations.

$$4\sigma_R \approx \frac{4R_R}{4} = R_R$$

$$4\sigma_{\bar{x}} \approx \frac{4R_{\bar{x}}}{4} = R_{\bar{x}}$$

The range scale should go from 0 to $(\bar{R} + R_R)$ or from 0 to $2R_R$; use the second choice, which is simpler. The $\bar{x}$ scale should go from $\bar{\bar{x}} - R_{\bar{x}}$ to $\bar{\bar{x}} + R_{\bar{x}}$ or from the mid-specification $-R_{\bar{x}}$ to mid-specification $+R_{\bar{x}}$. Again, use the second choice.

Mark the scale as follows. Divide the number of lines in the R chart section into $2R_R$ and round up to an easy number for setting up the chart (see Example 6.1, which follows). Start the R scale from 0 on the *bottom* line. Next, divide the number of lines in the $\bar{x}$ chart section into $2R_{\bar{x}}$. Round up to an easy number for charting. Start at the *middle* of the chart and label the middle line with the mid-specification value. Mark the $\bar{x}$ scale up and down from the mid-specification center line.

Keep a process log during the control charting and in it, be sure to note the time and make a comment about any occurrence that may have some effect on the process (either good or bad). The date and time should accompany each sample. The process log may be kept on the control chart or may be a separate comment sheet attached to the chart. When variation problems occur, the combination of a process log and control chart can be very beneficial to the operator or process control team as they attempt to isolate and eliminate the problems.

To illustrate the steps in this procedure, we will begin an extended example using the following data. The *first* control chart is to be made at a specified process point. The first eight samples are recorded in Table 6.1. Set the scale for the $\bar{x}$ chart and for the R chart. The specification limits are .0200 to .0300, and the target measurement is .025.

TABLE 6.1
Specification: .0200 to .0300

Sample values	.0218	.0247	.0244	.0254	.0265	.0259	.0266	.0259
	.0243	.0255	.0252	.0238	.0232	.0274	.0245	.0282
	.0232	.0282	.0265	.0249	.0294	.0228	.0231	.0264
	.0256	.0261	.0267	.0275	.0281	.0254	.0280	.0234
$\bar{x}$	.0237	.0261	.0257	.0254	.0268	.0254	.0256	.0260
R	.0038	.0035	.0023	.0037	.0062	.0046	.0049	.0048

The sample size is 4, so each $\bar{x}$ is found by adding the measurements and then dividing by 4. Use a calculator to check the $\bar{x}$ results and the R values.

The range of R for the first eight samples is

$$R_R = .0062 - .0023$$
$$R_R = .0039$$
$$2R_R = .0078$$

There are 9 lines on the range chart in Figure 6.1 on page 100. Divide 9 into $2R_R$.

$$9 \overline{)\, .0078}^{\,.0008+}$$

Round up to .001 units per line. Start at 0 at the bottom of the R chart and count up .001 units per line as shown.

.0015 _____
.0010 _____
.0005 _____
0 _____ (Bottom line on R chart)

$$\bar{R} = \frac{\Sigma R}{k} = \underline{\quad} = \underline{\quad}$$

$$\bar{\bar{x}} = \frac{\Sigma \bar{x}}{k} = \underline{\quad} = \underline{\quad}$$

Specification : .0200 to .0300

$$UCL_R = D_4 \times \bar{R} = \underline{\quad} \times \underline{\quad} = \underline{\quad} = \boxed{\quad}$$

$$A_2 \times \bar{R} = \underline{\quad} \times \underline{\quad} = \boxed{\quad}$$

$$UCL_{\bar{x}} = \bar{\bar{x}} + A_2 \bar{R} = \underline{\quad} + \boxed{\quad} = \boxed{\quad}$$

$$LCL_{\bar{x}} = \bar{\bar{x}} - A_2 \bar{R} = \underline{\quad} - \boxed{\quad} = \boxed{\quad}$$

Constants

n	A_2	$\tilde{A}_2$	D_4	d_2
3	1.023	1.19	2.574	1.693
4	0.729	—	2.282	2.059
5	0.577	.69	2.114	2.326

Chart of Averages — $\bar{x}$

Chart of Ranges — R

Sample Number	1	2	3	4	5	6	7	8	9	10	11	12	13	14	15	16	17	18	19	20	21	22	23	24	25
Sample measurements 1	.0218	.0247	.0244	.0254	.0265	.0259	.0266	.0259	.0302	.0221	.0219	.0205	.0264	.0251	.0259	.0254	.0263	.0258	.0273	.0213	.0223	.0252	.0248	.0253	.0260
2	.0243	.0255	.0252	.0238	.0232	.0274	.0245	.0282	.0271	.0247	.0242	.0253	.0267	.0274	.0221	.0257	.0267	.0243	.0266	.0256	.0251	.0224	.0232	.0262	.0229
3	.0232	.0282	.0265	.0249	.0294	.0228	.0231	.0264	.0250	.0256	.0223	.0241	.0253	.0236	.0245	.0263	.0254	.0249	.0264	.0294	.0248	.0263	.0250	.0221	.0232
4	.0256	.0261	.0267	.0275	.0281	.0254	.0280	.0234	.0254	.0246	.0258	.0236	.0278	.0265	.0255	.0230	.0240	.0230	.0232	.0275	.0241	.0247	.0208	.0243	.0251
5																									
Sum								.0260																	
Average, $\bar{x}$	.0237	.0261	.0257	.0254	.0268	.0254	.0256	.0260																	
Range, R	.0038	.0035	.0023	.0037	.0062	.0046	.0049	.0048																	

FIGURE 6.1

Calculate $\bar{x}$ and R and set the scales for the $\bar{x}$ and R charts. Plot and connect the points. Check your results with Figure 6.2.

The mid-specification value is $(.0200 + .0300)/2 = .0250$. Start the $\bar{x}$ chart with .0250 at the center of the vertical scale. Find the range of $\bar{x}$ for the first 8 samples:

$$R_R = .0268 - .0237$$
$$R_{\bar{x}} = .0031$$
$$2R_{\bar{x}} = .0062$$

There are 21 lines on the chart for $\bar{x}$ in Figure 6.1. Divide 21 into the $2R_{\bar{x}}$ value and round up to .0005 units per line. Start at the mid-specification value in the center and mark segments in increments of .0005 units per line in both directions as shown.

.0260 _____
.0255 _____
.0250 _____ Middle of $\bar{x}$ chart
.0245 _____
.0240 _____

6. Chart the points.

There are three charts presented for this $\bar{x}$ and R illustration. The first, Figure 6.1, has the measurements listed for the 25 samples. Calculate the missing $\bar{x}$ and R values. Set the $\bar{x}$ scale and the R scale as directed, plot the points, and draw the connecting lines from point to point on Figure 6.1 for two separate broken-line graphs (one for $\bar{x}$ and one for R). Check your results with the second chart, Figure 6.2 (see page 102).

7. Calculate the averages and the control limits.

To calculate $\bar{R}$, add all the range values and then divide by the number of values, k.

$$\bar{R} = \frac{\sum R}{k}$$
$$= \frac{.1004}{25}$$
$$= .00402$$

The calculations will be shown here in a step-by-step format. The same calculations are shown in concise form in Figure 6.3 on page 103.

Calculate UCL_R and LCL_R. The subscript R indicates that the control limits are for ranges. UCL_R = Upper control limit for ranges. The formulas for the control limits are

$$UCL_R = D_4\bar{R}$$
$$LCL_R = D_3\bar{R}$$

The values for the numerical constants in the formulas, D_4 and D_3, are found in Appendix B, Table 1.1.

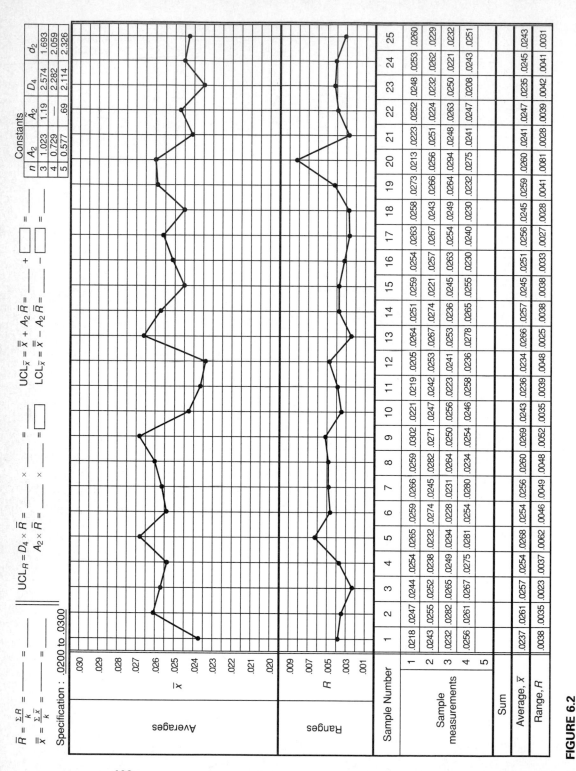

FIGURE 6.2

Calculate $\bar{R}$, $\bar{\bar{x}}$, UCL_R, $UCL_{\bar{x}}$, and $LCL_{\bar{x}}$. Draw the lines. Check your results with Figure 6.3.

102

$\bar{R} = \frac{\Sigma R}{k} = \frac{.1004}{25} = .00402$

$\bar{\bar{x}} = \frac{\Sigma \bar{x}}{k} = \frac{.6279}{25} = .0251$

Specification: .0200 to .0300

$UCL_R = D_4 \times \bar{R} = 2.282 \times .00402 = .0092$

$A_2 \times \bar{R} = .729 \times .00402 = .00293$

$UCL_{\bar{x}} = \bar{\bar{x}} + A_2 \bar{R} = .0251 + .00293 = .0280$

$LCL_{\bar{x}} = \bar{\bar{x}} - A_2 \bar{R} = .0251 - .00293 = .0222$

Constants

n	A_2	A_2	D_4	d_2
3	1.023	1.19	2.574	1.693
4	0.729	—	2.282	2.059
5	0.577	.69	2.114	2.326

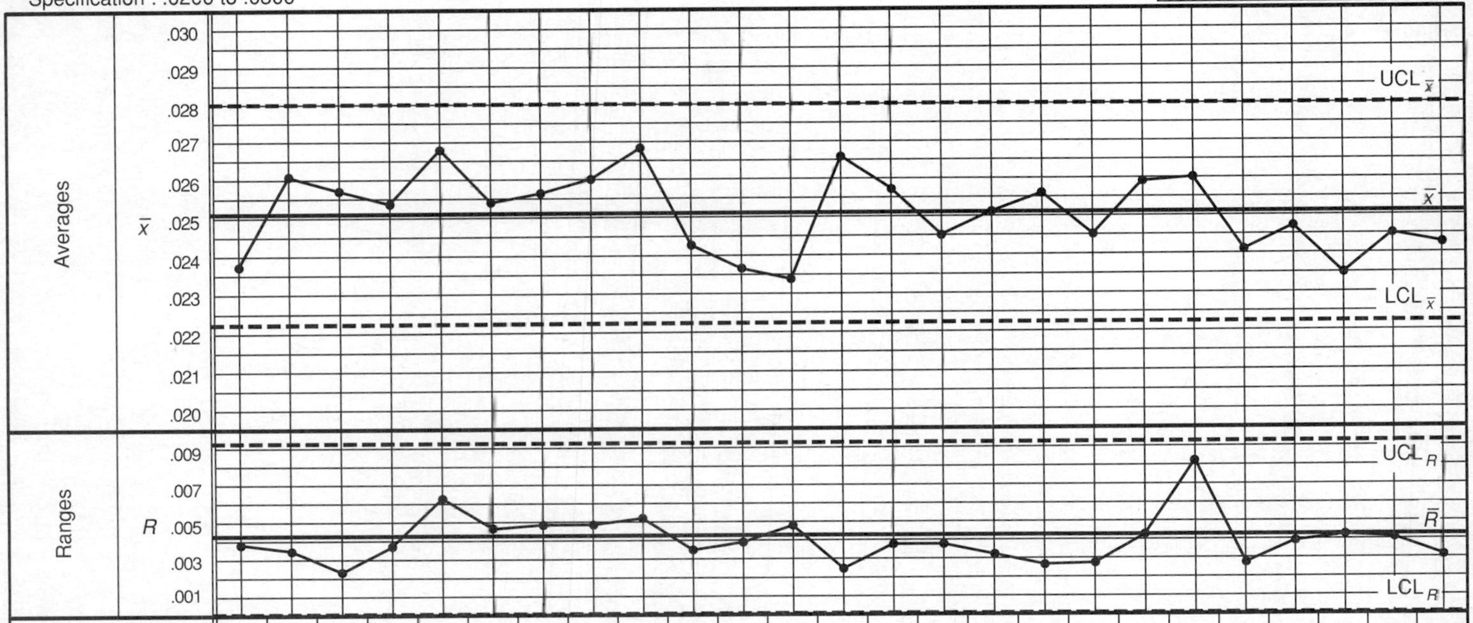

Sample Number	1	2	3	4	5	6	7	8	9	10	11	12	13	14	15	16	17	18	19	20	21	22	23	24	25
Sample measurements 1	.0218	.0247	.0244	.0254	.0265	.0259	.0266	.0259	.0302	.0221	.0219	.0205	.0264	.0251	.0259	.0254	.0263	.0258	.0273	.0213	.0223	.0252	.0248	.0253	.0260
2	.0243	.0255	.0252	.0238	.0232	.0274	.0245	.0282	.0271	.0247	.0242	.0253	.0267	.0274	.0221	.0257	.0267	.0243	.0266	.0256	.0251	.0224	.0232	.0262	.0229
3	.0232	.0282	.0265	.0249	.0294	.0228	.0231	.0264	.0250	.0256	.0223	.0241	.0253	.0236	.0245	.0263	.0254	.0249	.0264	.0294	.0248	.0263	.0250	.0221	.0232
4	.0256	.0261	.0267	.0275	.0281	.0254	.0280	.0234	.0254	.0246	.0258	.0236	.0278	.0265	.0255	.0230	.0240	.0230	.0232	.0275	.0241	.0247	.0208	.0243	.0251
5																									
Sum																									
Average, $\bar{x}$	.0237	.0261	.0257	.0254	.0268	.0254	.0256	.0260	.0269	.0243	.0236	.0234	.0266	.0257	.0245	.0251	.0256	.0245	.0259	.0260	.0241	.0247	.0235	.0245	.0243
Range, R	.0038	.0035	.0023	.0037	.0062	.0046	.0049	.0048	.0052	.0035	.0039	.0048	.0025	.0038	.0038	.0033	.0027	.0028	.0041	.0081	.0028	.0039	.0042	.0041	.0031

FIGURE 6.3

Mark all points that are out of control. Check your results with Figure 6.4.

For a sample of four ($n = 4$), $D_4 = 2.282$ and $D_3 = 0$.

$$\text{UCL} = D_4 \times \overline{R} \qquad\qquad \text{LCL} = D_3 \times \overline{R}$$
$$= 2.282 \times .00402 \qquad\qquad = 0 \times .00402$$
$$= .0092 \qquad\qquad\qquad = 0$$

Draw a solid line for $\overline{R}$ and a dashed line for UCL_R and LCL_R. Check for out-of-control patterns on the R chart, patterns characterized by points above the UCL_R, shifts (seven or more consecutive points above or below $\overline{R}$), or runs (seven or more consecutive points going up or going down). Because there are no apparent out-of-control patterns in this case (see Figure 6.3), proceed with the $\overline{x}$ chart. Had we discovered any points out of control, we would have marked them with an "X", found and eliminated the cause, removed the sample(s) from the data set, and recalculated $\overline{R}$.

The range chart must be in statistical control before any interpretation can be made on the $\overline{x}$ chart. Excessive variation can cause the $\overline{x}$ chart to appear out of control, but the underlying problem is then the variation, not necessarily a needed adjustment toward the target measurement.

In the next step, we will calculate $\overline{\overline{x}}$ and the control limits. To find $\overline{\overline{x}}$, the average of the $\overline{x}$ values, add all the $\overline{x}$ values and divide by the number of samples, k.

$$\overline{\overline{x}} = \frac{\sum \overline{x}}{k}$$
$$= \frac{.6279}{25}$$
$$= .0251$$

Calculate the control limits, $\text{UCL}_{\overline{x}}$ and $\text{LCL}_{\overline{x}}$. The $\overline{x}$ subscript indicates that the control limits are for sample averages. The formulas for the control limits are

$$\text{UCL}_{\overline{x}} = \overline{\overline{x}} + (A_2\overline{R})$$
$$\text{LCL}_{\overline{x}} = \overline{\overline{x}} - (A_2\overline{R})$$

Notice that the same product, $A_2\overline{R}$, is added to the mean for the $\text{UCL}_{\overline{x}}$ and subtracted from the mean for the $\text{LCL}_{\overline{x}}$. The value for the numerical constant, A_2, is found in Appendix B, Table 1.1. $A_2 = .729$ for $n = 4$.

$$\text{UCL}_{\overline{x}} = \overline{\overline{x}} + (A_2\overline{R}) \qquad\qquad \text{LCL}_{\overline{x}} = \overline{\overline{x}} - (A_2\overline{R})$$
$$= .0251 + (.729 \times .00402) \qquad\qquad = .0251 - .00293$$
$$= .0251 + .00293 \qquad\qquad\qquad = .0222$$
$$= .0280$$

Draw a solid line for $\overline{\overline{x}}$ and dashed lines for the control limits, $\text{UCL}_{\overline{x}}$ and $\text{LCL}_{\overline{x}}$. At this point, your control chart in Figure 6.1 should look like the completed control chart in Figure 6.3. Check for out-of-control patterns of the $\overline{x}$ chart: Points above $\text{UCL}_{\overline{x}}$ or below $\text{LCL}_{\overline{x}}$, shifts (seven or more consecutive points on one side of $\overline{\overline{x}}$), or runs (seven or more consecutive points going up or going down).

The second through the ninth points on the chart are all above $\bar{\bar{x}}$ and that indicates an out-of-control situation. Mark the points for samples 8 and 9 in the shift pattern with an "X" to show the points that are out-of-control. When an out-of-control situation such as this occurs, the operator, the process control team, or both analyze the chart and the process log to determine the cause of the problem and then work to eliminate the problem. Work procedures are amended to prevent the problem from recurring.

At this point, the control chart is used in two ways: to find out-of-control situations, as illustrated in this case, and to measure the process for capability. That measuring takes place after all the out-of-control situations have been resolved and the process is in statistical control. Statistical control on the chart means that all the points on the chart are *in control*. The easiest way to evaluate this is to eliminate all of the out-of-control points, recalculate the averages and control limits, and reanalyze the chart to see if the process is in statistical control.

When the out-of-control pattern is a run or shift, it takes several points before the situation can be recognized. If the initial out-of-control point can be determined on the control chart, remove all the out-of-control points back to that initial point. Otherwise, just remove the ones marked with an "X". Connect the points on either side of the removed points by a dotted line, eliminate the data values, and recalculate $\bar{x}$ and $\bar{R}$. Figure 6.4 on page 106 shows this adjustment.

Eliminate $\bar{x} = .0260$ and $\bar{x} = .0269$ from $\sum \bar{x}$.

$$
\begin{array}{rl}
.0260 & \\
+.0269 & \text{Add them.} \\
\hline
.0529 &
\end{array}
$$

$$
\begin{array}{rl}
.6279 & \text{Previous } \sum \bar{x}. \\
-.0529 & \text{Subtract their sum from } \sum \bar{x}. \\
\hline
.5750 & \text{The new } \sum \bar{x} \text{ value.}
\end{array}
$$

$$
\bar{\bar{x}} = \frac{\sum x}{k} \qquad \text{Recalculate } \bar{\bar{x}}.
$$

$$
= \frac{.5750}{23} \qquad \begin{array}{l} \text{The new value for } \sum \bar{x} \text{ is .5750.} \\ \text{The new value for } k \text{ is 23.} \end{array}
$$

$$
= .0250 \qquad \text{The new } \bar{\bar{x}} \text{ value.}
$$

Eliminate $R = .0048$ and $R = .0052$ from $\sum R$. Follow the procedure shown for eliminating $\bar{x}$ data.

$$
\begin{array}{rl}
.0048 & \text{Add them.} \\
+.0052 & \\
\hline
.0100 &
\end{array}
$$

$$
\begin{array}{rl}
.1004 & \text{Previous } \sum R. \\
-.0100 & \text{Subtract their sum from } \sum R. \\
\hline
.0904 & \text{The new } \sum R \text{ value.}
\end{array}
$$

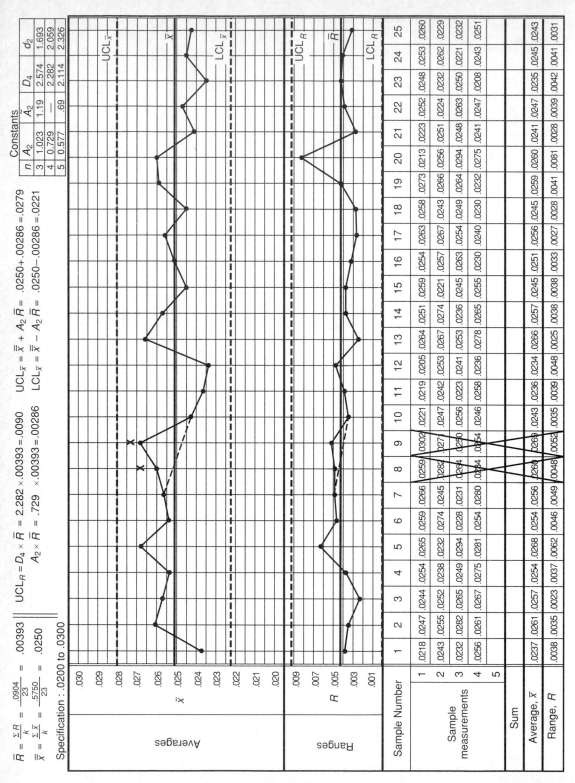

FIGURE 6.4
Out-of-control data are eliminated from the control chart *after* the cause has been determined and eliminated. Recalculate.

$$\bar{R} = \frac{\sum R}{k} \qquad \text{Recalculate } \bar{R}.$$

$$= \frac{.0904}{23}$$

$$= .00393 \qquad \text{The new } \bar{R} \text{ value.}$$

Recalculate the control limits.

$$\text{UCL}_R = D_4 \bar{R}$$
$$= 2.282 \times .00393$$
$$= .0090 \qquad \text{The new UCL}_R \text{ value.}$$

$$\text{UCL}_{\bar{x}} = \bar{\bar{x}} + (A_2 \bar{R})$$
$$= .0250 + (.729 \times .00393)$$
$$= .0250 + .00286$$
$$= .0279 \qquad \text{The new UCL}_{\bar{x}} \text{ value.}$$

$$\text{LCL}_{\bar{x}} = \bar{\bar{x}} - A_2 \bar{R}$$
$$= .0250 - .00286$$
$$= .0221 \qquad \text{The new LCL}_{\bar{x}} \text{ value.}$$

There is no substantial change in the average and control limit lines, and no other out-of-control point patterns are evident. If all the causes of the out-of-control points have been determined and eliminated, the process is now in statistical control and the capability analysis can commence. The elimination of the out-of-control data points may seem useless because the control limit lines and averages didn't really change; however, the change in $\bar{R}$ is quite important for the capability study because the standard deviation of all the measurements is determined from the $\bar{R}$ value.

The recalculation of the averages and the control limits was made easier because the initial sums, $\sum \bar{x}$ and $\sum R$, were noted on the worksheet. It was much easier to subtract the deleted data values from the original sums than to have to recalculate the sums from the remaining 23 data values. Whenever you do control chart calculations, be sure to write down the formulas, show your numerical substitutions, and keep your calculated results. This procedure allows easy checking and reference.

The Capability Analysis

For the first step in the capability analysis, check the histogram to be sure that the distribution of measurements is normal. The histogram in Figure 6.5 (page 108) indicates that the measurements in our study satisfy a normal distribution.

Calculate the *process* standard deviation. The analysis for statistical control deals with the distribution of sample means, $\bar{x}$. The control limits for $\bar{x}$ were three standard deviations *of $\bar{x}$* measured above and below $\bar{\bar{x}}$:

$$\bar{\bar{x}} \pm 3\sigma_{\bar{x}}$$

The three standard deviation value was approximated by the $A_2 \bar{R}$ product. Virtually all the $\bar{x}$ values are expected to fall between the control limits (99.7 percent of all $\bar{x}$'s,

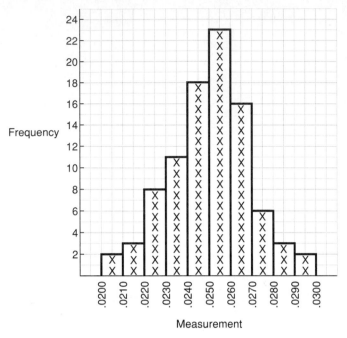

FIGURE 6.5
The histogram of all the control chart data values.

according to the normal curve analysis), so any $\bar{x}$ that was beyond was caused by some out-of-control condition. Now the emphasis switches to the individual measurements, x. The symbol $\bar{\bar{x}}$ indicates the average value of all the individual measurements as well as the average of the $\bar{x}$'s. The standard deviation of the individual measurements is approximated by

$$\sigma = \frac{\bar{R}}{d_2}$$

$$= \frac{.00393}{2.059}$$

$$= .00191$$

The value for d_2 is found in Appendix B, Table 1.1. The three standard deviation spread of the individual measurements, x, from their average value, $\bar{\bar{x}}$, is found by adding and subtracting 3σ or

$$\frac{3\bar{R}}{d_2}$$

Again, according to the normal curve analysis, 99.7 percent of all the individual measurements will lie between the $\bar{\bar{x}} \pm (3\bar{R})/d_2$ values. This spread of values can be compared with the specification limits to determine the process capability.

$$\begin{array}{ll}
\text{UCL}_x = \bar{\bar{x}} + 3\sigma & \text{LCL}_x = \bar{\bar{x}} - 3\sigma \\
\quad = .0250 + 3 \times .00191 & \quad = \bar{\bar{x}} - 3 \times .00191 \\
\quad = .0250 + .00573 & \quad = .0250 - .00573 \\
\quad = .0307 & \quad = .0193
\end{array}$$

Ninety-nine point seven percent of all process measurements should be between .0193 and .0307 and be normally distributed. The control limits extend beyond the specification limits; some of the process output is out of specification.

If the specification limits are put on a sketch of the normal curve for the individual measurements, as shown in Figure 6.6, the percent of product that is out of specification can be calculated. Use the z formula for analysis of the sections under the normal curve. Substitute the lower specification value for x and the values for $\bar{\bar{x}}$ and σ. Subtract first, then divide.

$$z = \frac{x - \bar{\bar{x}}}{\sigma}$$

$$= \frac{.0200 - .0250}{.00191}$$

$$= \frac{-.0050}{.00191}$$

$$= -2.62$$

The area from Table 3 in Appendix B is .0044, so .44 percent is out of specification on the low side.

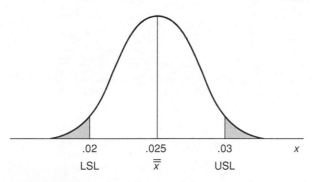

FIGURE 6.6
Specification limits on a normal curve.

To calculate the z value for the high side, substitute the upper specification limit for x and the values for $\bar{\bar{x}}$ and σ.

$$z = \frac{x - \bar{\bar{x}}}{\sigma}$$

$$= \frac{.0300 - .0250}{.00191}$$

$$= 2.62$$

The area is again .0044, meaning that .44 percent is out of specification on the high side. The total percent of product out of specification is

$$.44\% + .44\% = .88\%$$

This process analysis shows that the average measurement .0250 is equal to the mid-specification value, so no adjustment is needed there. However, with almost 1 percent of the product out of specification, process improvements are needed to decrease the amount of product variability. The three standard deviation spread of the measurements should be well within the specification limits. The ultimate goal is to have the ± three standard deviation spread of the measurements use less than 50 percent of the tolerance (the specification spread), as shown in Figure 6.7.

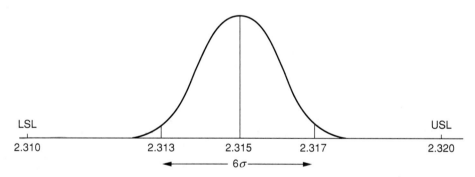

FIGURE 6.7
Process 1: a good process. Distribution is well within the specification limits.

Calculating the PCR and the Cpk

Process capability may also be measured using either the PCR or the Cpk. Both the PCR and the Cpk represent process capability ratios; these are quick and easy numbers used to classify the capability of a process. Both ratios are used in industry; for example, General Motors favors the PCR, and Ford uses the Cpk. Both measures compare the tolerance spread, or the difference between the specification limits, to the standard deviation of the measurements. The main difference between the two capability measures is that the Cpk will indicate trouble with an off-center distribution, and the PCR may not.

The following are the formulas for the two measures:

$$PCR = \frac{6\sigma}{\text{Tolerance}}$$

$$Cpk = \frac{|\text{ Nearest specification limit} - \bar{\bar{x}}\,|}{3\sigma}$$

EXAMPLE 6.1

Calculate the PCR and Cpk for the control chart in Figure 6.4.

Solution

The standard deviation for the measurements was calculated to be

$$\sigma = \frac{\bar{R}}{d_2}$$

$$= \frac{.00393}{2.059}$$

$$= .00191$$

$$3\sigma = .00573$$

$$6\sigma = .01146$$

The product specifications for these data were given in Figure 6.4. The tolerance is

$$\begin{array}{r} .0300 \\ -.0200 \\ \hline .0100 \end{array}$$

The formula for the PCR is

$$PCR = \frac{6\sigma}{\text{Tolerance}}$$

Substitute the values.

$$PCR = \frac{.01146}{.01}$$

$$= 1.146$$

The formula for the Cpk is

$$Cpk = \frac{|\text{ Nearest specification} - \bar{\bar{x}}\,|}{3\sigma}$$

Calculate the differences between each specification limit and the mean and use the smaller difference as the numerator of the Cpk formula.

$$
\begin{array}{llll}
\text{USL} & .0300 & .0250 & \bar{\bar{x}} \\
\bar{\bar{x}} & -.0250 & -.0200 & \text{LSL} \\
\hline
& .0050 & .0050 &
\end{array}
$$

This process is centered at the mid-specification value, so both differences are the same.

$$
\text{Cpk} = \frac{.0050}{.00573}
$$

$$
= .8726
$$

When the process is centered, as this one is, PCR = 1/Cpk.

Does the preceding example indicate a good process capability or a poor one? To determine the answer, we will look at a few illustrations.

The normal curve pattern contains virtually all the measurements (99.7 percent of them) in a 6σ spread, from 3σ units below the mean to 3σ units above. Process 1, shown in Figure 6.7, is a *good* process. The distribution is centered, and the 6σ spread of the measurements is well within the specification limits.

Determine 6σ, 3σ, and the tolerance from the sketch of the distribution.

$$
\begin{array}{ll}
\begin{array}{r}
2.317 \\
-2.313 \\
\hline
.004 = 6\sigma \\
.002 = 3\sigma
\end{array}
&
\begin{array}{r}
2.320 \\
-2.310 \\
\hline
.010 = \text{Tolerance}
\end{array}
\end{array}
$$

Now calculate the PCR and Cpk.

$$
\text{PCR} = \frac{6\sigma}{\text{Tolerance}} \qquad \text{Cpk} = \frac{|\text{Nearest spec. limit} - \bar{\bar{x}}|}{3\sigma}
$$

$$
= \frac{.004}{.010} \qquad\qquad = \frac{2.320 - 2.315}{.002}
$$

$$
= .40 \qquad\qquad\qquad = 2.5
$$

The PCR indicates that the process uses .4, or 40 percent, of the tolerance. The Cpk also indicates that the process uses 40 percent of the tolerance (1/Cpk = 1/2.5 = .4). The results are the same because the process is centered. This is classified as an "A" process: The PCR is less than 50 percent, and the Cpk is greater than 2.0.

This process classification system, the A, B, C, and D classification, is used by the Saginaw Division of General Motors and is illustrated in Table 6 in Appendix B.

Process 2, shown in Figure 6.8 on page 113, is a *poor* process because it crowds the LSL and overlaps the USL with its 6σ spread.

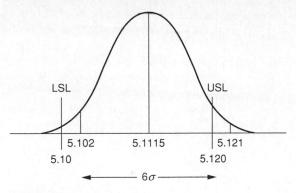

FIGURE 6.8
Process 2: a poor process. The distribution overlaps and crowds the specification limits.

Using the sketch of the distribution, we can determine 6σ, 3σ, and the tolerance.

$$
\begin{array}{ll}
5.1210 & 5.120 \\
-5.1020 & -5.100 \\
\hline
.0190 = 6\sigma & .020 = \text{Tolerance} \\
.0095 = 3\sigma &
\end{array}
$$

Calculate the PCR.

$$
\begin{aligned}
\text{PCR} &= \frac{6\sigma}{\text{Tolerance}} \\[2mm]
&= \frac{.019}{.020} \\[2mm]
&= .95
\end{aligned}
$$

Next, calculate the Cpk. Find the difference between the mean and each specification limit.

$$
\begin{array}{llll}
\text{USL} & 5.120 & 5.1115 & \bar{\bar{x}} \\
\bar{\bar{x}} & -5.1115 & -5.1000 & \text{LSL} \\
\hline
& .0085 & .0115 &
\end{array}
$$

Use the smaller difference in the Cpk formula.

$$
\begin{aligned}
\text{Cpk} &= \frac{.0085}{3\sigma} \\[2mm]
&= \frac{.0085}{.0095} \\[2mm]
&= .895
\end{aligned}
$$

The PCR indicates that the process uses .95, or 95 percent, of the tolerance; because the distribution is off-center, however, the Cpk indicates that the process uses 1.12, or 112 percent, of the tolerance (1/Cpk = 1/.895) on the "worst" side. The PCR shows that if the process were centered, it would use 95 percent of the tolerance. The Cpk shows the result of the existing, noncentered distribution: One hundred twelve percent of the tolerance is used (the distribution overlaps the specifications). This is a D process because the process capability is more than 91 percent, and Cpk is less than 1.10.

Process 3, illustrated in Figure 6.9, shows the discrepancy between the PCR and the Cpk values.

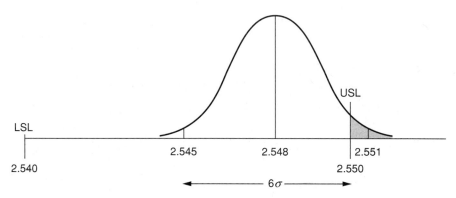

FIGURE 6.9
Process 3: a fair process, but off-center.

Determine 6σ, 3σ, and the tolerance from the sketch of the distribution.

$$
\begin{array}{ll}
2.552 & 2.550 \\
-2.545 & -2.540 \\
\hline
.007 = 6\sigma & .010 = \text{Tolerance} \\
.0035 = 3\sigma &
\end{array}
$$

Calculate the PCR.

$$
\begin{aligned}
\text{PCR} &= \frac{6\sigma}{\text{Tolerance}} \\
&= \frac{.007}{.010} \\
&= .70
\end{aligned}
$$

Seventy percent of the tolerance is used by the distribution of product measurements. To calculate the Cpk, find the difference between the mean and each specification limit.

$$\begin{array}{lrll} \text{USL} & 2.550 & 2.548 & \bar{\bar{x}} \\ \bar{\bar{x}} & -2.548 & -2.540 & \text{LSL} \\ & \overline{.002} & \overline{.008} \end{array}$$

Use the smallest difference in the Cpk formula.

$$\text{Cpk} = \frac{\text{smallest difference}}{3\sigma}$$

$$= \frac{.002}{.0035}$$

$$= .571$$

This is classified as a B process because the PCR indicates a capability between 51 percent and 70 percent of the tolerance. However, it may also be classified a D process because its Cpk is less than 1.10 and because 1.75, or 175 percent, of its tolerance ($1/\text{Cpk} = 1/.571$) is used by the distribution on the worst side.

From the three illustrations we can conclude that a good process has a process capability of 50 percent or less, in which the 6σ spread of variation is less than half the tolerance. A poor process has a process capability of 91 percent or more, which means that the data we calculated on the $\bar{x}$ and R chart in Figure 6.5 came from a process with a poor capability.

In general, the PCR shows what fraction of the tolerance is used by the product distribution. Because the product variability should be totally within tolerance, the numerator of the PCR formula should be less than the tolerance in the denominator and, ideally, less than half of it.

The Cpk formula uses the worst half of the product distribution: the one closest to the specification limit. The formula reverses tolerance and measurement variation in the fraction, so the reciprocal of the Cpk value gives the fraction or percent of the tolerance used by the distribution on that worst side.

A nice feature of using the PCR and Cpk as indicators of the process capability is the fact that they are basically independent of the shape of the distribution of measurements. Any distribution of measurements will have virtually all the measurements within three standard deviations of the mean, so both the PCR and Cpk will give a realistic comparison of the true measurement spread and the product tolerance. In contrast, the use of the z formula and the normal curve analysis requires that the distribution of measurements have a normal pattern.

EXAMPLE 6.2

Twenty-five samples with $n = 5$ are shown in Figure 6.10 (page 116). Create a control chart and analyze the capability of the process by completing the following steps.

1. Assume this is the first chart for the process and set the scale using the first eight samples.
2. Chart the points and draw the graphs.
3. Calculate the center lines and the control limit lines on the calculation sheet and draw the lines.

Constants

n	A_2	$\tilde{A}_2$	D_4	d_2
3	1.023	1.19	2.574	1.693
4	0.729	—	2.282	2.059
5	0.577	.69	2.114	2.326

$$\bar{R} = \frac{\Sigma R}{k} = \underline{\hspace{1cm}} = \underline{\hspace{1cm}}$$

$$\bar{\bar{x}} = \frac{\Sigma \bar{x}}{k} = \underline{\hspace{1cm}} = \underline{\hspace{1cm}}$$

Specification : .745 to .755

$$UCL_R = D_4 \times \bar{R} = \underline{\hspace{1cm}} \times \underline{\hspace{1cm}} = \underline{\hspace{1cm}}$$

$$A_2 \times \bar{R} = \underline{\hspace{1cm}} \times \underline{\hspace{1cm}} = \boxed{}$$

$$UCL_{\bar{x}} = \bar{\bar{x}} + A_2 \bar{R} = \underline{\hspace{1cm}} + \boxed{} = \underline{\hspace{1cm}}$$

$$LCL_{\bar{x}} = \bar{\bar{x}} - A_2 \bar{R} = \underline{\hspace{1cm}} - \boxed{} = \underline{\hspace{1cm}}$$

Chart of Averages — $\bar{x}$

Chart of Ranges — R

Sample Number	1	2	3	4	5	6	7	8	9	10	11	12	13	14	15	16	17	18	19	20	21	22	23	24	25
Sample measurements 1	.751	.750	.749	.748	.753	.755	.754	.748	.751	.751	.752	.750	.748	.749	.752	.752	.756	.749	.752	.754	.750	.750	.750	.754	.749
2	.747	.748	.749	.749	.749	.752	.751	.753	.750	.753	.752	.749	.749	.750	.751	.750	.754	.749	.750	.753	.750	.752	.751	.745	.749
3	.752	.749	.752	.749	.752	.753	.752	.749	.751	.751	.751	.749	.751	.750	.751	.750	.752	.750	.753	.750	.750	.751	.749	.747	.749
4	.750	.750	.750	.751	.751	.744	.750	.748	.752	.752	.751	.748	.747	.751	.752	.748	.744	.751	.750	.750	.750	.753	.748	.746	.749
5	.751	.752	.748	.748	.751	.749	.750	.748	.751	.751	.751	.751	.750	.751	.751	.750	.747	.749	.754	.751	.748	.750	.748	.755	.750
Sum																									
Average. $\bar{x}$	.7502	.7498	.7496	.7490	.7512	.7506	.7514	.7492	.7510	.7516	.7514	.7494	.7490	.7502	.7514	.7500	.7506	.7496	.7518	.7516	.7496	.7512	.7494	.7494	.7492
Range. R	.005	.004	.004	.003	.004	.011	.004	.005	.002	.002	.001	.003	.004	.002	.001	.004	.012	.002	.004	.004	.002	.003	.004	.010	.001

FIGURE 6.10

Set the scales, plot the points, and draw the graphs. Calculate averages and control limits and check your results with Figure 6.11.

116

4. Interpret the charts.
5. Make the histogram for all the data.
6. Calculate the process capability: the PCR, the Cpk, and the percent out of specification.
7. Check the results with Figures 6.13–6.15.

Solution
First, set the scale from the first eight samples.

$$\text{Range of } R: \quad R_R = .011 - .003$$
$$= .008$$

Scale the range chart from 0 to $2R_R$ (0 to .016). There are 9 lines available:

$$\frac{.001+}{9\,)\,.016}$$

Use .001 units per line for the range chart.

$$\text{Range of } \bar{x}: \quad R_{\bar{x}} = .7518 - .7486$$
$$= .0032$$

Scale .0032 units above and below the mid-specification value of .750. Twenty-one lines are available. Put .750 at the center and scale up to .753 and down to .747. Divide the number of lines into $2R_{\bar{x}}$.

$$\frac{.0003+}{21\,)\,.0064}$$

Use .0005 units per line on the $\bar{x}$ chart.

Second, make the control chart, plot the points, and draw the broken-line graphs on Figure 6.10. Check your results with Figure 6.11 on page 118. Step three is next: Calculate the center lines and the control limit lines using the format of Figure 6.11. Compare your results with Figure 6.12 (page 119).

Fourth, interpret the control chart for statistical control. Mark any points that are out of control with an "X".

The ranges of three samples are out of control. Assume that the out-of-control problems have been corrected, eliminate that data from the data set, and recalculate the center lines and the control limits. For the follow-up process capability, the process must be in statistical control, so only in-control points should be used. This is illustrated on Figure 6.13 (see page 120).

To calculate the new value of $\bar{R}$, deduct .033 (.011 + .012 + .010) from the previous $\sum R$.

$$
\begin{array}{rl}
.101 & \text{Previous } \sum R \\
-.033 & \text{Excluded } R \text{ values} \\
\hline
.068 & \text{The new } \sum R
\end{array}
$$

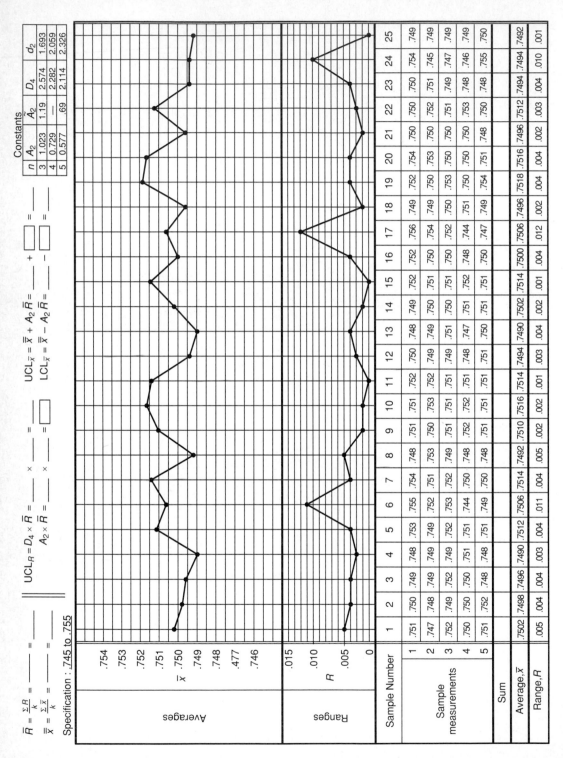

FIGURE 6.11
Calculate middle lines and control limits.

$$\bar{R} = \frac{\Sigma R}{k} = \underline{\qquad} =$$

$$\bar{\bar{x}} = \frac{\Sigma \bar{x}}{k} = \underline{\qquad} =$$

Specification : .745 to .755

$$UCL_R = D_4 \times \bar{R} = 2.114 \times .00404 = .0085$$
$$A_2 \times \bar{R} = .577 \times .00404 = .0023$$

$$UCL_{\bar{x}} = \bar{\bar{x}} + A_2 \bar{R} = .7503 + .0023 = .7526$$
$$LCL_{\bar{x}} = \bar{\bar{x}} - A_2 \bar{R} = .7503 - .0023 = .7480$$

Constants

n	A_2	$\tilde{A}_2$	D_4	d_2
3	1.023	1.19	2.574	1.693
4	0.729	—	2.282	2.059
5	0.577	.69	2.114	2.326

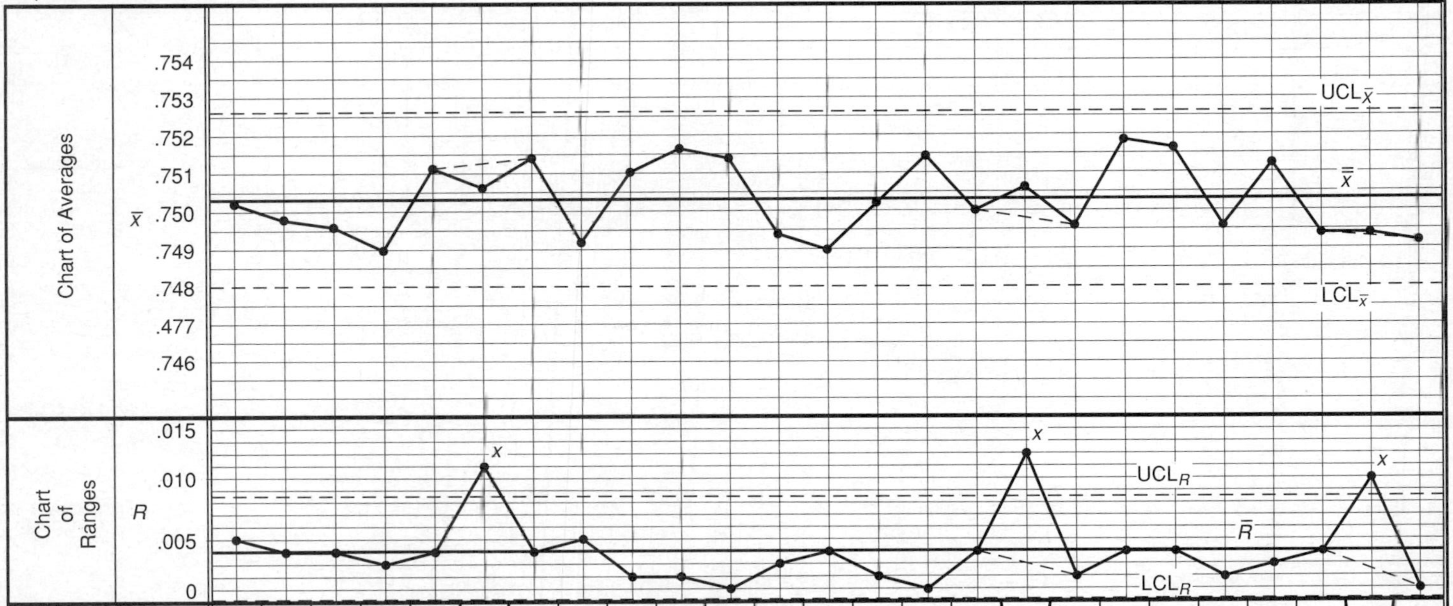

Chart of Averages (y-axis): .754, .753, .752, .751, .750 ($\bar{x}$), .749, .748, .747, .746
Lines shown: $UCL_{\bar{x}}$, $\bar{\bar{x}}$, $LCL_{\bar{x}}$

Chart of Ranges (y-axis): .015, .010 ($\bar{R}$), .005, 0
Lines shown: UCL_R, $\bar{R}$, LCL_R

Sample Number	1	2	3	4	5	6	7	8	9	10	11	12	13	14	15	16	17	18	19	20	21	22	23	24	25
Sample measurements 1	.751	.750	.749	.748	.753	.755	.754	.748	.751	.751	.752	.750	.748	.749	.752	.752	.756	.749	.752	.754	.750	.750	.750	.754	.749
2	.747	.748	.749	.749	.749	.752	.751	.753	.750	.753	.752	.749	.749	.750	.751	.750	.754	.749	.750	.753	.750	.752	.751	.747	.749
3	.752	.749	.752	.749	.752	.753	.752	.749	.751	.751	.751	.749	.751	.750	.751	.750	.752	.750	.753	.750	.750	.751	.749	.746	.749
4	.750	.750	.750	.751	.751	.754	.750	.748	.752	.752	.751	.748	.747	.751	.752	.748	.744	.751	.750	.751	.748	.753	.748	.755	.750
5	.751	.752	.748	.748	.751	.749	.750	.748	.751	.751	.751	.751	.750	.751	.751	.750	.747	.749	.754	.751	.748	.750	.748	.755	.750
Sum																									
Average.$\bar{x}$	.7502	.7498	.7496	.7490	.7512	.7500	.7514	.7492	.7510	.7516	.7514	.7494	.7490	.7502	.7514	.7500	.7500	.7496	.7518	.7516	.7496	.7512	.7494	.7494	.7492
Range.R	.005	.004	.004	.003	.004	.011	.004	.005	.002	.002	.001	.003	.004	.002	.001	.004	.012	.002	.004	.004	.002	.003	.004	.010	.001

FIGURE 6.12
Three samples are eliminated from the set of data. Recalculate averages and control limits.

119

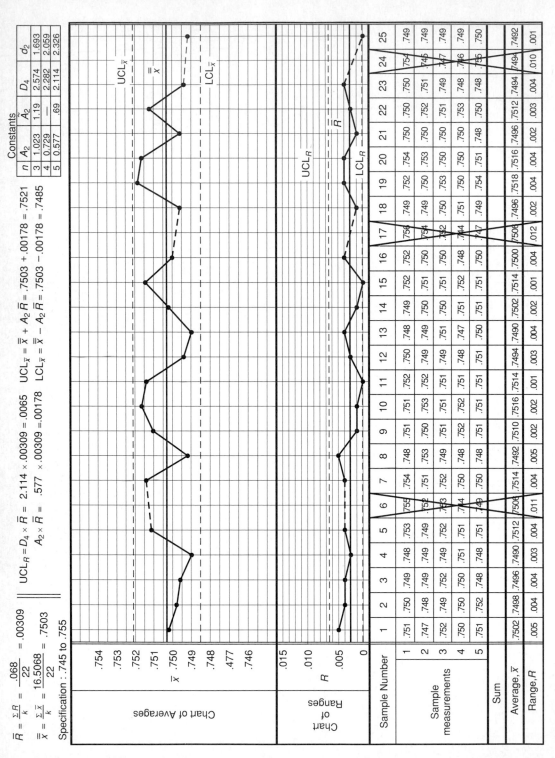

FIGURE 6.13
The control chart with new control limits.

After eliminating the out-of-control points, $k = 22$.

$$\text{New } \bar{R} = \frac{.068}{22}$$

$$\bar{R} = .003091$$

Calculate the new $\bar{\bar{x}}$ value. Deduct 2.2506 (.7506 + .7506 + .7494) from 18.7574.

$$\begin{array}{ll}
18.7574 & \text{Previous } \sum \bar{x} \\
-2.2506 & \text{Excluded } \bar{x} \text{ values} \\
\hline
16.5068 & \text{The new } \sum x
\end{array}$$

As above, $k = 22$.

$$\text{New } \bar{\bar{x}} = \frac{16.5068}{22}$$

$$\bar{\bar{x}} = .75031$$

Calculate the new control limits.

$$\begin{aligned}
\text{UCL}_R &= D_4 \bar{R} \\
&= 2.114 \times .003091 \\
&= .0065 \\
\text{UCL}_{\bar{x}} &= \bar{\bar{x}} + A_2 \bar{R} \\
&= .75031 + (.577 \times .003091) \\
&= .75031 + .00178 \\
&= .75209 \\
\text{LCL}_{\bar{x}} &= \bar{\bar{x}} - A_2 \bar{R} \\
&= .75031 - .00178 \\
&= .74853
\end{aligned}$$

Re-check for control on the $\bar{x}$ and R chart.

Everything seems fine: There are no points beyond the control limits and no trouble patterns for the points between the control limits on either chart. The process is in statistical control.

The fifth step instructs us to draw the histogram for all the in-control measurements to check for a normal distribution of data. Check the results with Figure 6.14 on page 122. There appears to be a slight skewness to the right, but the pattern is close enough to normal for a capability check with the normal curve analysis.

Sixth, determine the process capability.

$$\begin{aligned}
\sigma &= \frac{\bar{R}}{d_2} \\
&= \frac{.003091}{2.326} \\
&= .001329
\end{aligned}$$

FIGURE 6.14
The tally histogram of the in-control data.

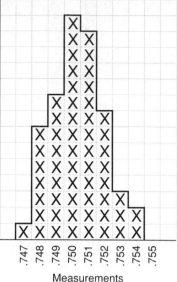

Measurements

$$
\begin{array}{r}
.755 \\
-\ .745 \\
\hline
.010 \quad \text{Tolerance}
\end{array}
$$

$$
\text{PCR} = \frac{6\sigma}{\text{Tolerance}}
$$

$$
= \frac{6 \times .001329}{.010}
$$

$$
= .797
$$

This shows the process using 80 percent of the tolerance.

Find the differences between the mean and the specification limits.

$$
\begin{array}{ll}
\text{USL} \quad .755 & .75031 \quad \bar{\bar{x}} \\
\bar{\bar{x}} \quad -.75031 & -.745 \quad \text{LSL} \\
\hline
.00469 & .00531
\end{array}
$$

Use the smaller difference in the Cpk formula.

$$
\text{Cpk} = \frac{\text{Minimum (specification limit} - \bar{\bar{x}})}{3\sigma}
$$

$$
= \frac{.00469}{3 \times .001329}
$$

$$
= \frac{.00469}{.003987}
$$

$$
= 1.176
$$

$$\frac{1}{\text{Cpk}} = \frac{1}{1.176}$$
$$= .8503$$

Eighty-five percent of the tolerance (.8503) is used by the process on the "short" side.

Both the PCR and the Cpk values classify this as a C process according to the classification chart in Appendix B, Table 6.

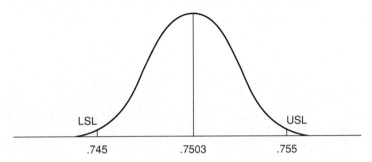

FIGURE 6.15
Find the percent of product beyond the specification limits.

What percent of the process is out of specification? Substitute the specification limits for x in the z formula, as suggested by the sketch of the normal curve in Figure 6.15. Use Table 3 in Appendix B to find the area.

$$z = \frac{x - \bar{\bar{x}}}{\sigma} \qquad\qquad z = \frac{x - \bar{\bar{x}}}{\sigma}$$

$$= \frac{\text{LSL} - \bar{\bar{x}}}{\sigma} \qquad\qquad = \frac{\text{USL} - \bar{\bar{x}}}{\sigma}$$

$$= \frac{.745 - .7503}{.001329} \qquad\qquad = \frac{.755 - .7503}{.001329}$$

$$= -3.99 \qquad\qquad = 3.54$$

$$\text{Area} = .00003 \qquad\qquad \text{Area} = .00020$$

A total of .00023, or .023 percent, is out of specification.

6.2 THE MEDIAN AND RANGE CHART

When the distribution of measurements is normal, the mean and the median will both be at the center. If there are no extreme data values in the samples (if the range is in control), the median values can be used for the average values. The median chart isn't quite as sensitive for interpretation as the averages, but it is preferred for many charting jobs, because it is simpler to use.

The $\tilde{x}$ and R Chart Procedure

The procedure for using $\tilde{x}$ and R charts is basically the same as the one for the $\overline{x}$ & R charts:

1. Select a process measurement to track.
2. Eliminate obvious sources of variability before charting.
3. Check the gauges. The gauges must be capable before the charting begins.
4. Devise a sample plan. The sample plan should be a random sample plan similar to the ones shown in Examples 4.1 and 4.2. The one additional consideration for medians is the requirement that for easy figuring, the sample size should be an odd number such as 3, 5, or 7. The median is then the middle value, not the average of the two in the middle.
5. Set up the charts and process log using the format that was introduced for the $\overline{x}$ and R charts.
6. Calculate the center lines and the control limits. A slight change in the formulas should be noted:

   - $\overline{\tilde{x}}$ is the average of the medians
   - $\overline{\tilde{x}} = (\sum \tilde{x})/k$
   - $UCL_{\tilde{x}} = \overline{\tilde{x}} + \tilde{A}_2\overline{R}$
   - $LCL_{\tilde{x}} = \overline{\tilde{x}} - \tilde{A}_2\overline{R}$

   Table 1.2 in Appendix B lists the values for numerical constant $\tilde{A}_2$. The R chart in the $\tilde{x}$ and R chart is the same as the R chart in the $\overline{x}$ and R chart.
7. The chart interpretation is the same as before. Out-of-control patterns include points beyond the control limits, trends, and shifts.
8. Check the histogram of the in-control data to see if the data is normally distributed.
9. Process capability is calculated as before, but with $\overline{\tilde{x}}$ instead of $\overline{\overline{x}}$.

We will explain this procedure by applying it to an example.

EXAMPLE 6.3

Twenty-five samples are recorded on the control chart in Figure 6.16. Set the scales, chart the points, and calculate the center lines and control limits. Then interpret the charts, and draw the histogram for all *in-control* data. Determine the process capability with the in-control data.

Solution

To set the scales, calculate the median and range for all the samples in Figure 6.16 (page 125). Check the results with Figure 6.17 (page 128). Use the first 10 samples (again, simulating a first run charting situation) to set the $\tilde{x}$ and R scales.

$$R_R = 59 - 20$$
$$= 39$$

$\bar{R} = \dfrac{\Sigma R}{k} =$ _____ = _____

$\bar{\bar{x}} = \dfrac{\Sigma \bar{x}}{k} =$ _____ = _____

Specification : 850 to 950

$UCL_R = D_4 \times \bar{R} =$ _____ × _____ = _____

$A_2 \times \bar{R} =$ _____ × _____ = _____

$UCL_{\bar{x}} = \bar{\bar{x}} + A_2\bar{R} =$ _____ + _____ = _____

$LCL_{\bar{x}} = \bar{\bar{x}} - A_2\bar{R} =$ _____ - _____ = _____

Constants

n	A_2	$\tilde{A}_2$	D_4	d_2
3	1.023	1.19	2.574	1.693
4	0.729	—	2.282	2.059
5	0.577	.691	2.114	2.326

Median Range

Sample Numbers	1	2	3	4	5	6	7	8	9	10	11	12	13	14	15	16	17	18	19	20	21	22	23	24	25
Sample measurements	915	900	905	871	940	912	897	920	928	890	895	901	906	932	906	907	885	904	913	882	907	913	910	918	889
	891	905	889	930	890	895	933	908	926	900	925	895	872	902	893	909	942	897	936	941	912	909	885	917	919
	920	911	902	882	909	892	879	894	920	890	908	892	927	932	917	904	916	912	932	917	896	912	908	914	898
	890	862	873	913	915	902	885	896	895	930	933	898	909	895	925	923	892	916	912	934	926	928	903	917	912
	916	898	915	900	895	896	900	906	922	903	896	892	904	902	910	888	911	920	896	894	928	915	926	925	884

Chart of Medians — $\tilde{x}$

Chart of Ranges — R

FIGURE 6.16

Calculate $\tilde{x}$ and R for each sample. Set the scales for each chart, plot the $\tilde{x}$ and R values, and draw the lines. Calculate center lines and control limits.

125

Scale from 0 to $2R_R$ (0 to 78). There are nine lines.

$$\frac{8+}{9 \overline{)\,78}}$$

Round up to 10. Use 10 units per line.

$$R_{\tilde{x}} = 922 - 896$$
$$= 26$$

Start at the mid-specification value of 900 and scale 26 units above and below. There are 21 lines.

$$\frac{2+}{21 \overline{)\,52}}$$

Round up to 4 units per line.

Chart the points on Figure 6.16 and check the results with Figure 6.17. When all the data are plotted, calculate the averages. There are 25 samples to average, so $k = 25$. The average of the medians:

$$\bar{\tilde{x}} = \frac{\sum \tilde{x}}{k}$$

$$= \frac{\tilde{x}_1 + \tilde{x}_2 + \tilde{x}_3 + \cdots + \tilde{x}_{25}}{25}$$

$$= \frac{915 + 900 + \cdots + 898}{25}$$

$$= \frac{22676}{25}$$

$$= 907.04$$

The average of the ranges:

$$\bar{R} = \frac{\sum R}{k}$$

$$= \frac{R_1 + R_2 + R_3 + \cdots + R_{25}}{25}$$

$$= \frac{30 + 49 + \cdots + 35}{25}$$

$$= \frac{920}{25}$$

$$= 36.8$$

Draw a solid line on each chart for $\bar{\tilde{x}}$ and $\bar{R}$.

To continue, calculate the upper and lower control limits for the ranges and medians. Use the calculation sheet on Figure 6.16. It has the same format as the one used with the $\bar{x}$ and R chart. Check your results with the following calculations.

The numerical constants for the control chart are found in Table 1.2, Appendix B. The sample size is $n = 5$.

$$D_4 = 2.114$$
$$D_3 = 0$$
$$\tilde{A}_2 = .691$$

The upper control limit for the range is 77.8.

$$\begin{aligned} \text{UCL}_R &= D_4\overline{R} \\ &= 2.114 \times 36.8 \\ &= 77.8 \end{aligned}$$

The lower control limit for the range is 0.

$$\begin{aligned} \text{LCL}_R &= D_3\overline{R} \\ &= 0 \times 36.8 \\ &= 0 \end{aligned}$$

The upper and lower control limits for the medians have the same $\tilde{A}_2\overline{R}$ product in the formulas.

$$\begin{aligned} \text{UCL}_{\tilde{x}} &= \bar{\tilde{x}} + \tilde{A}_2\overline{R} \\ &= 907.04 + (.691 \times 36.8) \\ &= 907.04 + 25.43 \\ &= 932.5 \end{aligned} \qquad \begin{aligned} \text{LCL}_{\tilde{x}} &= \bar{\tilde{x}} - \tilde{A}_2\overline{R} \\ &= 907.04 - 25.43 \\ &= 881.6 \end{aligned}$$

Draw a dashed line on the charts for each control limit. Check your results with Figure 6.17.

Now interpret the charts on Figure 6.17, analyzing the pattern of data points with respect to the center line and control limit lines. Look for points that fall outside the control limits and nonrandom patterns such as runs of seven or more points going up or going down, all above the middle line or all below the middle line. These would be considered out of control. Check your findings with Figure 6.18 (page 129). The cause of the out-of-control situations must be found and prevented from happening again. Reference to the control chart comments and observations will be helpful in determining the cause(s) for the out-of-control situations.

Always do the R chart first. The R chart must be in statistical control before the median chart can be realistically analyzed.

When all of the out-of-control occurrences have been eliminated, delete their data points from the set of data and recalculate the control limits. Eliminate the out-of-control data from the control chart by marking an "X" by each point and connecting the good points on either side by a dotted line.

$$\bar{R} = \frac{\Sigma R}{k} = \frac{920}{25} = 36.8$$

$$\tilde{\bar{x}} = \frac{\Sigma \tilde{x}}{k} = \frac{22676}{25} = 907.04$$

Specification: 850 to 950

$$UCL_R = D_4 \times \bar{R} = 2.114 \times 36.8 = 77.8$$
$$A_2 \times \bar{R} = .691 \times 36.8 = 25.43$$

$$UCL_{\tilde{x}} = \tilde{\bar{x}} + \tilde{A}_2 \bar{R} = 907.04 + 25.43 = 932.5$$
$$LCL_{\tilde{x}} = \tilde{\bar{x}} - \tilde{A}_2 \bar{R} = 907.04 - 25.43 = 881.6$$

Constants

n	A_2	D_4	$\tilde{A}_2$	d_2
3	1.023	2.574	1.19	1.693
4	0.729	2.282	—	2.059
5	0.577	2.114	.691	2.326

Sample Numbers	1	2	3	4	5	6	7	8	9	10	11	12	13	14	15	16	17	18	19	20	21	22	23	24	25
$\tilde{x}$	915	900	902	900	909	896	897	906	922	900	908	895	906	902	910	907	911	912	913	917	912	913	908	917	898
R	30	49	42	59	50	20	54	26	33	40	38	9	55	37	32	35	57	23	40	59	32	19	23	11	35
Sample measurements	915	900	905	871	940	812	897	920	928	890	895	901	906	932	906	907	885	904	913	882	907	913	910	918	889
	891	905	889	930	890	895	933	908	926	900	925	895	872	902	893	909	942	897	936	941	912	909	885	917	919
	920	911	902	882	909	892	879	894	920	890	908	892	927	932	917	904	916	912	932	917	896	912	908	914	898
	890	862	873	913	915	902	885	896	895	930	933	898	909	895	925	923	892	916	912	934	926	928	903	917	912
	916	898	915	900	895	896	896	906	922	903	896	892	904	902	910	888	911	920	896	894	928	915	926	925	884

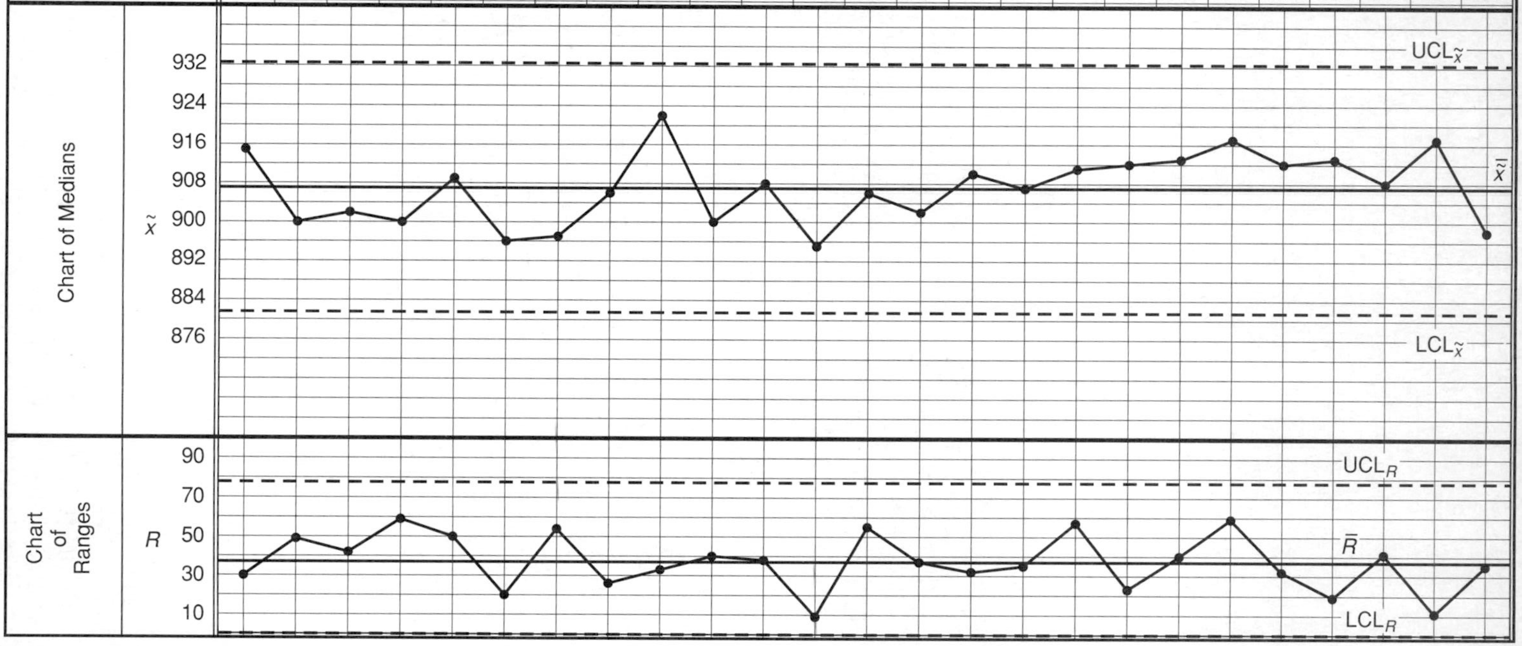

Chart of Medians (y-axis $\tilde{x}$: 932, 924, 916, 908, 900, 892, 884, 876) with lines $UCL_{\tilde{x}}$, $LCL_{\tilde{x}}$, $\tilde{\tilde{x}}$.

Chart of Ranges (y-axis R: 90, 70, 50, 30, 10) with lines UCL_R, $\bar{R}$, LCL_R.

FIGURE 6.17
Interpret the charts.

128

$$\bar{R} = \frac{\Sigma R}{k} = \frac{868}{23} = 37.74$$

$$\tilde{\bar{x}} = \frac{\Sigma \tilde{x}}{k} = \frac{20851}{23} = 906.6$$

Specification: 850 to 950

$$UCL_R = D_4 \times \bar{R} = 2.114 \times 37.74 = 79.8$$
$$A_2 \times \bar{R} = .69 \times 37.74 = 26.0$$

$$UCL_{\tilde{x}} = \tilde{\bar{x}} + \tilde{A}_2 \bar{R} = 906.6 + 26.0 = 932.6$$
$$LCL_{\tilde{x}} = \tilde{\bar{x}} - \tilde{A}_2 \bar{R} = 906.6 - 26.0 = 880.6$$

Constants

n	A_2	$\tilde{A}_2$	D_4	d_2
3	1.023	1.19	2.574	1.693
4	0.729	—	2.282	2.059
5	0.577	.691	2.114	2.326

Sample Numbers	1	2	3	4	5	6	7	8	9	10	11	12	13	14	15	16	17	18	19	20	21	22	23	24	25
Sample measurements	915	900	905	871	940	882	897	920	928	890	895	901	906	932	906	907	885	904	913	882	907	913	910	918	889
	891	905	889	930	890	895	933	908	926	900	925	895	872	902	893	909	942	897	936	941	912	909	885	917	919
	920	911	902	882	909	892	879	894	920	890	908	892	927	932	917	904	916	912	932	917	896	912	908	914	898
	890	862	873	913	915	902	885	896	895	930	933	898	909	895	925	923	892	916	912	934	926	928	926	917	912
	916	898	915	900	895	896	896	906	922	903	896	892	904	902	910	888	911	920	896	894	928	915	908	925	884
$\tilde{x}$	915	900	902	900	909	896	897	906	922	900	908	895	906	902	910	907	911	912	913	917	912	913	908	917	898
R	30	49	42	59	50	20	54	26	33	40	38	9	55	37	32	35	57	23	40	59	32	19	41	11	35

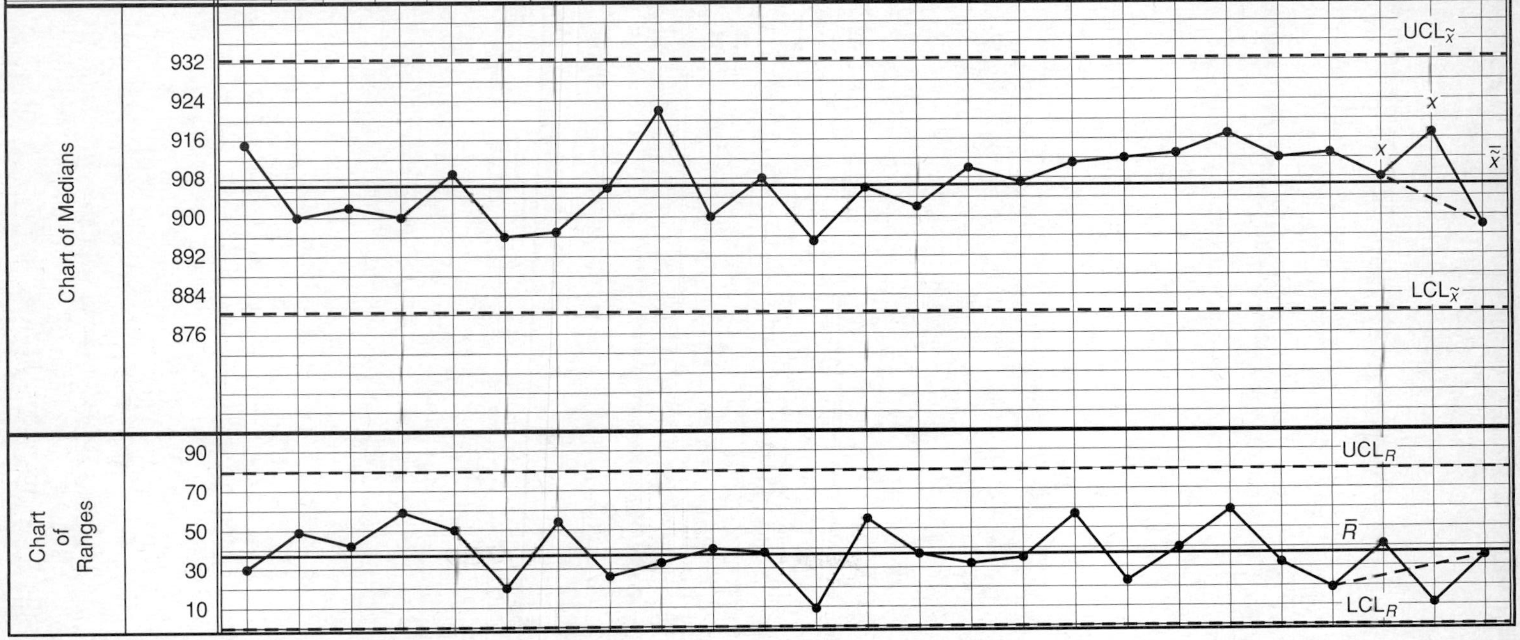

Chart of Medians

$UCL_{\tilde{x}}$
$\bar{\bar{x}}$
$LCL_{\tilde{x}}$

932 — 924 — 916 — 908 — 900 — 892 — 884 — 876

Chart of Ranges

UCL_R
$\bar{R}$
LCL_R

90 — 70 — 50 — 30 — 10

FIGURE 6.18
The $\tilde{x}$ and R chart is now in statistical control.

When all the data points are between the control limits in a random pattern, the process is in statistical control.

The R chart in Figure 6.17 is in statistical control. The $\tilde{x}$ chart, however, shows the pattern of a shift: eight points in a row on one side of $\overline{\tilde{x}}$. The 23rd and 24th sample points are classified out of control and marked with an "X," and the points on either side are connected with a dashed line. The data values for those samples are eliminated as well.

To recalculate, subtract the sum of the medians from the eliminated samples from the previous $\sum \tilde{x}$.

$$
\begin{array}{r}
908 \\
+917 \\
\hline
1825
\end{array}
\quad \text{Medians of eliminated samples}
$$

$$
\begin{array}{r}
22676 \\
-1825 \\
\hline
20851
\end{array}
\quad
\begin{array}{l}
\text{The original } \sum \tilde{x} \\
\\
\text{The new } \sum \tilde{x}
\end{array}
$$

$$
\text{The new } \overline{\tilde{x}} = \frac{\sum \tilde{x}}{k}
$$

$$
= \frac{20851}{23}
$$

$$
= 906.6
$$

Subtract the sum of the eliminated R values from $\sum R$.

$$
\begin{array}{r}
41 \\
+11 \\
\hline
52
\end{array}
\quad \text{Eliminated } R \text{ values}
$$

$$
\begin{array}{r}
920 \\
-52 \\
\hline
868
\end{array}
\quad \text{The new } \sum R
$$

$$
\text{The new } \overline{R} = \frac{\sum R}{k}
$$

$$
= \frac{868}{23}
$$

$$
= 37.74
$$

In both calculations, two samples were eliminated from the data set, so the new k value is 23.

Calculate the new control limits:

$$\text{UCL}_R = D_4\overline{R} = 2.114 \times 37.74 = 79.8$$

$$
\begin{aligned}
\text{UCL}_{\bar{x}} &= \overline{\overline{x}} + \tilde{A}_2\overline{R} \\
&= 906.6 + (.69 \times 37.74) \\
&= 906.6 + 26.0 \\
&= 932.6
\end{aligned}
$$

$$
\begin{aligned}
\text{LCL}_{\bar{x}} &= \overline{\overline{x}} - \tilde{A}_2\overline{R} \\
&= 906.6 - 26.0 \\
&= 880.6
\end{aligned}
$$

There is no appreciable change on the control chart with the new control limits and average values, and the process is now in statistical control. The analysis on Figure 6.17 should match Figure 6.18.

Make a histogram with the remaining in-control data values. The data range is eighty ($942 - 862$). For 115 data values, the G chart in Table 2, Appendix B indicates that 10 groups or classes should be used. Eighty divided by 10 is 8, so the group range should be greater than 8 if just 10 classes are wanted. A class range of 9 will be used. The classes will be

859 to 867

868 to 876

877 to 885

886 to 894

895 to 903

904 to 912

913 to 921

922 to 930

931 to 939

940 to 948

The tally histogram is shown on page 132 in Figure 6.19.

The shape of the histogram shows that the data is normally distributed, so the normal curve formulas can be used for the capability analysis as well as the PCR and Cpk.

The next step is to find out if the product being produced is good enough, which is determined by a process capability analysis. To do this, first calculate the standard deviation for all the measurements. The d_2 value from Table 1.2 in Appendix B is 2.326 for a sample size of 5. Divide the average range value by 2.326.

FIGURE 6.19
The data appears to be normally distributed.

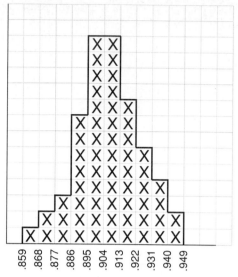

Measurements

$$\sigma = \frac{\overline{R}}{d_2}$$

$$= \frac{37.74}{2.326}$$

$$= 16.225$$

$$3\sigma = 48.7$$

$$6\sigma = 97.4$$

The tolerance is

$$\begin{array}{r} 950 \\ -850 \\ \hline 100 \end{array}$$

Calculate the PCR.

$$PCR = \frac{6\sigma}{\text{Tolerance}}$$

$$= \frac{97.4}{100}$$

$$= .974$$

The process uses 97.4 percent of the tolerance.

To calculate the Cpk, find the differences between the specification limits and $\overline{\overline{x}}$.

$$
\begin{array}{llll}
\text{USL} & 950 & 906.6 & \overline{\overline{x}} \\
\overline{\overline{x}} & -906.6 & -850 & \text{LSL} \\
\hline
& 43.4 & 56.6 &
\end{array}
$$

Use the smaller of the two differences in the Cpk formula.

$$
\begin{aligned}
\text{Cpk} &= \frac{\text{Smallest difference with } \overline{\overline{x}}}{3\sigma} \\[4pt]
&= \frac{43.4}{48.7} \\[4pt]
&= .891 \\[4pt]
\frac{1}{\text{Cpk}} &= \frac{1}{.891} \\[4pt]
&= 1.12
\end{aligned}
$$

The process uses 112 percent of the tolerance on the "short" side.

To find the percent of product that is out of specification, substitute the specification limits into the z formula.

$$
z = \frac{x - \overline{\overline{x}}}{\sigma} \qquad\qquad z = \frac{x - \overline{\overline{x}}}{\sigma}
$$

$$
\begin{aligned}
z_1 &= \frac{\text{LSL} - \overline{\overline{x}}}{\sigma} & z_2 &= \frac{\text{USL} - \overline{\overline{x}}}{\sigma} \\[6pt]
&= \frac{850 - 906.6}{16.225} & &= \frac{950 - 906.6}{16.225} \\[6pt]
&= -3.49 & &= 2.67
\end{aligned}
$$

Find the tail area values in the normal curve table in Table 3, Appendix B.

$$
\text{Area}_1 = .00024 \qquad \text{Area}_2 = .0038
$$

The total amount of product that is out of specification, .00024 + .0038, is .00404, or .4 percent.

The charting procedure, analysis, and interpretation of the $\tilde{x}$ and R chart and the $\overline{x}$ and R chart are primarily the same. The seven steps outlined for the $\overline{x}$ and R chart follow the same process as the nine points outlined for the $\tilde{x}$ and R chart with these minor differences:

1. An *odd* number sample size should be used when making the $\tilde{x}$ and R chart. The sample size, n, can be odd *or* even for the $\overline{x}$ and R chart.
2. The numerical constants for the control limits are different: A_2 for the $\overline{x}$ chart and $\tilde{A}_2$ for the $\tilde{x}$ chart.

3. The average values used are slightly different, but they represent the same quantity. The average of the sample means, $\bar{\bar{x}}$, and the average of the sample medians, $\bar{\tilde{x}}$, both represent the average of all the individual measurements.

4. The sample median, $\tilde{x}$, will not necessarily show a "freak" measurement (one measurement that differs drastically from the others) in the sample. The sample mean, $\bar{x}$, will show its existence. The R chart shows its existence in both cases.

EXAMPLE 6.4

The target measurement for shaft diameters is .500 inches, and the tolerance is .495 inches to .505 inches. Twenty-five samples are recorded on the control chart in Figure 6.20 (page 135). Make the $\tilde{x}$ and R chart and interpret the results. Check your results on steps 1 to 4 with the completed chart in Figure 6.21 (see page 137). The process capability analysis is completed after Figure 6.22 (page 138) has been assessed; check your results from step 5.

1. Calculate the median and range for each sample.
2. Set the $\tilde{x}$ and R scales and make the charts.
3. The calculation format is at the top of the control chart. Do the calculations and draw the averages and control limit lines.
4. Analyze the charts (R chart first) and mark any out-of-control points with an "X."
5. Remove any out-of-control data from the chart and calculate the process capability with the PCR, Cpk, and the percent out of specification. Remember to check the data histogram to see if the calculation of the out-of-specification percent is credible.

Solution

To set the scales, calculate the range of the $\tilde{x}$'s and the R's from the first eight samples:

$$R_{\tilde{x}} = .502 - .499$$
$$= .003$$
$$2R_{\tilde{x}} = 2 \times .003$$
$$= .006$$

Count the number of lines in the $\tilde{x}$ section of the control chart. Divide the number of lines into the .006.

$$\frac{.0002+}{21\,)\,.006}$$

Round up to .0005 units/line. It's easiest to use 2 lines per thousandth. Start at the mid-specification value of .500 at the center of the chart and use two lines for each .001. Calculate the range of the ranges and set the scale.

$$R_R = .006 - .002$$
$$= .004$$
$$2R_R = 2 \times .004$$
$$= .008$$

$$\bar{R} = \frac{\Sigma R}{k} = \underline{\hphantom{xxx}} = \underline{\hphantom{xxx}} \qquad\Vert\qquad UCL_R = D_4 \times \bar{R} = \underline{\hphantom{xx}} \times \underline{\hphantom{xx}} = \underline{\hphantom{xx}}$$

$$\tilde{\bar{x}} = \frac{\Sigma \tilde{x}}{k} = \underline{\hphantom{xxx}} = \underline{\hphantom{xxx}} \qquad\qquad\qquad A_2 \times \bar{R} = \underline{\hphantom{xx}} \times \underline{\hphantom{xx}} = \underline{\hphantom{xx}}$$

Specification : .495 to .505

$$UCL_{\tilde{x}} = \tilde{\bar{x}} + \tilde{A}_2 \bar{R} = \underline{\hphantom{xx}} + \boxed{\hphantom{xx}} = \boxed{\hphantom{xx}}$$

$$LCL_{\tilde{x}} = \tilde{\bar{x}} - \tilde{A}_2 \bar{R} = \underline{\hphantom{xx}} - \boxed{\hphantom{xx}} = \boxed{\hphantom{xx}}$$

Constants

n	A_2	$\tilde{A}_2$	D_4	d_2
3	1.023	1.19	2.574	1.693
4	0.729	—	2.282	2.059
5	0.577	.69	2.114	2.326

Sample Numbers	1	2	3	4	5	6	7	8	9	10	11	12	13	14	15	16	17	18	19	20	21	22	23	24	25
Sample measurements	.502	.500	.496	.501	.501	.499	.502	.500	.500	.501	.498	.501	.502	.494	.498	.500	.499	.501	.504	.499	.497	.502	.501	.502	.502
	.503	.501	.500	.500	.501	.501	.500	.499	.499	.500	.500	.502	.502	.499	.496	.498	.502	.500	.500	.499	.499	.500	.505	.502	.496
	.499	.497	.502	.500	.500	.502	.504	.501	.495	.500	.499	.500	.503	.503	.499	.502	.504	.501	.499	.495	.501	.501	.502	.501	.499
	.498	.499	.499	.500	.501	.504	.503	.497	.498	.500	.501	.501	.501	.496	.500	.500	.502	.501	.500	.498	.500	.500	.501	.500	.498
	.503	.500	.499	.502	.498	.501	.500	.501	.501	.497	.502	.501	.503	.505	.499	.501	.500	.503	.502	.498	.501	.501	.500	.503	.499
$\tilde{x}$																									
R																									

Chart of Medians — $\tilde{x}$

Chart of Ranges — R

FIGURE 6.20
Make the $\tilde{x}$ and R chart.

Count the number of lines on the R section of the control chart. Divide the number of lines into the .008.

$$10 \overline{)\,.008} = .0008$$

Round up to .001 units/line. Start at 0 on the bottom line and use one line for each .001. Make the $\tilde{x}$ and R chart on Figure 6.20.

When the chart is completed, compare your results with the chart in Figure 6.21. Do the calculations for the average and control limits of the range chart first. Analyze the range chart and eliminate any out-of-control points before proceding with the $\tilde{x}$ chart. Assume that the out-of-control problem in the process has been solved and eliminated. Bringing the R chart into control this way before starting calculations on the $\tilde{x}$ chart saves time. Otherwise, the calculations on the $\tilde{x}$ will be done twice: before and after out-of-control data are removed as a result of the R chart analysis. The median chart calculations, shown on Figure 6.21, indicate that one data point has been removed from the chart. Further chart analysis reveals no other out-of-control situations.

For the process capability, the new value of R is

$$\begin{array}{rl} .107 & \text{Original } \sum R \\ -.011 & \text{The out-of-control } R \text{ value} \\ \hline .096 & \text{The new } \sum R \end{array}$$

$$\bar{R} = \frac{\sum R}{k}$$

$$= \frac{.096}{24}$$

$$= .004$$

$$\sigma = \frac{\bar{R}}{d_2}$$

$$= \frac{.004}{2.326}$$

$$= .00172$$

$$3\sigma = .00516$$

$$6\sigma = .01032$$

$$\begin{array}{rl} .505 & \text{USL} \\ -4.95 & \text{LSL} \\ \hline .010 & \text{Tolerance} \end{array}$$

$$\text{PCR} = \frac{6\sigma}{\text{Tolerance}}$$

$$= \frac{.01032}{.010}$$

$$= 1.032$$

$$\bar{R} = \frac{\Sigma R}{k} = \frac{.107}{25} = .00428 \qquad UCL_R = D_4 \times \bar{R} = 2.114 \times .00428 = .00905 \qquad UCL_{\tilde{x}} = \tilde{\bar{x}} + \tilde{A}_2 \bar{R} = .50042 + .00276 = .5032$$

$$\tilde{\bar{x}} = \frac{\Sigma \bar{x}}{k} = \frac{12.01}{24} = .50042 \qquad \tilde{A}_2 \times \bar{R} = .69 \times .004 = .00276 \qquad LCL_{\tilde{x}} = \tilde{\bar{x}} - \tilde{A}_2 \bar{R} = .50042 - .00276 = .4977$$

Specification : .495 to .505

Constants

n	A_2	$\tilde{A}_2$	D_4	d_2
3	1.023	1.19	2.574	1.693
4	0.729	—	2.282	2.059
5	0.577	.69	2.114	2.326

Sample Numbers	1	2	3	4	5	6	7	8	9	10	11	12	13	14	15	16	17	18	19	20	21	22	23	24	25
Sample measurements	.502	.500	.496	.501	.501	.499	.502	.500	.500	.501	.498	.501	.502	.494	.498	.500	.499	.501	.504	.499	.497	.502	.501	.502	.502
	.503	.501	.500	.500	.501	.501	.500	.499	.499	.500	.500	.502	.502	.499	.496	.498	.502	.500	.500	.499	.499	.500	.505	.502	.496
	.499	.497	.502	.500	.500	.502	.504	.501	.495	.500	.499	.500	.503	.503	.499	.502	.504	.501	.499	.495	.501	.501	.502	.501	.499
	.498	.499	.499	.500	.501	.504	.503	.497	.498	.500	.501	.501	.501	.496	.500	.500	.502	.501	.500	.498	.500	.500	.501	.500	.498
	.498	.500	.499	.502	.498	.501	.500	.501	.501	.497	.502	.501	.503	.505	.499	.501	.500	.503	.502	.498	.501	.501	.500	.503	.499
$\tilde{x}$	.502	.500	.499	.500	.501	.501	.502	.500	.499	.500	.500	.501	.502	.499	.499	.500	.502	.501	.500	.498	.500	.501	.501	.502	.499
R	.005	.004	.006	.002	.003	.005	.004	.004	.006	.004	.004	.002	.002	.011	.004	.004	.005	.003	.005	.004	.004	.002	.005	.003	.006

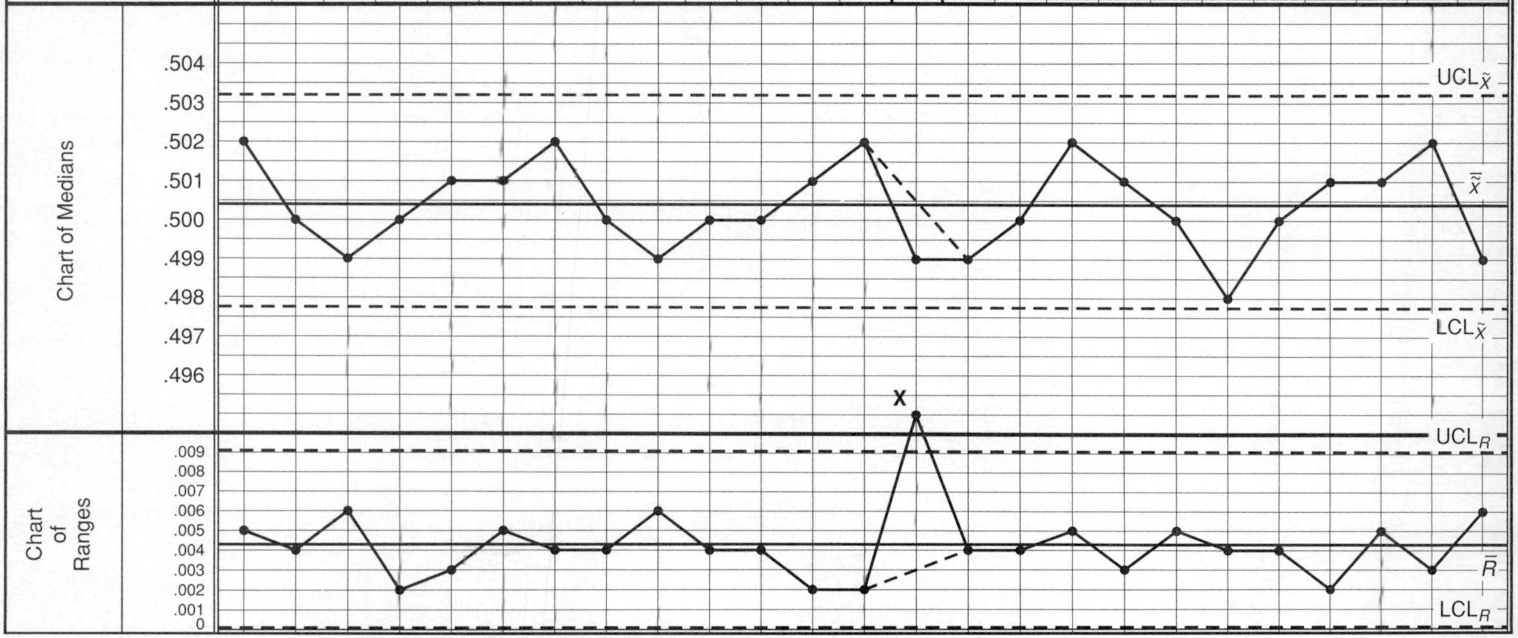

Chart of Medians — $UCL_{\tilde{x}}$, $\tilde{\bar{x}}$, $LCL_{\tilde{x}}$

Chart of Ranges — UCL_R, $\bar{R}$, LCL_R

FIGURE 6.21

Recalculate. The chart is now in statistical control.

137

The PCR indicates that this is a D process that uses 103 percent of the tolerance.

To calculate the Cpk, find the differences between the specification limits and $\bar{\bar{x}}$. Use the smaller difference in the Cpk formula.

$$
\begin{array}{ll}
.50042 \quad \bar{\bar{x}} & .505 \quad \text{USL} \\
\underline{-.495} \quad \text{LSL} & \underline{-.50042} \quad \bar{\bar{x}} \\
.00542 & .00458
\end{array}
$$

$$
\text{Cpk} = \frac{\text{Smallest} \mid \text{specification limit} - \bar{\bar{x}} \mid}{3\sigma}
$$

$$
= \frac{.00458}{.00516}
$$

$$
= .8876
$$

The Cpk indicates that this is a D process that uses $1/\text{Cpk} = 1/.8876 = 1.13$, or 113 percent, of the tolerance on the "worst" side of the mean, where the mean is closest to the specification limit.

FIGURE 6.22
The tally histogram shows that the distribution is normal.

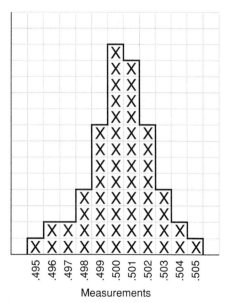

Measurements

The tally histogram in Figure 6.22 shows that the distribution of the data has a normal shape, so the calculation of the percent of product that is out of specification should give credible results. Substitute the specification limits for x in the z formula.

$$z = \frac{x - \bar{\bar{x}}}{\sigma}$$

$$= \frac{USL - \bar{\bar{x}}}{\sigma}$$

$$= \frac{.505 - .50042}{.00172}$$

$$= 2.66$$

The area is .0039 according to Table 3 in Appendix B, which indicates that .39 percent of the product is out of specification on the high side.

$$z = \frac{x - \bar{\bar{x}}}{\sigma}$$

$$= \frac{LSL - \bar{\bar{x}}}{\sigma}$$

$$= \frac{.495 - .50042}{.00172}$$

$$= -3.15$$

The area is .00082, which indicates that .082 percent of the product is out of specification on the low side. The total percent of product that is out-of-specification is

$$.39\% + .082\% = .472\%$$

6.3 $\bar{x}$ AND s CHARTS

The $\bar{x}$ and s charts follow the same step-by-step procedure that was outlined for the $\bar{x}$ and R charts, and the $\bar{x}$ chart section is exactly the same for both charts. The difference between the two charts is the measurement of the variability: The $\bar{x}$ and s chart uses the sample standard deviation, s, instead of the sample range, R. Also, use of the $\bar{x}$ and s charts requires that the person doing the charting use a statistical calculator or an on-station computer. Our discussion will focus on the use of a statistical calculator.

EXAMPLE 6.5

For this problem, we will use the data from the previous shaft diameter problem. Make the $\bar{x}$ and s chart and analyze the process capability after achieving statistical control.

Solution
The data are presented in Figure 6.23 (page 140). Calculate $\bar{x}$ and s for each sample using a statistical calculator. Be sure to clear the statistical registers before starting each new sample. One way to see if the registers are clear is to press the $\bar{x}$ key. If a numerical value appears, the calculator has not been cleared. If either a zero or an error message comes up, the statistical registers are clear. Enter the five sample values with the data

Constants

n	A_3	B_3	B_4	C_4
3	1.954	0	2.568	.8862
4	1.628	0	2.266	.9213
5	1.427	0	2.089	.9400

$\bar{s} = \frac{\Sigma s}{k} = $ _____ = _____

$\bar{\bar{x}} = \frac{\Sigma \bar{x}}{k} = $ _____ = _____

Specification : .495 to .505

$UCL_s = B_4 \times \bar{s} = $ _____ × _____ = _____

$A_3 \times \bar{s} = $ _____ × _____ = _____

$UCL_{\bar{x}} = \bar{\bar{x}} + A_3\,\bar{s} = $ _____ + _____ = _____

$LCL_{\bar{x}} = \bar{\bar{x}} - A_3\,\bar{s} = $ _____ − _____ = _____

Sample Numbers	1	2	3	4	5	6	7	8	9	10	11	12	13	14	15	16	17	18	19	20	21	22	23	24	25
Sample measurements	.502	.500	.496	.501	.501	.499	.502	.500	.500	.501	.498	.501	.502	.494	.498	.500	.499	.501	.504	.499	.497	.502	.501	.502	.502
	.503	.501	.500	.500	.501	.501	.500	.499	.499	.500	.500	.502	.502	.499	.496	.498	.502	.500	.500	.499	.499	.500	.505	.502	.496
	.499	.497	.502	.500	.500	.502	.504	.501	.495	.500	.499	.500	.503	.503	.499	.502	.504	.501	.499	.495	.501	.501	.502	.501	.499
	.498	.499	.499	.500	.501	.504	.503	.497	.498	.500	.501	.501	.501	.496	.500	.500	.502	.501	.500	.498	.500	.500	.501	.500	.498
	.503	.500	.499	.502	.498	.501	.500	.501	.501	.497	.502	.501	.503	.505	.499	.501	.500	.503	.502	.498	.501	.501	.500	.503	.499
$\bar{x}$																									
s																									

Chart of Averages — $\bar{x}$

Chart of Standard Deviations — s

FIGURE 6.23
Make the $\bar{x}$ and s chart.

entry key. Press the $\bar{x}$ key and record the sample mean. Press the s or σ_{n-1} key and record the sample standard deviation. Be careful, because the calculator will probably have two different standard deviation keys. Check your results with Figure 6.24.

Set the scales from the first eight samples and chart the points. Find the range of $\bar{x}$ and double it to set the scale.

$$R_{\bar{x}} = .5018 - .4992$$
$$= .0026$$
$$2R_{\bar{x}} = 2 \times .0026$$
$$= .0052$$

Divide by the number of lines on the chart. Round up to .0005 units/line.

$$\frac{.0002+}{21 \overline{)\,.0052}}$$

Next find the range of s and double it.

$$R_s = .0023 - .0009$$
$$= .0014$$
$$2R_s = 2 \times .0014$$
$$= .0028$$

Divide by the number of lines on the chart. Round up to .0005 units/line.

$$\frac{.0002+}{10 \overline{)\,.0028}}$$

Start the $\bar{x}$ chart in the center at the mid-specification value of .500. Start the s chart on the bottom line at 0. Complete the control chart in Figure 6.23 for x and s. Check your results with Figure 6.24 on page 142.

The formulas for calculating the values for the averages and the control limits are given at the top of the control chart in Figure 6.23. Do the s chart first and bring it into statistical control by eliminating any out-of-control points. Assume that the cause for the out of control situation has been found and eliminated.

Do your calculations, draw the average and control limit lines, and analyze the chart for points out of control. Check your results with Figure 6.24.

The calculation section has been completed on Figure 6.24. The $\bar{s}$ calculation shows $\bar{s}$ calculated from all 25 s values. The UCL$_s$ is .0035. When the average and control limit lines are drawn on the s chart, the point for sample 14 is beyond the control limit. Assuming that the cause for the out-of-control point was eliminated from the process, delete the sample 14 data. The average, $\bar{\bar{x}}$, is determined from the remaining 24 sample values. Also, $\bar{s}$ is recalculated by subtracting .0046 (from sample 14) from the previous sum and dividing by 24.

$\bar{s} = \dfrac{\Sigma s}{k} = \_\_\_\_ = \_\_\_\_$

$\bar{\bar{x}} = \dfrac{\Sigma x}{k} = \_\_\_\_ = \_\_\_\_$

Specification: .495 to .505

$UCL_s = B_4 \times \bar{s} = 2.089 \times .00169 = .0035$

$A_3 \times \bar{s} = 1.427 \times .00157 = .00224$

$UCL_{\bar{x}} = \bar{\bar{x}} + A_3 \bar{s} = .5003 + .00224 = .50254$

$LCL_{\bar{x}} = \bar{\bar{x}} - A_3 \bar{s} = .5003 - .00224 = .49806$

Constants

n	A_3	B_3	B_4	C_4
3	1.954	0	2.568	.8862
4	1.628	0	2.266	.9213
5	1.427	0	2.089	.9400

Sample Numbers	1	2	3	4	5	6	7	8	9	10	11	12	13	14	15	16	17	18	19	20	21	22	23	24	25
Sample measurements	.502	.500	.496	.501	.501	.499	.502	.500	.500	.501	.498	.501	.502	.494	.498	.500	.499	.501	.504	.499	.497	.502	.501	.502	.502
	.503	.501	.500	.500	.501	.501	.500	.499	.499	.500	.500	.502	.502	.499	.496	.498	.502	.500	.500	.499	.499	.500	.505	.502	.496
	.499	.497	.502	.500	.500	.502	.504	.501	.495	.500	.499	.500	.503	.503	.499	.502	.504	.501	.499	.495	.501	.501	.502	.501	.499
	.498	.499	.499	.500	.501	.504	.503	.497	.498	.500	.501	.501	.501	.496	.500	.500	.502	.501	.500	.498	.500	.500	.501	.500	.498
	.503	.500	.499	.502	.498	.501	.500	.501	.501	.497	.502	.501	.503	.505	.499	.501	.500	.503	.502	.493	.501	.501	.500	.503	.499
$\bar{x}$	.5010	.4994	.4992	.5006	.5002	.5014	.5018	.4996	.4986	.4996	.5000	.5010	.5022	.4994	.4984	.5002	.5014	.5012	.5010	.4973	.4996	.5008	.5018	.5016	.4988
s	.0023	.0015	.0022	.0009	.0013	.0017	.0018	.0017	.0023	.0015	.0016	.0007	.0008	.0046	.0015	.0015	.0019	.0011	.0020	.0016	.0017	.0008	.0019	.0011	.0022

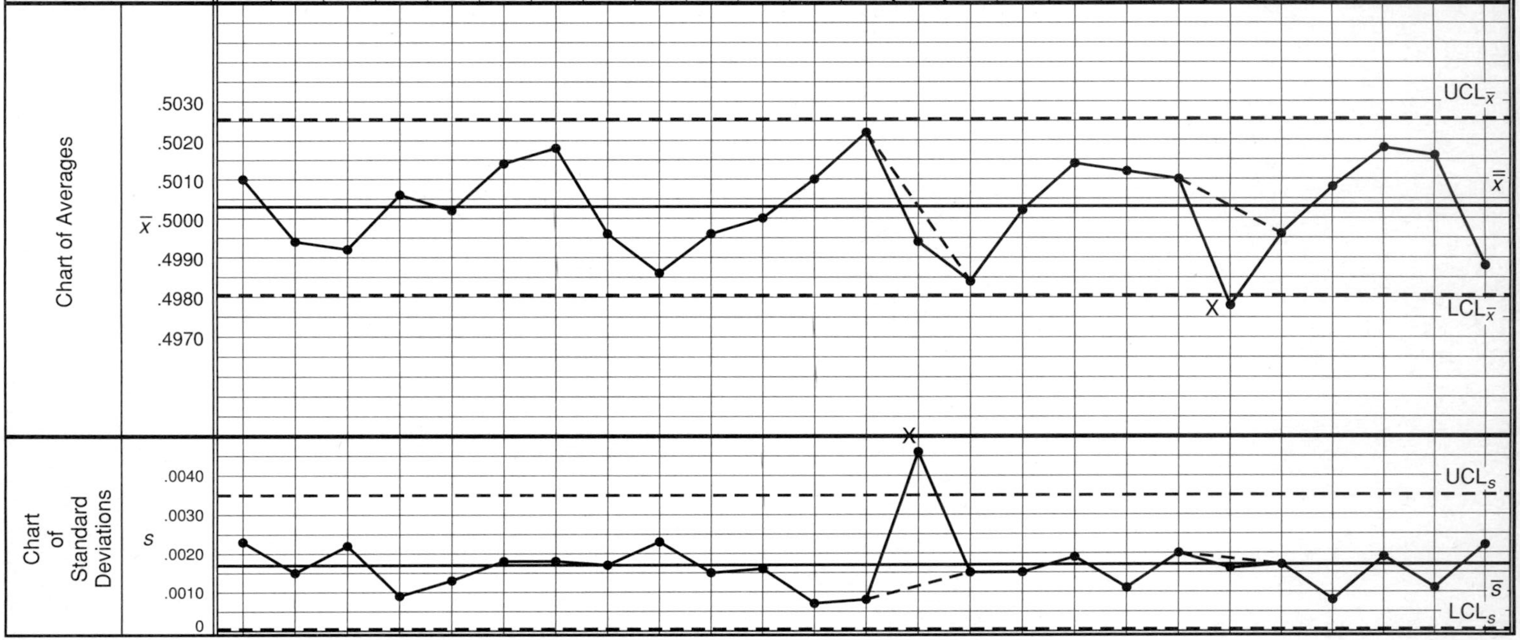

Chart of Averages

.5030
.5020
.5010
$\bar{x}$ .5000
.4990
.4980
.4970

$UCL_{\bar{x}}$
$\bar{\bar{x}}$
$LCL_{\bar{x}}$

Chart of Standard Deviations

.0040
.0030
s .0020
.0010
0

UCL_s
$\bar{s}$
LCL_s

FIGURE 6.24

The $\bar{x}$ and s chart is now in statistical control.

$$
\begin{array}{ll}
.0423 & \text{Original } \sum s \\
-.0046 & \text{Sample 14} \\
\hline
.0377 & \text{New } \sum s
\end{array}
$$

$$
\text{The new } \bar{s} = \frac{.0377}{24}
$$
$$
= .00157
$$

The new $\bar{s}$ is then used to calculate $A_3\bar{s}$ for the $\bar{x}$ chart control limits.

   Analyze the $\bar{x}$ chart for points that are out-of-control; look for points beyond the control limits and runs or shifts of seven or more consecutive points. A more complete chart analysis will be discussed in Chapter 9.

   One additional point is out of control, as shown in Figure 6.24. With that data point eliminated and the process in statistical control, the process capability can be determined.

   The first step in the capability analysis is to determine the standard deviation of the *individual* measurements. The s values calculated for the control chart were *sample* standard deviations. Fortunately, a simple conversion is available, similar to the one used with the R charts.

$$
\sigma = \frac{\bar{s}}{C_4}
$$

The numerical constant C_4 depends on the sample size and is shown in a table in the calculation section of the control chart in Figure 6.25 (page 146). A more complete table of constants is shown as part of Table 1.3 in Appendix B.

$$
\sigma = \frac{.00157}{.94}
$$
$$
= .00167
$$
$$
3\sigma = .00501
$$
$$
6\sigma = .01002
$$

$$
\begin{array}{ll}
.505 & \text{USL} \\
-.495 & \text{LSL} \\
\hline
.010 & \text{Tolerance}
\end{array}
$$

$$
\text{PCR} = \frac{6\sigma}{\text{Tolerance}}
$$
$$
= \frac{.01002}{.01}
$$
$$
= 1.002
$$

This indicates a D process that uses 100.2 percent of the tolerance.

$$
\begin{array}{ll}
.505 & \text{USL} \\
-.5004 & \bar{\bar{x}} \\
\hline
.0046 &
\end{array}
\qquad
\begin{array}{ll}
.5004 & \bar{\bar{x}} \\
-.495 & \text{LSL} \\
\hline
.0054 &
\end{array}
$$

The smallest difference is used in the calculation of the Cpk.

$$\text{Cpk} = \frac{\text{smallest difference}}{3\sigma}$$

$$= \frac{.0046}{.00501}$$

$$= .918$$

$$\frac{1}{\text{Cpk}} = \frac{1}{.918}$$

$$= 1.09$$

This calculation shows that the process uses 109 percent of the tolerance on the worst side.

The histogram for this data was shown in Figure 6.22 to have a normal shape. The normal curve analysis can be used to find the percent of product that is out of specification.

$$z = \frac{\text{USL} - \bar{\bar{x}}}{\sigma}$$

$$= \frac{.505 - .5004}{.00167}$$

$$= 2.93$$

$$\text{Area} = .0017$$

This analysis indicates that .17 percent of the product is out of specification on the high side.

$$z = \frac{\text{LSL} - \bar{\bar{x}}}{\sigma}$$

$$= \frac{.495 - .5004}{.00167}$$

$$= -3.44$$

$$\text{Area} = .00029$$

On the low side, .029 percent is out of specification. The total is approximately .2 percent out of specification.

This same set of data was analyzed twice: first with the $\tilde{x}$ and R chart in Example 6.4 and then here with the $\bar{x}$ and s chart. The results are comparable. The slight difference is due to the varying estimations of the standard deviation of the individual measurements: One is calculated from R and the other from s.

	$\bar{x}$ and s	$\tilde{x}$ and R
PCR	100.2%	103%
Cpk	109%	113%
percent out	.2%	.5%

The $\bar{x}$ chart seems a little more sensitive than the $\tilde{x}$ chart. ιart showed one point out of specification that the median chart missed. It also seemeα more obvious with the $\bar{x}$ chart that the process was still not in statistical control. Two point patterns suggest control problems: (1) too many points near the control limits and (2) rhythmic ups and downs. These out-of-control patterns will be discussed thoroughly in Chapter 9.

EXAMPLE 6.6

The data values presented in Figure 6.25 are lengths of cam roller bushings that have a tolerance of 1.328 to 1.334 inches. The measurements are to the nearest ten-thousandth, so *coded* measurements are used. Appendix A discusses the use of coded measurements. The base measurement is 1.3300, and the coded values represent the last two digits. For example, 1.3324 codes to 24. Measurements smaller than 1.3300 will have a negative coded value, so 1.3286, for example, codes to -14 (14 below 00). Coded averages are multiplied by .0001 and added to the base, 1.3300, for the true mean value: The true value for coded $\bar{x} = 13$ is $\bar{x} = 1.3313$. Coded standard deviations are simply multiplied by .0001: A coded $s = 3.6$ is really $s = .00036$. Make an $\bar{x}$ and s chart and interpret the results.

Solution

The calculations on the first few samples are illustrated here. The entire set of data is in coded form on the control chart in Figure 6.25. Complete the calculations for $\bar{x}$ and s for the remaining samples on Figure 6.25 and check your results with Figure 6.26 (page 148). Enter the coded measurements into your statistical calculator with the data entry key. Then press $\bar{x}$ and s (or σ_{n-1}) and record the values.

Sample 1	Coded form	Coded $\bar{x}$	Coded s
1.3329	29		
1.3330	30		
1.3328	28		
1.3337	37		
1.3329	29	30.6	3.65

Sample 2			
1.3329	29		
1.3319	19		
1.3325	25		
1.3321	21		
1.3335	35	25.8	6.42

$$\bar{s} = \frac{\Sigma s}{k} = \underline{\qquad} = \underline{\qquad}$$

$$\bar{\bar{x}} = \frac{\Sigma \bar{x}}{k} = \underline{\qquad} = \underline{\qquad}$$

Specification : 1.328 to 1.334

$$UCL_s = B_4 \times \bar{s} = \underline{\qquad} \times \underline{\qquad} = \underline{\qquad}$$
$$A_3 \times \bar{s} = \underline{\qquad} \times \underline{\qquad} = \underline{\qquad}$$

$$UCL_{\bar{x}} = \bar{\bar{x}} + A_3\,\bar{s} = \underline{\qquad} + \underline{\qquad} = \boxed{}$$
$$LCL_{\bar{x}} = \bar{\bar{x}} - A_3\,\bar{s} = \underline{\qquad} - \underline{\qquad} = \boxed{}$$

Constants

n	A_3	B_3	B_4	C_4
3	1.954	0	2.568	.8862
4	1.628	0	2.266	.9213
5	1.427	0	2.089	.9400

Sample Numbers	1	2	3	4	5	6	7	8	9	10	11	12	13	14	15	16	17	18	19	20	21	22	23	24	25
Coded 0 = 1.3300	29	29	28	28	22	33	33	33	27	28	38	36	25	26	20	16	29	17	21	29	24	27	20	28	08
	30	19	27	27	26	36	27	20	21	21	29	27	25	35	31	19	29	04	28	16	10	25	21	20	30
	28	25	14	14	08	32	20	21	31	17	25	24	11	20	19	23	05	27	16	19	30	21	18	29	16
	37	21	18	18	27	27	33	27	30	34	26	26	27	25	30	16	19	26	17	33	16	27	26	27	09
	29	35	34	34	24	28	21	33	27	25	27	21	36	24	35	25	21	16	21	15	21	30	31	22	00
Average Range $\bar{x}$ s																									

Chart of Averages — $\bar{x}$

Chart of Standard Deviations — s

FIGURE 6.25

Calculate $\bar{x}$ and s for each sample and make an $\bar{x}$ and s chart. Calculate averages and control limits and determine process capability.

Sample 3	Coded form	Coded $\bar{x}$	Coded s
1.3328	28		
1.3327	27		
1.3314	14		
1.3318	18		
1.3334	34	24.2	8.07

Continue the rest of the $\bar{x}$ and s calculations with the coded data given in Figure 6.25. Set the scales in coded form and make the $\bar{x}$ an s chart. The formulas, constants, and calculation format are shown at the top of the control chart in Figure 6.25. Do the calculations, draw the center lines and control limit lines, and interpret the results. Check your results with the completed chart in Figure 6.26.

Chart Interpretation.   On the s chart, $\bar{s} = 6.39$ (coded). The base is ten-thousandths, so multiplication by the base factor .0001 will change the coded value to the actual value.

$$\bar{s} = 6.39 \times .0001$$
$$= .000639 \quad \text{(actual)}$$

There are no apparent out-of-control patterns on the s chart. Proceed with the $\bar{x}$ chart.

On the $\bar{x}$ chart, $\bar{\bar{x}} = 24.5$ (coded). Multiply the coded value by the base factor .0001 and add the product to the base value of 1.3300 to change the coded value back to the actual value.

$$\bar{\bar{x}} = (24.5 \times .0001) + 1.3300$$
$$= 1.33245 \quad \text{(actual)}$$

One source of trouble that is apparent in the $\bar{x}$ chart is the discovery that the cut for bushing length is set too high. The average value, $\bar{\bar{x}}$, should be near the mid-specification value of 1.3310.

A second trouble indicator is the shift pattern that shows up in samples 6 through 15. Seven consecutive points on one side of the average line indicate a shift, and the seventh point and any successive points in the shift pattern are marked with an "X."

A third trouble indicator occurs at sample 25, where the point falls beyond the control limits.

Each trouble indicator must be investigated. If the out-of-control situation is determined and resolved, the out-of-control data values can be removed from the chart and the remaining in-control data can be used to calculate the process capability. Assume that the trouble has been eradicated, cross out the out-of-control data values and calculate the process capability.

$$\bar{s} = \frac{\Sigma s}{k} = \frac{159.83}{25} = 6.39$$

$$\bar{\bar{x}} = \frac{\Sigma \bar{x}}{k} = \frac{611.4}{25} = 24.5$$

Specification : 1.328 to 1.334

$$UCL_s = B_4 \times \bar{s} = 2.089 \times 6.39 = 13.34$$
$$A_3 \times \bar{s} = 1.427 \times 6.39 = 9.12$$

$$UCL_{\bar{x}} = \bar{\bar{x}} + A_3 \bar{s} = 24.5 + 9.12 = 33.6$$
$$LCL_{\bar{x}} = \bar{\bar{x}} - A_3 \bar{s} = 24.5 - 9.12 = 15.4$$

Constants

n	A_3	B_3	B_4	C_4
3	1.954	0	2.568	.8862
4	1.628	0	2.266	.9213
5	1.427	0	2.089	.9400

Sample Numbers	1	2	3	4	5	6	7	8	9	10	11	12	13	14	15	16	17	18	19	20	21	22	23	24	25
Coded 0 = 1.3300	29	29	28	28	22	33	33	33	27	28	38	36	25	26	20	16	29	17	21	29	24	27	20	28	08
	30	19	27	27	26	36	27	20	21	21	29	27	25	35	31	19	29	04	04	16	10	25	21	20	30
	28	25	14	14	08	32	20	21	31	17	25	24	17	25	19	23	05	27	27	19	30	21	18	29	16
	37	21	18	18	27	27	33	27	30	34	26	26	27	25	30	16	19	26	26	33	16	27	26	27	09
	29	35	34	34	24	28	21	33	27	25	27	21	36	24	35	25	21	16	21	15	21	30	31	22	00
$\bar{x}$	30.6	25.8	24.2	24.2	21.4	31.2	28.8	28.8	27.2	25.0	29.0	26.8	24.8	26.0	27.0	19.8	20.6	18.0	20.6	22.4	20.2	26.0	25.2	25.2	12.6
s	3.65	6.42	8.07	8.07	7.73	3.70	5.50	5.50	3.90	6.52	5.24	5.63	8.96	5.52	7.11	4.09	9.84	9.30	4.72	8.11	7.63	3.32	6.06	3.96	11.26

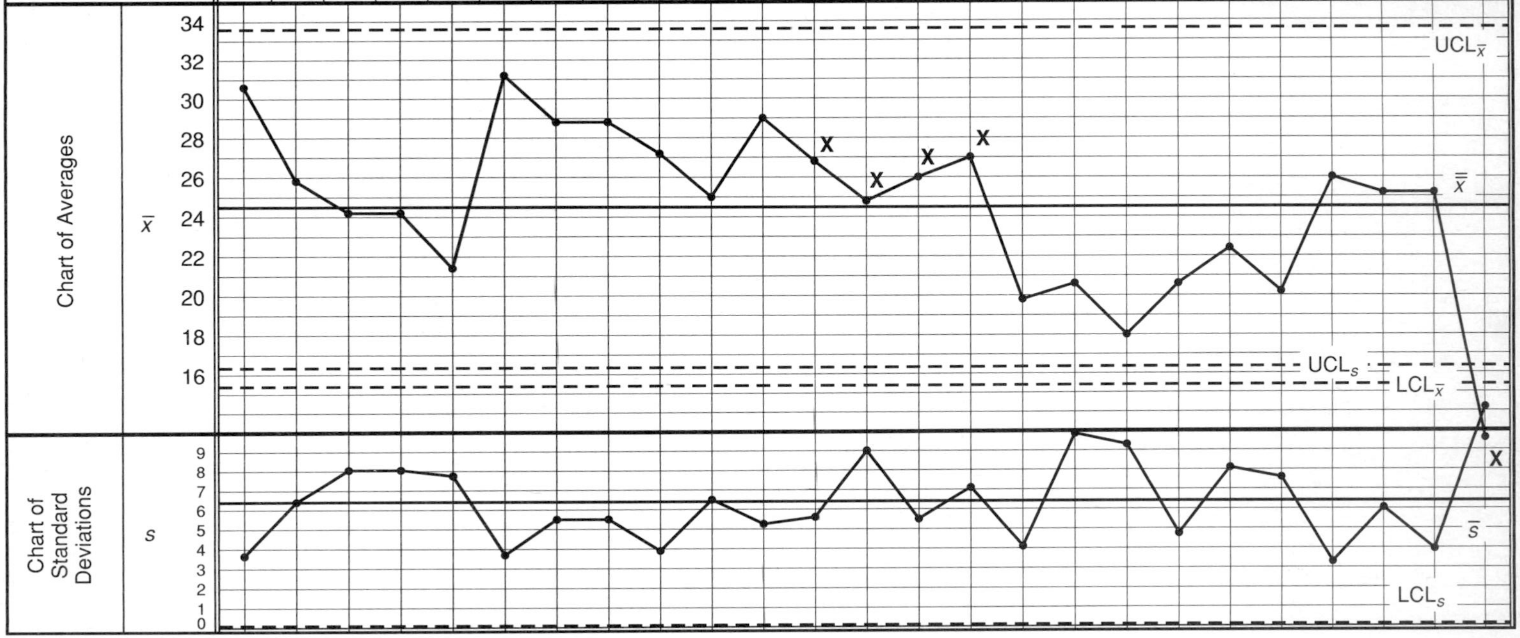

Chart of Averages — $\bar{x}$ (scale: 34, 32, 30, 28, 26, 24, 22, 20, 18, 16)

Chart of Standard Deviations — s (scale: 9, 8, 7, 6, 5, 4, 3, 2, 1, 0)

$UCL_{\bar{x}}$ $\bar{\bar{x}}$ UCL_s $LCL_{\bar{x}}$ $\bar{s}$ LCL_s

FIGURE 6.26

Recalculate averages and control limits and calculate PCR and Cpk. Make a histogram to check for a normal pattern; determine the percent out of specification.

Process Capability.   Remove the out-of-control data values.

Excluded $\bar{x}$'s	Excluded s's
26.8	5.63
24.8	8.96
26.0	5.52
27.0	7.11
12.6	11.26
117.2	38.48

611.4	previous $\sum \bar{x}$	159.83	previous $\sum s$
−117.2	excluded $\bar{x}$'s	−38.48	excluded s's
494.2	new $\sum \bar{x}$	121.35	new $\sum s$

$$\bar{\bar{x}} = \frac{\sum \bar{x}}{k}$$

$$= \frac{494.2}{20}$$

$$= 24.71 \quad \text{new } \bar{\bar{x}}$$

$$\bar{s} = \frac{\sum s}{k}$$

$$= \frac{121.35}{20}$$

$$= 6.07 \quad \text{new } \bar{s}$$

There is no appreciable change in the averages or control limits, so further analysis for out-of-control point patterns is unnecessary.

The standard deviation for the individual measurements is found with the formula $\sigma = \bar{s}/C_4$.

$$\sigma = \frac{\bar{s}}{C_4}$$

$$= \frac{6.07}{.9400}$$

$$= 6.457 \quad \text{(coded)}$$

Apply the base factor

$$\sigma = .0001 \times 6.457$$
$$= .0006457 \quad \text{(actual)}$$

1.334	USL
−1.328	LSL
.006	Tolerance

$$PCR = \frac{6\sigma}{\text{Tolerance}}$$

$$= \frac{6 \times .0006457}{.006}$$

$$= .6457$$

This classifies the process as a B process (see Table 6 in Appendix B), which uses 65 percent of the tolerance.

1.334	USL		1.3324	$\bar{\bar{x}}$
−1.3324	$\bar{\bar{x}}$		−1.328	LSL
.0016			.0044	

The smaller difference is used in the Cpk calculation.

$$Cpk = \frac{\text{smallest difference}}{3\sigma}$$

$$= \frac{.0016}{3 \times .0006457}$$

$$= .826$$

$$\frac{1}{Cpk} = \frac{1}{.826}$$

$$= 1.21$$

The Cpk classifies this as a D process, which uses 121 percent of the tolerance on the worst side. The Cpk value, along with the PCR measurement, verifies the previous conclusion that the cut on the bushings is set too high. The process is good enough to center the distribution at the mid-specification value: The PCR shows that 65 percent of the tolerance is used by the distribution of measurements. The Cpk indicates that the present setting is producing some bushings that are out of specification on the high side: The 3σ spread of measurements above the mean overlaps the upper specification limit. The present setting is costly because the out-of-specification bushings must be found (inspection costs) and reworked to bring them into specification (processing costs).

Although the histogram of the in-control data, shown in Figure 6.27 on page 151, indicates a slight skewness to the left, the pattern is close enough to the normal distribution to apply the normal curve analysis.

$$z = \frac{USL - \bar{\bar{x}}}{\sigma}$$

$$= \frac{1.334 - 1.3324}{.0006457}$$

$$= 2.48$$

FIGURE 6.27
The histogram of the In-control data.

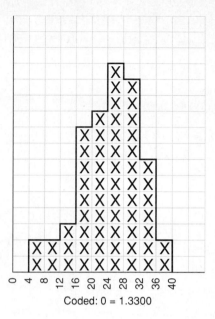

Coded: 0 = 1.3300

The area, according to Appendix B, Table 3, is .0066. This indicates that .66 percent of the bushings must be found and reworked to bring them into specification.

$$z = \frac{\text{LSL} - \bar{\bar{x}}}{\sigma}$$

$$= \frac{1.328 - 1.3324}{.0006457}$$

$$= -6.81$$

$$\text{Area} = .00000$$

The z value is off the chart, so the measurable tail area is 0. This large negative value for z also shows that there is room to shift the process toward the mid-specification value, 1.3310. With the process centered, there should be no problem with out-of-specification bushings.

Control charts, along with accompanying histograms of the data they contain, serve two basic purposes. First, they indicate trouble, and the patterns that occur offer hints of the source of trouble. In this situation, the control charts demand action. If there is no operator or management response to trouble patterns, charting is a waste of time and effort. SPC is used as "window dressing," and no quality improvement results. Second, control charts and histograms present proof of good quality. Purchasing departments should demand this proof and be able to interpret it. Sales and marketing departments should understand it and use it convincingly.

EXERCISES

1. What two types of variation show up on a variables control chart such as the $\bar{x}$ and R chart?
2. What does it mean when a process is said to be in statistical control?
3. What nine steps are involved in charting a process?
4. The specification limits for a process are given as 2.745 to 2.765. The following are the first seven samples:

Sample	1	2	3	4	5	6	7
	2.754	2.751	2.758	2.743	2.748	2.762	2.749
	2.759	2.753	2.753	2.747	2.743	2.761	2.753
	2.748	2.747	2.747	2.752	2.749	2.758	2.768
	2.759	2.751	2.750	2.749	2.751	2.755	2.763

Set up the scales that could be used on the $\bar{x}$ and R chart when there are 15 lines on the R chart and 25 lines on the $\bar{x}$ chart.

5. Given that $\bar{\bar{x}}$ is 4.725, $\bar{R} = .0096$, and $n = 4$, calculate
   (a) σ
   (b) UCL_R, LCL_R
   (c) $UCL_{\bar{x}}$, $LCL_{\bar{x}}$

6. Given that USL = 6.450, $\bar{R} = .042$, $n = 5$, LSL = 6.350, and $\bar{\bar{x}} = 6.391$, find
   (a) PCR and the percent of tolerance used
   (b) Cpk and the percent of tolerance used
   (c) The percent of product out of specification.

7. Given the set of data on Figures 6.28 (page 153), 6.29 (page 154), and 6.30 (page 155), make the indicated control charts. Include center lines and all control limit lines.

8. For the charts completed in Exercise 7, eliminate any out of control points and calculate process capability for each:
   (a) Cpk and the percent of tolerance used
   (b) PCR and the percent of tolerance used
   (c) The percent of product out of specification

Constants

n	A_2	$\tilde{A}_2$	D_4	d_2
3	1.023	1.19	2.574	1.693
4	0.729	–	2.282	2.059
5	0.577	.69	2.114	2.326

$\bar{R} = \dfrac{\Sigma R}{k} =$ _____

$\tilde{\bar{x}} = \dfrac{\Sigma \tilde{x}}{k} =$ _____

Specification : .7450 to .7470

$UCL_R = D_4 \times \bar{R} =$ _____ $\times$ _____ $=$ _____

$\tilde{A}_2 \times \bar{R} =$ _____ $\times$ _____ $=$ _____

$UCL_{\tilde{x}} = \tilde{\bar{x}} + \tilde{A}_2 \bar{R} =$ _____ $+$ _____ $=$ _____

$LCL_{\tilde{x}} = \tilde{\bar{x}} - \tilde{A}_2 \bar{R} =$ _____ $-$ _____ $=$ _____

Data rows:

.7465	.7460	.7455	.7450	.7455	.7460	.7465	.7460	.7470	.7455	.7450	.7455	.7450	.7455	.7450	.7460	.7450	.7455	.7450	.7465	.7460	.7450	.7460	.7460
.7450	.7465	.7450	.7450	.7460	.7465	.7470	.7465	.7460	.7455	.7465	.7460	.7465	.7470	.7455	.7455	.7445	.7445	.7455	.7460	.7465	.7455	.7465	.7465
.7455	.7445	.7450	.7450	.7465	.7460	.7465	.7460	.7475	.7450	.7460	.7450	.7460	.7465	.7450	.7450	.7450	.7455	.7460	.7460	.7450	.7455	.7460	.7475

$\tilde{x}$

R

Chart of Medians — $\tilde{x}$

Chart of Ranges — R

FIGURE 6.28

Exercise 7(a). Make a median and range chart.

153

$\bar{R} = \frac{\Sigma R}{k} = \underline{\qquad} = \underline{\qquad}$

$\bar{\bar{x}} = \frac{\Sigma \bar{x}}{k} = \underline{\qquad} = \underline{\qquad}$

Specification : .7450 to .7470

$UCL_R = D_4 \times \bar{R} = \underline{\qquad} \times \underline{\qquad} = \underline{\qquad}$

$A_2 \times \bar{R} = \underline{\qquad} \times \underline{\qquad} = \underline{\qquad}$

$UCL_{\bar{x}} = \bar{\bar{x}} + A_2 \bar{R} = \underline{\qquad} + \boxed{} = \underline{\qquad}$

$LCL_{\bar{x}} = \bar{\bar{x}} - A_2 \bar{R} = \underline{\qquad} - \boxed{} = \underline{\qquad}$

Constants

n	A_2	A_2	D_4	d_2
3	1.023	1.19	2.574	1.693
4	0.729	—	2.282	2.059
5	0.577	.69	2.114	2.326

Chart of Averages — $\bar{x}$

Chart of Ranges — R

Sample Number		1	2	3	4	5	6	7	8	9	10	11	12	13	14	15	16	17	18	19	20	21	22	23	24	25
Sample measurements	1	.7465	.7460	.7455	.7465	.7460	.7455	.7455	.7460	.7465	.7455	.7445	.7455	.7450	.7455	.7460	.7470	.7460	.7470	.7460	.7465	.7450	.7460	.7450	.7460	.7460
	2	.7450	.7465	.7450	.7470	.7465	.7440	.7465	.7470	.7460	.7455	.7465	.7465	.7460	.7470	.7465	.7460	.7445	.7455	.7450	.7460	.7460	.7465	.7455	.7465	.7465
	3	.7455	.7445	.7450	.7460	.7465	.7460	.7465	.7455	.7460	.7455	.7460	.7450	.7450	.7460	.7465	.7475	.7445	.7455	.7465	.7460	.7455	.7455	.7455	.7460	.7475
	4																									
	5																									
Sum																										
Average, $\bar{x}$																										
Range, R																										

FIGURE 6.29

Exercise 7(b). Make an $\bar{x}$ and R chart.

$$\bar{S} = \frac{\Sigma s}{k} = \underline{\hspace{2cm}} = \underline{\hspace{2cm}}$$

$$\bar{\bar{x}} = \frac{\Sigma \bar{x}}{k} = \underline{\hspace{2cm}} = \underline{\hspace{2cm}}$$

Specification : .7450 to .7470

$$UCL_s = B_4 \times \bar{s} = \underline{\hspace{1cm}} \times \underline{\hspace{1cm}} = \underline{\hspace{1cm}}$$

$$A_3 \times \bar{s} = \underline{\hspace{1cm}} \times \underline{\hspace{1cm}} = \underline{\hspace{1cm}}$$

$$UCL_{\bar{x}} = \bar{\bar{x}} + A_3\,\bar{s} = \underline{\hspace{1cm}} = \underline{\hspace{1cm}} + \boxed{}$$

$$LCL_{\bar{x}} = \bar{\bar{x}} - A_3\,\bar{s} = \underline{\hspace{1cm}} = \underline{\hspace{1cm}} - \boxed{}$$

Constants

n	A_3	B_3	B_4	C_4
3	1.954	0	2.568	.8862
4	1.628	0	2.266	.9213
5	1.427	0	2.089	.9400

	.7455	.7450	.7445	.7465	.7450	.7455	.7455	.7460	.7455	.7460	.7475	.7465	.7455	.7455	.7465	.7475
	.7460	.7445	.7450	.7450	.7440	.7465	.7460	.7445	.7460	.7465	.7460	.7465	.7465	.7455	.7465	.7460
	.7465	.7460	.7455	.7460	.7455	.7455	.7445	.7470	.7470	.7460	.7465	.7450	.7460	.7450	.7460	.7460
	.7450	.7465	.7470	.7455	.7455	.7465	.7470	.7460	.7460	.7460	.7455	.7460	.7460	.7455	.7460	.7460
	.7455	.7450	.7465	.7470	.7465	.7450	.7460	.7450	.7445	.7470	.7455	.7450	.7465	.7455	.7465	.7475
$\bar{x}$																
s																

Chart of Averages — $\bar{x}$

Chart of Standard Deviations — s

FIGURE 6.30
Exercise 7(c). Make an $\bar{x}$ and s chart.

7

PRECONTROL CHARTS AND INDIVIDUALS AND MOVING RANGE (*x* AND *MR*) CHARTS

OBJECTIVES

- Know the standard precontrol method.
- Learn the "and" and "or" rules for compound probability.
- Apply the modified precontrol method for tight control.
- Learn the *x* and *MR* charting method.
- Understand the limitations of both precontrol and *x* and *MR* charts.

The precontrol method and the *x* and *MR* chart are similar to the charting techniques discussed in Chapter 6 because, like the $\bar{x}$ and R, the $\tilde{x}$ and R, and the $\bar{x}$ and s charts, these two charts use the actual measurements and are classified as variables control charts. However, their use is somewhat different. The $\bar{x}$ and R and the $\tilde{x}$ and R charts are usually the first choices among control charts for variables because they provide the most information for analyzing, improving, and controlling a process. The precontrol method and the *x* and *MR* chart, on the other hand, work best under different circumstances.

The precontrol method is best used for monitoring the process after it has been brought under control and improved to an acceptable quality level. The *x* and *MR* chart can be used when there is a limited amount of data or when the data consists of only single values. In a short-run manufacturing situation in which a small number of pieces are made, the *x* and *MR* chart can give valuable analysis for both control and improvements during the run. Over a longer period of time, after several short runs are made, the data may be grouped into samples and reanalyzed using an $\bar{x}$ and R chart. Situations that produce single data values include accounting figures for specified times and process measurements such as temperature, voltage, and pressure. The *x* and *MR* chart works well for these situations, too.

7.1 PRECONTROL[1]

Precontrol charting is an excellent monitoring method for a process that is in statistical control and has been judged capable. When a process has been charted with the $\bar{x}$ and R or the $\tilde{x}$ and R charts, brought under control, and improved to the point at which it is considered best to make improvements elsewhere, the switch to a precontrol chart for monitoring is a welcome change because it is so much easier to use.

The Precontrol Procedure

Step 1 Be sure the process capability is safely less than the specification: Six standard deviations must be less than .88 times the tolerance, or even less if the process is subject to drifts.

Step 2 Divide the tolerance by four to set up four equal zones. Figure 7.1 illustrates how the zones can be color coded of easier analysis: Sections 2 and 3 make up the green (go) zone, and sections 1 and 4 are designated the yellow (caution) zone. The areas to the left of 1 and the right of 4 are the red (stop) zones.

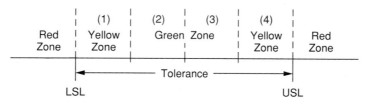

FIGURE 7.1
Precontrol zones.

Step 3 Remember the following precontrol rules:

1. A set-up job is safe to run when five consecutive pieces have measurements in the target (green) zone.
2. When the process is running, sample one or two consecutive pieces.

   ■ If the first piece measures in the green zone, let the process run. Don't bother to check the second piece.
   ■ If the first piece measures in the yellow zone, check the second. If the second is in the green zone, let the process run, but if it is not in the green zone, adjust the process and return to the set-up procedure.
   ■ If the first piece is in the red zone, adjust the process and return to the set-up procedure.

---

[1] Robert W. Traver, "Pre-Control. A Good Alternative to $\bar{x}$ and R Charts," *Quality Progress* (September, 1985): 11–13. Reprinted with the permission of the American Society for Quality Control.

These rules for checking a running process are capsulized in the chart below. A is the first measurement and B is the second.

Measurement	Zone	Decision
A	Green	Run (B not needed).
A	Yellow	Check the next piece.
B	Green	Run.
A	Yellow	Check the next piece.
B	Yellow	Adjust or correct.
		A and B in same yellow zone, $\bar{x}$ is out of control.
		A and B in opposite yellow zones, the range, R, is out of control and variation has increased.
A	Red	Adjust or correct.

Figure 7.2 compares the normal curve and the four zones.

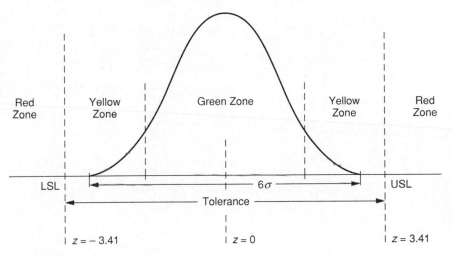

FIGURE 7.2
The normal distribution and the precontrol zones ($6\sigma = .88T$).

Calculating Zones

Suppose the 6σ spread of the normal distribution of the measurements is within the tolerance. The precontrol rules specify that 6σ should be less than $.88 \times$ tolerance, so for this explanation, the maximum spread of measurements will be used: $6\sigma = .88 \times$ tolerance. The laws of probability can be used to explain the precontrol rules.

In order to set up the zones, we must use algebra to solve the equation in the preceding paragraph. The following equation has the same form as the one we want to solve.

$$3x = 15$$
$$3(5) = 15$$
$$x = 5$$

The solution in this case is obvious: A 5 makes the statement true when it replaces the variable x, so the value of x must be 5.

In order to solve more complicated equations in which the answer isn't obvious, algebraic rules are formed to change the equation from its complicated form to a simple form, or answer statement. The answer statement isolates the variable on one side of the "=" and the answer on the other side. The equation $3x = 15$ can be solved by eliminating the number 3, which can be accomplished by using the opposite operation (in this case, division). The equation states that the quantities on each side are exactly the same amount, so any mathematical operation that changes one side must be performed on the other side as well.

$3x = 15$ To solve for x, eliminate the 3. Because 3 is *multiplied* by x, use the opposite operation, division, to eliminate it.

$\dfrac{3x}{3} = \dfrac{15}{3}$ Divide both sides of the equation by 3.

$x = 5$ The solution.

This algebra technique can be used to solve the equation $6\sigma = .88 \times$ tolerance. Let the variable T represent the tolerance.

$.88T = 6\sigma$ To solve for T, eliminate the number .88 by division.

$\dfrac{.88T}{.88} = \dfrac{6\sigma}{.88}$ Divide both sides of the equation by .88.

$T = 6.82\sigma$ The right side of the equation was simplified by dividing the .88 into 6.

The resulting equation, $T = 6.82\sigma$, means that the tolerance, T, is 6.82 standard deviation units. As we learned in our study of the normal curve in Chapter 5, standard deviation units are the z values that are used in the normal Curve Table. So, with $z = 0$ at the center of the curve and the 6.82 split half to each side, the z values at the specification units are 3.41 at the USL and -3.41 at the LSL. This is illustrated in Figure 7.2. Four equal width zones are needed, so divide the z values by 2 to get the green-yellow boundaries.

$$\frac{-3.41}{2} = -1.70 \qquad \frac{3.41}{2} = 1.70$$

Left green boundary   Right green boundary

According to the normal curve table in Appendix B (Table 3), the tail area for $z = 1.70$ is .0446. That gives the total area for both the yellow and red zones on one side. We can calculate the area in the red zone and subtract it from .0446 to find the area in one yellow zone. This is shown in Figure 7.3.

$$z = 3.41 \qquad \text{The red zone boundary}$$
$$\text{Tail area} = .00032$$
$$z = 1.70 \qquad \text{The yellow and red zone boundary}$$
$$\text{Tail area} = .0446$$

$$
\begin{array}{ll}
.0446 & \text{Area in yellow and red zones} \\
-\ .00032 & \text{Area in red zone} \\
\hline
.04428 & \text{Area in yellow zone (one side)}
\end{array}
$$

The area in each yellow zone is therefore .04428, or about 4 percent.

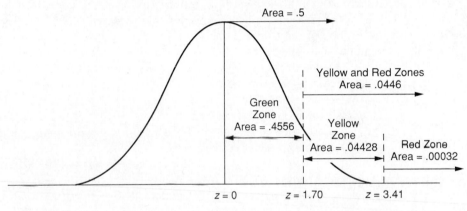

FIGURE 7.3
The area under the right side of the normal curve in the precontrol zones.

The total area under the normal curve is 1, and the center line divides it in half, so the area under the right half of the curve is .5. Figure 7.3 shows that the tail area to the right of the green zone is .0446. By subtracting that number from .5, we can determine the area in the green zone on one side.

$$
\begin{array}{ll}
.5000 & \\
-\ .0446 & \\
\hline
.4554 & \text{Area in green zone (right half)}
\end{array}
$$

To find the total area in the green zone, we simply need to multiply the area in the right half by two.

$$2 \times .4554 = .9108 \quad \text{Total area in green zone (both halves)}$$

7.2 COMPOUND PROBABILITY

The laws of probability can be used to explain the precontrol rules. What is the chance that a single piece will be in the green zone? The preceding calculations show a 91 percent chance, making it highly likely. This is what we expect to happen when the process is running well.

What is the chance that a single piece will be in the red zone? The LSL and USL correspond to $z = 3.41$, which we found in the normal curve table to be .00032, or .032 percent. There is a red zone at both tails, so the total chance that a measurement will fall in the red zone is .064 percent. This is classified as a rare event and is not very likely to occur if the process is running right. When it does occur, we can conclude that the process changed somehow and needs to be adjusted. The red zone is a trouble indicator; the process should be stopped and the trouble eliminated.

The concept of probability that has been used up to this point refers directly to the normal curve. The area under specific sections corresponds to the percent of data that falls in those sections, which is the same as the percent chance that an individual measurement will fall in those specific sections. To illustrate, in the foregoing work, the area of the yellow zone on the right side is .04428. Because the total area under the curve is 1, the fraction of the total area that is in the right yellow zone is .04428, or 4.428 percent, of the area. The curve represents the distribution of product produced, so 4.428 percent of all the product will have measurements that are in the right yellow zone. If one specific piece is randomly chosen from production, the probability, or chance, that its measurement will be in the right yellow zone will be 4.428 percent.

To answer the probability questions that lead to the precontrol rules, a few more probability concepts must be developed. By definition, the *probability*, or chance, that some event will happen is equal to the number of ways the event can occur divided by the total number of events that can occur. For example, if a coin is tossed, the chance of getting a tail is 50 percent. There is one way a tail can occur (the numerator = 1), and there are two events: a head or a tail (the denominator = 2). Therefore, the probability of getting a tail is $\frac{1}{2}$, or 50 percent.

EXAMPLE 7.1

A bag of marbles contains four red, five white, and three blue marbles. If one marble is randomly drawn from the bag, what is the probability of getting a red one?

Solution
There are four ways a red marble could be drawn (the numerator = 4), and 12 events that can occur because each of the 12 different marbles could be drawn (the denominator = 12). The probability of getting a red marble is $\frac{4}{12}$, or $\frac{1}{3}$.

It doesn't take too much imagination to create a complicated event in which the probability will be difficult to calculate. If four marbles are drawn, what is the chance of not getting a red one? Or, what is the chance that the third one will be blue? Questions such as these require compound probability laws to resolve them. For immediate purposes, we will introduce two laws of compound probability. For convenient notation let *P(A)* represent the probability of event *A*.

Rule 1: If event A and event B cannot occur simultaneously,

$$P(A \text{ or } B) = P(A) + P(B)$$

We will use several examples to explain this rule.

EXAMPLE 7.2

If one marble is drawn from the bag of four red, five white, and three blue marbles, what is the probability that it will be either a red or a blue marble?

Solution

$$P(\text{Red or Blue}) = P(\text{Red}) + P(\text{Blue})$$

$$P(\text{Red}) = \frac{4}{12}$$

$$P(\text{Blue}) = \frac{3}{12}$$

$$P(\text{Red or Blue}) = \frac{4}{12} + \frac{3}{12}$$

$$= \frac{7}{12}$$

This could also be found by using the definition. There are seven possible successful events (draw any of the four red and three blue marbles) and 12 possible events all together.

EXAMPLE 7.3

If one card is drawn from a well-shuffled standard deck of cards, what is the probability that it is a King, a Queen, or a Jack?

Solution

$$P(\text{King}) = \frac{4}{52} \quad \text{There are four Kings in the deck of 52 cards.}$$

$$P(\text{Queen}) = \frac{4}{52} \quad \text{There are four Queens in the deck.}$$

$$P(\text{Jack}) = \frac{4}{52} \quad \text{There are four Jacks in the deck.}$$

$$P(\text{King or Queen or Jack}) = P(\text{King}) + P(\text{Queen}) + P(\text{Jack})$$

$$= \frac{4}{52} + \frac{4}{52} + \frac{4}{52}$$

$$= \frac{12}{52}, \text{ or } \frac{3}{13}$$

The second law of compound probability is

Rule 2: If A and B are successive events and the $P(B)$ is unaffected by event A,

$$P(A \text{ and then } B) = P(A) \cdot P(B)$$

When two pieces are checked, the probability of an event, such as getting two measurements in the yellow zone, is found by multiplying their individual probabilities. This idea is illustrated with a coin toss example. If the coin is tossed once, the chance of getting a head is 50 percent. The chance of getting a head is one chance out of two possibilities, or $\frac{1}{2}$. If the coin is tossed twice, the chance of getting two heads is $\frac{1}{2} \cdot \frac{1}{2} = \frac{1}{4}$, or 25 percent. The $\frac{1}{4}$ chance can also be seen by observing that there is just one favorable outcome in the four possibilities:

The possible outcomes when a coin is tossed twice.

Head and head
Head and tail
Tail and head
Tail and tail

Head and head is one chance out of four possibilities.

Now back to the zones. What is the chance of getting the first measurement in the yellow zone and the second in the green zone? Because the yellow zone could be in the left strip or the right, the total probability of being in the yellow first, by rule 1, is

$$P(Y_{\text{left}} \text{ or } Y_{\text{right}}) = P(Y_{\text{left}}) + P(Y_{\text{right}})$$
$$= .0443 + .0443$$
$$= .0886$$

The chance of being in the yellow zone first and the green zone second is found by multiplying their probabilities (rule 2).

$$P(Y \text{ and then } G) = P(Y) \cdot P(G)$$
$$= .0886 \cdot .9108$$
$$= .0807$$

It's not highly likely to occur, at approximately 8 percent, but 8 times out of 100 is often enough to expect it to happen occasionally. This probability is not an indication of trouble with the process.

What is the chance of getting two successive pieces in the yellow zones? This can happen four different ways:

$$
\begin{array}{ccc}
Y_{\text{right}} & \text{and} & Y_{\text{right}} \\
Y_{\text{right}} & \text{and} & Y_{\text{left}} \\
Y_{\text{left}} & \text{and} & Y_{\text{right}} \\
Y_{\text{left}} & \text{and} & Y_{\text{left}}
\end{array}
$$

In each case we can use rule 2 and substitute the area values we found earlier for the yellow zone.

$$P(Y \text{ and then } Y) = P(Y) \cdot P(Y)$$
$$= .0443 \cdot .0443$$

The probability of two yellows, then, is .0443 × .0443 × 4 = .0078, or approximately .8 percent. This means that with the process running as it should, .8 percent of the time a sample of two consecutive pieces will be in the yellow zones. This is considered a small enough chance to be classified as a trouble indicator: Getting two in the yellow zones is a rare enough event to believe that a problem with the process caused it to happen. Further, the type of trouble is usually indicated by a pattern: Two in the same yellow zone may indicate process drift, and two in opposite yellow zones suggest increased variability.

7.3 MODIFIED PRECONTROL FOR TIGHT CONTROL

When a process has been classified as an A or B process (as defined in Appendix B, Table 6) *and* when tight control is desired, the 6σ value should be used to set up the zones instead of the tolerance. Otherwise, the process may regress to a C or D classification, and the precontrol monitoring will not necessarily indicate the change. This is shown in Figures 7.4, 7.5, and 7.6 (see page 166 for Figures 7.5 and 7.6).

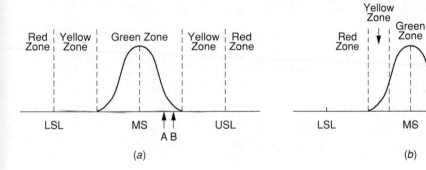

FIGURE 7.4
(*a*) Zones calculated from the specification limits. Trouble is not indicated; both measurements are in the green zone. (*b*) Zones calculated from the mid-specification (MS) point $\pm 3\sigma$. Trouble is indicated; both measurements are in the same yellow zone.

Each figure shows product distributions that come from A processes (processes in which the 6σ spread is less than half the tolerance). In order to maintain the A process classification, any trouble with the process should be noted as soon as possible. In all three illustrations, the zones in the (*a*) diagrams are figured from the tolerance and the zones in the (*b*) diagrams are figured from the 6σ product distribution spread. In each

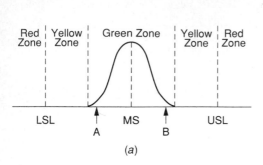

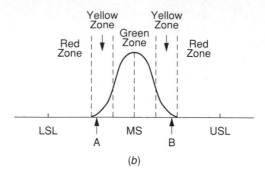

FIGURE 7.5
(a) Zones calculated from the specification limits. No trouble is indicated; both measurements are in the green zone. (b) Zones calculated from MS $\pm 3\sigma$. Measurements in opposite yellow zones indicate trouble.

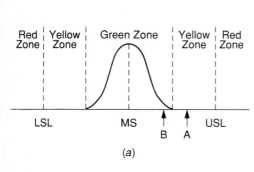

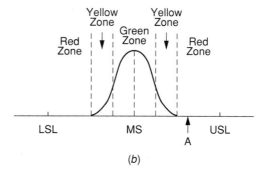

FIGURE 7.6
(a) Zones calculated from specification limits. Trouble is not indicated; A is in the yellow and B in the green. (b) Zones calculated from MS $\pm 3\sigma$. Point A is in the red zone, signaling trouble.

case the A and B indicators show trouble on the (b) diagram, but the same measurements (in the same position on the tolerance scale) are considered acceptable on the (a) diagram. The zones calculated from the tolerance neglected to indicate the trouble. The pictures show that if the goal is to stay within the tolerance, the (a) diagram, with the zones calculated from the tolerance, will suffice. If the goal is to maintain a tight distribution well within the tolerance limits, the (b) diagram, with the zones calculated from 6σ, is needed.

EXAMPLE 7.4

Apply precontrol to a run of top adapters. The top adapters are being turned out on an automatic screw machine. The specification limits are .212 to .218, and the goal is to stay within those limits. Measurements are sampled hourly.

Solution
Set up the zones from the tolerance. First divide the tolerance by four.

$$\frac{.218 - .212}{4} = \frac{.006}{4}$$
$$= .0015$$

Start at the lower specification limit and add .0015 for the first yellow zone. Next add .003 (.0015 twice) for the green zone and .0015 again for the other yellow zone. See Figure 7.7.

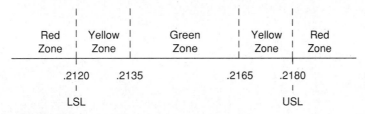

FIGURE 7.7
Precontrol zones based on the tolerance.

Sample	A Value	Zone	B Value	Zone	Decision
1	.214	Green	Not needed		OK
2	.2125	Yellow	.2125	Yellow	Reported trouble
3	.2120	Yellow	.2120	Yellow	Reported trouble
4	.2125	Yellow	.2120	Yellow	Reported trouble
5	.2123	Yellow	.2124	Yellow	Reported trouble
6	.2125	Yellow	.2125	Yellow	Given OK to sharpen

Five consecutive pieces are needed in the green zone for the restart.

Measurement:	.2140	.2136	.2134	.2139	.2138	.2138	.2139	.2135	OK
Zone:	(G)	(G)	(Y)	(G)	(G)	(G)	(G)	(G)	to run

7	.2136	Green	Not needed		OK
8	.2138	Green	Not needed		OK
9	.2135	Green	Not needed		OK
10	.2130	Yellow	.2139	Green	OK
11	.2137	Green	Not needed		OK
12	.2138	Green	Not needed		OK
13	.2133	Yellow	.2135	Green	OK
14	.2135	Green	Not needed		OK
15	.2140	Green	Not needed		OK

Samples 2 through 6 had both A and B in the same yellow zone, which indicated a process shift. The process shift was the result of a dull tool. After sharpening the tool, consecutive pieces were measured until five consecutive pieces measured in the green zone, which indicated that the process shifted back into the target (green) zone. The chart shows that for at least four hours, the measurements crowded the lower specification limit. The past discussion on product distributions indicates that some of the product was most likely out of specification during that period. The decision to shut down and sharpen should have been made sooner.

EXAMPLE 7.5

Use the modified precontrol to maintain tight control of an A process. The process has specification limits of .008 to .010 and a standard deviation $\sigma = .000158$.

Solution

The process capability is

$$PCR = \frac{6\sigma}{\text{tolerance}}$$

$$= \frac{6 \times .000158}{.002}$$

$$= \frac{.000948}{.002}$$

$$= .474$$

The process uses 47.4 percent of the tolerance and is classified as an A process. The goal is to maintain the A process classification, so the 6σ spread is used to set up the precontrol zones, as illustrated in Figure 7.8 on page 169.

$$\frac{6\sigma}{4} = \frac{6 \times .000158}{4}$$

$$= \frac{.000948}{4}$$

$$= .000237$$

$$3\sigma = 2 \times \frac{6\sigma}{4}$$

$$= 2 \times .000237$$

$$= .000474$$

$$MS = \text{Mid-specification point}$$

$$= \frac{.008 + .010}{2}$$

$$= .009$$

$$\text{Green zone} = MS \pm \frac{6\sigma}{4}$$

$$= .009 \pm .00024$$

$$= .00876 \text{ to } .00924$$

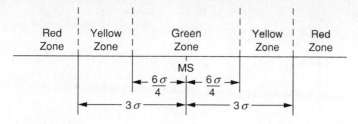

FIGURE 7.8
Precontrol zones based on MS $\pm 3\sigma$.

$$
\begin{aligned}
\text{Yellow zone (left)} &= \text{MS} - 3\sigma \\
&= .009 - .00047 \\
&= .00853 \\
&= .00853 \text{ to } .00876
\end{aligned}
$$

$$
\begin{aligned}
\text{Yellow zone (right)} &= \text{MS} + 3\sigma \\
&= .009 + .00047 \\
&= .00947 \\
&= .00924 \text{ to } .00947
\end{aligned}
$$

The red zones are to the left of .00853 and to the right of .00947. Use Figure 7.9 to zone the A and/or B measurement and indicate the decision for samples 1 to 15 (see the display on page 170).

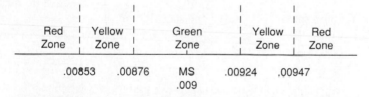

FIGURE 7.9
Precontrol chart based on MS $\pm 3\sigma$.

The process in Example 7.5 should be shut down at the first indication of trouble. Two measurements occur in opposite yellow zones at sample 7, which indicates that something has changed to increase the variation. Examination of the process indicates a loose fixture, which will be tightened. The required five consecutive piece startup procedure follows.

If the tolerance had been used to set up the zones in this case, the loose fixture would not have been found until the variation had increased enough to show the problem with the wider zones. In the meantime the process would have deteriorated to a C or D classification and quality would have suffered.

Sample	A Value	Zone	B Value	Zone	Decision
1	.0093	Yellow	.0090	Green	OK
2	.0091	Green	Not needed		OK
3	.0089	Green	Not needed		OK
4	.0088	Green	Not needed		OK
5	.0090	Green	Not needed		OK
6	.0089	Green	Not needed		OK
7	.0084	Yellow	.0093	Yellow	Tightened loose fixture.
.0090	.0091	.0090	.0089 .0091		OK
8	.0090	Green	Not needed		OK
9	.0092	Green	Not needed		OK
10	.0093	Yellow	.0090	Green	OK
11	.0089	Green	Not needed		OK
12	.0090	Green	Not needed		OK
13	.0091	Green	Not needed		OK
14	.0087	Yellow	.0091	Green	OK
15	.0090	Green	Not needed		OK

In some situations precontrol may be the first choice for use as a control chart. An automatic screw machine, for example, may be considered in control with only occasional shutdowns for tool sharpening or adjustment. The precontrol chart will tell when a shutdown is needed and if the initial in-control assumption is correct. Successive readings in different zones indicate excessive variability. Drifts or shifts of the measurements from the desired mid-specification value eventually show up as two successive measurements in the same yellow zone or in a yellow and red zone on the same side. If the in-control assumption is wrong, a switch to an $\bar{x}$ and R chart may provide better information for bringing the process under control.

7.4 CHARTS FOR INDIVIDUAL MEASUREMENTS: x AND MR CHARTS

When constructing an x and MR chart, only the individual measurements, x, are charted. The chart uses the moving range, MR, which is the difference between consecutive pieces, to determine the control limits for the chart. The position of the x values and their average, $\bar{x}$, shows the location of the measurements with respect to the desired mid-specification value. The width of the control limits indicates the extent of common cause variation. Piece-to-piece variation shows up in the lengths of the broken-line segments that connect the points. All of these aspects are analyzed to bring the process under statistical control.

There are two basic uses for the x and MR chart. First, its use is effective for cases in which the number of items produced is too small to form the 25 or more samples necessary for an $\bar{x}$ and R chart. In this instance, the individuals chart may be the only chart needed to bring the process under statistical control. However, the individuals chart may be used for a preliminary analysis with the small, initial set of data and then followed up with an $\bar{x}$ and R chart when enough data accumulates over time. The first analysis with the individuals chart may be enough to achieve statistical control, but the additional analysis information from an $\bar{x}$ and R chart may be needed for process improvements and for a decrease in common cause variation.

Second, the x and MR chart is ideal for cases in which the data naturally occur as single values. An individuals chart may be used in various accounting situations in which daily, weekly, or monthly figures are analyzed. In production critical measurements may occur as single values such as temperature, humidity, batch measures, and voltage: An individuals chart is the best choice for charting these.

Procedure for the Individuals and Moving Range Chart

1. Take measurements of consecutive pieces.

More than 10 measurements are required for a chart, but approximately 20 or more measurements are commonly used. If the chart is developed as the measurements are taken, wait until the first 10 are taken and then set up the chart.

2. Record the measurements, x, and the moving range, MR, on the chart.

The MR values will be offset one position with the *first* position blank. The moving range, MR, is the difference between consecutive measurements without regard to sign (the absolute value of the differences).

$$MR_1 = |x_2 - x_1|$$
$$MR_2 = |x_3 - x_2|$$
$$MR_3 = |x_4 - x_3|$$

The values are entered on the chart as shown in Figure 7.10 for the first few values.

x		x_1	x_2	x_3	x_4	
MR			MR_1	MR_2	MR_3	

FIGURE 7.10
Selected data values on an x and MR chart.

EXAMPLE 7.6

Given the data values in order of production, enter the values on an individuals and moving range chart. The measurements are 4.213, 4.219, 4.209, 4.207, 4.215, and 4.215.

$MR_1 =$	4.219	$MR_2 =$	4.219	$MR_3 =$

$$MR_1 = \begin{array}{r} 4.219 \\ -4.213 \\ \hline .006 \end{array} \quad MR_2 = \begin{array}{r} 4.219 \\ -4.209 \\ \hline .010 \end{array} \quad MR_3 = \begin{array}{r} 4.209 \\ -4.207 \\ \hline .002 \end{array} \quad MR_4 = \begin{array}{r} 4.215 \\ -4.207 \\ \hline .008 \end{array}$$

In each case the smaller of the two consecutive values is subtracted from the larger to get the absolute value. Figure 7.11 shows the chart entries.

x	4.213	4.219	4.209	4.207	4.215	4.215
MR	–	.006	.010	.002	.008	.000

FIGURE 7.11
Entries for the x and MR chart.

3. Set the scale for the chart.

Don't scale it too wide; use about 10 divisions between the largest and smallest measurements. First locate the middle of the chart so it has a value about halfway between the largest and smallest measurements. This can be done by averaging the two:

$$\text{Middle chart value} \approx \frac{\text{Largest} + \text{Smallest}}{2}$$

The scale is approximately

$$\frac{\text{Largest} - \text{Smallest}}{10}$$

units per line. Round up or down to find an easy number for charting. Extend the scale so it includes the specification limits.

EXAMPLE 7.7

Using the data in Example 7.6, set the scale for an x and MR chart.

Solution

$$\text{Middle chart value} = \frac{4.219 + 4.207}{2}$$

$$= 4.213$$

$$\text{Scale} = \frac{4.219 - 4.207}{10}$$

$$= .0012 \text{ units per line}$$

Round to .001 units per line.

Unless the process is classified as an A or B process, the individual measurements can approach or overlap the specification limits. The specification limits, therefore, may be used to set the scale for an x and MR chart. See Figure 7.12 on page 173.

FIGURE 7.12
Set the scale for the *x* and *MR* chart: Start at the middle of the chart and count .001 units per line in both directions.

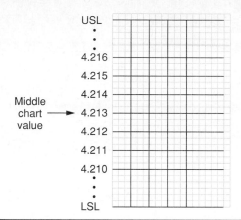

EXAMPLE 7.8 A measurement has specification limits of .749 to .751. Set up an *x* and *MR* chart in preparation for tracking the measurement.

Solution

$$MS = \frac{USL + LSL}{2}$$

$$= \frac{.751 + .749}{2}$$

$$= .750$$

$$Scale = \frac{USL - LSL}{10}$$

$$= \frac{.751 - .749}{10}$$

$$= \frac{.002}{10}$$

$$= .0002 \text{ units per line}$$

Start at the MS value of .750 and count .0002 units per line in both directions.

---

4. Plot only the individual measurements, *x*, and connect them with a broken-line graph. The MR values are used for the calculation of control limits.
5. Calculate $\bar{x} = (\sum x)/N$ where N is the number of values. Draw a solid line for $\bar{x}$.
6. Calculate the *MR* average.

$$\overline{MR} = \frac{\sum MR}{N - 1}$$

$N-1$ is the divisor because the number of MR values is one less than the number of x values.

7. Calculate the control limits.

$$UCL_x = \bar{x} + 2.659 \cdot \overline{MR}$$
$$LCL_x = \bar{x} - 2.659 \cdot \overline{MR}$$

The number 2.659 that is multiplied by $\overline{MR}$ is a statistical constant that is the same for all UCL_x and LCL_x calculations. Draw dashed lines for the control limits.

8. Interpret the chart.
   a. Look for trends of seven or more consecutive points going up or going down. Look for shifts of seven or more consecutive points above $\bar{x}$ or below $\bar{x}$. The shifts or trends may indicate that an adjustment is necessary.
   b. Check the point-to-point fluctuations indicated by the length of the broken-line segments. If they are getting larger, variation may be increasing.
   c. Check to see if the pattern of points avoids one of the control limits. This may indicate a skewed distribution.
   d. Look for cycles and grouping, or bunching, of points. Either pattern can be an indicator of process problems.
   e. Look for an absence of points near $\bar{x}$. That may mean that there are two or more specific groups, each with its own distribution, blended at or before the point at which the measurements are taken.
   f. Mark the specification limits on the control chart. The relationship of the individual values to the specification limits shows up directly on the chart when the product specification limits are included.

Caution must be taken with interpretation because the control limits are less precise and less sensitive than for $\bar{x}$ and R charts. The shape of the distribution is also more critical. A normal distribution of measurements is needed because the calculations for the control limits is based on the normal probability distribution. When possible, check the interpretations with a follow-up $\bar{x}$ and R chart.

9. A preliminary capability analysis may be done. The more reliable capability analysis with the $\bar{x}$ and R chart is done in Step 10.

Any capability study from an x and MR chart must be considered preliminary information. The chart provides a hint of how the process is behaving, but nothing conclusive. Bad news is cause for immediate action, but good news should be received with a wait-and-see attitude.

A normal curve analysis for the percent of product that is out of specification cannot realistically be applied to the data from an x and MR chart because there is usually not enough data to verify that the measurements follow a normal distribution. The PCR and Cpk *can* be used to assess the capability, however, because they compare the tolerance with the 6σ spread of the data. The PCR uses the entire 6σ value and the Cpk uses half of it, assessing only the side of the mean that is closest to the specification limit.

Virtually all of the data of any distribution, normal or otherwise, will be within 3σ of the mean, so the PCR and Cpk values can be treated as realistic capability measures. It must be stressed, however, that even those measures must be considered temporary because of the relatively small amount of data used in the calculations.

The control limit lines on all of the charts represent a six standard deviation spread of the variable being charted. In this case, with the individual values being charted, $UCL_x - LCL_x = 6\sigma$.

$$PCR = \frac{6\sigma}{Tolerance}$$

$$Cpk = \frac{|\,Nearest\ specification\ limit - \bar{x}\,|}{3\sigma}$$

10. Follow up with an $\bar{x}$ and R chart when sufficient data are available.

Assign the individual measurements to the samples. If a sample of five is used, the first five measurements taken are sample one, the second five measurements are sample two, and so on. Note any breaks in the production schedule on the chart. When 25 or more samples have been formed, calculate $\bar{x}$, R, and the control limits and analyze the results.

Use of the *x* and *MR* Charts

Both charts are useful. When time is a factor, process information can be determined sooner with the x and MR chart. Some process problems, indicated by trends, cycles, and mixture, show up better (or sooner) on the x and MR chart. However, unnatural pattern analysis is more reliable on the $\bar{x}$ and R chart.

EXAMPLE 7.9

Demonstrate the x and MR chart for the first 36 data values from Figure 6.1.

Solution

Follow the ten steps outlined. First, record the consecutive data values on the x and MR chart. The data are presented in Figure 7.13 (page 176).

Second, calculate the MR values and enter them on the chart. Remember to offset the MR values one place to the right.

$$x_2 - x_1 = MR_1 \qquad .0243 - .0218 = .0025$$
$$x_2 - x_3 = MR_2 \qquad .0243 - .0232 = .0011$$
$$x_4 - x_3 = MR_3 \qquad .0256 - .0232 = .0024$$
$$x_4 - x_5 = MR_4 \qquad .0256 - .0247 = .0009$$

In each case, take consecutive measurements and subtract the smaller from the larger. Continue the calculations on Figure 7.13 and check your results with Figure 7.14 (page 177).

Third, set the scale. The largest measurement is .0294 and the smallest is .0218. The average of these two measurements will give the approximate middle of the chart.

$$\overline{MR} = \frac{\Sigma MR}{k-1} = \underline{\qquad} = \underline{\qquad}$$

$$\overline{x} = \frac{\Sigma x}{k} = \underline{\qquad} = \underline{\qquad}$$

Specification : .0200 to .0300

$$2.659 \times \overline{MR} = 2.659 \times \underline{\qquad} = \boxed{\qquad}$$

$$UCL_x = \overline{x} + 2.659\overline{MR} = \underline{\qquad} + \boxed{\qquad} = \boxed{\qquad}$$

$$LCL_x = \overline{x} - 2.659\overline{MR} = \underline{\qquad} - \boxed{\qquad} = \boxed{\qquad}$$

Time																																				
Sample Numbers	1	2	3	4	5	6	7	8	9	10	11	12	13	14	15	16	17	18	19	20	21	22	23	24	25	26	27	28	29	30	31	32	33	34	35	36
x	.0218	.0243	.0232	.0256	.0247	.0255	.0282	.0261	.0244	.0252	.0265	.0267	.0254	.0238	.0249	.0275	.0265	.0232	.0294	.0281	.0259	.0274	.0228	.0254	.0266	.0245	.0231	.0280	.0259	.0282	.0264	.0234	.0302	.0271	.0250	.0254
MR	✕	.0025	.0011	.0024	.0009																															

FIGURE 7.13

Set the scale and chart the x values. Calculate the MR values, $\overline{x}$, $\overline{MR}$, and control limits. Check your results with Figure 7.14.

$$\overline{MR} = \frac{\Sigma MR}{k-1} = \frac{.0770}{35} = .0022$$

$$\overline{x} = \frac{\Sigma x}{k} = \frac{.9263}{36} = .0257$$

Specification: .0200 to .0300

$$2.659 \times \overline{MR} = 2.659 \times .0022 = .0059$$

$$UCL_x = \overline{x} + 2.659\overline{MR} = .0257 + .0059 = .0316$$
$$LCL_x = \overline{x} - 2.659\overline{MR} = .0257 - .0059 = .0198$$

Sample Numbers	x	MR
1	.0218	
2	.0243	.0025
3	.0232	.0011
4	.0256	.0024
5	.0247	.0009
6	.0255	.0008
7	.0282	.0027
8	.0261	.0021
9	.0244	.0017
10	.0252	.0008
11	.0265	.0013
12	.0267	.0002
13	.0254	.0013
14	.0238	.0016
15	.0249	.0011
16	.0275	.0026
17	.0265	.0010
18	.0232	.0033
19	.0294	.0062
20	.0281	.0013
21	.0259	.0022
22	.0274	.0015
23	.0228	.0046
24	.0254	.0026
25	.0266	.0012
26	.0245	.0021
27	.0231	.0014
28	.0280	.0049
29	.0259	.0021
30	.0282	.0023
31	.0264	.0018
32	.0234	.0030
33	.0302	.0068
34	.0271	.0031
35	.0250	.0021
36	.0254	.0004

Time

UCL_x $\overline{x}$ LCL_x

x: .0300 .0290 .0280 .0270 .0260 .0250 .0240 .0230 .0220 .0210

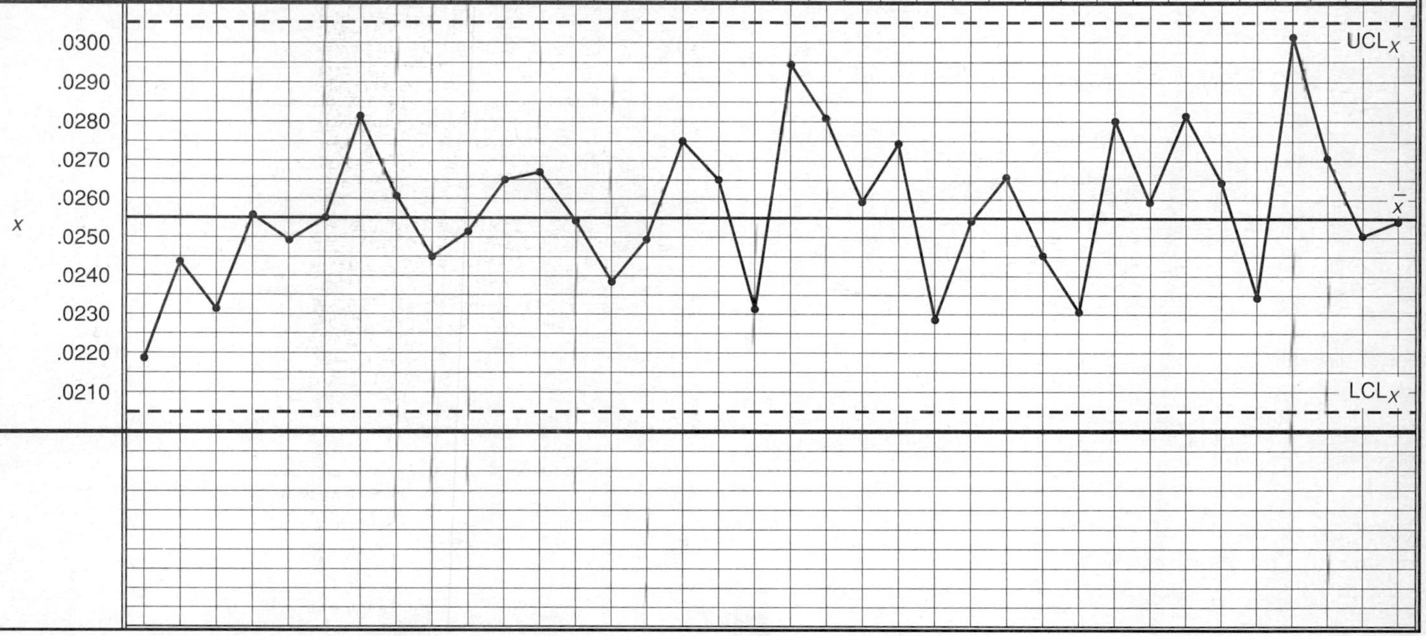

FIGURE 7.14
The completed x and MR chart.

$$\frac{.0302 + .0218}{2} = \frac{.0520}{2}$$

$$= .0260$$

Aiming for a chart of about 10 lines, divide the difference of the largest and smallest by 10.

$$\frac{.0302 - .0218}{10} = \frac{.0084}{10}$$

$$= .00084 \text{ units per line}$$

For easy scale values we can either round up to .001 units per line or down to .0005 units per line. This chart will be centered at .0260 and will use .0005 units per line. Set up the scale on Figure 7.13 and check the results on Figure 7.14.

Fourth, graph the x values and connect the points with a broken-line graph.

For step five, find $\bar{x}$ and draw the solid line.

$$\bar{x} = \frac{\sum x}{N}$$

$$= \frac{.9263}{36}$$

$$= .0257$$

Sixth, calculate $\overline{MR}$.

$$\overline{MR} = \frac{\sum MR}{N - 1}$$

$$= \frac{.0770}{35}$$

$$= .0022$$

Following step seven, calculate the control limits and draw the dashed lines.

$$\text{UCL}_x = \bar{x} + 2.659 \cdot \overline{MR}$$
$$= .0257 + 2.659 \times .0022$$
$$= .0257 + .0059$$
$$= .0316$$

$$\text{LCL}_x = \bar{x} - 2.659 \cdot \overline{MR}$$
$$= .0257 - 2.659 \times .0022$$
$$= .0257 - .0059$$
$$= .0198$$

Eighth, check for statistical control. There are no apparent out-of-control patterns on the chart such as points beyond the control limits, shifts, or trends. However, the lengths of the connecting lines on the broken-line graph indicate excessive variation.

This is borne out in the following capability study. The process shift that showed up on the $\bar{x}$ and R chart on the same data (shown in Figure 6.1) failed to show up on this chart. The shift on the $\bar{x}$ chart was accompanied by an increase in variability on the R chart. Analyzed together, the x and MR chart and the $\bar{x}$ and R chart show the basic problem to be one of excessive variation.

The ninth step directs us to determine the process capability. Subtract the control limits for the 6σ value.

$$.0316 - .0198 = .0118$$
$$= 6\sigma$$

The specification limits for the data were given as .0200 to .0300, so the tolerance will be $.0300 - .0200 = .0100$.

$$\text{PCR} = \frac{6\sigma}{\text{Tolerance}}$$
$$= \frac{.0118}{.01}$$
$$= 1.18$$

The PCR is 118 percent. According to the classification chart (Appendix B, Table 6), this classifies as a D process. Notice that this value is close to the PCR of 112.5 percent that was calculated from the data on the $\bar{x}$ and R chart in Example 6.1. The Cpk calculation follows.

$$\frac{6\sigma}{2} = \frac{.0118}{2}$$
$$= .0059$$
$$= 3\sigma$$

Calculate the differences between $\bar{x}$ and the specification limits.

USL $- \bar{x}$	$\bar{x} -$ LSL
$.0300 - .0257$	$.0257 - .0200$
$.0043$	$.0057$

$$\text{Cpk} = \frac{\text{Smallest difference}}{3\sigma}$$
$$= \frac{.0043}{.0059}$$
$$= .73$$

The chart in Appendix B shows that the Cpk analysis also classifies this as a D process. This Cpk value compares with the value of .89 that was calculated using all the data in Example 6.1.

EXAMPLE 7.10

The first 30 measurements are taken from Figure 6.11 for an x and MR analysis to compare with the $\bar{x}$ and R analysis in Chapter 6. Specification limits are .745 to .755. The measurements are entered in order on Figure 7.15 (page 181). Complete each of the following steps and compare your results with the calculations below and Figure 7.16 (page 182).

1. Calculate the MR values.
2. Set the x scale using the specification limits.
3. Chart the x values and draw the broken-line graph.
4. Calculate $\bar{x}$ and draw the solid line.
5. Calculate the control limits and draw the dashed lines.
6. Interpret the results.
7. Calculate the process capability.

Solution

Calculations

$$MS = \frac{.745 + .755}{2}$$

$$= .750 \text{ (center of chart)}$$

$$\frac{.755 - .745}{10} = \frac{.010}{10}$$

$$= .001 \text{ units per line}$$

$$\bar{x} = \frac{\sum x}{N}$$

$$= \frac{.751 + .747 + \cdots + .749}{30}$$

$$= \frac{22.502}{30}$$

$$= .750$$

$$\overline{MR} = \frac{\sum MR}{N-1} = \frac{.004 + .005 + \cdots + .005}{29}$$

$$= \frac{.070}{29}$$

$$= .0024$$

$$\begin{aligned} UCL_x &= \bar{x} + 2.659 \cdot \overline{MR} \\ &= .750 + 2.659 \times .0024 \\ &= .750 + .006 \\ &= .756 \end{aligned}$$

$$\begin{aligned} LCL_x &= \bar{x} - 2.659 \cdot \overline{MR} \\ &= .750 - .006 \\ &= .744 \end{aligned}$$

$$\overline{MR} = \frac{\Sigma MR}{k-1} = \underline{\hspace{2cm}} = \underline{\hspace{1cm}}$$

$$\overline{\overline{x}} = \frac{\Sigma x}{k} = \underline{\hspace{2cm}} = \underline{\hspace{1cm}}$$

Specification : .745 to .755

$$2.659 \times \overline{MR} = 2.659 \times \underline{\hspace{1cm}} = \underline{\hspace{2cm}}$$

$$UCL_x = \overline{\overline{x}} + 2.659\overline{MR} = \underline{\hspace{1cm}} + \underline{\hspace{1cm}} = \underline{\hspace{1cm}}$$

$$LCL_x = \overline{\overline{x}} - 2.659\overline{MR} = \underline{\hspace{1cm}} - \underline{\hspace{1cm}} = \underline{\hspace{1cm}}$$

Time																														
Sample Numbers	1	2	3	4	5	6	7	8	9	10	11	12	13	14	15	16	17	18	19	20	21	22	23	24	25	26	27	28	29	30
x	.751	.747	.752	.750	.751	.750	.748	.749	.750	.752	.749	.749	.752	.750	.748	.748	.749	.749	.751	.748	.753	.749	.752	.751	.751	.755	.752	.753	.744	.749
MR	✕																													

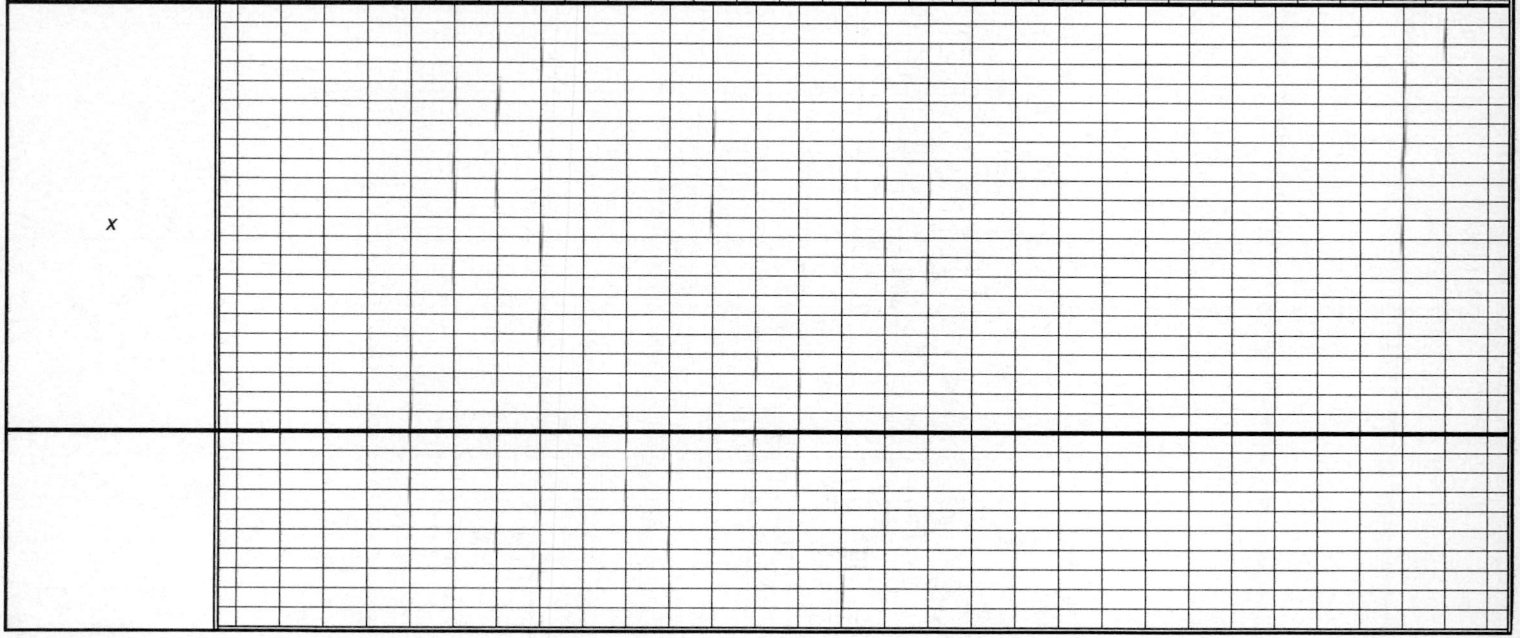

FIGURE 7.15
Make the x and MR chart.

181

$$\overline{MR} = \frac{\Sigma MR}{k-1} = \frac{.070}{29} = .0024$$

$$\overline{x} = \frac{\Sigma x}{k} = \frac{22.502}{30} = .750$$

Specification : .745 to .755

$$2.659 \times \overline{MR} = 2.659 \times .0024 = .0064$$

$$UCL_x = \overline{x} + 2.659\overline{MR} = .750 + .0064 = .756$$
$$LCL_x = \overline{x} - 2.659\overline{MR} = .750 - .0064 = .744$$

Sample Numbers	1	2	3	4	5	6	7	8	9	10	11	12	13	14	15	16	17	18	19	20	21	22	23	24	25	26	27	28	29	30
x	.751	.747	.752	.750	.751	.750	.748	.749	.750	.752	.749	.749	.752	.750	.748	.748	.749	.749	.751	.748	.753	.749	.752	.751	.751	.755	.752	.753	.744	.749
MR		.004	.005	.002	.001	.001	.002	.001	.001	.002	.003	0	.003	.002	.002	0	.001	0	.002	.003	.005	.004	.003	.001	0	.004	.003	.001	.009	.005

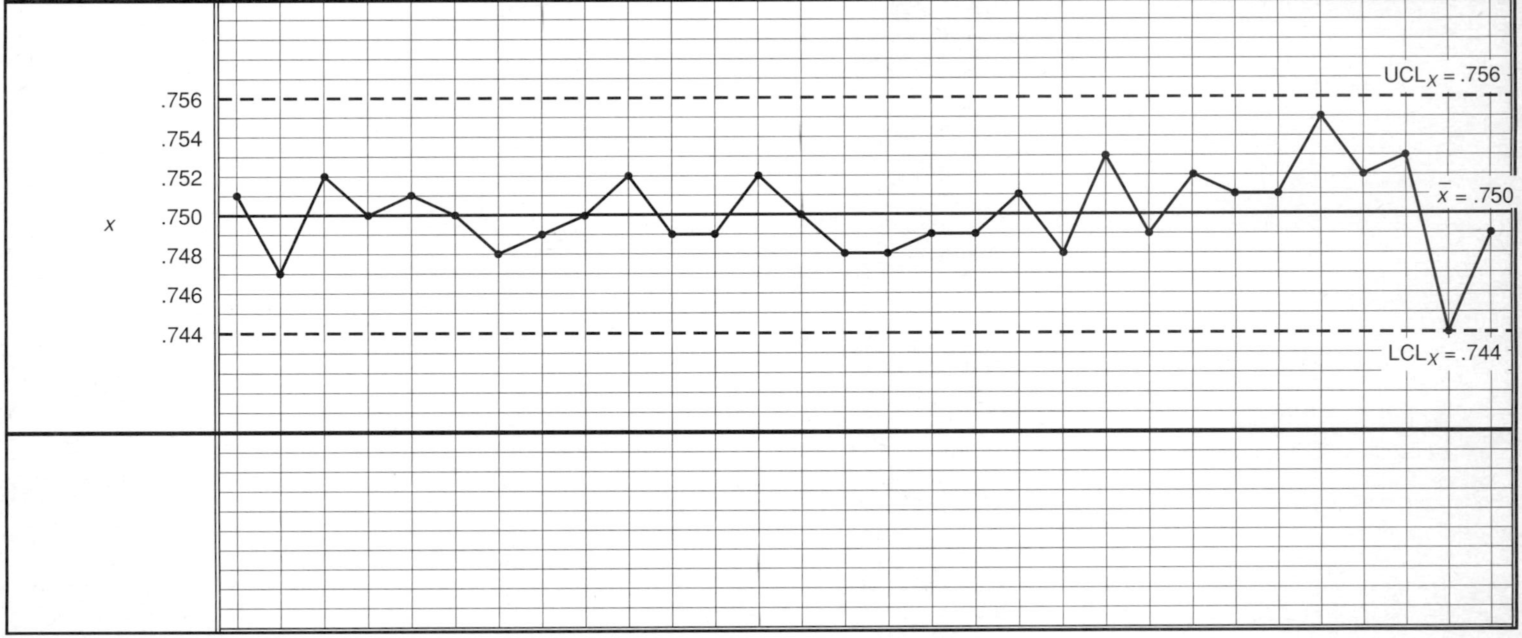

$UCL_x = .756$

$\overline{x} = .750$

$LCL_x = .744$

FIGURE 7.16
The x and MR chart for Example 7.10.

Interpretation   There are no apparent out-of-control patterns on the chart. There are almost enough points above the mid-line toward the end of the chart to qualify as a shift, but the sudden change to the .744 value breaks that pattern. The .744 value is not beyond the control limit, but the length of the connecting lines at the right end of the chart indicates an increase in variation. This corresponds to the out-of-control point on the range chart in Example 6.4 (Figure 6.12).

Process Capability   The process capability can be determined from the PCR and Cpk calculations because they are somewhat independent of the shape of the product distribution. The control limits are for the individual measurements, so they coincide with $\bar{x} + 3\sigma$ and $\bar{x} - 3\sigma$. Their difference is 6σ.

$$
\begin{array}{ll}
.756 \quad \text{UCL} & .755 \quad \text{USL} \\
\underline{-.744} \quad \text{LCL} & \underline{-.745} \quad \text{LSL} \\
.012 \quad 6\sigma & .010 \quad \text{Tolerance}
\end{array}
$$

$$
\text{PCR} = \frac{6\sigma}{\text{Tolerance}}
$$

$$
= \frac{.012}{.010}
$$

$$
= 1.2
$$

The process uses 120 percent of the tolerance.

Because $\bar{x}$ is the same as the mid-specification value, the process is on target and the Cpk will yield the same information as the PCR.

The chart in Table 6 of Appendix B labels this a D process. This is a trouble indicator because the D process can overlap the specification limits and out-of-specification products may be made.

EXERCISES

1. The specification limits for a process are .925 to .945. The following fifteen samples of two are given in order by column for precontrol analysis. The goal is to stay within the specification limits. Set up the precontrol zones using the tolerance and analyze each sample pair.
   (a) Indicate the zone for each measurement used.
   (b) Indicate when the B measurement is not needed.
   (c) Indicate your decision after each measurement or pair to let the process run or to report trouble.

Measurement	A	B	A	B	A	B
	.932	.940	.937	.939	.938	.935
	.935	.931	.936	.925	.929	.942
	.942	.935	.918	.934	.931	.940
	.938	.936	.937	.932	.943	.944
	.927	.933	.927	.929	.944	.949

2. A process has an A classification and is in statistical control. The decision is made to switch from $\bar{x}$ and R charting to the precontrol chart, but the A classification must be maintained. Specification limits are .520 to .540, and the analysis of the $\bar{x}$ and R chart gives $\bar{\bar{x}} = .530$ and $\sigma = .0015$. Twenty pairs of measurements are given in order by column. Set up the precontrol chart from $\bar{\bar{x}} \pm 3\sigma$ (because the A classification must be maintained) and analyze each sample pair.

(a) Indicate the zone for each measurement used.

(b) Indicate when the B measurement is not needed.

(c) Indicate your decision after each measurement or pair to let the process run or to report trouble.

Measurement	A	B	A	B	A	B
	.531	.532	.528	.530	.531	.530
	.530	.532	.527	.527	.536	.532
	.529	.528	.529	.530	.532	.531
	.532	.531	.531	.530	.533	.526
	.530	.531	.530	.529	.529	.528
	.527	.529	.530	.529	.529	.530
	.531	.531	.534	.533		

3. If both the A and B measurements are in the same yellow zone on a precontrol chart, what type of trouble is indicated?

4. What type of trouble is indicated by A and B measurements in opposite yellow zones on a precontrol chart?

5. On an x and MR chart, what trouble is indicated by long line segments on the broken-line graph?

6. For the following set of data, ordered by column, make and interpret an x and MR chart using Figure 7.17 (see page 185). Use the specification limits .849 to .851 to set the chart scale. Also, calculate process capability (PCR) after removing any out-of-control data (assume that any problem has been resolved). Use the following measurements:

.8503	.8500	.8508	.8502	.8507
.8498	.8506	.8498	.8503	.8508
.8497	.8497	.8502	.8504	.8507
.8502	.8508	.8498	.8504	.8508
.8499	.8493	.8500	.8505	.8506
.8501	.8492	.8502	.8507	.8507

$\overline{MR} = \frac{\Sigma MR}{N-1} = ____ = ____$

$\overline{x} = \frac{\Sigma x}{N} = ____ = ____$

$2.659 \times \overline{MR} = 2.659 \times ____ = \square$

$UCL_X = \overline{x} + 2.659\overline{MR} = ____ + \square = ____$

$LCL_X = \overline{x} - 2.659\overline{MR} = ____ - \square = ____$

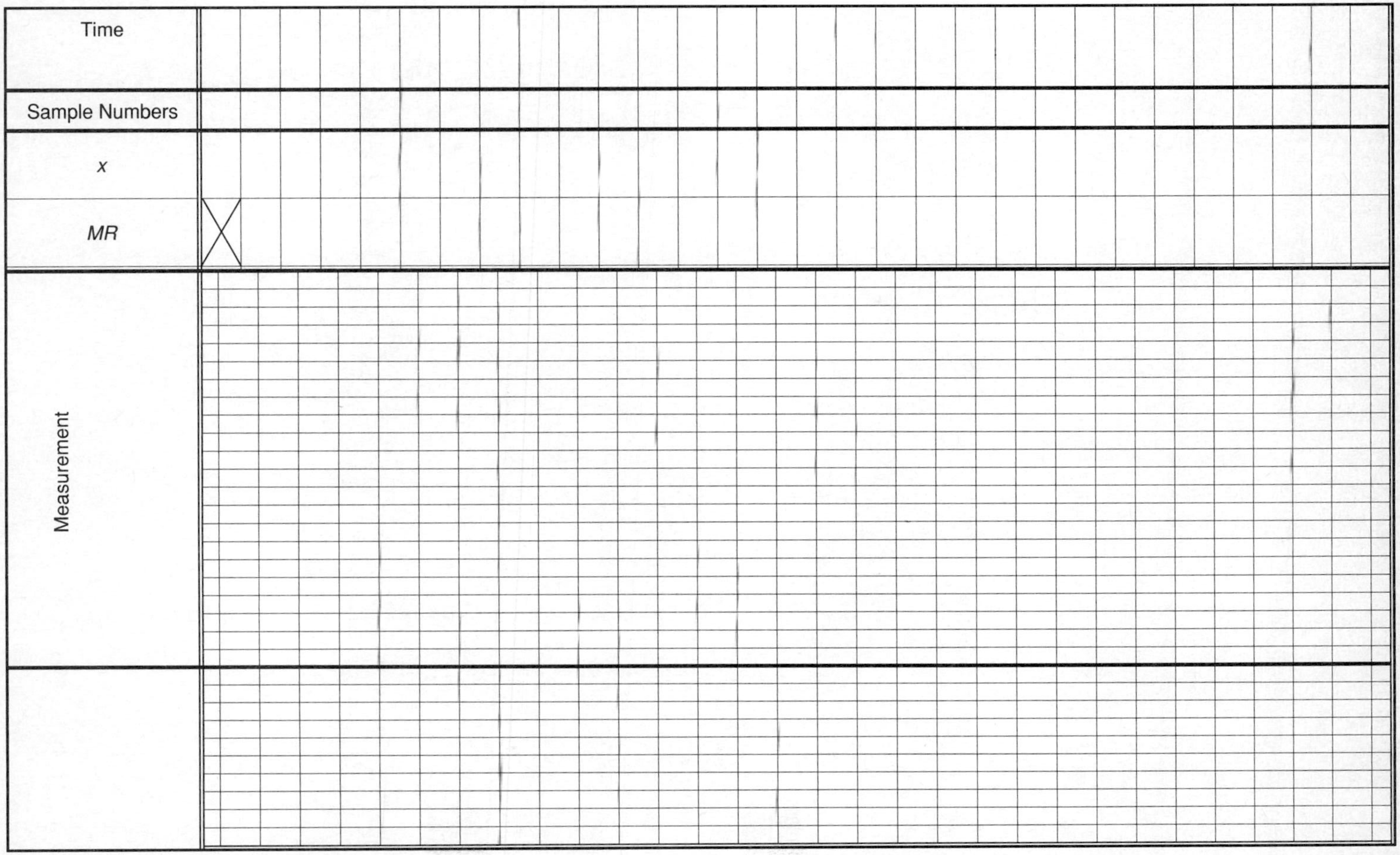
Time
Sample Numbers
x
MR
Measurement

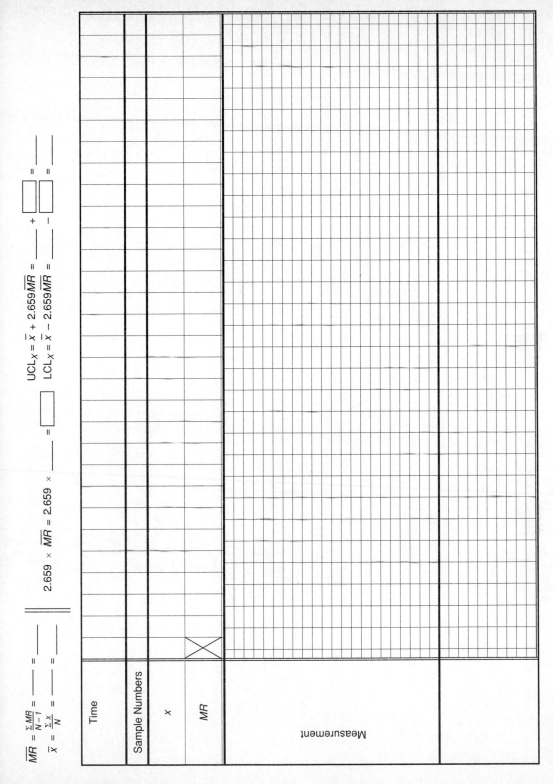

FIGURE 7.17
Make an *x* and *MR* chart for Exercise 6.

7. Make an x and MR chart on Figure 7.18 (page 187) for the following set of data. The specification limits are .021 to .027. The following measurements are for consecutive pieces and are listed in order by column:

.0258	.0213	.0252	.0253
.0243	.0256	.0224	.0262
.0249	.0274	.0263	.0221
.0230	.0275	.0247	.0243
.0273	.0223	.0248	.0260
.0266	.0251	.0232	.0229
.0264	.0248	.0250	
.0232	.0241	.0228	

Use the given specification limits to set the chart scale. Interpret the chart. If any points are out of control, remove them from the data set (assume that the out-of-control problem has been resolved) and calculate process capability.

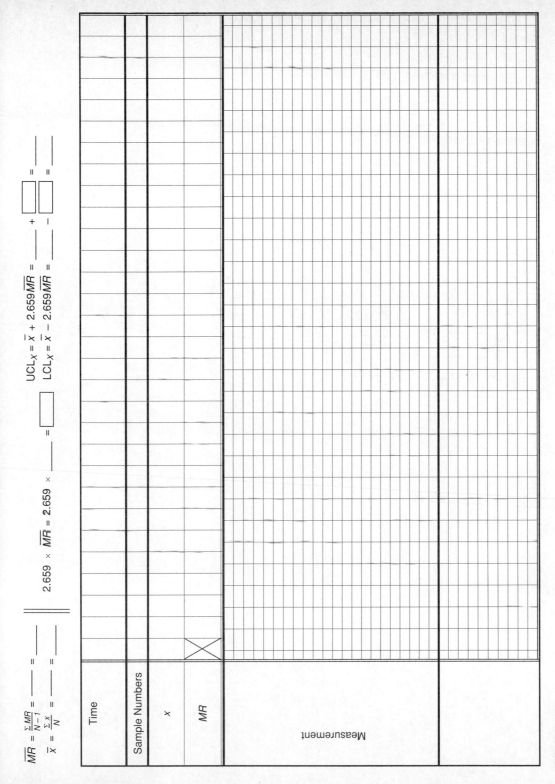

$\overline{MR} = \frac{\Sigma MR}{N-1} = \underline{\hspace{1cm}} = \underline{\hspace{1cm}}$

$\overline{x} = \frac{\Sigma x}{N} = \underline{\hspace{1cm}} = \underline{\hspace{1cm}}$

$2.659 \times \overline{MR} = 2.659 \times \underline{\hspace{1cm}} = \underline{\hspace{1cm}}$

$UCL_x = \overline{x} + 2.659\overline{MR} = \underline{\hspace{1cm}} + \underline{\hspace{1cm}} = \boxed{}$

$LCL_x = \overline{x} - 2.659\overline{MR} = \underline{\hspace{1cm}} - \underline{\hspace{1cm}} = \boxed{}$

Time																								
Sample Numbers																								
x																								
MR																								

Measurement

FIGURE 7.18
Make an x and MR chart for Exercise 7.

8

ATTRIBUTES CONTROL CHARTS

OBJECTIVES

- Know the four types of attributes charts.
- Make a *p* chart.
- Make an *np* chart.
- Make a *c* chart.
- Make a *u* chart.

The four types of attributes control charts will be discussed in this chapter. Attributes charts, as compared to the previously discussed variables charts, do not use the actual measurements in their construction. Measurements are simply classified as acceptable or not acceptable (pass-fail, or go–no go). Then either the number of failures or the fraction, or percent, of failures is charted.

Attributes control charts are used when measurements are too difficult to take, when measurements do not apply to the situation (such as visual checks for mars or flaws), or when measurements are too costly to take because of time lost. Because measurements aren't used in the charting process, attributes charts are not as sensitive to analysis as the variables control charts.

A *defect* is a single failure to specification. It differs from a defective item in that a defect is one specification discrepancy and a defective item contains one or more defects. An item sampled for a *p* or an *np* chart is classified as acceptable if it contains no defects but is counted as a single defective item if it contains one or more defects.

8.1 THE FOUR TYPES OF ATTRIBUTES CHARTS

The *p* Chart

The *p* chart is the most commonly used attributes chart. The value *p* is the fraction, or percent, of the number of items checked that are defective (or unacceptable). Large samples of 50 or more are needed. When the *p* value is very small, the sample size must be increased so that primarily nonzero values of *p* are charted. For example, if $\bar{p} = .0002$, the sample size necessary for charting is in the range of $n = 20,000$. The sample size may vary in a *p* chart. Sampling in time blocks naturally leads to different sample sizes: In time block sampling, the sample consists of all the items produced in a specific time period.

The *np* Chart

The *np* chart is sometimes used instead of the *p* chart because it is easier; *np* is simply the number, rather than the fraction, of defective items in the sample. When a sample is taken and the number of defective items is counted, it is easier to chart that number than to divide it by the sample size to change it into *p*, the fraction defective. The *p* and the *np* charts differ by that constant divisor, so they do the same job with respect to control, process analysis, assessing priority, and so forth. The one detail necessary for an *np* chart is the requirement that all samples be the *same size*. If the sample sizes differ, the *p* chart must be used.

The *c* Chart

The *c* chart tracks the number of defects in constant size units. There may be a single type of defect or several different types, but the *c* chart tracks the total number of defects in each unit. The unit may be a single item or a specified section of an item.

The *u* Chart

When samples of constant size units are taken, *u* is the *average* number of defects per unit. The *u* chart is quite similar to the *c* chart in function.

Applications of the Charts

The following examples list several situations in which the various attributes charts apply. In the first case, a printed circuit board is produced in high volume. The fraction defective has been reduced to approximately .007 and control is to be maintained at that level. Samples of 700 circuit boards are tested. The test criterion is pass-fail: The circuit either works or is defective. Here a *p* chart may be used to track the *proportion* of defective circuits in each sample or an *np* chart may track the *number* of defective circuits in each sample.

In the second situation, there has been a problem with incorrect invoices. To isolate the problem, the invoices are separated according to vendor. Samples of 50 invoices are selected for each vendor. Invoices are classified as correct or incorrect. Again, a *p* chart may be formed for each vendor to track the *proportion* of incorrect invoices in each sample, or an *np* chart may be formed for each vendor to track the *number* of incorrect invoices in each sample.

A new automatic frame welder has been installed in the third case, and an initial performance standard must be established for the operation of the welder. According to the test criterion, a weld is either acceptable or faulty. Several samples of 100 welds are checked: One has two faulty welds and three have one faulty weld. The sample size is increased to 500. Here a *p* chart may track the *fraction* of faulty welds in each sample, or an *np* chart may track the *number* of faulty welds in each sample.

In the final example of attributes chart applications, a textile machine produces bolts of fabric. A quality check for flaws is to be made. A random square yard is checked in each bolt, and the number of flaws in that square yard is counted. The various types of flaws are defined by picture example. In this case a *c* chart is formed to track the *number* of flaws per square yard. The *c* chart is too inconsistent for a quality analysis in this case, so a more intensive sampling plan is devised. Four random square yards are checked in each bolt, and five consecutive bolts complete the sample for a total of twenty square yards checked in each sample. Dividing the total number of flaws in each sample, by 20 gives the value *u*, the number of flaws per square yard in the sample. A *u* chart is formed to chart the *average* number of flaws per square yard.

8.2 THE *p* CHART

The *p* chart tracks the fraction of nonconforming items in a sample. Samples may consist either of *n* consecutive items taken at specified times during the day according to a random sample plan or of 100 percent of the production for a specified time period (hour, day, week, and so forth).

The conforming/nonconforming decision may be based on one characteristic or on several, but a defective item is counted as defective only once, even though it may contain several defects.

Preparation for the *p* Chart

The preparatory steps are similar to those of the variables charts.

1. Establish an environment suitable for action.

The appropriate people must be trained in charting techniques and interpretation and made aware of their importance in the quality improvement process.

2. Define the process.

Brainstorming with the quality control team can be effective for developing flow charts, cause and effect diagrams, or storyboards for process analysis.

3. Determine the most promising characteristics to be managed.

Use of Pareto charts (bar charts that classify defects) can be helpful in setting priorities. Be sure to consider customer needs for both the final customer and the downstream customers (the people using the item in subsequent process steps) along with current and potential problem areas. Quality control personnel trained in statistics can check for correlation between characteristics. When high correlation (mathematical interdependence) exists, charting one characteristic may be sufficient. The topic of correlation is discussed briefly in Appendix A.

4. Define the measurement system.

This may be something simple, such as a go–no go gauge at a specific measurement point, or something quite difficult for consistency, such as a judgment call on pass/fail. When individual judgment is used for deciding whether a product conforms, inspectors must have total agreement as to exactly what is defective and what is not. For example, if a visual check is made for surface flaws of the item produced, clear pictures should be available to illustrate what is acceptable and what is not, or sample pass and fail pieces should be used for comparison. Occasional consistency checks among the inspectors can keep the measurement system fine-tuned.

5. Minimize any unnecessary variation before the charting begins.

Don't wait for the charts to point out obvious problems when those problems can be eliminated beforehand. What is obvious to one inspector may not be obvious to another, however, and in that case, the chart can be used to supply the proof that trouble exists so that action may be authorized.

The p Chart Procedure

There are six basic steps in the p chart procedure.

1. Gather the data. Select the size, frequency and number of samples.

Large samples of 50, 100, or more are common. The sample size should be large enough to ensure that most of the samples will have a nonzero number of defectives. The chart will be easier to interpret if the average number of defectives in the sample is five or more. If an estimate of $\bar{p}$, the average proportion of defective items, can be made, the necessary sample size, n, can be determined by choosing an n value large enough to make the product, $n\bar{p}$, approximately 5. The calculations and interpretation of the chart are easier when the sample size is kept constant. When constant sample times are used and the sample size varies, a single set of control limits can be used as long as the individual sample sizes do not differ too much. If any individual samples or groups of samples differ in size by more than 25 percent of the average sample size, $\bar{n}$, separate control limit calculations will be needed. Chart interpretation is trickier because it is more difficult to relate the point pattern to fluctuating control limits.

Sampling frequency should make sense in terms of production schedules. The chart should give as accurate a picture as possible of the process at the specific point in question. In order to do this, every item produced during the charting program must have an equal chance of being chosen in a sample. A random sampling plan similar to the plans discussed in Example 4.1 should therefore be used.

The number of samples on a _p_ chart should be 20 or more, but if time is a factor, a preliminary analysis may be made after ten samples have been charted. The data collection period should be long enough to track all possible sources of variation.

2. Calculate _p_ for each sample.

Record the sample size, _n_, and the number of defective items, _np_, on the chart. Calculate and record _p_.

$$p = \frac{np}{n}$$

3. Set the scale for the control chart.

After several _p_ values have been calculated, make the _p_ scale from 0 to approximately twice the largest _p_ value. For easier interpretation, do not make the scale too wide.

4. Plot the _p_ values and connect them with a broken-line graph.
5. Calculate $\bar{p}$, the average _p_ value, and the control limits after about 20 points have been charted. The number of samples is _k_. Draw a solid line at $\bar{p}$ and dashed lines at the control limits.

$$\bar{p} = \frac{\sum np}{\sum n}$$

$$= \frac{np_1 + np_2 + np_3 + \cdots + np_k}{n_1 + n_2 + \cdots + n_k}$$

$$\text{UCL}_p = \bar{p} + 3\sqrt{\frac{\bar{p}(1 - \bar{p})}{n}}$$

$$\text{LCL}_p = \bar{p} - 3\sqrt{\frac{\bar{p}(1 - \bar{p})}{n}}$$

If the sample size is constant, the denominator in the preceding control limit formulas is _n_. When a constant sample size is _not_ used, then the average sample size is used in the control limit calculations. For _k_ samples,

$$\bar{n} = \frac{\sum n}{k}$$

When the sample size variation is minimal, the one set of control limits is adequate. However, any individual sample sizes that vary by more than 25 percent from $\bar{n}$ require separate control limits. This isn't the best type of _p_ chart because it is harder to interpret than a _p_ chart with constant sample size, but unequal sample sizes can be used when necessary.

6. Interpret the chart.

Shifts   Because p represents the defective proportion, a shift of seven or more points to a higher or lower level could mean that something has affected the proportion defective or that the definition of what is defective has somehow changed, either intentionally or unintentionally.

Trends   A run of seven or more points up or down indicates that something is causing the proportion that is defective to change in a gradual manner.

An erratic pattern indicates that something irregular is affecting the process. There are several possible trouble spots: Poorly trained operators may be responsible for widely fluctuating values of p, different inspection criteria may be used by some inspectors, or an assembly point may be using poorly controlled parts. The erratic pattern usually signals a need for either separate p charts at various upstream positions in the process or a switch to a variables control chart for further analysis.

Interpretation of p charts demands more caution than interpretation of the variables control charts. Do not assume too quickly that the p chart is in control. Sometimes a situation that appears to be in control is just a balance of different characteristics that are individually out of control. It's important to stay aware of the number of different characteristics that are involved in a specific pass/fail decision. Decision standards should be checked periodically to ensure that they have not changed.

Often, several p charts are dealt with simultaneously. Do not concentrate on just the charts with high $\bar{p}$ values: It may be more beneficial to work with a chart that has a low $\bar{p}$ value but shows a lack of control. A similar concept was discussed with the variables control charts. The first step toward achieving control on a variables chart is control of the variation on the R chart. A fluctuating p chart signals a variation problem. Solving the variation problem can have a ripple effect and possibly reduce some of the $\bar{p}$ values on other charts.

EXAMPLE 8.1

Figure 8.1 on page 195 contains data that show samples of 200, the number of defective items, and the first few p values.

$$p_1 = \frac{np_1}{n} \qquad p_3 = \frac{np_3}{n}$$

$$= \frac{2}{200} \qquad = \frac{4}{200}$$

$$= .01 \qquad = .02$$

$$p_2 = \frac{np_2}{n} \qquad p_4 = \frac{np_4}{n}$$

$$= \frac{5}{200} \qquad = \frac{0}{200}$$

$$= .025 \qquad = .000$$

Solution

Calculate the rest of the p values and check your results with Figure 8.2 (page 197). The proportion, p, varies from 0 to .04. Aiming for approximately 10 lines on the chart, divide 10 into the range of p and round up to .005 units per line.

Calculations

$$\bar{p} = \frac{\Sigma np}{\Sigma n} = \frac{\quad}{\quad} =$$

$$1 - \bar{p} =$$

$$\bar{p} \times (1-\bar{p}) = \underline{\quad} \times \underline{\quad} =$$

$$\frac{\bar{p} \times (1-\bar{p})}{n} = \frac{\quad}{\quad} =$$

$$\sqrt{\frac{\bar{p} \times (1-\bar{p})}{n}} = \sqrt{\quad} =$$

$$3 \times \sqrt{\frac{\bar{p} \times (1-\bar{p})}{n}} = 3 \times \underline{\quad} = \boxed{}$$

$$UCL_p = \bar{p} + 3\sqrt{\frac{\bar{p} \times (1-\bar{p})}{n}} = \underline{\quad} + \underline{\quad}$$

$$LCL_p = \bar{p} - 3\sqrt{\frac{\bar{p} \times (1-\bar{p})}{n}} = \underline{\quad} - \underline{\quad}$$

$$= \quad$$

= 0 if negative

Date																				
Checker																				
n	200	200	200	200	200	200	200	200	200	200	200	200	200	200	200	200	200	200	200	200
np	2	5	4	0	1	6	4	2	5	8	4	5	2	4	5	3	6	0	3	
p	.01	.025	.02	.00																

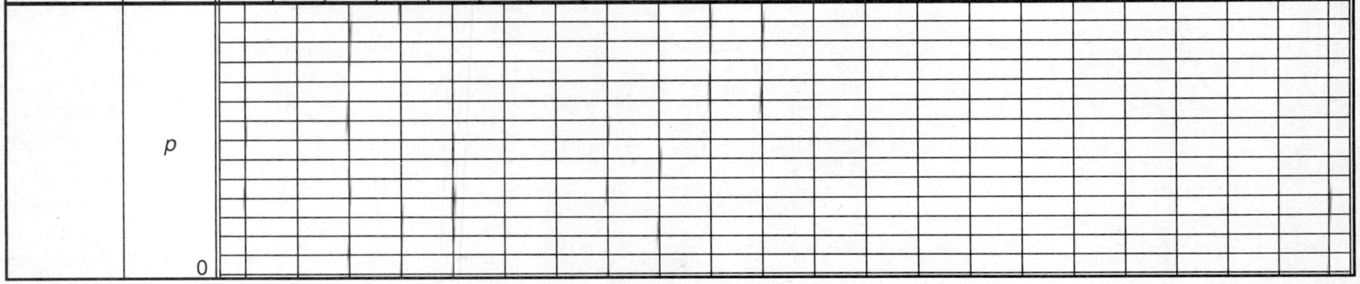

p

0

FIGURE 8.1

Follow the procedure for Example 8.1 and check the results with Figure 8.2.

$$\begin{array}{r} .004 \\ 10\overline{)\ .04} \end{array}$$

This should allow enough room for control limits without making the chart too wide. Put the scale on the chart in Figure 8.1 and graph the p values. Connect the points with a broken-line graph. Check your results with Figure 8.2.

Calculate $\bar{p}$ and draw the solid line.

$$\begin{aligned} \bar{p} &= \frac{\sum np}{\sum n} \\ &= \frac{2 + 5 + 4 + 0 + 1 + \cdots + 3}{20 \times 200} \\ &= \frac{76}{4000} \\ &= .019 \end{aligned}$$

The denominator, $200 + 200 + 200 + \cdots$, is calculated by multiplying 200 by 20.

Next, calculate the control limits and draw the dashed lines.

$$\text{UCL}_p = \bar{p} + 3\sqrt{\frac{\bar{p}(1 - \bar{p})}{n}} \qquad \text{LCL}_p = \bar{p} - 3\sqrt{\frac{\bar{p}(1 - \bar{p})}{n}}$$

The more complicated second term will be calculated first, then added to and subtracted from $\bar{p}$.

1. Find $1 - \bar{p}$.

$$\begin{aligned} 1 - \bar{p} &= 1 - .019 \\ &= .981 \end{aligned}$$

2. Multiply by $\bar{p}$.

$$\begin{aligned} \bar{p}(1 - \bar{p}) &= .019 \times .981 \\ &= .018639 \end{aligned}$$

3. Divide by n.

$$\begin{aligned} \frac{\bar{p}(1 - \bar{p})}{n} &= \frac{.018639}{200} \\ &= .000093195 \end{aligned}$$

4. Calculate the square root.

$$\begin{aligned} \sqrt{\frac{\bar{p}(1 - \bar{p})}{n}} &= \sqrt{.000093195} \\ &= .0096538 \end{aligned}$$

Calculations

$$\bar{p} = \frac{\Sigma np}{\Sigma n} = \frac{76}{4000} = .019$$

$$1 - \bar{p} = .981$$

$$\bar{p} \times (1 - \bar{p}) = .019 \times .981 = .018639$$

$$\frac{\bar{p} \times (1 - \bar{p})}{n} = \frac{.018639}{200} = .000093195$$

$$\sqrt{\frac{\bar{p} \times (1 - \bar{p})}{n}} = \sqrt{.000093195} = .0096538$$

$$3\sqrt{\frac{\bar{p} \times (1 - \bar{p})}{n}} = 3 \times .0096538 = .029$$

$$UCL_p = \bar{p} + 3\sqrt{\frac{\bar{p} \times (1 - \bar{p})}{n}}$$
$$= .019 + .029 = .048$$

$$LCL_p = .019 - .029$$
$$= -.01$$
$$= 0 \text{ (because of negative value)}$$

Date																				
Checker																				
n	200	200	200	200	200	200	200	200	200	200	200	200	200	200	200	200	200	200	200	200
np	2	5	4	0	1	6	4	2	5	7	8	4	5	2	4	5	3	6	0	3
p	.01	.025	.02	.00	.005	.03	.02	.01	.025	.035	.04	.02	.025	.01	.02	.025	.01	.03	.00	.015

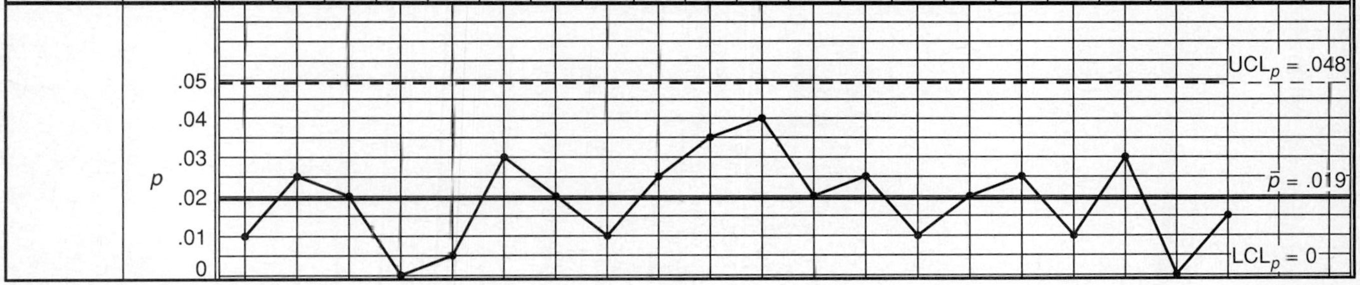

$UCL_p = .048$

$\bar{p} = .019$

$LCL_p = 0$

FIGURE 8.2
The *p* chart for Example 8.1.

With the .000093195 in the calculator display, press the radical button on the calculator, "$\sqrt{\ }$".

5. Multiply by 3.

$$3\sqrt{\frac{\bar{p}(1-\bar{p})}{n}} = 3 \times .0096538$$
$$= .029$$

6. Add .029 to $\bar{p}$ for UCL_p.

$$UCL_p = .019 + .029$$
$$= .048$$

7. Subtract .029 from $\bar{p}$ for LCL_p. When the LCL comes out negative, use LCL = 0.

$$LCL_p = .019 - .029$$
$$= -.01$$
$$= 0$$

Check your results with Figure 8.2.

   Interpretation is the final step. There are no obvious out-of-control patterns such as points beyond the control limits, seven points in a row above or below the mean, or seven points steadily increasing or decreasing. There may be a downward trend beginning with the eleventh sample, but the chart will have to be extended for several more samples to see if a trend really is occurring.

8.3 THE *np* CHART

The *np* chart can be used in place of the *p* chart whenever the sample size is constant. The *np* chart is the preferred chart because it is easier to construct. An easy conversion is available for changing the charting results to a proportion format. That conversion will be demonstrated at the end of Example 8.2.

EXAMPLE 8.2   Make an *np* chart for the data in Figure 8.3 (page 199). The data have been copied from Figure 8.1. Follow the directions below and complete the chart; check your results with Figure 8.4 (page 201).

Solution

The *np* values range from 0 to 8, so scale the *np* chart in one unit values from 0 to 10. Chart the *np* values and draw the broken-line graph. Find the value of the centerline, $\overline{np}$, and draw a solid line.

Calculations

$$\overline{np} = \frac{\Sigma\, np}{k} = \underline{\hspace{2cm}} = \underline{\hspace{2cm}}$$

$$\overline{p} = \frac{\overline{np}}{n} = \underline{\hspace{2cm}} = \underline{\hspace{2cm}}$$

$$1 - \overline{p} = \underline{\hspace{2cm}}$$

$$\overline{np} \times (1-\overline{p}) = \underline{\hspace{1.5cm}} \times \underline{\hspace{1.5cm}}$$

$$\sqrt{\overline{np} \times (1-\overline{p})} = \sqrt{\underline{\hspace{1cm}}} = \underline{\hspace{1.5cm}}$$

$$3\sqrt{\overline{np} \times (1-\overline{p})} = 3 \times \underline{\hspace{1.5cm}} = \boxed{}$$

$$UCL_p = \overline{np} + 3\sqrt{\overline{np} \times (1-\overline{p})} = \underline{\hspace{1cm}} + \underline{\hspace{1cm}} = \underline{\hspace{1cm}}$$

$$LCL_p = \overline{np} - 3\sqrt{\overline{np} \times (1-\overline{p})} = \underline{\hspace{1cm}} - \underline{\hspace{1cm}} = \underline{\hspace{1cm}}$$

$$= 0 \text{ if negative}$$

Date																			
Checker																			
n	200	200	200	200	200	200	200	200	200	200	200	200	200	200	200	200	200	200	200
np	2	5	4	0	1	6	4	2	5	7	8	4	5	2	4	3	6	0	3

np

FIGURE 8.3

Follow the directions given in Example 8.2. Check your results with Figure 8.4.

$$\overline{np} = \frac{\sum np}{k}$$

$$= \frac{2 + 5 + 4 + \cdots + 3}{20}$$

$$= \frac{76}{20}$$

$$= 3.8$$

Calculate the control limits and draw the dashed lines.

$$\text{UCL}_{np} = \overline{np} + 3\sqrt{\overline{np}(1 - \overline{p})} \qquad \text{LCL}_{np} = \overline{np} - 3\sqrt{\overline{np}(1 - \overline{p})}$$

1. Calculate $\overline{p}$.

$$\overline{p} = \frac{\overline{np}}{n}$$

$$= \frac{3.8}{200}$$

$$= .019$$

2. Subtract $\overline{p}$ from 1.

$$1 - \overline{p} = 1 - .019$$

$$= .981$$

3. Multiply by $\overline{np}$.

$$\overline{np}(1 - \overline{p}) = 3.8 \times .981$$

$$= 3.7278$$

4. Calculate the square root.

$$\sqrt{\overline{np}(1 - \overline{p})} = \sqrt{3.7278}$$

$$= 1.931$$

5. Multiply by 3.

$$3\sqrt{\overline{np}(1 - \overline{p})} = 3 \times 1.931$$

$$= 5.793$$

6. Add to $\overline{np}$ for the UCL_{np}.

$$\text{UCL}_{np} = 3.8 + 5.8$$

$$= 9.6$$

Calculations

$$\overline{np} = \frac{\Sigma\, np}{k} = \frac{76}{20} = 3.8$$

$$\bar{p} = \frac{\overline{np}}{n} = \frac{3.8}{200} = .019$$

$$1 - \bar{p} = .981$$

$$\overline{np} \times (1-\bar{p}) = 3.8 \times .981 = 3.7278$$

$$\sqrt{\overline{np} \times (1-\bar{p})} = \sqrt{3.7278} = 1.931$$

$$3\sqrt{\overline{np} \times (1-\bar{p})} = 3 \times 1.931 = 5.793$$

$$UCL_p = \overline{np} + 3\sqrt{\overline{np} \times (1-\bar{p})}$$

$$= 3.8 + 5.8 = 9.6$$

$$LCL_p = \overline{np} - 3\sqrt{\overline{np} \times (1-\bar{p})}$$

$$= 3.8 - 5.8 = -2$$

$$= 0 \text{ if negative}$$

Date																					
Checker																					
n	200	200	200	200	200	200	200	200	200	200	200	200	200	200	200	200	200	200	200	200	
np	2	5	4	0	1	6	4	2	5	7	8	4	5	2	4	5	3	6	0	3	

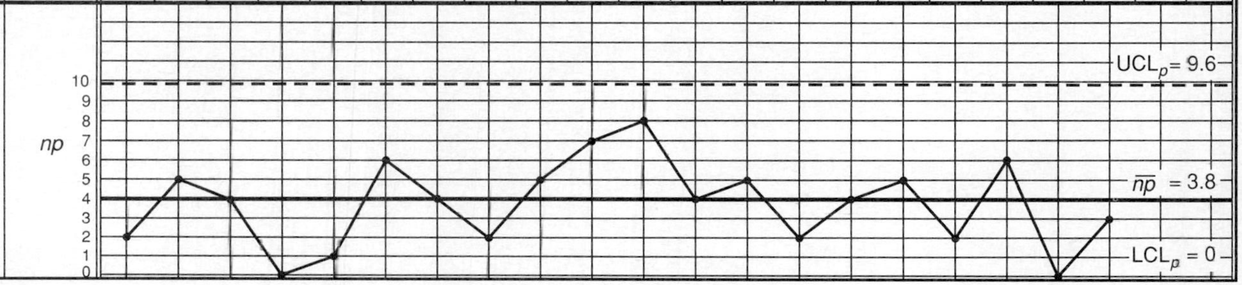

FIGURE 8.4
The *np* chart for Example 8.2.

7. Subtract from $\overline{np}$ for the LCL_{np}.

$$LCL_{np} = 3.8 - 5.8$$
$$= -2$$
$$= 0$$

Just as before, if the LCL comes out negative, use LCL $= 0$.

The np chart interpretation is the same as that for the p chart. There are no apparent out-of-control situations, but if the chart is continued for several more samples, a downward trend may show up.

Process capability is a measure of how well the process is doing with respect to some standard. With variables control charts, the standard is always the specification limits. With attributes control charts, both the p and np charts have a standard of zero defects. The measure of process capability is the number of defects produced per sample on the average, $\overline{np}$, or the fraction (or percent) of defects produced on the average, $\overline{p}$.

If you compare the p chart and the np chart carefully you will notice that the scales match exactly and the broken-line graphs look the same. Further, the averages and control limits match. The information from an np chart can be translated to the corresponding p chart information by dividing by the sample size, n. Also, p chart information can be translated to np values by multiplying by the sample size, n.

$$\overline{np} = 3.8$$
$$\frac{\overline{np}}{n} = \frac{3.8}{200}$$
$$= .019$$
$$= \overline{p}$$
$$UCL_{np} = 9.6$$
$$\frac{UCL_{np}}{n} = \frac{9.6}{n}$$
$$= .048$$
$$= UCL_p$$

EXAMPLE 8.3 For another example of the connection between p values and np values, suppose that a p chart has $\overline{p} = .032$ and the UCL_p is .0654 for constant samples of $n = 250$. What is the average number of defectives per sample and the number of defects three standard deviations above the mean?

Solution
The average number of defects per sample is $\overline{np}$.

$$\overline{np} = n \times \overline{p}$$
$$= 250 \times .032$$
$$= 8$$

The upper control limit gives the number of defects three standard deviations above the mean.

$$\text{UCL}_{np} = n \times \text{UCL}_p$$
$$= 250 \times .0654$$
$$= 16.3$$

8.4 THE *c* CHART

The *c* chart tracks the number of defects in some unit. In the following example, the unit used is one shirt.

EXAMPLE 8.4

A shirt manufacturer is trying to upgrade the quality of the dress shirts it produces in order to introduce a new line in men's stores. After the cloth quality is improved, the management decides that with the introduction of the new cloth into the process, the number of defects should be tracked. The inspectors are provided with a list of items to check on each shirt and shown samples of acceptable quality. Ten consecutive shirts are checked several times a day according to a random sample plan, and the following data are collected. With the following data in Table 8.1, construct a *c* Chart. The data are in order by column. The number of defects on each shirt is *c*.

TABLE 8.1
Number of flaws per shirt

c	*c*	*c*	*c*	*c*	*c*	*c*	*c*	*c*	*c*
0	2	0	3	0	1	2	0	0	2
5	0	1	2	0	0	0	4	4	2
0	1	0	0	1	3	4	0	0	2
0	1	1	5	3	2	2	0	1	3
0	4	1	2	0	1	0	0	2	3
3	0	0	1	5	3	2	4	0	1
0	0	1	4	4	3	0	2	1	1
0	2	1	3	2	0	0	2	2	1
0	0	0	4	6	2	0	3	0	1
2	0	5	6	2	0	1	2	4	1

The *c* values range from 0 to 6, so set the scale in units from 0 to 7. A quick scan of the data shows that $\overline{c}$ should be relatively small and that the upper control limit should be less than 7. There's enough room on the chart to put three *c* charts for shirts 1 to 30, 31 to 65, and 66 to 100. Set three different scales from 0 to 7 on the chart in Figure 8.5 (page 204), plot the *c* values, and draw the broken-line graph. Check your results with Figure 8.6 on page 205.

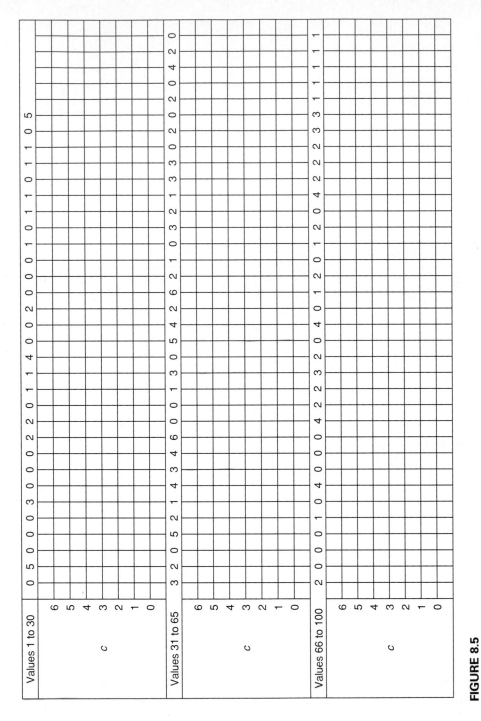

FIGURE 8.5

Construct the *c* chart, calculate the average and control limits, and draw the lines. Check your results with Figure 8.6.

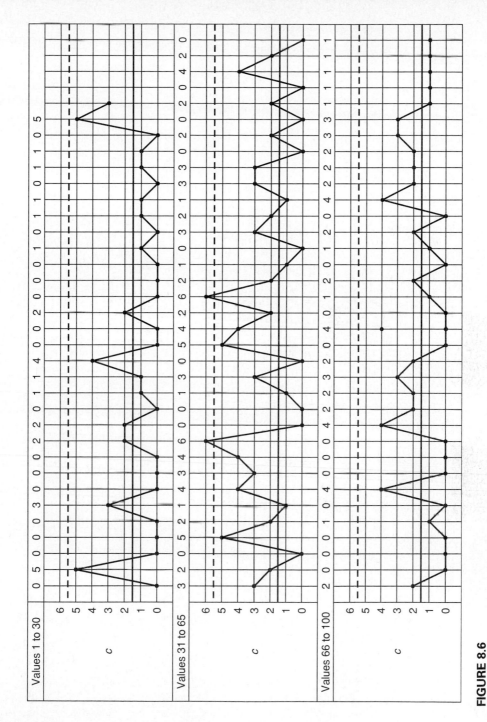

FIGURE 8.6

The completed c chart for Example 8.4.

Calculate $\bar{c}$ and draw the solid line on each of the three c charts (one $\bar{c}$ for all the data). For k units,

$$\bar{c} = \frac{\sum c}{k}$$
$$= \frac{157}{100}$$
$$= 1.57$$

Calculate the control limits and draw the dashed lines.

$$\begin{aligned} \text{UCL}_c &= \bar{c} + 3\sqrt{\bar{c}} & \text{LCL}_c &= \bar{c} - 3\sqrt{\bar{c}} \\ &= 1.57 + 3\sqrt{1.57} & &= 1.57 - 3\sqrt{1.57} \\ &= 1.57 + (3 \times 1.253) & &= 1.57 - (3 \times 1.253) \\ &= 1.57 + 3.76 & &= 1.57 - 3.76 \\ &= 5.33 & &= -2.19 \\ & & &= 0 \end{aligned}$$

A negative LCL is calculated, so LCL $= 0$.

A few shirts fall in the out-of-control category because their number of flaws exceeds the control limit value of 5.33. The process capability is the average number of defects, $\bar{c}$, and a $\bar{c}$ of 1.57 defects per shirt must be improved before the men's stores market can be attempted.

8.5 THE *u* CHART

The data from Example 8.4 can also be analyzed with a u chart by grouping the shirts into samples. In this example the data are grouped into samples of $n = 10$ shirts. The previous table from the c chart is reorganized into samples by taking ten consecutive shirts per sample. The first ten samples in the following table are taken from Example 8.4 and an additional ten samples have been added.

EXAMPLE 8.5

Make a u chart for the data in Table 8.2 (page 207). For each u value in the table, the total number of defects in the sample is divided by the sample size, 10. The average number of defects per shirt in each sample is u.

Solution

The data have been entered on the chart in Figure 8.7 (page 208). Set the scale on the chart. The maximum u value in the table is 3.0, so a scale of .2 units per line is convenient. Make the scale from 0 to 3.0. Chart the points and check your results with the completed chart in Figure 8.8 on page 209.

Calculate $\bar{u}$ and the control limits.

TABLE 8.2
Samples of grouped data—$n = 8$

Sample	$\sum c$	u	Sample	$\sum c$	u
1	10	1.0	11	9	.9
2	10	1.0	12	8	.8
3	10	1.0	13	11	1.1
4	30	3.0	14	7	.7
5	23	2.3	15	12	1.2
6	15	1.5	16	10	1.0
7	11	1.1	17	9	.9
8	17	1.7	18	15	1.5
9	14	1.4	19	14	1.4
10	17	1.7	20	14	1.4

$$\sum n = 10 \times 20$$
$$= 200$$

$$\bar{u} = \frac{\sum c}{\sum n}$$

$$= \frac{262}{200}$$

$$= 1.31$$

$$\text{UCL}_u = \bar{u} + 3\sqrt{\frac{\bar{u}}{n}}$$

$$= 1.31 + 3\sqrt{\frac{1.31}{10}}$$

$$= 1.31 + 3\sqrt{.131}$$

$$= 1.31 + (3 \times .36)$$

$$= 1.31 + 1.08$$

$$= 2.39$$

$$\text{LCL}_u = \bar{u} - 3\sqrt{\frac{\bar{u}}{n}}$$

$$= 1.31 - 1.08$$

$$= .23$$

Draw a solid line at $\bar{u}$ and dashed lines at the control limits. Your completed chart should look like Figure 8.8.

The process capability is $\bar{u}$, which is 1.31 flaws per shirt. Because the capability is considered too large, a follow-up study is planned that will chart individual flaws as a first step toward process improvement.

Calculations

$$\bar{u} = \frac{\Sigma c}{\Sigma n} = \underline{\hspace{1cm}} = \underline{\hspace{1cm}}$$

$$\frac{\bar{u}}{n} = \underline{\hspace{1cm}}$$

$$\sqrt{\frac{\bar{u}}{n}} = \underline{\hspace{1cm}}$$

$$3\sqrt{\frac{\bar{u}}{n}} = \underline{\hspace{1cm}}$$

$$UCL_u = \bar{u} + 3\sqrt{\frac{\bar{u}}{n}} = \underline{\hspace{1cm}} + \underline{\hspace{1cm}} = \underline{\hspace{1cm}}$$

$$UCL_u = \bar{u} - 3\sqrt{\frac{\bar{u}}{n}} = \underline{\hspace{1cm}} - \underline{\hspace{1cm}} = \underline{\hspace{1cm}}$$

Sample	1	2	3	4	5	6	7	8	9	10	11	12	13	14	15	16	17	18	19	20
n	10	10	10	10	10	10	10	10	10	10	10	10	10	10	10	10	10	10	10	10
c	10	10	10	30	23	15	11	13	14	17	9	8	11	7	12	10	9	15	14	14
u	1	1	1	3	2.3	1.5	1.1	1.3	1.4	1.7	.9	.8	1.1	.7	1.2	1	.9	1.5	1.4	1.4

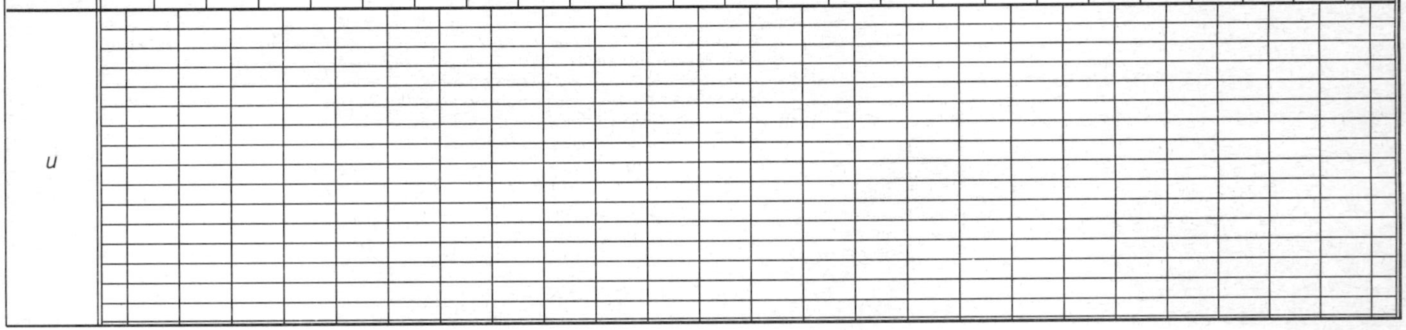

u

FIGURE 8.7

Complete the *u* chart as instructed in Example 8.5.

Calculations

$$\bar{u} = \frac{\Sigma c}{\Sigma n} = \frac{262}{200} = 1.31$$

$$\frac{\bar{u}}{n} = \frac{1.31}{10} = 1.31$$

$$\sqrt{\frac{\bar{u}}{n}} = \sqrt{1.31} = .36$$

$$3\sqrt{\frac{\bar{u}}{n}} = 3 \times .36 = 1.08$$

$$UCL_u = \bar{u} + 3\sqrt{\frac{\bar{u}}{n}} = 1.31 + 1.08 = 1.39$$

$$LCL_u = \bar{u} - 3\sqrt{\frac{\bar{u}}{n}} \quad 1.31 - 1.08 = .23$$

Sample	1	2	3	4	5	6	7	8	9	10	11	12	13	14	15	16	17	18	19	20
n	10	10	10	10	10	10	10	10	10	10	10	10	10	10	10	10	10	10	10	10
c	10	10	10	30	23	15	11	13	14	17	9	8	11	7	12	10	9	15	14	14
u	1	1	1	3	2.3	1.5	1.1	1.3	1.4	1.7	.9	.8	1.1	.7	1.2	1	.9	1.5	1.4	1.4

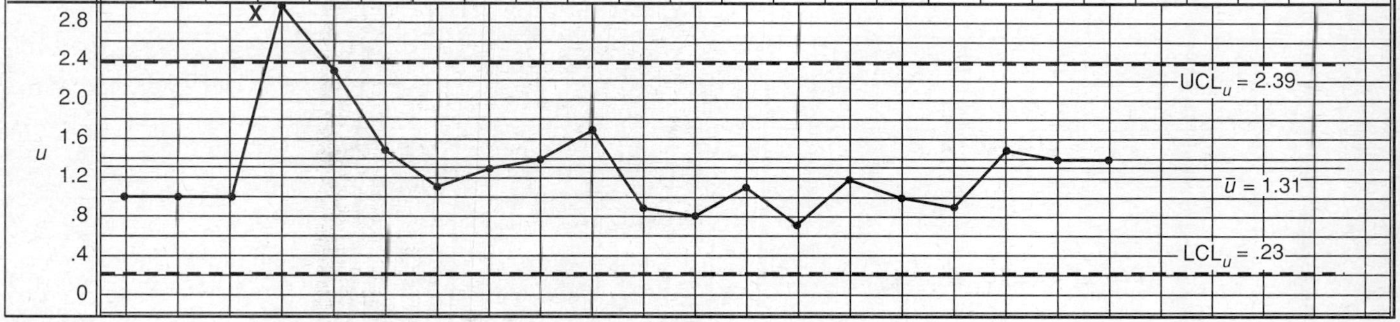

2.8
2.4
2.0
1.6
u
1.2
.8
.4
0
X
$UCL_u = 2.39$
$\bar{u} = 1.31$
$LCL_u = .23$

FIGURE 8.8
The completed chart for Example 8.5.

Calculations

$$\bar{p} = \frac{\Sigma np}{\Sigma n} = \frac{\rule{1cm}{0.4pt}}{\rule{1cm}{0.4pt}} = \rule{1cm}{0.4pt}$$

$$1 - \bar{p} = \rule{1cm}{0.4pt}$$

$$\bar{p} \times (1 - \bar{p}) = \rule{1cm}{0.4pt} \times \rule{1cm}{0.4pt} = \rule{1cm}{0.4pt}$$

$$\frac{\bar{p} \times (1 - \bar{p})}{n} = \frac{\rule{1cm}{0.4pt}}{\rule{1cm}{0.4pt}} = \rule{1cm}{0.4pt}$$

$$\sqrt{\frac{\bar{p} \times (1 - \bar{p})}{n}} = \sqrt{\rule{1cm}{0.4pt}} = \rule{1cm}{0.4pt}$$

$$3\sqrt{\frac{\bar{p} \times (1 - \bar{p})}{n}} = 3 \times \rule{1cm}{0.4pt} = \boxed{}$$

$$UCL_p = \bar{p} + 3\sqrt{\frac{\bar{p} \times (1 - \bar{p})}{n}} = \rule{1cm}{0.4pt} + \boxed{}$$

$$UCL_p = \rule{1cm}{0.4pt}$$

$$LCL_p = \bar{p} - 3\sqrt{\frac{\bar{p} \times (1 - \bar{p})}{n}} = \rule{1cm}{0.4pt} - \boxed{}$$

$$LCL_p = \rule{1cm}{0.4pt}$$

np	12	10	8	14	21	16	18	15	12	19	16	10	22	17	14	20	21	12	8	10	16	12	18	14	15
n	400	400	400	400	400	400	400	400	400	400	400	400	400	400	400	400	400	400	400	400	400	400	400	400	400
p																									

FIGURE 8.9

Make the p chart for Exercise 1.

EXERCISES

1. The number of defectives, np, and the sample size, n, are given on the chart in Figure 8.9 (page 210).
   (a) Set the scale and make a p chart.
   (b) Calculate $\bar{p}$ and the control limits. Draw the lines.
   (c) Mark any out-of-control situations.
   (d) What is the process capability?
2. The data from Exercise 1 are given in Figure 8.10 on page 212.
   (a) Make an np chart.
   (b) Calculate $\overline{np}$ and the control limits. Draw the lines.
   (c) Mark any out-of-control situations.
   (d) What is the process capability?
   (e) Make sure that the graphs on Figures 8.9 and 8.10 look the same and that $\overline{np}$ and UCL_{np} convert to $\bar{p}$ and UCL_p by dividing by n.
3. The number of defects per item is shown on Figure 8.11 on page 213.
   (a) Make a c chart.
   (b) Calculate $\bar{c}$ and the control limits. Draw the lines.
   (c) Interpret for statistical control.
   (d) What is the process capability?
4. Samples of size 8 are shown in Table 8.3 on page 213 with the number of defects in each item listed. Each column is a sample.
   (a) Make a u chart for the 20 samples using Figure 8.12 (page 214).
   (b) Calculate $\bar{u}$ and the control limits.
   (c) Interpret for statistical control.
   (d) What is the process capability?

Calculations

$$\overline{np} = \frac{\Sigma\, np}{k} = \frac{\underline{\quad}}{\underline{\quad}} = \underline{\quad}$$

$$\bar{p} = \frac{\overline{np}}{n} = \underline{\quad}$$

$$1 - \bar{p} = \underline{\quad}$$

$$\overline{np}\,(1-\bar{p}) = \underline{\quad} \times \underline{\quad} = \underline{\quad}$$

$$\sqrt{\overline{np}\,(1-\bar{p})} = \sqrt{\underline{\quad}} = \underline{\quad}$$

$$3\sqrt{\overline{np}\,(1-\bar{p})} = 3 \times \underline{\quad} = \boxed{}$$

$$UCL_p = \overline{np} + 3\sqrt{\overline{np}\,(1-\bar{p})}$$

$$UCL_p = \underline{\quad} + \underline{\quad} = \underline{\quad}$$

$$LCL_p = \overline{np} - 3\sqrt{\overline{np}\,(1-\bar{p})}$$

$$LCL_p = \underline{\quad} - \underline{\quad} = \underline{\quad} = 0 \text{ if negative}$$

$$n = 400$$

np	12	10	8	14	21	16	18	15	12	19	16	10	22	17	14	20	21	12	8	10	16	12	18	14	15

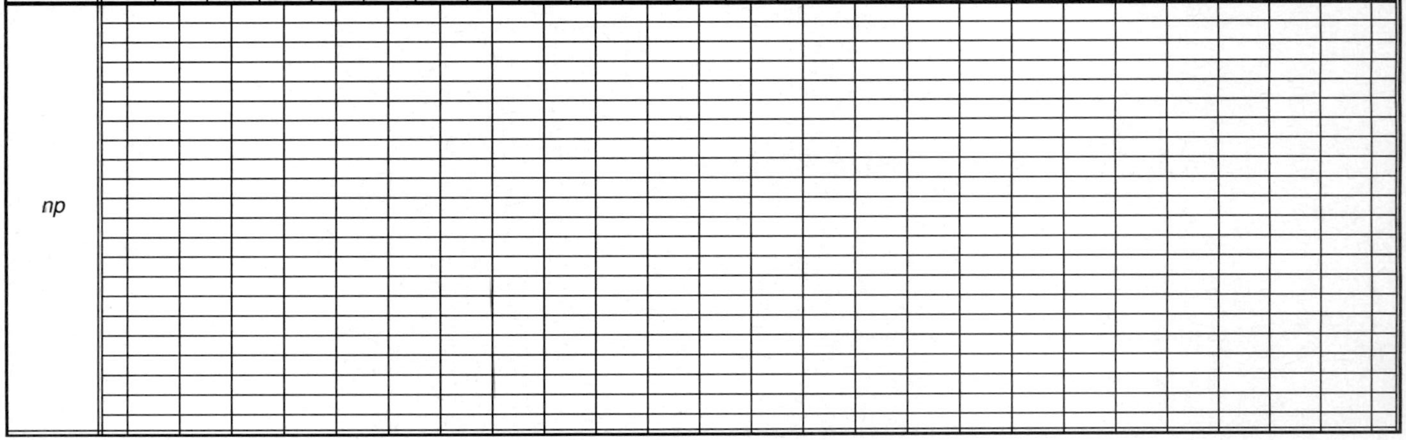

np

FIGURE 8.10
Make the *np* chart for Exercise 2.

Calculations

$$\bar{c} = \frac{\Sigma c}{k} = \underline{\quad} = \underline{\quad} \qquad UCL_C = \bar{c} + 3\sqrt{\bar{c}} = \underline{\quad} + \underline{\quad} = \underline{\quad}$$

$$\sqrt{\bar{c}} = \sqrt{\underline{\quad}} = \underline{\quad} \qquad LCL_C = \bar{c} - 3\sqrt{\bar{c}} = \underline{\quad} - \underline{\quad} = \underline{\quad}$$

$$3\sqrt{\bar{c}} = 3 \times \underline{\quad} = \underline{\quad}$$

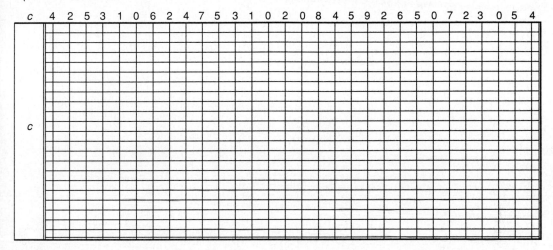

| c | 4 | 2 | 5 | 3 | 1 | 0 | 6 | 2 | 4 | 7 | 5 | 3 | 1 | 0 | 2 | 0 | 8 | 4 | 5 | 9 | 2 | 6 | 5 | 0 | 7 | 2 | 3 | 0 | 5 | 4 |

c

FIGURE 8.11
Make the *c* chart for Exercise 3.

TABLE 8.3
Number of defects per item

0	2	1	6	4	5	5	0	1	3	2	4	0	1	2	5	8	6	2	0
2	1	2	4	2	1	5	0	5	2	0	3	6	1	4	2	4	6	1	4
6	2	0	2	0	4	2	2	2	2	0	2	2	0	8	1	6	2	4	2
2	4	5	1	2	8	1	6	3	5	2	1	4	1	6	4	2	0	4	3
4	3	0	3	4	6	6	0	5	6	4	5	0	3	4	0	1	2	2	0
0	8	7	5	4	3	4	2	1	4	4	6	4	4	5	1	2	7	1	0
3	4	3	5	4	3	0	2	1	4	2	4	4	7	3	2	4	4	0	2
0	1	3	0	1	0	0	3	2	0	1	1	2	3	1	3	0	0	2	1

| Σc | | | | | | | | | | | | | | | | | | | | |
| u | | | | | | | | | | | | | | | | | | | | |

Calculations

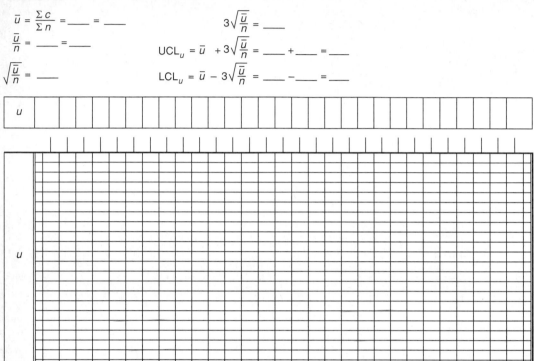

$$\bar{u} = \frac{\Sigma c}{\Sigma n} = \underline{\qquad} = \underline{\qquad}$$

$$\frac{\bar{u}}{n} = \underline{\qquad} = \underline{\qquad}$$

$$\sqrt{\frac{\bar{u}}{n}} = \underline{\qquad}$$

$$3\sqrt{\frac{\bar{u}}{n}} = \underline{\qquad}$$

$$UCL_u = \bar{u} + 3\sqrt{\frac{\bar{u}}{n}} = \underline{\qquad} + \underline{\qquad} = \underline{\qquad}$$

$$LCL_u = \bar{u} - 3\sqrt{\frac{\bar{u}}{n}} = \underline{\qquad} - \underline{\qquad} = \underline{\qquad}$$

FIGURE 8.12
Make the *u* chart for Exercise 4.

9

INTERPRETING CONTROL CHARTS

OBJECTIVES

- Distinguish between a random pattern of points on a control chart and a trouble-indicating pattern.
- Classify the various trouble-indicating patterns.
- Understand how probability concepts are used to classify the trouble-indicating patterns.
- Identify the basic possible causes of an out-of-control pattern of points on a control chart.

The points on a control chart should follow a completely random pattern if a process is in statistical control, and that random distribution of points should follow the normal distribution. When the population of measurements has some other stable distribution pattern, one of the trouble-indicating patterns discussed in this chapter will show it.

When a process is out of control, the pattern of points on the control chart will be affected in some way. Freaks, shifts, trends, and cycles are some of the recognizable control chart patterns. Along with other patterns, these four signify that a change has occurred in the process. Each of these trouble patterns must be spotted as nonrandom as soon as possible, without misinterpreting a truly random pattern. Rules concerning the minimum number of points that are needed to indicate a trouble pattern will be discussed in the following sections along with the mathematics of chance that were used to form the rules.

Remember one of the basic rules in chart interpretation: *Always get the range chart in statistical control first*. The accompanying averages or median chart cannot be analyzed if the range chart is out of control. Excessive variation or changes in variation affect the $\bar{x}$ or $\tilde{x}$ chart by changing the control limits. This occurs because $\bar{R}$ is used

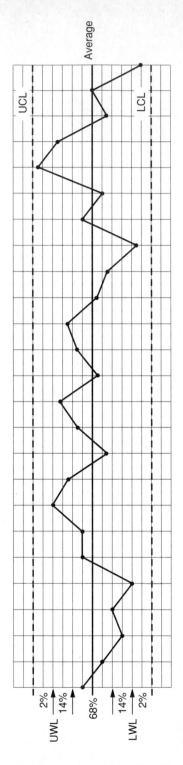

FIGURE 9.1
A random distribution of points.

in the formulas for control limits: $CL = \bar{x} \pm A_2\bar{R}$ and $CL = \tilde{x} \pm \tilde{A}_2\bar{R}$. A range chart that is out of control can make the $\bar{x}$ chart look out of control as well. It can also hide an out-of-control situation because $\bar{R}$ may be based on bad data. Efforts to control the average measurement size when variability is out of control can be a complete waste of time. Solving the variation problem will often eliminate what was originally thought to be an accompanying problem with average measurement.

9.1 THE RANDOM DISTRIBUTION OF POINTS

Figure 9.1 illustrates a random distribution of points on a control chart. The expected percentages in the different sections are shown on the left side. Some charts include upper warning lines (UWL) and lower warning lines (LWL) to help recognize some of the trouble patterns. The characteristics of a normally distributed random pattern of points include the following:

- The sequence of points is not predictable.
- The majority of the points (about 68 percent) should be within one standard deviation of the center line.
- About 28 percent should be between 1σ and 2σ units from the center line, with about 14 percent on each side.
- About 2 percent should be near each of the control limit lines.
- Virtually none of the points should be beyond the control limits.

When control charts are analyzed, points classified as out of control should be marked with an "X". A consistent marking pattern should be used. The X should be placed outside the broken-line graph, away from the center line. If a single point is out of control, just that point is marked. If several points are out of control within a classification such as a shift or trend, the first point that satisfies the rule and all points after it are marked out of control by the same classification. In Figure 9.2, for example, the first out-of-control classification is a shift: seven or more consecutive points on one side of the center line. The seventh and eighth points in the shift pattern are marked for that classification. The second out-of-control classification is a freak: a single point beyond the control limit. Just that one point is marked. Sometimes the out-of-control patterns are circled, either instead of or in conjunction with the X marks.

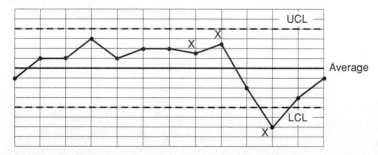

FIGURE 9.2
Out-of-control points marked with X's.

When a control chart indicates that a process is out of statistical control, the ideal action is to stop the process and eliminate the cause. However, this is not always possible. First, it may not be easy to determine the cause. Each different out-of-control pattern has its own "laundry-list" of possible causes, and several out-of-control occurrences may be needed before enough information is gathered to pinpoint the trouble. Second, some out-of-control situations can be temporarily tolerated because the measurements aren't critical with respect to the quality of the final product. Third, the relative position of the process within the quality program is important. If SPC is just being introduced to the process, there may be several problems contributing to poor quality at one of the process points. If the process was running with some degree of satisfaction before the application of SPC, it may make sense to continue the process while the sources of trouble are being determined and eliminated.

9.2 FREAKS

A *freak* is a single point that is beyond a control limit. It signifies that something changed dramatically in the process for a short time or that a mistake was made.

The most common process cause of freaks is a sudden change in material. If the raw material is subject to occasional inconsistencies or if the control of the mix of material is affected by either human error or flow gauge irregularity, freaks will result. These process problems indicated by freaks should be tracked because they can seriously affect the quality of the product.

A freak can also falsely signal process trouble when a mistake is made in measurement, recording, arithmetic, or plotting. When a freak occurs, always check for errors of this type first. Figure 9.3 shows two separate occasions in which freaks occur.

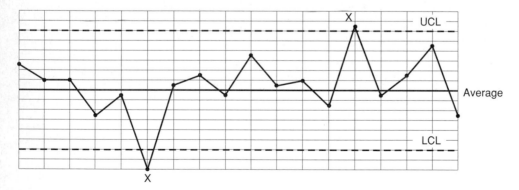

FIGURE 9.3
Freaks.

The display on page 219 lists the most common causes of freaks in three types of charts.

R **chart:**

- A sudden change in material
- A mistake in measurement
- An error in recording
- An error in arithmetic
- An error in plotting
- An incomplete or omitted operation
- Damage in handling

$\bar{x}$ **chart with *R* chart in control:**

- Same as the *R* chart list

p **chart:**

- Variation in sample size
- Sample taken from a different population
- An occasional very good or very poor lot

The identification of freaks is based on the mathematics associated with the normal distribution. On an $\bar{x}$ and *R* chart, the distribution of points will be normal even if the population of measurements is not. This is the result of the Central Limit Theorem in statistics, which states that the distribution of sample means from any population will be approximately normal. The larger the sample, the more closely the sample mean distribution matches the normal distribution.

The control limits for $\bar{x}$ and *R* are three standard deviations from the center line. The work with the normal curve revealed that 99.7 percent of all the values lie within three standard deviations of the center. Therefore, the chance that a point lies beyond the control limits is .3 percent, a very small chance of occurrence. When a freak occurs, the question arises, "Did a rare event occur or did something happen to cause the freak to occur?" The second reason is assumed, and the cause for the freak is investigated. If no cause is found and the freak doesn't happen again, then the first reason, that rare events do happen, is accepted.

EXAMPLE 9.1

Indicate the most likely cause for the freaks in Figures 9.4 to 9.7 on pages 220 and 221 from the following list:

1. Change in material.
2. Mistake in measurement.
3. Recording error.
4. Arithmetic error.
5. Plotting error.

FIGURE 9.4

Suggest a likely cause of the freak.

Measurements

.218	.218	.215	.217	.216
.214	.220	.211	.214	.215
.213	.218	.219	.211	.219
.219	.216	.207	.214	.218
$\overline{X}$ .216	.218	.213	.214	.217

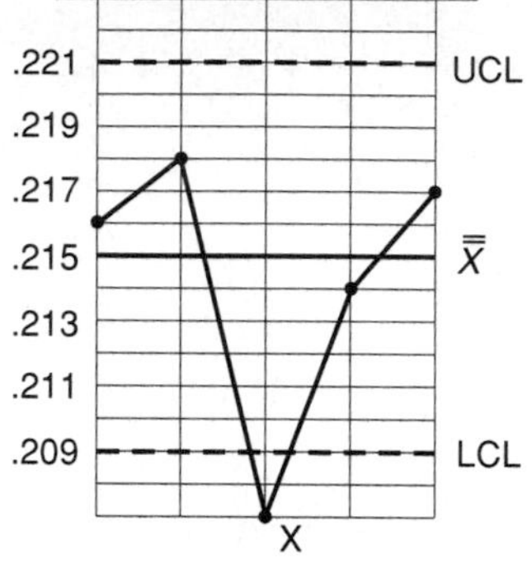

FIGURE 9.5

Suggest a likely cause of the freak.

Measurements

.216	.221	.234	.220	.214
.220	.217	.218	.212	.214
.214	.212	.216	.210	.212
.214	.216	.220	.214	.208
$\overline{X}$ .216	.214	.222	.214	.212

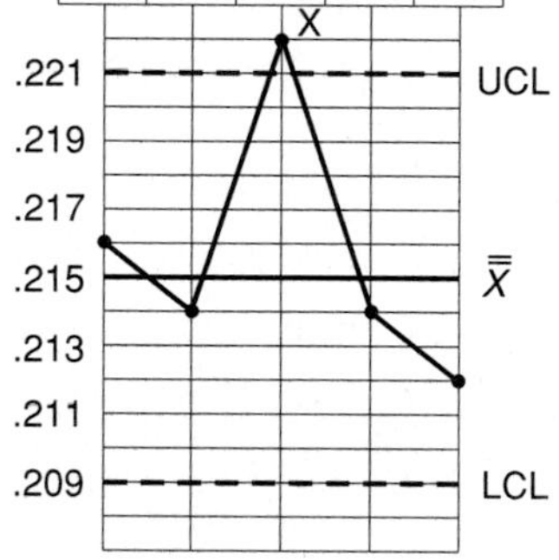

FIGURE 9.6

Suggest a likely cause of the freak.

Measurements

.213	.219	.218	.209	.220	.216
.215	.209	.220	.214	.215	.214
.218	.207	.214	.213	.217	.222
.210	.213	.208	.216	.216	.212
$\overline{X}$ .214	.212	.208	.213	.217	.216

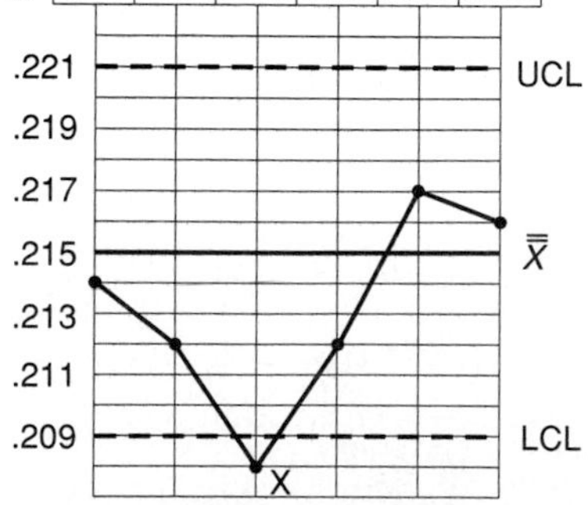

FIGURE 9.7
Suggest a likely cause of the freak.

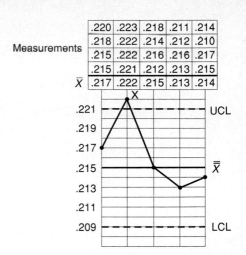

Measurements

.220	.223	.218	.211	.214
.218	.222	.214	.212	.210
.215	.222	.216	.216	.217
.215	.221	.212	.213	.215
$\overline{X}$	.217	.222	.215	.213	.214

Solution

In Figure 9.4 the average value of .213 is incorrectly plotted. Perhaps the last sample value is plotted instead of $\overline{x}$.

The most likely cause for the freak in Figure 9.5 is either a measuring error or a recording error. The other measurements in that sample are within limits.

The sample measurements at the freak in Figure 9.6 are incorrectly averaged.

All four measurements at the freak in Figure 9.7 are high. This most likely points to a temporary change in material.

9.3 BINOMIAL DISTRIBUTION APPLICATIONS

A binomial experiment is one in which there are only two outcomes. Tossing a coin is a binomial experiment: The two outcomes are a head and a tail. Any situation in which the outcomes can be categorized as successes or failures with no other possibilities can be classified as binomial. If the experiment is repeated several times and the individual probabilities of success and failure are known, probabilities of specific events can be determined. Binomial distribution tables are available for cases in which the individual probabilities range from .1 to .9, and algebraic structures can be used when probabilities are in hundredths or smaller units. For example, if a coin is tossed eight times, a binomial table may be used to find the probability of events such as getting five heads and three tails. Our present needs can be better served, however, by relying on a few basic rules of chance and applying them to any binomial situations that occur. The "and" and "or" rules of compound probability discussed in Section 7.2 can be applied to binomial probabilities.

The easiest illustration of a binomial problem is the coin-tossing problem. Suppose a coin is tossed five times. What is the chance of getting five heads? This can be answered by using the "and" rule for probability:

$$P(A \text{ and } B) = P(A) \times P(B)$$

When successive events occur, such as tossing a coin several times, and when the probability of any one of the events is unaffected by the preceding events, the probability of that successive event is found by multiplying the individual probabilities. If H is a head,

$$
\begin{aligned}
P(5H) &= P(H \text{ and } H \text{ and } H \text{ and } H \text{ and } H) \\
&= P(H) \times P(H) \times P(H) \times P(H) \times P(H) \\
P(H) &= .5 \\
P(5H) &= .5 \times .5 \times .5 \times .5 \times .5 \\
&= .01325
\end{aligned}
$$

The problem becomes more complicated when both heads and tails are involved in the outcome. Suppose the coin is tossed three times. Find the probability of getting two tails (T) and one head. There are three ways that this event can occur:

$$H \text{ and } T \text{ and } T$$
$$T \text{ and } H \text{ and } T$$
$$T \text{ and } T \text{ and } H$$

This combines the "or" rule, in which the probabilities are added,

$$P(A \text{ or } B) = P(A) + P(B)$$

with the "and" rule.

$$
\begin{aligned}
P(2T \text{ and } 1H) &= P(H \cdot T \cdot T) + (P(T \cdot H \cdot T) + P(T \cdot T \cdot H) \\
&= (.5 \times .5 \times .5) + (.5 \times .5 \times .5) + (.5 \times .5 \times .5) \\
&= 3 \times .125 \\
&= .375
\end{aligned}
$$

In the last equation, the 3 is the number of ways of getting two tails and one head. The probability, .125, is the same for each way.

What is the chance of getting two heads and three tails when the coin is tossed five times? This can happen in 10 ways:

$$
\begin{array}{ll}
H\,H\,T\,T\,T & T\,T\,H\,T\,H \\
H\,T\,H\,T\,T & T\,T\,T\,H\,H \\
H\,T\,T\,H\,T & T\,T\,H\,H\,T \\
H\,T\,T\,T\,H & T\,H\,H\,T\,T \\
T\,H\,T\,T\,H & T\,H\,T\,H\,T
\end{array}
$$

The probability of *each* of the 10 events is found by applying the "and" rule:

$$.5 \times .5 \times .5 \times .5 \times .5 = .03125$$

The probability that one of the 10 will occur is then

$$
\begin{aligned}
P(2H \text{ and } 3T) &= 10 \times .03125 \\
&= .3125
\end{aligned}
$$

The 10 represents the number of possible ways of getting two heads and three tails. The probability, .03125, is the same for each way.

Multiplying by the number of ways that the event can happen is a short cut for the "or" rule. The repeated addition of the "or" probability can be done by multiplying by the number of products that are being added, because they are all the same product.

In general, the binomial distribution is a probability distribution that applies to a two-outcome situation with repeated trials. The outcomes may be labeled specifically, such as heads and tails, or generally, such as success and failure. The repeated trials may be tossing a coin several times or considering the position of several consecutive points on a control chart. Of course, it's the latter application that pertains to SPC.

In a normal distribution most points should be close to the mean; 68 percent should be within one standard deviation of the center. How many points should be beyond the 1 σ boundaries before trouble is suspected to have changed the process measurements? The percent chance from both the normal curve and the binomial distribution can be used to answer this question. The binomial situation works because the position of a point on a control chart can be categorized in one of two ways: It is either inside the $\pm$ 1 σ boundary or outside.

Several points on the control chart that fall beyond the 1 σ limit may indicate a problem with the process because only 16 percent of the points are expected to be in that area on one side of the mean. One classification for this situation is called *freak patterns*. Testing for freak patterns involves one side of the center line. The control chart is informally divided into sections that are 1 σ in width. Because each control limit is 3 standard deviations from the center line, there are six sections on an $\bar{x}$ chart and usually five complete sections on an R chart. Remember, the lower control limit on the R chart can't be below zero, so the section below $\bar{R}$ is usually narrower than the 3 σ width above.

The 3 σ widths above and below the center line are divided into thirds as shown in Figure 9.8. Each section is now 1 σ wide. The 2 σ lines are sometimes referred to as the upper and lower warning lines and marked UWL and LWL. Each of the 1 σ widths are called zones and are lettered C, B, and A from the center line out.

The probability of getting four out of five points in zone B or beyond can be calculated using the binomial distribution application and information from the normal

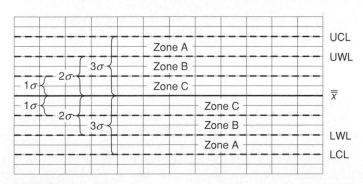

FIGURE 9.8
Control chart zones.

curve. The area beyond 1 σ can be found with the normal curve table in Appendix B. The z value is the number of standard deviations from the center, so $z = 1$. The area is .16, and the probability that a measurement falls in that tail area is .16. The total area under the curve is 1. The probability that a measurement is not in that area can be found by subtraction.

$$
\begin{array}{rl}
1.00 & \text{Total area under the curve} \\
- \ .16 & \text{Area in Zone B and beyond (on one side of } \bar{x}) \\
\hline
.84 & \text{Area outside of the zone B and beyond.}
\end{array}
$$

The shaded area under the curve in Figure 9.9 corresponds to the probability that a measurement is in zone B and beyond on one side of the mean, as defined in Figure 9.8.

FIGURE 9.9
Area under the normal curve beyond 1 σ.

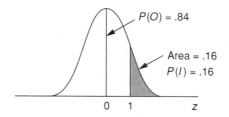

Let I represent a measurement inside zone B or beyond.

Let O represent a measurement outside that zone in the direction of the center.

This sets up the binomial situation: A point is in zone B or beyond with a probability of .16 or a point is not in that section with a probability of .84.

There are five ways in which four measurements may be inside and one measurement outside:

$$
\begin{array}{c}
I\ I\ I\ I\ O \\
I\ I\ I\ O\ I \\
I\ I\ O\ I\ I \\
I\ O\ I\ I\ I \\
O\ I\ I\ I\ I
\end{array}
$$

Each of the five ways represents an "and" probability such as

$$P(I \text{ and } I \text{ and } I \text{ and } I \text{ and } O) = .16 \times .16 \times .16 \times .16 \times .84$$
$$P(I \cdot I \cdot I \cdot I \cdot O) = .00055$$
$$P(4 \text{ out of 5 in B or beyond}) = 5 \times .00055$$
$$= .0028$$

The 5 represents the number of ways of getting four inside and one outside. The probability, .00055, is the same for each way.

The calculation shows that the chance of getting four out of five points in zone B or beyond in a random distribution is about .3 percent, a slim chance. When that occurs on a control chart, the question again arises, "Did a rare event occur, or did the process change somehow to cause that pattern?" The four of five pattern is considered a trouble indicator, and the chart should subsequently be marked as out of control and an investigation started to determine the cause.

Points that crowd the control limit line can also indicate trouble. Find the probability that two out of three points will be in the A zone or beyond on one side of the mean. The probability behind the two of three rule can be calculated in the same way as the previous four of five rule.

A z value of 2 corresponds to $2\,\sigma$ units from the center to zone A or beyond, as defined in Figure 9.8. According to the normal curve table, when $z = 2$, the tail area is .023. That is the probability that a measurement is inside zone A or beyond. Subtraction from 1 gives the probability that a measurement is outside of zone A on the center line side. This is illustrated in Figure 9.10.

FIGURE 9.10
Area under the normal curve beyond $2\,\sigma$.

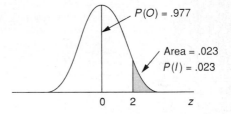

$$
\begin{array}{rl}
1.000 & \text{Total area under the normal curve} \\
-\ .023 & \text{Area in zone A or beyond on one side of mean} \\
\hline
.977 & \text{Area outside of zone A on the center line side}
\end{array}
$$

$$P(I) = .023$$
$$P(O) = .977$$

There are three ways in which there may be two measurements inside the zone and one measurement outside:

$$I\ I\ O$$
$$I\ O\ I$$
$$O\ I\ I$$

$$
\begin{aligned}
P(I \text{ and } I \text{ and } O) &= .023 \times .023 \times .997 \\
&= .00053
\end{aligned}
$$

$$
\begin{aligned}
P(2 \text{ of 3 in A or beyond}) &= 3 \times .00053 \\
&= .0016
\end{aligned}
$$

The probability of getting two of three points outside the warning line, or $2\,\sigma$ line, in a random distribution of points is .16 percent. This is used as a trouble indicator because the probability is so small that it is assumed that something in the process caused that distribution of points.

9.4 FREAK PATTERNS

The preceding work with the binomial distribution leads to two out-of-control tests that are labeled *freak patterns*.

Test 1: If four out of five consecutive points are in zone B or beyond on the same side of the center line, a freak pattern is formed.

Test 2: A freak pattern is formed if two out of three consecutive points fall in zone A or beyond on the same side of the center line.

The charts shown for Examples 9.2 through 9.8 (Figures 9.11 through 9.17) are repeated three times in each figure. Analyze (*a*) to see if you can spot the out-of-control situations. The out-of-control sections are circled in (*b*), and the out-of-control points are correctly marked with X's in (*c*).

EXAMPLE 9.2 Mark the points that are out of control in Figure 9.11.

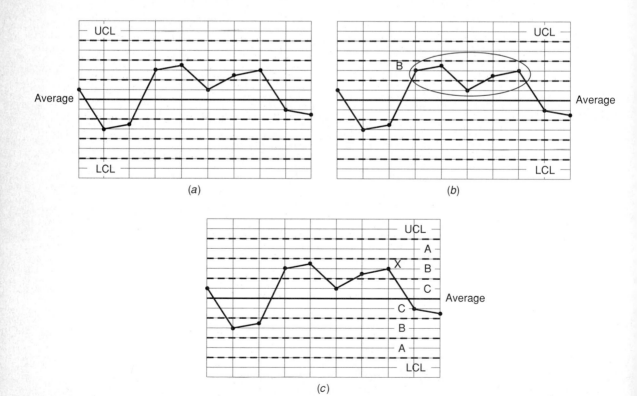

FIGURE 9.11
The chart for Example 9.2.

Solution

According to Test 1, any sequence of five consecutive points which has four of the points in zone B or beyond on the same side of the center line forms a four of five freak pattern. The fourth through eighth points on the chart satisfy that description. The second and third points in Figure 9.11 cannot be counted with the circled points because the four points in zone B or beyond have to be on the same side of the center line. Only one of the five points can be on the center line side of the B boundary. Try to interpret (*a*) as it's pictured in (*c*). The fifth point in the pattern is circled because it is the fourth point in the B zone. Cover (*b*) and (*c*) and see if the freak pattern in (*a*) is obvious.

EXAMPLE 9.3

Sometimes more than one out-of-control pattern exists within the same set of points. Analyze the points in Figure 9.12.

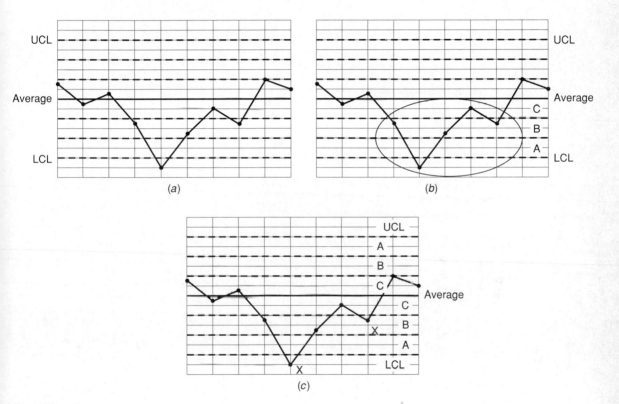

FIGURE 9.12
The chart for Example 9.3.

Solution

The first point marked in Figure 9.12(*c*) is classified as a freak because it is a single point beyond the control limit. The second point marked satisfies the four of five rule for a freak pattern. The first point marked is also part of the four of five freak pattern and is counted as one of the four points beyond the 1 σ line.

EXAMPLE 9.4   Mark the points that are out of control in Figure 9.13.

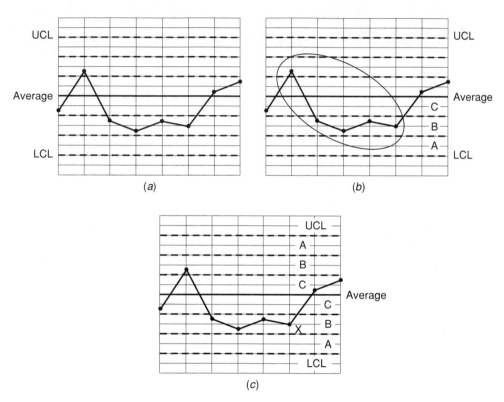

FIGURE 9.13
The chart for Example 9.4.

Solution
The four consecutive points in zone B in Figure 9.13 satisfy the four of five rule because the second point on the chart can be counted as the first of the five.

EXAMPLE 9.5   Mark the points that are out of control in Figure 9.14 (see page 229).

Solution
The first X in Figure 9.14 marks a freak. The second and third X's are part of a freak pattern satisfying the four of five rule. When the out-of-control pattern continues, the additional points that are out of control are marked too.

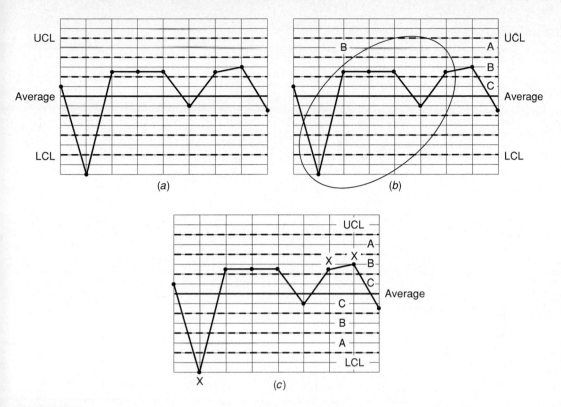

FIGURE 9.14
The chart for Example 9.5.

EXAMPLE 9.6 Identify the points that are out of control in Figure 9.15 (see page 230).

Solution
In Figure 9.15(*b*) the circled section shows that a freak pattern is formed by the two of three rule. Two of the three points circled are in zone A. The third point in that pattern is marked with an X to signal the out-of-control situation.

EXAMPLE 9.7 Identify the points that are out of control in Figure 9.16 (see page 231).

Solution
In Figure 9.16 a freak pattern is formed according to the two of three rule. The first three points circled satisfy the two of three rule. The fourth point is part of the same out-of-control pattern and is marked as well.

EXAMPLE 9.8 Mark the points that are out of control in Figure 9.17 (see page 232).

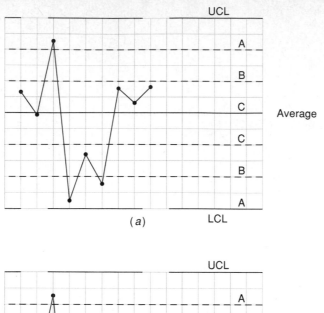

(a)

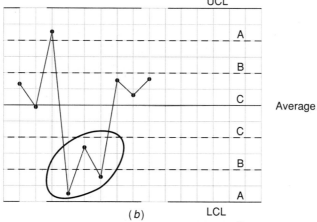

(b)

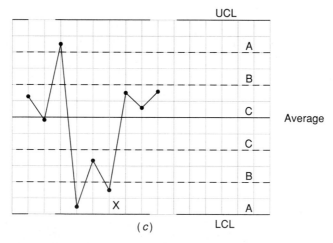

(c)

FIGURE 9.15
The chart for Example 9.6.

230

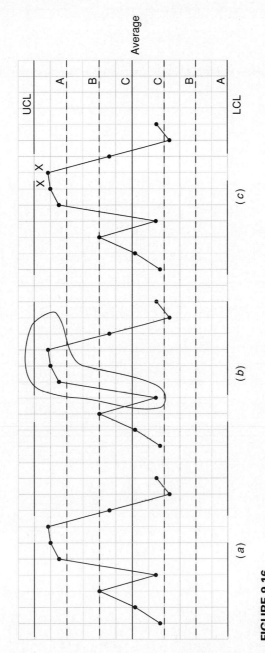

FIGURE 9.16
The chart for Example 9.7.

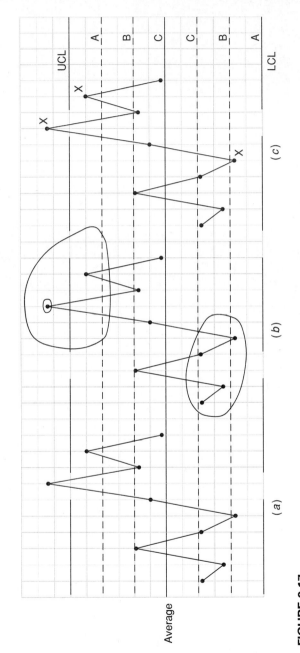

FIGURE 9.17
The chart for Example 9.8.

Solution
There are three different out-of-control situations in Figure 9.17. The first group circled in (b) is a freak pattern by the four of five rule; only the fifth point in that group is marked. The second group circled has a freak embedded within a two of three freak pattern. The freak is marked along with the third point in the freak pattern.

Each out-of-control pattern has its own list of common causes. Some process problems may produce more than one out-of-control pattern, and, consequently, that problem will be on more than one list. The following chart lists the most common causes of freak patterns.

R chart:

- Operator errors
- Poor technique owing to improper training or instruction
- Excessive vibration and increased variability caused by inadequate fixtures
- Inconsistent materials or materials from different suppliers
- Defective parts used in assembly
- Measurement or gauge problems
- "Chasing" the target measurement and excessive variability caused by overadjustment of the machine

$\bar{x}$ chart with the R chart in control:

- The preceding possible causes
- Planned rework resulting from deliberate crowding of one side of the specifications as a hedge against producing scrap

p chart:

- Poor maintenance of the machine
- Defective parts in an assembly
- Variations in sample size
- Nonrandom sampling
- Sampling different distributions

9.5 SHIFTS

Shifts, sets of seven or more consecutive points that are all on one side of the center line, indicate that the center of the distribution has changed. Something was introduced to the process that changed the whole process. Shifts are usually temporary. The points on the control chart change to a different level for a while, then change back again. When diagnosing a shift, look for something that affects the whole process. Any special cause of the shift in the process is generally in one of six major categories:

Operator	Method	Machine
Material	Tooling	Environment

A change in one of those categories can affect the entire process and shift the points on the control chart.

Shifts can indicate improvements as well as problems in the process. A shift away from the target line on the $\bar{x}$ chart signifies that the parts being measured and charted are now too large or too small, depending on the direction of the shift. A shift *up* on the R chart is a trouble indicator because product variation has increased. However, a shift *down* on the R chart indicates process improvement: Variation has decreased. A shift on a p chart may be an improvement or worsening of the defective proportion, but quick judgments are not advisable because a change in the inspection criteria, for example, has an accompanying shift on the p chart without any real change in the product.

The seventh point and any following points in the same shift pattern should be marked as out of control. This is illustrated in Figure 9.18.

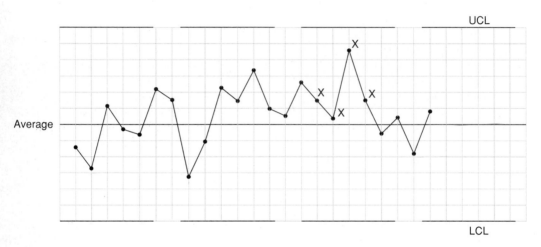

FIGURE 9.18
A shift.

The mathematical justification for the seven in a row rule is based on a random pattern of points about a center line. Each point has a 50 percent chance of being on one side of the center line. Points that appear to fall on the line are not really an exception to this because both the measurement and the calculation of the average can theoretically be carried to enough places (such as thousandths or ten-thousandths) to show whether the point is above or below the line. The chance of getting seven consecutive points above the line can be calculated with the "and" rule.

$$P(7 \text{ points above}) = P(\text{point 1 is above } and \text{ point 2 is above } and \ldots)$$
$$= .5 \times .5 \times .5 \times .5 \times .5 \times .5 \times .5 = (.5)^7$$
$$= .008$$
$$= .8 \text{ percent}$$

The probability is small enough to classify the event of getting seven consecutive points on one side of the center line as a rare event. As before, with the other patterns, this is classified as a trouble indicator. Something has changed the process and the cause of the change must be found.

The following are possible causes of shifts.

R chart:

- A careless or poorly trained operator
- Maintenance problems
- Change in material:
  Poorer material will shift up
  Better material will shift down
  A mixture of material will shift up
- Fixtures not holding the work in place
- Downshifts caused by better labor quality
- Downshifts owing to improved process capability

$\bar{x}$ chart when *R* chart is in control:

- A change in the machine setting or speed
- A new operator or inspector
- A change in method
- A new lot of material
- A new setup
- Use of a different gauge

p chart:

- Any changes listed for the $\bar{x}$ chart
- A change in standards

The start of a shift is not obvious. Although the seventh point in the pattern is the official designator of the shift, the actual process shift may have begun at any of the preceding points in the shift pattern. It is not always at the first point in the pattern because the first few points may have been part of the normal random fluctuations. Be sure to check the process log at each point in the shift pattern.

EXAMPLE 9.9   Identify the points that are out of control in Figure 9.19 (see page 236). Cover (*b*) and analyze (*a*) first.

Solution

The first point marked in Figure 9.19(*b*) is for a freak pattern using the two of three rule. That freak pattern is embedded in a shift, and the second and third X's mark the shift.

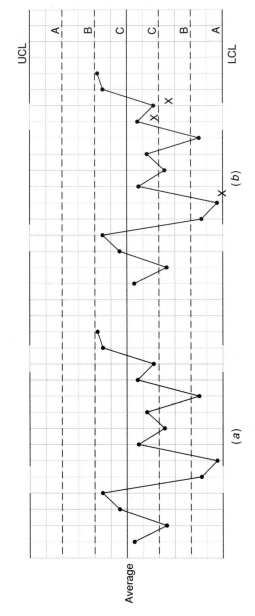

FIGURE 9.19
The chart for Example 9.9.

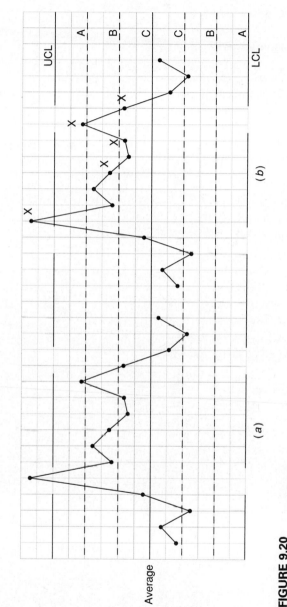

FIGURE 9.20

The chart for Example 9.10 (see page 238).

EXAMPLE 9.10 Identify the points that are out of control in Figure 9.20 on page 237. Cover (*b*) and analyze (*a*) first.

Solution

There are three out-of-control patterns in Figure 9.20. The first point marked is a freak, and the second point marked indicates a freak pattern by the four of five rule. The seventh, eighth, and ninth points, the next three marked points, denote a shift pattern. Figure 9.20 also illustrates that freaks and freak patterns can be forerunners to a shift pattern and can call attention to the trouble before the shift may be recognized. It is also important to realize that shift patterns are functions of time. For example, if samples are taken hourly, the shift pattern may not be recognized until several hours after the process shift has occurred. If a shift is suspected after three or four points have started the pattern, a change to more frequent sampling will verify the shift sooner.

EXAMPLE 9.11 Using the list below, identify the most likely cause for the points that are out of control in Figures 9.21 through 9.24 on pages 238 through 240.

       1. Machine adjustment
       2. Arithmetic error
       3. Improvement in process capability
       4. New operator

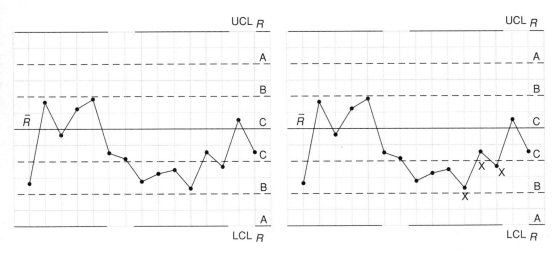

FIGURE 9.21
A chart for Example 9.11.

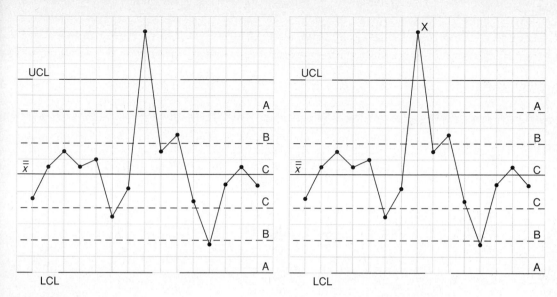

FIGURE 9.22
A chart for Example 9.11.

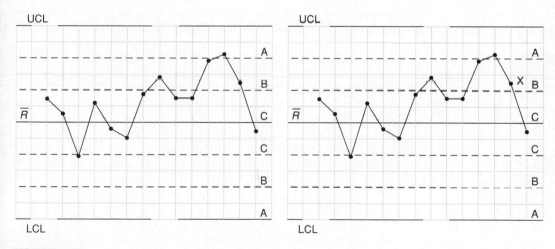

FIGURE 9.23
A chart for Example 9.11.

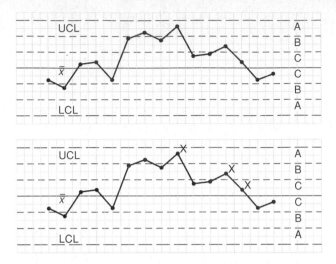

FIGURE 9.24
A chart for Example 9.11.

Solution
Figure 9.21, an *R* chart, has a freak pattern by the four of five rule that is part of a shift. The basic pattern is the shift pattern. Because the shift is down on an *R* chart, variability has decreased. Look for something that has improved the process. Choice 3 from the list of causes is the correct one.

There is one freak on the $\bar{\bar{x}}$ chart in Figure 9.22. The other points seem randomly well behaved, so the most likely cause is 2, the arithmetic error.

Figure 9.23 shows a shift upward on a range chart. This is an indication that variation has increased. The most likely cause from the list is a new operator, 4.

The $\bar{x}$ chart in Figure 9.24 has a shift as the main trouble pattern. The first X marks a freak pattern by the four of five rule. This could be caused by either a machine adjustment, 1, or a new operator, 4.

9.6 RUNS AND TRENDS

A *run* occurs when several points steadily increase or decrease on a control chart. Seven is the usual number that is used to indicate a run, but 10 of 11 may be used as well. There may also be a gradual trend with fluctuations within it, but identifying trends becomes a judgment call because they don't have a specific number requirement. In the case of a gradual trend, the process is usually labeled out of control because of some other pattern, such as a shift, before it is classified as a trend.

Figure 9.25 shows a run: Seven or more points are steadily increasing. The seventh increasing point is marked along with the next two points, which are part of the same run pattern. The base point of the run, the eighth point from the left on the chart, is not counted as part of the run.

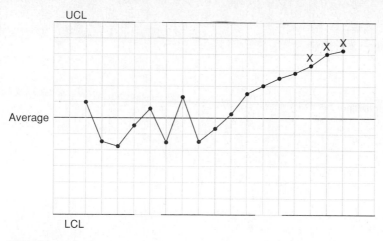

FIGURE 9.25
A run.

The general pattern in Figure 9.26 is a trend (see page 242). The random fluctuations that occur within it, however, make it fail both the seven in a row run test and the 10 of 11 run test. Its "official" out-of-control pattern is a shift, with seven or more consecutive points above the center line. The distinction between the run pattern and the shift pattern can be important in analyzing the cause for the out-of-control situation. The shift classification implies that something in the process suddenly changed. The trend classification implies that there is a gradual change occurring. The two different clues can lead in different directions when the source of the trouble is unknown.

A run suggests that something in the process is changing gradually. If the run is on an $\bar{x}$ chart and the range chart is in control, the problem may be tool wear. If it's a boring tool such as a drill, gradual wear will make the holes smaller and the run will be in a downward direction. If it's a cutting tool, gradual wear will make the pieces larger and the run will move upward.

A run can point out good news as well as bad. On an R chart, a downward trend indicates that variation is decreasing in the product. This may signal process improvements owing to use of SPC, better operator training, or improved maintenance. An upward run on an R chart signals that things are getting worse: Variation is increasing. Fixtures may be loosening, operator fatigue may be setting in, or tool wear may be causing more variability.

The probability calculation for seven steadily increasing (or decreasing) points uses the same concept that is used with the shift: The "and" rule applies. The symbol ">" represents "larger than,"

P(7 increasing) $= P$ (first point $>$ base point *and* second $>$ first *and* third
$>$ second *and* ... *and* seventh $>$ sixth)

By the "and" rule, the individual probabilities are multiplied.

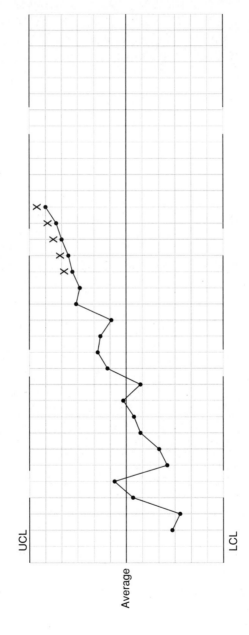

FIGURE 9.26
The general pattern is a run, but the official pattern is a shift.

$$P(7 \text{ increasing}) = P \text{ (first } > \text{ base point)} \times P(\text{second } > \text{ first})$$
$$\times \cdots \times P(\text{seventh } > \text{ sixth})$$

The individual probabilities are impossible to determine using the normal distribution because the probability that a second point is larger than the first depends on the position of the first. This is illustrated in Figure 9.27.

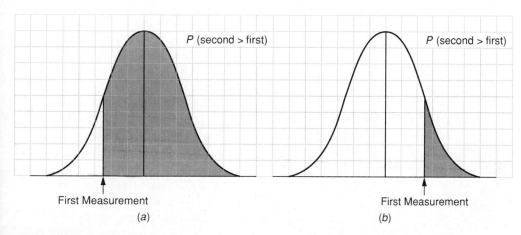

FIGURE 9.27
The shaded areas show the probability that the second measurement is larger than the first for two different first measurements.

Figure 9.27 shows two different positions of the first measurement on the measurement scale. Drawing (a) shows the first measurement value less than the average value, and (b) shows the first measurement larger than the average value. In each diagram the shaded area represents the probability that the second measurement is larger than the first. There are so many possible positions for the first variable that it is impossible to tell exactly what the probability will be. The same situation occurs when considering the probability that the third measurement is larger than the second or the fourth is larger than the third. A different approach to the problem is needed.

A trend implies a gradual change in measurement from some base level. If there is some temporary working average at that base level, in case the process isn't at $\overline{\overline{x}}$, then diagram (b) in Figure 9.27 will represent the probability that a second measurement is larger than the first in an increasing trend. Each new point will be further above that initial, average value, and the probability that it is larger than the previous point will therefore be less than .5. Using .5 for each probability value will ensure that the true probability will be less than the calculated value. The symbol for "less than" is "<".

$P(\text{1st point} > \text{base point}) < .5$

$P(\text{2nd point} > \text{1st point}) < .5$

$P(\text{3rd point} > \text{2nd point}) < .5$

$P(\text{7 increasing points}) = P(\text{1st} > \text{base value}) \times P(\text{2nd} > \text{1st})$
$$\times P(\text{3rd} > \text{2nd}) \times \cdots \times P(\text{7th} > \text{6th})$$

$P(\text{7 increasing points}) < .5 \times .5 \times \cdots \times .5 = (.5)^7$

$< .008$

The probability of getting seven increasing points or seven decreasing points in a row is less than .8 percent, a rare event. Therefore, this pattern is an indicator that the process is changing.

The probability for the 10 of 11 rule combines the "and" rule for the 11 consecutive points with the "or" rule, which takes into account the fact that the one point that isn't increasing (or decreasing) with the others could be first *or* second *or* third or any of the 11 points. If *I* represents increasing points and *D* represents decreasing, the sequence of points will be, for example,

$$I\ I\ I\ I\ I\ I\ I\ I\ I\ I\ D$$
$$\text{or} \quad I\ I\ I\ I\ I\ I\ I\ I\ I\ D\ I$$
$$\text{or} \quad I\ I\ I\ I\ I\ I\ I\ I\ D\ I\ I$$
$$\text{or} \quad I\ I\ I\ I\ I\ I\ I\ D\ I\ I\ I$$

These are four of 11 possibilities.

$$P(\text{10 of 11 increasing}) < 11 \times (.5)^{11}$$
$$< .0054$$

Eleven is the number of possibilities, and each way has a probability less than .5. The probability of getting 10 out of 11 points that are steadily increasing (or decreasing) is therefore less than .5 percent.

The following list summarizes the specifications for runs and trends.

1. Seven consecutive points that steadily increase or decrease indicate a run.
2. Ten out of eleven points that steadily increase or decrease form a run.
3. A long fluctuating pattern that is steadily increasing or decreasing is a trend.

Runs and trends may stem from a variety of causes:

R chart, *upward* trend (process deteriorating):

- Gradually increasing material variability
- Loosening fixtures

- Operator fatigue (check day-to-day time patterns)
- Machine wear
- Gauge wear

R chart, *downward* trend (process improving):

- Improvements owing to SPC and the quality program
- Better training of operators
- Better maintenance program
- Gradual introduction of better material

$\bar{x}$ chart with the R chart in control:

- Gradual introduction of new material
- Tool wear
- Machine due for adjustment.

p chart:

- Changing defective proportion
- Changing requirements or standards

9.7 CYCLES

Cycles on a control chart are patterns that repeat on a regular basis. They signal that something is systematically affecting the process. The key to finding the problem that is causing the cycles is concentration on the factors that change the process periodically. Power fluctuations, varying speeds on conveyor belts, operator fatigue patterns, and temperature changes are likely causes.

There is no number rule for cycles; it involves a recognition of repeating patterns. Figure 9.28 illustrates the cycle pattern (see page 246). The figure also shows several out-of-control points by the two of three, the four of five, and the shift patterns. Cycles may be short-term in duration and clearly show up on a control chart such as in Figure 9.28. It's also possible to have long-range cycles in which several or many charts must be considered simultaneously. To check on long-term cycles such as seasonal effects, it may be necessary to condense data from many charts to one. This can be done by charting daily, weekly, or monthly averages.

In some cases, trouble patterns of one type exist within another. For example, runs or trends may be the trouble pattern diagnosed on a chart, but they may be just one section of a cycle pattern. Spotting the overall cycle pattern may add that extra clue needed to diagnose the process trouble. Looking at the data from a different perspective provides information that can be used to solve the problem.

Repeating patterns are usually quite obvious when they occur on a single chart. When several charts are compared simultaneously, they should be checked for repeating patterns.

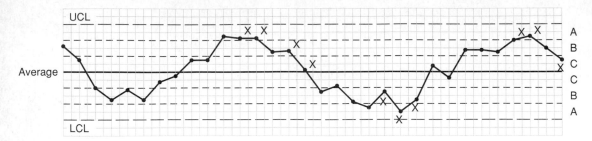

FIGURE 9.28
A cycle.

There are various causes of cycles:

R chart:

- Operator fatigue and shift changes
- Measurement gauge rotation.
- Eccentric tooling wear, periodic changes
- Maintenance schedules
- Periodic speed changes

$\bar{x}$ chart with the *R* chart in control:

- The listed *R* chart causes
- Seasonal or environmental changes
- Worn threads and locking devices
- Power fluctuations
- Reliance on different suppliers

p chart:

- Material variations
- Different suppliers
- Change in sampling methods

A manufacturing process is often likened to a river or a stream with the product becoming more complete as it moves downstream. The workers who are positioned downstream from a specific process point are the internal customers. A good quality program emphasizes a quality product for both the downstream customer and the eventual purchaser of the finished product. When an out-of-control pattern shows up on a control chart the problem will be at the process point being charted or at some point(s) upstream. When all the possible solutions at the process point have been eliminated and the problem still exists, an upstream search for the problem source must be undertaken.

9.8 GROUPING

This is another case in which one trouble classification may be embedded in another. *Grouping*, or *bunching*, occurs when the points on a chart occur in clusters. Large fluctuations between clusters may qualify as one of the instability patterns: freaks or freak patterns. However, the overall pattern of grouping may be the pattern that provides the necessary information for solving the problem.

Grouping indicates that several different distributions are present. They may be strictly upstream problems that are converging at a point in the process or may signify inconsistent workmanship or materials.

Figure 9.29 illustrates bunching. The circles are included for emphasis. The only out-of-control point marks a freak pattern within the bunching pattern.

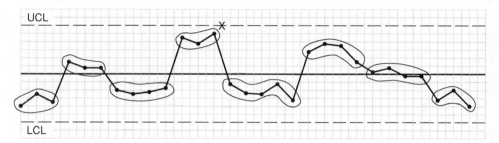

FIGURE 9.29
Bunching.

The causes of bunching are the following:

R chart:

- Differences in work quality
- Inconsistent materials

x̄ chart with the R chart in control:

- Differences in work quality
- Inconsistent materials
- Shifting fixtures
- Inconsistencies in method
- Several upstream problems

EXAMPLE 9.12   In Figure 9.30 on page 248, cover (*b*) while you analyze (*a*).

Solution

The main problem structure is the bunching that has been emphasized with the circles in Figure 9.30. The first X marks a freak pattern by the four of five rule. The second X is a freak as well as a continuation of the four of five pattern. The third X can be considered

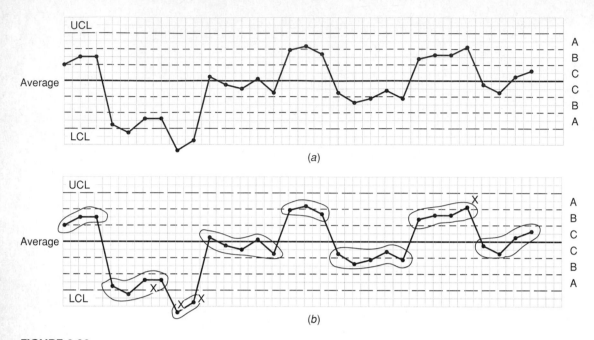

FIGURE 9.30
The chart for Example 9.12.

a continuation of the four of five pattern or as the third point in a two of three freak pattern. The last X marks a freak pattern by the four of five rule. The bunches seem to follow a cyclic pattern as well.

EXAMPLE 9.13   In Figure 9.31 cover (b) while you analyze (a).

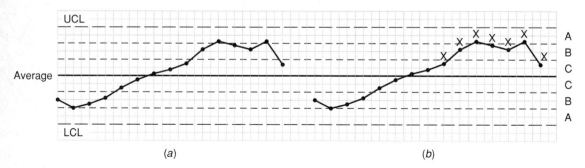

FIGURE 9.31
The chart for Example 9.13.

Solution
In Figure 9.31, the main pattern is a run. The first three X's mark the run. The next four X's simultaneously show a shift and a freak pattern by the four of five rule. The shift is

the pattern of secondary importance because the process held at that new level after the gradual run brought it there.

EXAMPLE 9.14   In Figure 9.32, cover (*b*) and analyze (*a*).

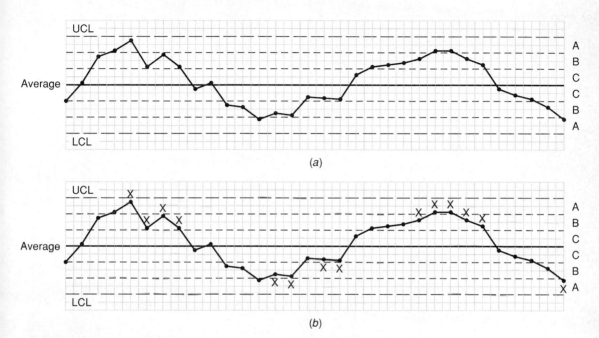

FIGURE 9.32
The chart for Example 9.14.

Solution
The main pattern in Figure 9.32 is a cycle. Within that pattern, the first X marks a two of three freak pattern and the second through fourth X's mark a freak pattern by the four of five rule. The next pair of X's also marks out-of-control points by the four of five rule; these points are followed by two X's marking a shift pattern. The cluster of five X's starts as a freak pattern by the four of five rule with the latter three points simultaneously fitting the shift pattern. The last X signifies a run.

9.9 INSTABILITY

An erratic pattern that has large fluctuations on a control chart is classified as *instability*, or *unstable mixture*. Freaks or freak patterns may exist within the erratic pattern, but the main message comes from the extended and frequent ups and downs. Instability is generally hard to track because it usually has several causes. A pattern of instability often indicates that the trouble lies upstream from the chart that indicates the trouble. For example, there may be several product distributions at an assembly point, all capable of changing with respect to each other. The trouble may be in one or several of the separate pieces. Unstable mixture, illustrated in Figure 9.33, has a good, descriptive name. The two X's mark freaks that occur within the unstable mixture pattern.

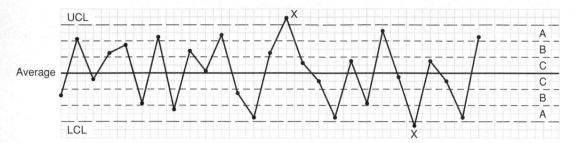

FIGURE 9.33
An unstable mixture.

When a process is in statistical control, 68 percent of the points on the control chart, roughly two-thirds of the data, should be within one standard deviation of the mean. Also, only 5 percent of the points should lie in the two 1σ bands that are adjacent to the control limit lines (A zones). To test for unstable mixture, look for violations in that normal pattern. This process consists of a search for two characteristics:

1. More than one-third of the points lie outside the *center* $\pm 1\sigma$ band *or* more than 5 percent of the points fall in or beyond the *outer* 1σ bands.
2. The chart has a steep, zig-zag pattern.

Look for several causes of instability, often upstream. The following are possible causes.

R charts, $\bar{x}$ charts, p charts:

- Frequent breakdowns and start-ups (R and $\bar{x}$)
- Overadjustment ($\bar{x}$)
- A mixture of materials or parts from different machines or spindles (R and $\bar{x}$ and p)
- Loose fixtures (R and $\bar{x}$)
- Poor sampling procedures ($\bar{x}$)
- Inconsistent materials (R and $\bar{x}$)
- A faulty gauge (R and $\bar{x}$)
- Inconsistent inspection standards (p)

9.10 STABLE MIXTURES

A mixture pattern that has erratic ups and downs similar to the instability pattern but has very few points in the middle of the chart is a *stable mixture*. The points crowd or overlap the control limits. This pattern usually indicates a mixing of two different stable distributions: one for the upper set of points and one for the lower set. Five or more consecutive points outside the C zones (beyond the 1 σ lines) on either side of the center line signal a stable mixture pattern, as Figure 9.34 illustrates. The first X in Figure 9.34 signals a two of three freak pattern, and the remaining X's indicate a stable mixture pattern.

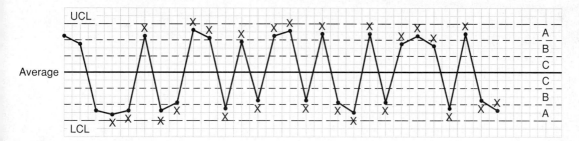

FIGURE 9.34
A stable mixture.

The probability of getting five consecutive points beyond the C zones can be calculated using the "and" rule.

P(5 points beyond the C zones) = P(1st and 2nd and 3rd and 4th and 5th are beyond)

Using the normal distribution, the probability of one point falling beyond the C zones is the chance that it will fall in either of the shaded sections indicated in Figure 9.35. The boundaries of the C zones are 1 σ from the average value, which correspond to z values of ± 1. The number of standard deviations from the center is z.

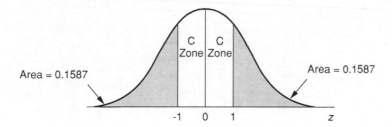

FIGURE 9.35
The probability of a point falling beyond $\pm 1 \sigma$.

When $z = 1$, the shaded tail area on one side is .1587. Double this for the probability that a point is in either shaded area.

$$.1587 \times 2 = .3174$$
$$P(\text{5 points beyond C}) = .3174 \times .3174 \times .3174 \times .3174 \times .3174$$
$$= (.3174)^5 = .00322$$
$$= .32 \text{ percent}$$

The small probability classifies this as a rare event and an indicator that something is affecting the process.

Test for a stable mixture by looking for two characteristics:

1. Five or more consecutive points that are outside the center $\pm$ 1 σ band
2. Steep zig-zag lines on the control chart with very few points in the middle of the chart

A stable mixture pattern on R, $\bar{x}$, or p charts may be caused by mixing two stable distributions from the following list:

- Different suppliers
- Different inspectors
- Different operators
- Different lines
- Different lots
- Different gauges or inspection standards

9.11 STRATIFICATION

In a *stratification* pattern, the points hug the averages line on a control chart. There is a notable absence of points near the control limits. The rule for spotting this pattern is to look for 14 or more consecutive points in the two C zones, within $\pm$ 1 σ of the average value. Figure 9.36 illustrates a stratification pattern on a control chart.

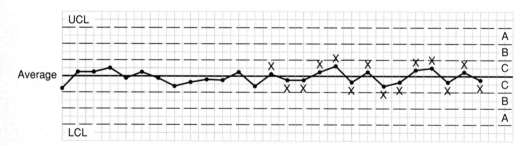

FIGURE 9.36
Stratification.

To the untrained eye, a stratification pattern seems to identify a smoothly running process. If the process has really improved, however, a downward trend or shift on the range chart will accompany the stratification pattern on the $\bar{x}$ chart. The follow-up step calls for new calculations for $\bar{x}$ and $\bar{R}$ at the new level of control. A recalculation of the control limits will make both the $\bar{x}$ and R chart look normal again with two-thirds of the points in the $\pm$ 1 σ center strip and the other one-third beyond. Of course, the new charts will reflect the tighter control of the improved process because the control limits will be numerically closer to the average line for both $\bar{x}$ and R.

Stratification on the $\bar{x}$ chart without the downward move on the range chart denotes trouble because it is a non-normal pattern. There may be a measuring problem: The measuring scale may be too crude for the job. Two general rules of measurement must be followed. The first, called the *rule of ten*, states that the measuring instrument should measure to one-tenth of the tolerance. The second states that there should be at least 10 units of measurement between $\bar{x} - 3\ \sigma$ and $\bar{x} + 3\ \sigma$. Initially, if a process hasn't been charted, there should be at least 10 units of measurement within the tolerance. Then as the process capability improves, the rule of 10 units or more between $\bar{x} \pm 3\ \sigma$ should be used.

EXAMPLE 9.15

Given the tolerance .215 ± .001, what unit of measurement should be on the gauges?

Solution

$$\frac{\text{Tolerance}}{10} = \frac{.002}{10}$$
$$= .0002$$

The gauges should be marked in 2 ten-thousandths.

EXAMPLE 9.16

Suppose the process capability uses 65 percent of the tolerance (PCR = .65, a B process according to Table 6 in Appendix B). What should the unit of measurement be?

Solution

$$\frac{\text{Tolerance} \times .65}{10} = \frac{.002 \times .65}{10}$$
$$= \frac{.0013}{10}$$
$$= .00013$$

The gauges should be marked in ten-thousandths.

Another source of trouble that may result in stratification is dishonest recording. An employee may arbitrarily record values close to the average to try to look good or may rework pieces that aren't good enough and record the better, reworked measurement. People working in purchasing or incoming inspection should take extra care to spot doctored control charts.

A third possible cause for stratified $\bar{x}$ charts is nonrandom sampling. This sometimes happens inadvertently when a sampler tries to make sure that each of several different distributions are represented in every sample. For example, in a multiple spindle operation, if each sample has one piece from each spindle, the range may be large owing to large differences in the individual spindle averages. If the variability on each spindle is low, the average from each sample will be close to $\bar{\bar{x}}$, and the control limits, calculated with $\bar{R}$, will be far from the center line. This may result in a stratified pattern. A stratified control chart may therefore show that several different distributions are being mixed in a nonrandom, representative way.

To summarize, possible causes of stratification are the following:

R charts, $\bar{x}$ charts:

- Falsification of data
- Gauge scale too crude for the job
- Nonrandom, representative sampling

The probability calculation for the 14-point rule uses the probabilities from the normal curve and the "and" rule. If $z = 1$, the tail area in the normal curve is .1587. Doubled, .3174, it is the combined tail area for both sides. The total area under the curve is 1, so the area in the middle $\pm 1\ \sigma$ section is

$$
\begin{array}{r}
1.0000 \\
-\ .3174 \\
\hline
.6826
\end{array}
$$

The chance of getting a single measurement in the center $\pm 1\ \sigma$ section is .6826.

The probability of getting 14 consecutive measurements in that center section is calculated using the "and" rule.

$$
\begin{aligned}
P(14 \text{ in the C zones}) &= P(\text{first in } and \text{ second in } and \text{ third in} \\
&\qquad and \ldots and \text{ fourteenth in}) \\
&= P(\text{first in}) \times P(\text{second in}) \times \cdots \times P(\text{fourteenth in}) \\
&= (.6826)^{14} \\
&= .0048
\end{aligned}
$$

The probability, about .5 percent, is small enough to classify this as a rare event and an indicator of trouble.

EXAMPLE 9.16

For each of the charts in Figures 9.37 to 9.41 on pages 255 through 257, cover (b) and analyze (a).

Solution

Figure 9.37 shows a stable mixture. After the eighth point on the chart, there is an absence of points in the C zones. The first and last X's mark a freak pattern by the two of three rule. The other X's show the stable mixture when five consecutive points

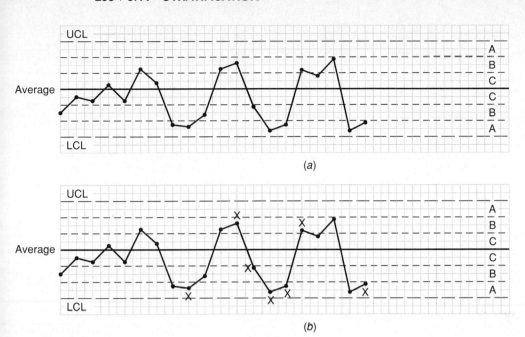

FIGURE 9.37
A chart for Example 9.16.

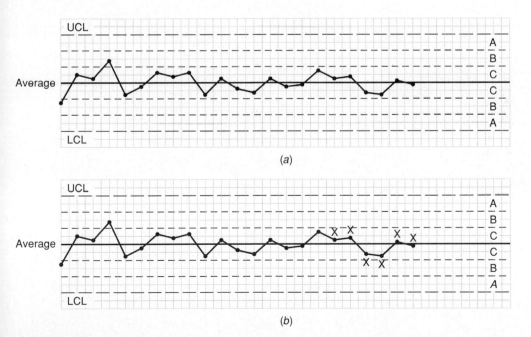

FIGURE 9.38
A chart for Example 9.16.

are beyond the C zones. This chart may also be interpreted as bunching within a cycle pattern. The analyses lead in different directions in the search for a solution. The mixture analysis will attempt to identify two separate distributions that may have worked their way into the process. The cyclic bunching approach suggests a time analysis, an operator check, and possibly a gauge check. Both approaches may lead to the conclusion that material from two different lines or suppliers was being systematically mixed.

The X's in Figure 9.38 mark the out-of-control points by the 14-point stratification rule.

In Figure 9.39 the main problem structure seems to be bunching. Within that overall bunching format, however, are shifts, freaks, and freak patterns. The X's are numbered for easy reference. The first two X's show a freak pattern by the two of three rule. The third X marks a freak pattern by the four of five rule. The fourth, fifth, and sixth X's may be part of a freak pattern by the four of five rule, and the fifth and sixth indicate a shift. The seventh and eighth X's signal a stable mixture. For the group of X's on the right, X number nine marks a freak pattern by the two of three rule, and number 10 indicates a stable mixture. The next three are all freaks, and the last two point out a shift.

The main problem in Figure 9.40 is instability. The erratic ups and downs and the fact that 16 of the 22 points, or 73 percent of them, are beyond the $\pm 1 \sigma$ center strip signal a strong possibility that several factors are affecting the process. Within the instability pattern the first X marks a freak and the other two mark freak patterns by the two of three rule.

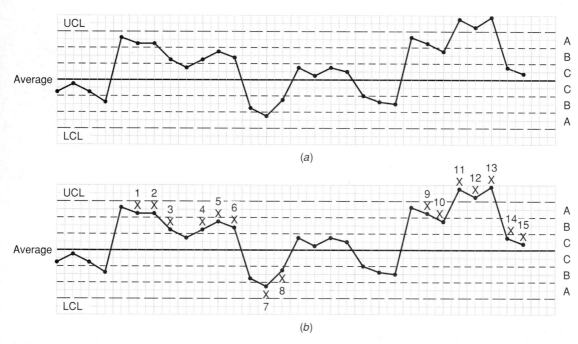

(a)

(b)

FIGURE 9.39
A chart for Example 9.16.

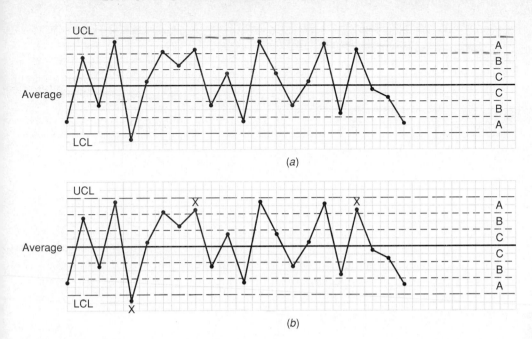

FIGURE 9.40
A chart for Example 9.16.

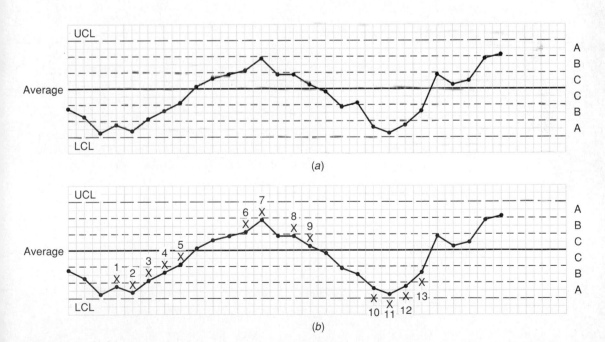

FIGURE 9.41
A chart for Example 9.16.

The X's in Figure 9.41 are numbered for easy reference (see page 257). A cycle is the basic pattern, within which shifts and freak patterns exist. The first four X's show freak patterns by the two of three rule and the four of five rule, and the fourth and fifth are part of a shift. The first two X's in the middle group, numbers 6 and 7, mark a run; the next two, a shift. Numbers 10 and 11 show a run, number 12 is part of a freak pattern by the two of three rule, and the last marks both a freak pattern by the four of five rule and a shift.

9.12 USING CONTROL CHART PATTERNS IN PROBLEM SOLVING

These basic control chart patterns that have been identified signal process changes or process troubles. For most patterns, a rule based on the laws of probability dictates the minimum number of points needed to declare an out-of-control situation. Each probability calculation shows that if the process is behaving normally, the chance of getting that specific point pattern is less than 1 percent, a rare event. The probability calculation leads to two possible conclusions:

1. The process is still behaving normally and a rare event occurred when the point pattern was formed.
2. Something affected the process and caused it to change. It's no longer in statistical control.

The second conclusion is always assumed to be correct, and the process is investigated to find the cause for the out-of-control point pattern. Investigators should be aware, however, that occasionally (in fewer than 1 percent of the cases) the first conclusion is the correct one. The probability calculation for each point pattern gives the chance of getting a false signal from the control charts.

This chapter emphasizes individual charts and their interpretations. It is important to realize, however, that on-the-Job application of these concepts is usually more complex than simplified textbook examples. Chart analysis provides clues that can be effectively used to solve problems. Each out-of-control pattern has primary causes, but when a direct, easy solution isn't apparent, tunnel vision will only frustrate efforts. The problem-solving team should keep the broad picture of the process in mind. Each phase of the process is interconnected with several others, so problem solving often becomes a systematic, upstream search.

When digging for the cause of a tough problem, remember that troubles with the process will always fall into one or more of the basic categories:

Operators	Machines
Methods	Materials
Tooling	Environment

At each step of the investigation, starting at the point at which the charts indicate trouble, use the chart clues and the six basic categories. Decide which categories apply most directly at that point in the process and whether the out-of-control pattern may indicate trouble in those categories.

Many of the topics in the following chapter come into play during the search for the root cause of problems. Critical at this point is a thorough understanding of the entire process. Teamwork, combined with the various problem-solving procedures at each process point, is needed for an effective search.

EXERCISES

1–17. Analyze the following control charts and mark the points that are out of control. List three possible causes for each out-of-control chart.

1. Figure 9.42

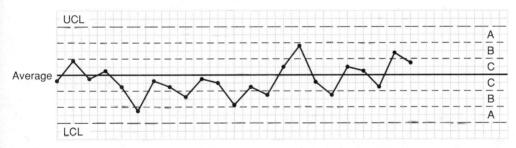

2. Figure 9.43

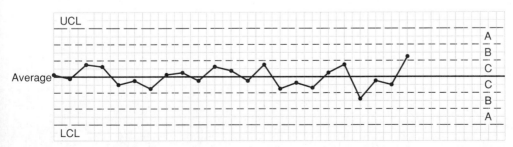

3. Figure 9.44

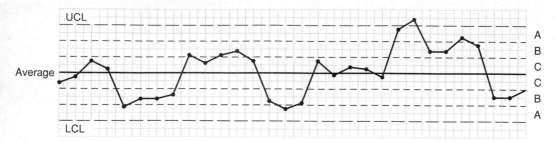

4. Figure 9.45

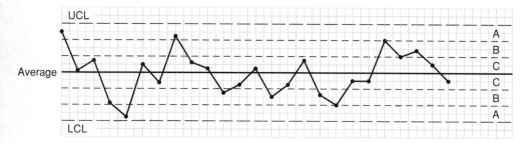

5. Figure 9.46

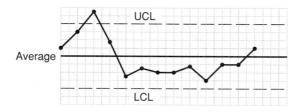

6. Figure 9.47

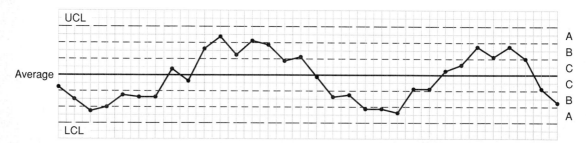

7. Figure 9.48

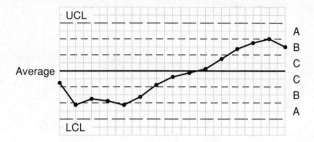

8. Figure 9.49

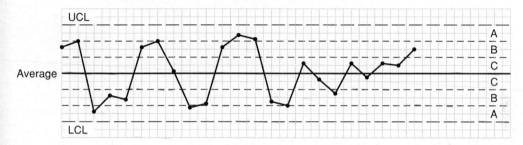

9. Figure 9.50

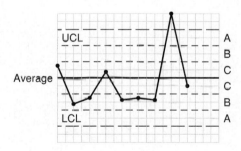

10. Figure 9.51

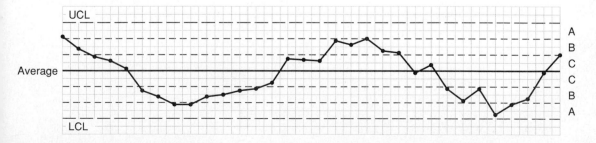

11. Figure 9.52

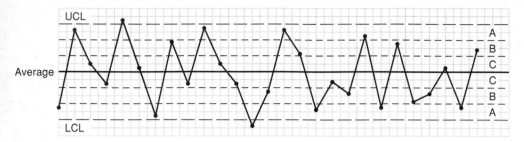

12. Figure 9.53

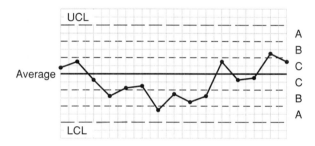

13. Figure 9.54

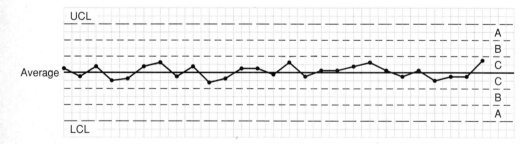

14. Figure 9.55

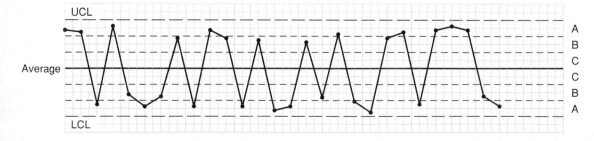

15. Figure 9.56

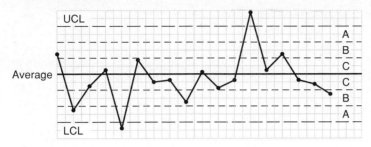

16. Figure 9.57

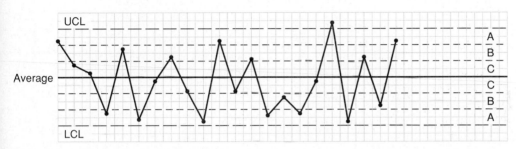

17. Figure 9.58

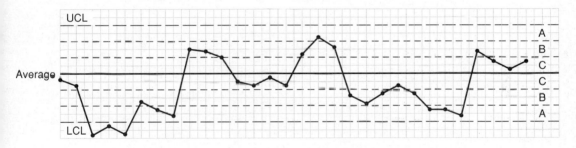

18. Calculate the probability of getting four consecutive points outside the two C zones.
19. Calculate the probability of getting two consecutive points above zone B on the upper half of a control chart.
20. Calculate the probability of getting 13 consecutive points in the two C zones.
21. Calculate the probability of getting six out of seven points above the mean on a control chart.
22. Calculate the probability of getting four consecutive points in a lower C zone *and* the next four consecutive points in the upper B zone.
23. Calculate the probability of getting a point in the lower B zone, the next point in the upper B zone, and the third point back in the lower B zone.

10

PROBLEM SOLVING

OBJECTIVES

- Know the problem solving sequence.
- Work with the following problem-solving tools:
  Brainstorming
  Flowcharts
  Storyboards
  Cause and effect diagrams
  Pareto charts
- Analyze a problem with histograms.
- Verify incoming quality by comparing histograms and data calculations.
- Make a scatterplot and recognize good correlation.

Problem-solving methods are used in every stage of quality improvement. A logical, systematic approach to problem solving follows the basic sequence of problem recognition, problem isolation, and problem solution. This chapter investigates various problem-solving tools and methods that can be used effectively in the problem-solving sequence.

10.1 THE PROBLEM-SOLVING SEQUENCE

The sequence follows six steps:

1. Problem recognition
2. Problem definition
3. Problem analysis
4. Choice for action
5. Problem solution
6. Prevention of backsliding

Step 1: Problem Recognition

Problem recognition can be as hazy as a feeling that a process can run better or that the situation can somehow be improved. For example, management may believe that the company's market share for a specific product can be increased. Production managers may believe that the operation can run more smoothly and efficiently. Operators may suspect that their phase of the operation can be improved. Problem recognition can also be as obvious as looking at the scrap bin and realizing that some specific part of the process is causing substandard product. Most often, problems are embedded in a process and must be searched out using problem-solving methods.

Some quality improvement programs emphasize that it is management's job to find problems.[1] One approach to this concept is MBWA: management by walking around. Managers at various levels actively seek out problems instead of passively waiting until the problem comes to them. The more comprehensive approach is for management to create an organizational structure that will involve all employees in problem solving. Companies facing today's competition cannot rely on a few people to find and solve problems: Everyone in the organization must be trained to use problem-solving techniques and then shown how their efforts fit into a coordinated, companywide, problem-solving structure.

When a company puts quality first in its set of goals and incorporates an ongoing quality process, tools for problem solving are systematically used for problem recognition. Control charts are also helpful in problem recognition. The control chart analysis techniques discussed in Chapter 9 are used for both problem recognition and problem analysis.

Step 2: Problem Definition

When a problem is found, it must be clearly defined. A good definitive problem statement is the first step in the problem's solution: It identifies a specific goal so that particular steps can be taken toward achieving that goal. Problems must be carefully analyzed to isolate the root cause. Most problems are complicated by symptoms that hide the root cause of the problem, and time spent trying to eliminate a symptom without attacking the root cause is often time wasted. A good problem definition helps separate symptoms from potential root causes.

Step 3: Problem Analysis

Problem analysis involves collecting appropriate data and using those data with the problem-solving tools to suggest various ways of resolving the problem. Control charts and their analyses of potential causes for out-of-control situations are used with flowcharts and cause and effect diagrams to track down root causes for problems.

---

[1] W. Edwards Deming, *Quality, Productivity, and Competitive Position* (Cambridge, MA: Massachusetts Institute of Technology, 1982).

Step 4: Choose Appropriate Action

The next step in the problem-solving sequence is the choice of the most promising method of solution. There may be several avenues of attack. Broad representation on the quality control team pays off at this stage. Each potential course of action must be examined from different perspectives in order to zero in on the best one.

Step 5: Problem Solution

The problem solution must be formally recorded along with the problem definition and the pertinent analysis information. It can be important for future reference as well as for the following step.

Step 6: Prevent Backsliding

The final phase in the problem-solving sequence is prevention of back-sliding. Ensure maintenance of the new methods and techniques that have been incorporated to eliminate the problem.

10.2 TEAMWORK AND TOOLS FOR PROBLEM SOLVING

Teamwork is perhaps the most important ingredient embedded in every step of the problem-solving process. The need for total teamwork is not always obvious, but many processes are in a problem situation because teamwork was not used enough when the process was initially created. Total teamwork gives everyone involved in an organization the opportunity to contribute to the resolution of company problems. It is always a challenge for management to organize the problem-solving format in a way that allows and even encourages input from all employees. Involving more people in organized, problem-solving efforts increases the likelihood that problems will be eliminated. Process problem-solving teams should be formed with appropriate subteams as needed, depending on the size and complexity of the process.

Problem-solving teams should consist of members from all phases of the process. Supervisors, operators, and personnel from management, purchasing, design, sales, engineering, and quality control should all be involved. Representatives can provide input from their respective points of view for a more complete picture of the problem and for a better chance of solving it. For example, employees at the workstation are often the most knowledgeable about the process and process problems at that point. Given training in statistical process control and permission to track the measurements in their area, they can provide much valuable input to the problem-solving process. Their involvement will help them understand their part of the process more thoroughly, and they will provide positive assistance to the supervisors and engineers who are focusing on the process as a whole. The diverse makeup of the problem-solving team is also important when deciding on a method of problem solution. Both the support and the capability of each department must be carefully considered before the choice is made.

There are various tools the team can use for problem solving. These tools involve ways of collecting, organizing, and analyzing information about a process. The problem-solving tools include the following:

- Brainstorming
- Flowcharts
- Storyboards
- Cause and effect diagrams
- Pareto charts
- Graphs, charts, and control charts

10.3 BRAINSTORMING

Brainstorming, developed in the 1930s, is a team technique that generates a large number of ideas on a topic. Its use by a problem-solving team ensures that everyone becomes involved, and with the diverse points of view of the different team members, nothing of importance should be overlooked. There are seven rules for brainstorming.

1. Choose a leader from within the group. The leader is responsible for the following tasks:

- Keeping the group focused on the topic
- Demanding adherence to the brainstorming rules
- Directing the action and individual input
- Starting and finishing the session
- Making sure that everyone clearly understands the topic
- Allowing time for participants to write down their initial ideas

2. Choose an official recorder from within the group.

All ideas are to be recorded. The ideas should be listed for group use during the session and provided as minutes in preparation for the next session. Two recorders can be used; one for the official list and one for the action list during the session.

3. As ideas are offered, no comments or disparaging remarks are allowed.

Nothing must dampen the spirit of participation or discourage team members from offering ideas on the topic. Quantity of ideas is more important than quality at this point. Occasionally, ideas that sound crazy at first mention are later found to have merit.

4. Call on each person in turn for an idea.

Insist on a response at each person's turn. Participants who have no ideas to contribute must say "pass." There are three good reasons for the "pass" routine: First, it forces shy people to "break the ice," which makes it easier for them eventually to contribute. Second, it keeps the pressure on for a contributing response because nobody wants to pass all the time. Third, when each person, in turn, passes, the meeting should end.

5. Provide writing material so that participants can jot down ideas as they think of them.

If team members try to remember a particular thought until it's their turn, they may forget their ideas as they mentally react to other ideas presented. The real power of a brainstorming session is in the "hitchhiking" of ideas. One person's idea presented in the group can inspire other ideas. Write the ideas that are presented on a blackboard or screen so that group members can still build on others' ideas after that specific topic has passed.

6. Regulate blurts!

Should group members be allowed to blurt out their ideas? Yes and no. If they are allowed to interject ideas indiscriminately, not everyone will contribute. Blurting has a detrimental effect on the more reticent members of the group. This opposes the fourth rule, in which everyone is encouraged to offer ideas. On the other hand, if members must wait their turn to present ideas, the atmosphere becomes a little more subdued; there's a lack of energizing excitement with a resulting loss of creativity. Also, if they are given a chance to think twice about an idea while waiting for their turn, participants may judge their ideas as not worth mentioning, thus defeating the quantity of ideas aspect of brainstorming. A good compromise is to proceed systematically in turn but to allow blurts that hitchhike on an idea just presented. Be sure to allow the recorder to catch up before going on to the next team member.

7. Follow brainstorming sessions with evaluating sessions in which the generated ideas are sorted by priority.

Eliminate no ideas until the problem is solved. Ideas that are considered unlikely or lacking in promise may be set aside, but not erased. Reconsideration from another point of view or further hitchhiking may occur.

Listing group priorities can be done by a weighted voting process. Provide team members with a list of the ideas and instruct them to place a number on each one:

0   This idea will not help in solving the problem.

1   There is a chance that this idea will be useful.

2   This idea should be of some help.

3   This idea will definitely help in solving the problem.

Add the votes. The totals for each idea provide a ranking.

EXAMPLE 10.1

Seven ideas are to be ranked. The votes of the six-member team are recorded in the following display.

Solution

Idea	Votes	Total	Rank
1	0,1,0,0,1,2	4	6
2	2,3,1,3,2,2	13	2
3	2,0,2,3,2,3	12	3
4	3,3,2,3,3,3	17	1
5	2,1,3,2,1,2	11	4
6	1,2,0,2,2,2	9	5
7	3,2,2,1,3,2	13	2

Ties may be given the same rank, as shown in the table with ideas 2 and 7. They may also be arbitrarily ranked in the increasing order, or a show-of-hands vote may establish which is ranked before the other.

10.4 FLOWCHARTS

A *flowchart* is a diagraming tool that is used to trace a process from start to finish. It can be used for an entire, complicated process or for some segment of the process. Different symbols specify what is being done to the product as it progresses from the input stage to the output stage of the process. When problems exist within a process or process segment, the problem-solving team should clearly understand what is being done to the product at the various stages in the process. A completed flowchart should make the step-by-step procedure within the process clear to the entire team.

In the problem-solving sequence, making a flowchart of the process is usually one of the first steps. Brainstorming is very useful in developing the flowchart, and using it ensures that important process details are not omitted.

Completed flowcharts can be helpful in finding the root causes of problems. Brainstorming sessions with a flowchart in hand allow the team to trace the product back and forth in the process until the cause of the problem is found or until several good candidates for the root cause have been uncovered, leading the way to further data gathering and analysis.

Two types of flowcharts will be demonstrated: a straight-forward procedure in which symbolism is unnecessary and a more complicated process that uses defined symbols to indicate the action at each step. The first step to take with either one is to brainstorm for steps in the process and for a logical process sequence.

EXAMPLE 10.2   Make a symbol-free flowchart for the process of making coffee in a coffee-maker at work.

Solution
Step 1. Brainstorm for process steps.

Buy the coffee.	Buy the filters.
Clean the pot.	Clean the basket.
Buy the sugar and creamer.	Put in the coffee.
Put in the filter.	Fill the reservoir with water.
Turn it on.	Put the basket in place.
Put the pot in place.	Wait until it is finished.
Pour the coffee.	Add sugar and creamer as needed.
Tidy up.	Drink the coffee.

Step 2. Make the flowchart.

Materials	Process	Controls
	Make sure everything is clean.	
Filter	Put in a filter.	
Coffee	Measure the coffee into the filter.	
Water	Fill the reservoir.	
	Put the basket in place.	
	Put the pot in place.	
	Turn the coffee-maker on.	
	Wait until it is done.	
Cup	Pour the coffee.	
Sugar	Add sugar if needed.	
Creamer	Add creamer if needed.	
	Adjust:	Taste
	amount of coffee (for next time)	
	sugar and creamer	
	Tidy up.	
	Drink the coffee.	
	Clean the basket and pot when the pot is empty or at the end of the day.	
	Buy needed materials for tomorrow.	

More complicated processes can be flowcharted with the use of standardized symbols to indicate what is being done to the product. This type of chart requires that everyone using it understand the symbols, which are displayed in Figure 10.1 (page 272).

FIGURE 10.1
Flowchart symbol definition. *Source*: "Problem Solving Tools and Techniques," Saginaw Division, General Motors Corporation, Decatur, Alabama, pp. 20–23.

○	Operation
[I]	Inspection
/S\	Storage
⇨	Product Movement
D	Delay
→	To Next Process Step

EXAMPLE 10.3

Make a flowchart, complete with symbols, for the process of buying a new car.

Solution
Step 1. Brainstorm for process steps.

Read the new car literature.

Decide on down payment.

Check your budget for maximum payments.

Visit a new car dealer.

Pick a car you like.

Discuss purchase price.

Find out about the payments.

Wait for the new car preparation.

Check *Compucar* (gives dealer costs on model and options).

Find out about extendable warranties.

Investigate the length of payment period.

Check on loan rates.

Check the papers on price of your present car.

Narrow your choices of cars.

Look at the cars on the lot.

Drive the car.

Discuss trade price.

Sign the papers and buy the car.

Pick up the car.

Do a final inspection.

Drive the car home.

Step 2. Make the flowchart, as shown in Figure 10.2 on page 273.

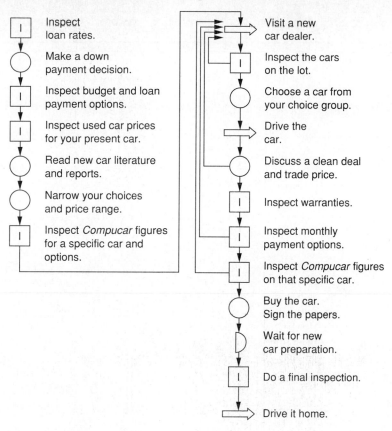

FIGURE 10.2
Flowchart for buying a new car.

10.5 STORYBOARDS

Walt Disney is credited with the development of the *storyboard*. When he made his feature-length animated pictures, he started by outlining the story on a board that ran the length of the wall. He and his associates would then fill in various substories and details. The format allowed them enough flexibility to try different ideas, change their minds, rearrange events, and see how it would logically fit in the storyline. As they worked in the details, the complete story developed on the storyboard.

The storyboard concept works very well in outlining a process for both initial setup and problem solving. A flexible structure such as a corkboard wall is effective, but chalkboards, markerboards, and even scotch tape and chart paper may be used. The storyboard is similar to a flowchart, but its format allows more attention to detail. Subroutines can either be included in the main process structure or be shown separately. Both options are illustrated in Figure 10.3 (see page 274).

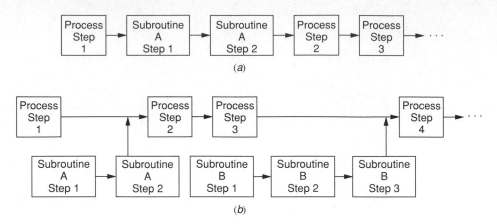

FIGURE 10.3
Storyboard patterns.

The choice of storyboard structure depends on the degree of complication in the process and subroutines. Color coding subroutines in either structure can also be helpful. The goal is clarity; everyone involved should be able to follow the process from start to finish when the storyboard is completed.

When a storyboard is going to be developed, brainstorming and teamwork are necessary ingredients. If a new process is being developed or an existing process is being outlined for troubleshooting, a diverse team with representatives from all phases of the process should be involved. Just as with the other problem-solving tools, it's important to have ideas and questions from different viewpoints.

Process problems can be tracked on the storyboard from their point of discovery in the process back to their root cause. When the path back is unclear, the storyboard can be helpful in deciding where additional information is needed.

10.6 THE CAUSE AND EFFECT DIAGRAM

The *cause and effect diagram* is a useful tool in a brainstorming session because it organizes the ideas presented. It is sometimes called a *fishbone diagram* because of its shape or an *Ishikawa diagram* after Professor Ishikawa of Japan, who first used the technique in the 1960s. The basic shape of the cause and effect diagram is shown in Figure 10.4 (page 275).

The diagram is a format for logically aligning the possible causes of a problem or effect. A basic way to organize the "ribs," or main categories, is to assign them the four M's: methods, machines, measurement, and materials. As the ideas are presented, they are inserted as the "bones," or possible causes of the effect, in the appropriate category. The bones can be subcategorized as causes of a cause are presented. The subdividing continues until the root cause to the problem is found. There may not always be a single root cause, but at least a few potential root causes will surface, and a decision for action can be made.

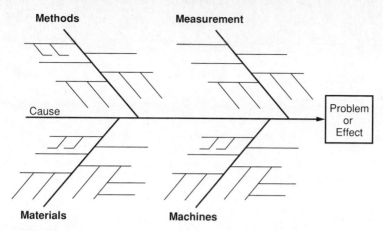

FIGURE 10.4
The cause and effect diagram.

The four M's are generally used as the initial main categories for a cause and effect diagram. Other categories specific to the particular process may be added if the team decides they're important. Environment is one example of a possible other category. It may be considered important enough to be a main category of problem causes, or it may be a subcategory in any or all of the other categories, depending on the process being analyzed.

When a problem has been isolated, a series of brainstorming sessions may be necessary before it is ultimately solved. Occasionally, for a complex process, the ideas generated in a brainstorming session may come too fast to be entered on the cause and effect diagram. If the session leader has to slow things down in order to make sure an idea fits in the right category or subcategory position, the spontaneous flow of ideas may be hindered. Housekeeping details at this point can slow the generation of ideas. This may occur, for example, at the very first session or at the beginning of a session when there is a large initial volume of ideas. The session leader may at that time switch to a list or a roughly categorized list. Later in the session when new ideas are scarce or at the next session, the group can decide where each idea belongs on the cause and effect diagram. That organization step of entering the ideas on the diagram can be very beneficial in generating new ideas. As categories and subcategories are arranged, the logical structure often suggests the root cause to the problem or specific phase of the problem.

EXAMPLE 10.4   Make a cause and effect diagram for the following problem: The car won't start.

Solution
A group brainstorms the problem using the four M's to create rough categories of possible causes. Enter the causes from the list on a cause and effect diagram. If that organization

step makes you think of any other possible causes, enter them as well. Figure 10.5 shows a completed diagram.

Measurement	Methods
Faulty gas gauge	Flooded engine
	Standard: clutch must be in
	Automatic: must be in neutral or park
	Wrong car
	Wrong key
	Seatbelt not fastened

Machines	Materials
Carburetor problem	No gas
Wiring problem	No oil
Computer malfunction	Oil too thick (cold)
Electrical trouble	Dead battery
	Loose battery connection
	Faulty spark plugs
	Plugged gas line
	Air cleaner too dirty

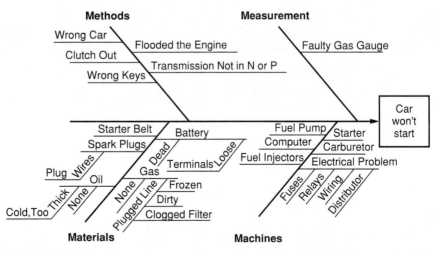

FIGURE 10.5
Cause and effect diagram for Example 10.4.

10.7 PARETO CHARTS

The Pareto chart, a bar graph that ranks problems in decreasing order of frequency, was adapted to quality control by Dr. Joseph M. Juran,[2] a noted authority and leader in the resurgence of quality in U.S. industry. The Pareto principle, credited to Italian economist Vilfredo Pareto, involves the concept that the comparative distributions of certain economic factors, such as wealth, follow an inverse relationship. Pareto discovered that 80 percent of the wealth in his country in the early 1900s was concentrated in 20 percent of the population. Dr. Juran discovered that the 80 percent–20 percent split also occurs in quality control. Eighty percent of the scrap is caused by 20 percent of the problems, and 80 percent of the dollar loss caused by poor quality is concentrated in 20 percent of the quality problems. Of course, the 80 percent–20 percent split is not exact; the percentages vary quite a bit. The important outcome of a Pareto chart is its assessment of process problem priorities. It separates the vital few problems from the trivial many. Another plus for the Pareto chart is its elimination of *recentivity*, the tendency to overestimate the importance of the most recent problem.

When a problem analysis is done for a Pareto chart, data are gathered that give the number of occurrences for each problem and the dollar loss associated with it. When all the data have been gathered, percentages can be tabulated for both the number data and the dollar loss data.

The procedure for making a Pareto chart is as follows:

1. Decide on the subject of the chart. Usually the need to set data priorities suggests the use of a Pareto chart. Determine what data are to be collected.

   ■ Where is the problem?
   ■ What are the categories?

   Where should the data be gathered?

   ■ Should they come directly off a line?
   ■ Should they come from a bin of nonconformities that have accumulated in the specified time period?

2. Be sure the time period for all the categories is the same: Use the number of nonconformities per hour, per shift, or per week.
3. What type of chart is needed? Should you track the numbers in each category, the percent in each category, or the costs in each category? A cost chart is usually included with either a numbers chart or a percent chart.
4. Make a table by gathering the data and tallying the numbers in each category. Find the total number of nonconformities and calculate the percent of the total in each category. Make a cost of nonconformities column and a cumulative percent column.
5. Arrange the table of data from the largest category to the smallest.
6. Set the scales and draw a Pareto chart.

---

[2] Joseph M. Juran, ed., *Quality Control Handbook*, 3d ed. (New York: McGraw Hill, 1974), 2-16–2-19.

7. Include all pertinent information on the chart. Are the categories clear? Has the time frame been specified?
8. Analyze the chart. The largest bars represent the vital few. The cumulative percent line levels off and emphasizes the trivial many. If the chart does not show a vital few, check to see if it is possible to recategorize for another analysis.

EXAMPLE 10.5

An analysis of nonconforming shirts in a week's production revealed the following causes. The nonconforming shirts were discounted according to defect and sold to Bargain Bin Incorporated and the dollar loss noted.

Defect	Number of Shirts	Percent of All Shirts	Dollar Loss	Cumulative Percent
Loose threads	2300	46%	$9200	46%
Hemming wrong	1650	33%	$9900	79%
Material flaw	300	6%	$2400	85%
Collar wrong	250	5%	$1250	90%
Cuffs wrong	200	4%	$1200	94%
Buttons	100	2%	$ 400	96%
Stitching	100	2%	$ 400	98%
Button holes	50	1%	$ 400	99%
Material tear	50	1%	$ 600	100%
TOTALS	5000	100%	$25750	

Solution

The data have been organized in the table according to the number of defects in each category. The percentages were calculated as follows:

1. Add the values in the number of defective shirts column to get the total number of defects.
2. Divide each number of defects by the total from step 1 and multiply by 100 to get the percent of the total number of defects.

The percents of defective shirts with loose threads or hemming problems, for example, are calculated according to the two steps:

$$\text{Loose threads} \quad \frac{2300}{5000} \times 100 = 46\%$$

$$\text{Hemming} \quad \frac{1650}{5000} \times 100 = 33\%$$

The percents were totaled in the last column.

46%		Loose threads
79%	= 46% + 33%	Threads and hems
85%	= 79% + 6%	Threads, hems, and flaws
90%	= 85% + 5%	Threads, hems, flaws, and collars

The Pareto charts can be formed in a few different ways. Figure 10.6 shows the basic chart with the number of defective shirts on the vertical scale and the different categories on the horizontal scale. Figure 10.7 on page 280 shows the dollar

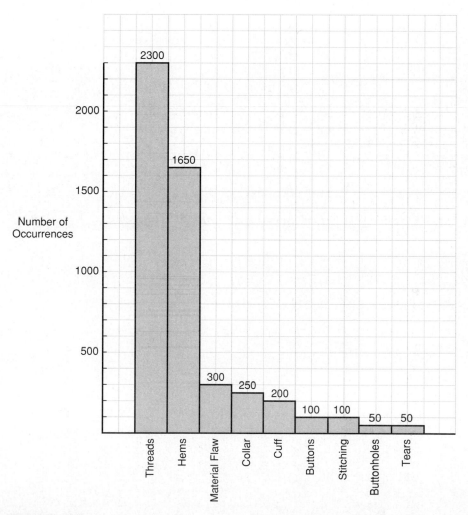

FIGURE 10.6
A Pareto chart for Example 10.5 of the number of nonconforming shirts per week with the number of defects per category per week.

loss on the vertical axis and the categories on the horizontal axis. Notice that the order has changed among the categories as the charted values go from largest to smallest. Figure 10.8 (page 281) is a combination of two Pareto charts. The left scale tracks the number of defects per category with the bar graph, and the right scale tracks the accumulated percent of all defects with a line graph. It is common practice to combine a cumulative percent chart with a percent of defects chart and also with a dollar loss chart. In all cases, the cumulative percent line levels off at the trivial many.

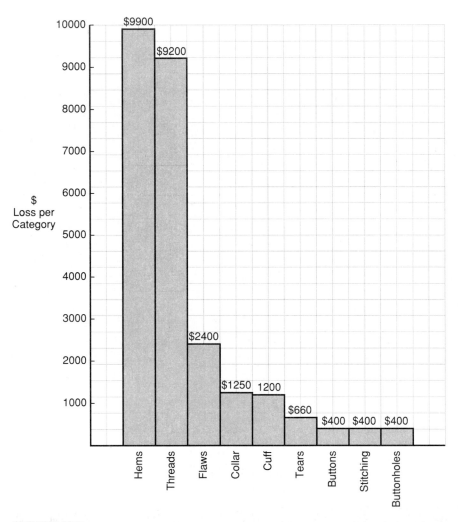

FIGURE 10.7
A Pareto chart for Example 10.5 showing the dollar loss per category per week.

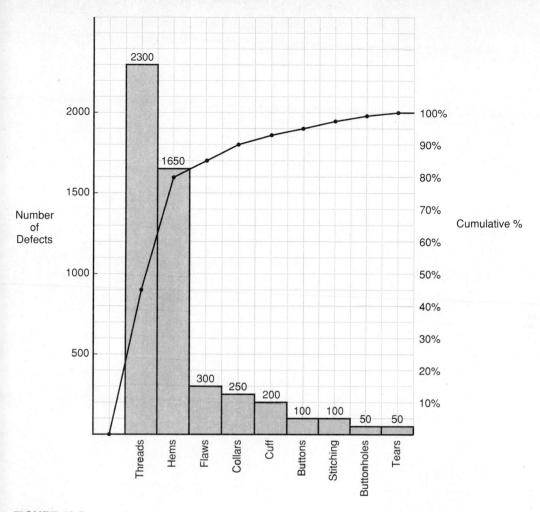

FIGURE 10.8
A Pareto chart for Example 10.5 showing the number of defects and the cumulative percent.

EXAMPLE 10.6 In a customer satisfaction survey at a local fast food restaurant, the following complaints were lodged.

Complaint	Number of Complaints
Cold food	105
Flimsy utensils	2
Food tastes bad	10
Salad not fresh	94
Poor service	13
Food too greasy	9
Lack of courtesy	2
Lack of cleanliness	25

Category	Number	Percent	Cumulative %
Cold food	105	$\frac{105}{260}$ → 40%	40%
Salad not fresh	94	$\frac{94}{260}$ → 36%	76%
Cleanliness	25	$\frac{25}{260}$ → 10%	86%
Service	13	$\frac{13}{260}$ → 5%	91%
Taste	10	$\frac{10}{260}$ → 4%	95%
Greasy	9	$\frac{9}{260}$ → 4%	99%
Utensils	2	$\frac{2}{260}$ → 1%	100%
Courtesy	2	$\frac{2}{260}$ → 1%	101%
Totals	260	101%	101%

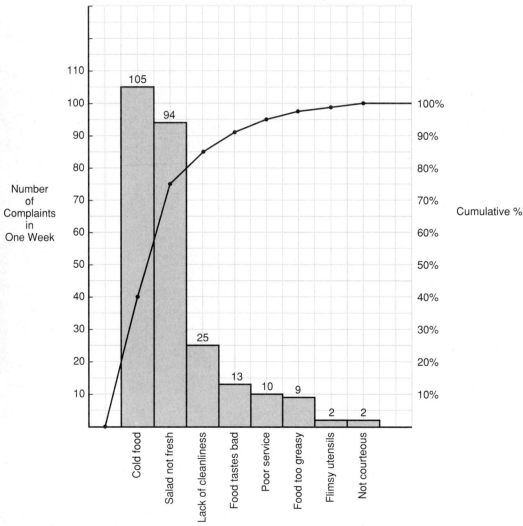

FIGURE 10.9
The Pareto chart for Example 10.6.

282

Using these data,

1. Make a table with the data ordered.
2. Include columns for percent of complaints and cumulative percent. Because of rounding, the cumulative percent may exceed 100 percent.
3. Make a Pareto chart for the number of complaints and include the cumulative percent graph.
4. Check your results with the completed table and chart in Figure 10.9 (page 282).

10.8   OTHER GRAPHS FOR PROBLEM SOLVING

All processes communicate to the analyst through the data that are gathered. Those data have to be organized so the message is clear; charts and graphs are the tools used to do this. The analyst must learn how to interpret charts and graphs to recognize the existence of a problem and then use the shapes and patterns on those charts and graphs to help solve the problem.

Every chart and graph has an expected shape or pattern. There is also a normal amount of naturally occurring variation from the expected form, so differentiating between normal pattern variation and a trouble-indicating pattern is a learned skill. Many times, the real skill is in spotting the trouble early, before measurements are out of specification.

Histograms

Histograms are important for analyzing trouble with a process, but they are also useful as a problem-solving tool.

Measurement data are usually expected to follow a normal distribution with the majority of measurements very close to the average value. As the distance from the average value increases, the number of measurements decreases. The distribution of the data should be symmetric about the mean with approximately the same number of measurements on the high side and the low side.

Some variation is expected within the general pattern of the normal histogram. When a tally histogram is made from a set of measurements, the distribution may look strange initially, but as more data are tallied the shape of the distribution is expected to look more normal.

When data do not follow the normal pattern, it is suspected that something out of the ordinary is causing that pattern change. This is the first step in problem recognition using histograms.

Sometimes several histograms are needed for problem solving for the same set of data. By looking at the data in specific groups, more information is gained that can lead to the problem's solution. This concept is demonstrated in the following example.

EXAMPLE 10.7   The control charts and the data values for a run of top adapters are shown in Figures 10.10 (page 284) and 10.11 (page 285). The charts were maintained by two machine operators on different shifts. The calculations for the averages are shown at the top of Figure 10.10 using all 40 data values from both charts. Is there a problem with this part of the process?

$$\bar{R} = \frac{\Sigma R}{k} = \frac{.0175}{40} = .00044$$
$$\bar{\bar{x}} = \frac{\Sigma \bar{x}}{k} = \frac{8.560}{40} = .214$$

$$UCL_R = D_4 \times \bar{R} = 2.114 \times .00044 = .0009$$
$$A_2 \times \bar{R} = .577 \times .00044 = .00025$$

$$UCL_{\bar{x}} = \bar{\bar{x}} + A_2 \bar{R} = .214 + .00025 = .21425$$
$$LCL_{\bar{x}} = \bar{\bar{x}} - A_2 \bar{R} = .214 - .00025 = .21375$$

Constants

n	A_2	$\tilde{A}_2$	D_4	d_2
3	1.023	1.19	2.574	1.693
4	0.729	—	2.282	2.059
5	0.577	.69	2.114	2.326

Time	0745	0945	1120	1305	1350	1445	4:45	5:45	7:00	8:00	9:30	10:30	9:30	10:30	11:30	12:30	1:15	2:00	2:45	5:00	6:00	7:00	8:00	9:30	10:30
Date/ Shift	7/29	#1					7/29	#2					7/30	#1						7/30	#2				
Top Adaptor Machine #15	.2134	.215	.214	.2138	.215	.2145	.214	.214	.215	.214	.214	.214	.2146	.2146	.2144	.2146	.2146	.2147	.2149	.215	.215	.215	.215	.215	.215
	.2136	.215	.2138	.2143	.214	.214	.215	.2145	.214	.214	.214	.214	.2146	.2146	.2146	.2147	.2148	.2147	.2147	.215	.215	.215	.215	.215	.215
1" Mics .001 units Spec: .215 {+.001 −.003	.2138	.2153	.2136	.2143	.214	.2147	.2145	.2145	.215	.214	.214	.214	.2145	.2146	.2146	.2148	.2147	.2147	.2148	.215	.2145	.215	.215	.215	.215
	.2136	.2134	.214	.214	.2142	.215	.214	.2145	.2145	.214	.214	.214	.2145	.2146	.2146	.2147	.2146	.2147	.2147	.215	.215	.215	.215	.215	.215
	.2147	.214	.214	.2136	.2145	.2143	.214	.2145	.214	.214	.2135	.214	.2146	.2145	.2147	.2146	.2148	.2147	.2147	.215	.2148	.215	.215	.215	.215
$\bar{x}$	.2138	.2145	.2139	.214	.2143	.2145	.2143	.2144	.2145	.214	.2139	.214	.2146	.2146	.2146	.2147	.2147	.2147	.2148	.215	.2149	.215	.215	.215	.215
R	.0013	.0019	.0004	.0007	.001	.001	.001	.0005	.001	.000	.0005	.000	.0001	.0001	.0003	.0002	.0002	0	.0002	0	.0005	0	0	0	0

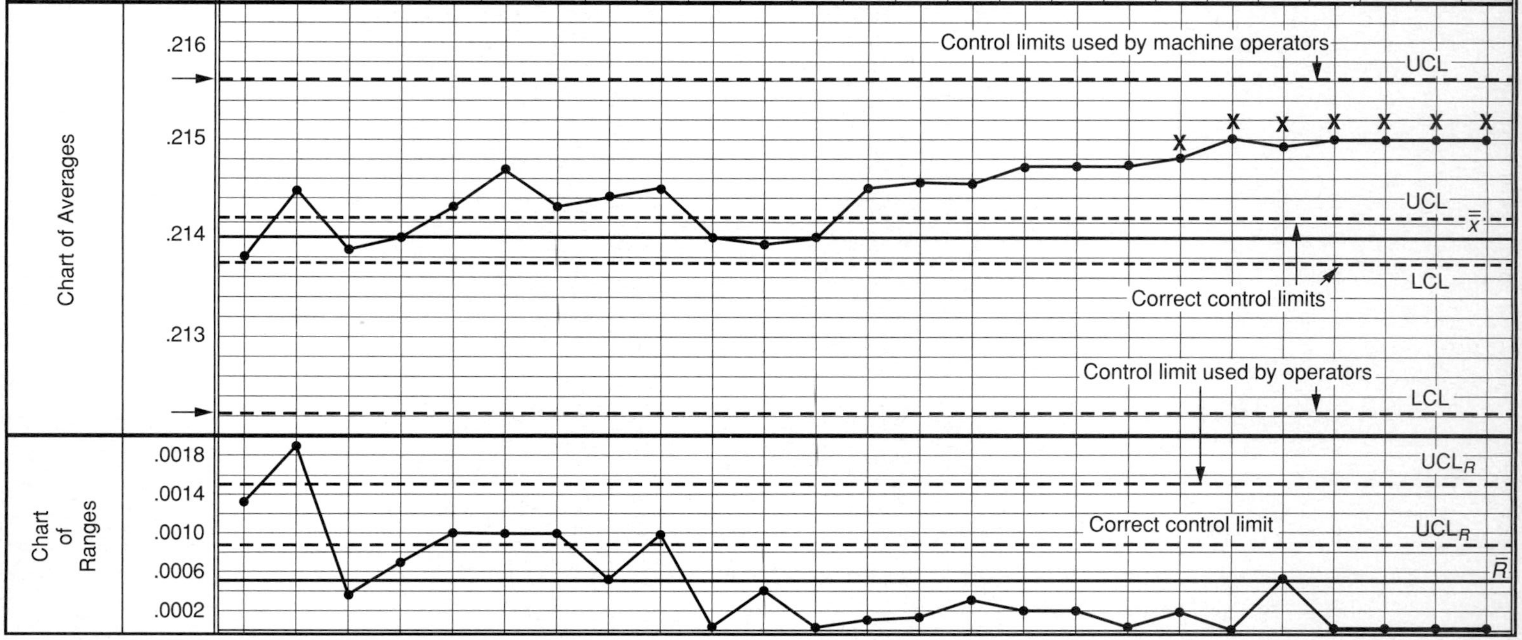

Chart of Averages
.216
.215
.214
.213
Control limits used by machine operators
UCL
UCL
$\bar{\bar{x}}$
LCL
Correct control limits
Control limit used by operators
LCL
Chart of Ranges
.0018
.0014
.0010
.0006
.0002
UCL_R
Correct control limit
UCL_R
$\bar{R}$

FIGURE 10.10
The $\bar{x}$ and R chart for top adapters, 7/29 to 7.30.

Time	4:45	6:30	7:30	8:30	9:30	10:30	9:00	10:00	11:00	12:00	1:00	2:00	4:30	5:30	9:30
Date/ Shift	7/31	#1					8/1	#2					8/1	#1	
Top Adaptor	.214	.2125	.212	.2125	.2123	.2125	.2136	.2138	.2135	.213	.2137	.2138	.2133	.2135	.214
Machine #15	.214	.2125	.212	.212	.2124	.2125	.2134	.2138	.2135	.2139	.2137	.2136	.2135	.2135	.2147
1" Mics	.214	.2125	.2125	.212	.2123	.2123	.2136	.2139	.2136	.2136	.2134	.2138	.214	.214	.2136
.001 units $\{$ +.001	.214	.2121	.2123	.212	.2123	.2123	.2135	.2135	.2136	.2136	.2139	.2139	.2134	.214	.2135
Spec: .215 $\{$ −.003	.214	.2125	.2122	.212	.2123	.2125	.2134	.2138	.2134	.2134	.2135	.2138	.2134	.2135	.214
Sum	1.07	1.0621	1.061	1.0605	1.0616	1.0621	1.0675	1.0688	1.0676	1.0675	1.0682	1.0689	1.0676	1.0685	1.0698
Average, $\bar{x}$	.214	.21242	.2122	.2121	.21232	.21242	.2135	.21376	.21352	.2135	.21364	.21378	.21352	.2137	.21396
Range, R	0	.0004	.0005	.0005	.0001	.0002	.0002	.0004	.0002	.0009	.0005	.0003	.0007	.0005	.0012

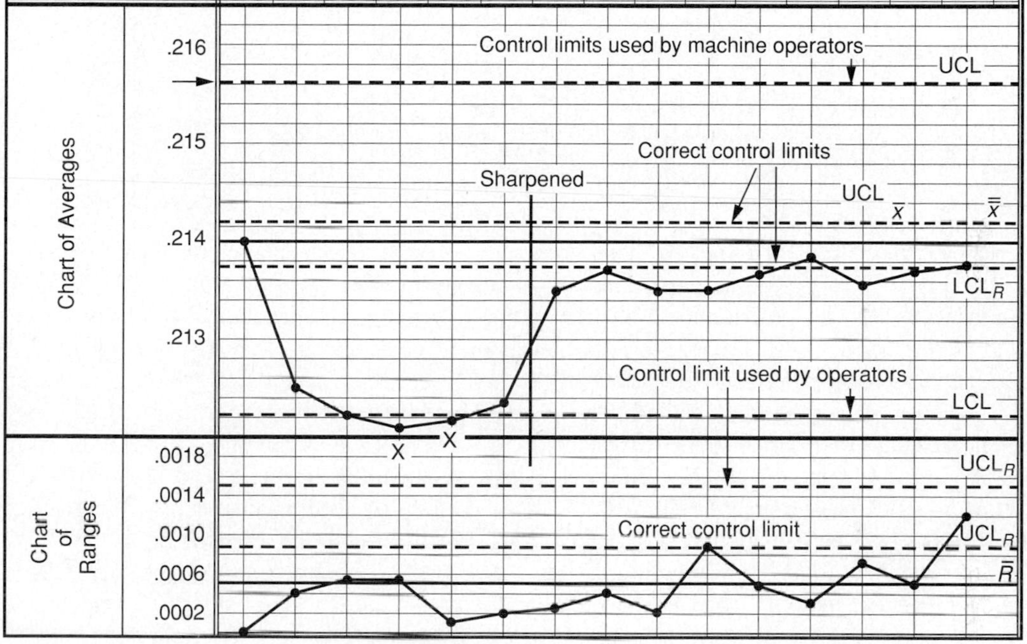

FIGURE 10.11
The $\bar{x}$ and R chart for top adapters, 7/31 to 8/1.

Solution

The operators marked several out-of-control situations on the control charts. One point is out of control on the range chart, and several are out of control on the $\bar{x}$ chart. Shifts on the $\bar{x}$ chart seem to be the main problem. One major problem that showed up on the second shift on 7/31 is a slow reaction to a trouble indicator. Also, the operator failed to mark the 7:30 P.M. reading out of control (a two of three freak pattern). Consequently, the majority of the pieces made during that shift must have been out of specification. Another major problem is that the operators miscalculated the control limits. The narrower control limits show many points out of control and give an earlier warning of trouble with the process. Histograms will be used for further problem analysis and for planning solution steps.

The histogram of all the data values could have a distribution that is crowded right with a longer tail section to the left, as shown in Figure 10.12. The statistical terminology for this shape is "skewed left."

FIGURE 10.12
A histogram with a skewed-left pattern.

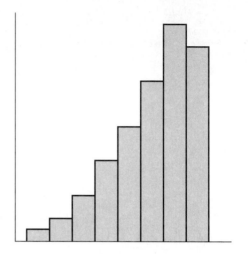

The reason for a skewed shape instead of a symmetrical shape is the asymmetrical tolerance: $.215^{+.001}_{-.003}$. The target value is .215, but values can be as high as .216 or as low as .212. The distribution of measurements is usually independent of the tolerance, but tolerances can be changed when management considers it permissible to accept a specific non-normal distribution pattern. In this case, a first analysis may indicate either a symmetric or a skewed pattern. The control chart indicates that the average of all the data is .214, so this machine may actually be working on a symmetrical distribution of .214 ± .002. This may indicate a problem. Are the operators trying to use .215 or .214 as a target measurement? Figure 10.13, the histogram of all the data, seems to indicate that the skewed distribution is the correct one for this operation (see page 287).

The shape of the histogram in Figure 10.13 brings two problems to light. First, the low end of Figure 10.13 doesn't match the shape of Figure 10.12, which may indicate that some out-of-specification pieces are being forced into the acceptable range. Second, the histogram shows excessive variation in measurements because virtually all of the tolerance is used and because the section in which the bulk of the data occurs (.2135 to .2155) is too wide.

As the work with the normal curve in Chapter 5 showed, the tail sections of the curve predict the percent of product that is out of specification. Area under the curve corresponds to the percent of product in that section, a concept that applies to many statistical curves. A statistical curve fitted to the histogram, demonstrated in Figure 10.14 (page 288), suggests that this machine is regularly producing top adapters that are out of specification. The area in the tail section can be estimated by counting squares. There are about 110 squares under the curve and about 8 squares beyond the specification limits, so approximately $\frac{8}{110}$, or 7 percent, of the top adapters are out of specification.

As the histogram in Figure 10.13 was being developed from the data, the measurements seemed somewhat streaky. This information may help solve the problem. The process capability is excellent.

FIGURE 10.13
The histogram for the top adapters in Example 10.7.

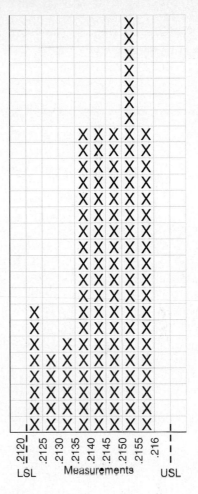

$$\sigma = \frac{\overline{R}}{d_z}$$

$$= \frac{.00044}{2.326}$$

$$= .000189$$

$$6\sigma = 6 \times .000189$$

$$= .001135$$

$$PCR = \frac{6\sigma}{\text{Tolerance}}$$

$$= \frac{.001135}{.004}$$

$$= .28$$

FIGURE 10.14
A skewed-left statistical curve is fitted to the data.

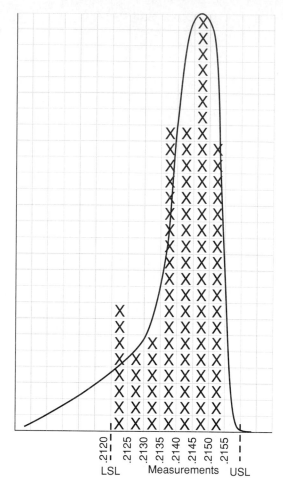

The process uses only 28 percent of the tolerance. However, problems of excessive variation caused by shifts and out-of-specification products have been identified. The cause of the problems may be attributed to the machine, the operators, or the gauges. The streaky behavior of the data implies that the measurements are grouped somehow. Another view of the data seems warranted.

Figure 10.15 on page 289 shows histograms of the data separated by operator. The histograms indicate that there could be a problem with the operators. The top adapters produced by the second shift operator have more variability than those produced by the first shift operator. Again, the data seemed to come in streaks as these histograms were developed; several sets of successive measurements were the same. Also, the pattern for both operators indicates either a gauge problem with the alternating high and low columns or a mixture of different distributions. The first operator's histogram is bimodal, with two high points, or modes. The second operator's histogram is trimodal, with three high columns. Two or more modes can indicate a mix of two or more distributions. There does appear to be

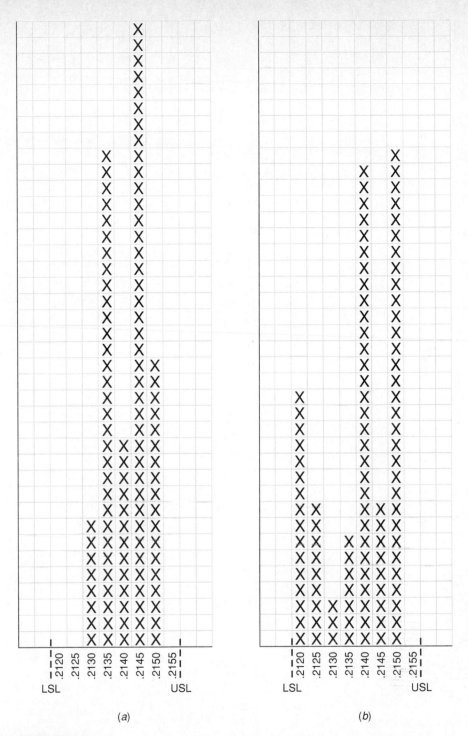

FIGURE 10.15
Data separated by operators: (a) first shift operator; (b) second shift operator.

a different distribution of measurements for the second shift operator on 7/31 that was partially corrected by the tool sharpening.

The data are again separated by operator in Figures 10.16 and 10.17 (page 292).

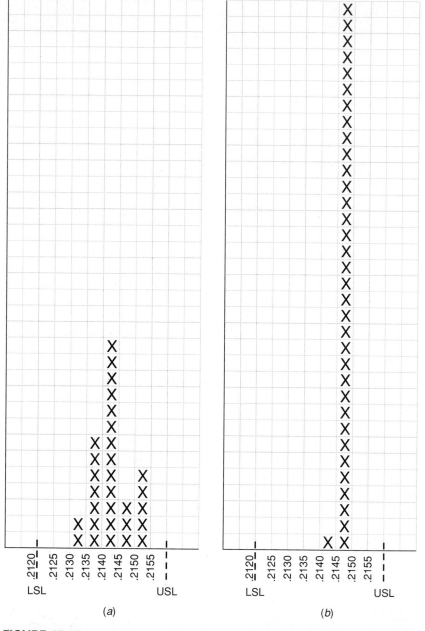

FIGURE 10.16

Data for the first shift operator: (a) 7/29; (b) 7/30; (c) 8/1.

FIGURE 10.16 *(continued)*

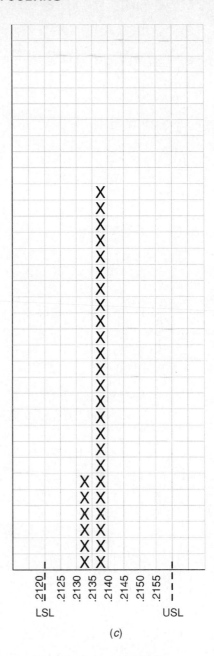

(c)

The first shift operator, in Figure 10.16, has more variability on the first day than on the other two days. The control chart indicates an initial set up on that first day, which may account for that difference. The second shift operator exhibits more trouble with variability, but only on 7/31 does the distribution of measurements have a trouble-indicating pattern. The note on the control chart indicates that a tool was sharpened, and

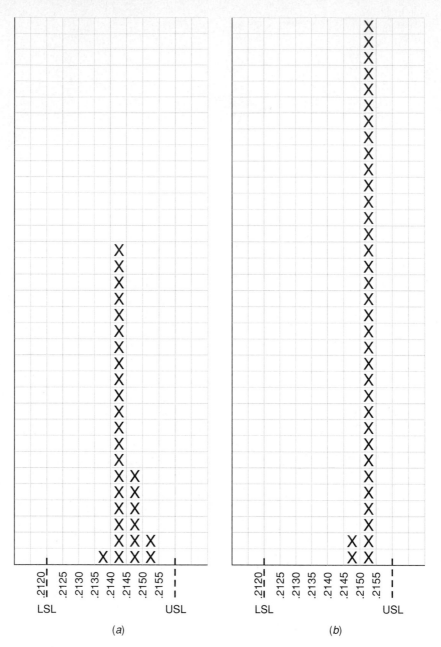

FIGURE 10.17
Data for the second shift operator: (a) 7/29; (b) 7/30; (c) 7/31; (d) 8/1.

the measurements move back toward the center line after that. The out-of-control X's on the control chart show that the measurements are still too low.

Another problem shows up by comparing histograms on the same day shifts. Com-

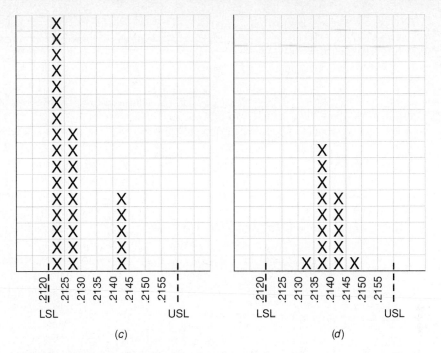

FIGURE 10.17 *(continued)*

paring first shift to second on 7/29, 7/30, and 8/1 illuminates a consistent shift to the right each day. This indicates a possible gauge problem, with the second shift operator reading a value higher than the first shift operator. This possibility may be tested by running a gauge capability study with the two operators. Another possible cause of the histogram's shift may be some kind of machine creep, in which the measurements gradually get larger as the day wears on. This case does not seem to warrant such an option because there does not appear to be a steady increase in measurements per shift.

The measurements also suggest one more problem. The first shift operator is estimating the measurements to the nearest .0001, whereas the second shift operator is only occasionally giving them to the nearest .0005. The data can be better interpreted with the more precise measurements. The rule of 10 states that the measuring unit should be one-tenth of the tolerance, or about .0005.

Finally, a major contributor to the total variation is some kind of a day-to-day shift in the measurements. This can be seen by comparing each day's result for the first shift operator in Figure 10.16 and again for the second shift operator in Figure 10.17. This may be caused by the day's set-up procedure, by something within the machine, or by a gauge problem.

The problem analysis and steps toward solution have been encapsulated in the display on page 294.

Trouble Indicators	Source
1. The control chart is out of control.	Control chart
2. The operators may be aiming for a target of .214 instead of .215.	Control chart
3. The operators failed to mark all the out-of-control points and miscalculated the control limits.	Control chart
4. Are out-of-specification pieces being accepted on the low end?	Histogram figures 10.13 and 10.14
5. There is excessive variation.	Histogram figure 10.13
6. An estimated 7 percent is out of specification.	Histogram figure 10.14
7. Is there an operator problem? One shows more product variability than the other.	Histogram figure 10.15
8. There could be a gauge problem.	Histogram figures 10.15, 10.16, 10.17
9. There may be a mixture of different distributions.	Histogram figure 10.15
10. The first operator had more variability on the first day.	Histogram figure 10.16
11. The second operator had a trouble distribution on 7/31.	Control chart, Histogram figure 10.17
12. The second shift operator is measuring with less precision.	Data on control chart
13. A day-to-day pattern shift is adding to the product variability.	Histogram figures 10.16 and 10.17
14. There is a slow reaction to trouble indicators.	Control chart

Problem Number	Action
1, 2, 5, 6, 9, 10	Check the set-up, start-up, and adjustment procedures.
4, 6, 11	Double check the output from 7/31.
3, 4, 7, 11, 12	Check on the second shift operator with respect to training, experience, ability, work habits, gauge reading.
5, 8, 9, 12, 13	Do a gauge capability study with the two operators.
1, 3, 11, 14	Check the operating procedures. The operator should check the machine log and anticipate when sharpening or adjustment is necessary and then take action at the first sign of trouble. Check on the SPC training for the operators and their supervisors.

Another illustration of the use of histograms for problem analysis is in materials acceptance. Incoming inspection plans are changing drastically. The quality demands on incoming parts and materials are increasing to a point at which the standard attribute inspection process cannot detect unacceptable quality levels unless the sample size is increased drastically. Consequently, quality assurance is becoming a way of life for vendors. Companies with assembly operations rely on vendors for the various bits and pieces that blend together for their final products. The final products are facing world competition, and quality must be inherent.

Companies are now demanding proof of quality from their vendors. They can no longer rely on incoming inspection alone: It is too costly and allows too much chance for accepting poor quality parts. A shipment that has been rejected because the inspection sample has an unacceptable number of defectives can often be reshipped as is, with perhaps a little reorganization, and stand a good chance of being accepted the second time.

The proof of quality that vendors provide includes copies of the control charts from their shop floor, statements giving mean and standard deviation information on their product's measurements, and histograms depicting their product's measurement distribution. Vendors are rated according to their own record of quality. A combination of that record and proof of quality is replacing the customary incoming inspection. Receiving companies can still verify the vendor claims by using histograms and calculations with sample measurements.

When a lot is chosen for a verification sample, the sample size should be large enough to create a histogram of the measurements that will imply the distribution of the population of measurements: A sample size between 100 and 200 should be sufficient. Measurements are recorded for all pieces in the *random* sample, and a histogram is made for those measurements. That histogram should compare favorably with the histogram of data provided by the vendor. Vendors should be required to provide histograms and control charts of specific critical measurements. Process mean, standard deviation, and capability can be determined from the charts and compared with the manufacturer's claims. They can also be calculated from the data in the sample histogram. The histogram mean, standard deviation, and distribution should be approximately the same as the population mean, standard deviation, and distribution.

Compare and Assess

Vendor's claim   Distribution of measurements from vendor's histograms

$\bar{\bar{x}}$

σ and process capability

Vendor's charts   Distribution of measurements from the data on the vendor's control charts

$\bar{\bar{x}}$

σ and process capability

Sample histogram   Distribution of measurements from the random sample of incoming pieces

$\bar{\bar{x}}$

σ and process capability

There should be close agreement among the three sets of information.

Sample Numbers	1	2	3	4	5	6	7	8	9	10	11	12	13	14	15	16	17	18	19	20	21	22	23	24	25
$\bar{\bar{x}} = .74999$	.751	.750	.749	.751	.750	.749	.749	.748	.750	.752	.751	.750	.750	.749	.751	.749	.749	.750	.749	.750	.752	.750	.751	.750	.749
	.750	.749	.750	.749	.751	.751	.750	.750	.750	.751	.749	.751	.750	.749	.750	.749	.751	.751	.749	.749	.750	.750	.750	.749	.750
	.751	.750	.750	.748	.751	.752	.750	.750	.751	.750	.749	.748	.749	.752	.750	.750	.751	.752	.750	.749	.750	.750	.750	.749	.749
$\bar{R} = .001769$	.750	.751	.749	.750	.751	.750	.749	.750	.751	.750	.749	.750	.751	.750	.751	.750	.750	.749	.750	.750	.750	.750	.749	.751	.751
	.750	.750	.750	.749	.751	.750	.749	.749	.751	.750	.750	.751	.751	.751	.750	.750	.750	.749	.749	.749	.749	.750	.750	.751	.751
$\bar{x}$	.7504	.7500	.7496	.7494	.7508	.7504	.7494	.7494	.7506	.7506	.7496	.7500	.7498	.7502	.7504	.7496	.7502	.7502	.7494	.7494	.7502	.7500	.7500	.7500	.7502
R	.001	.002	.001	.003	.001	.003	.001	.002	.001	.002	.002	.003	.002	.003	.001	.001	.002	.003	.001	.001	.003	.000	.002	.002	.002

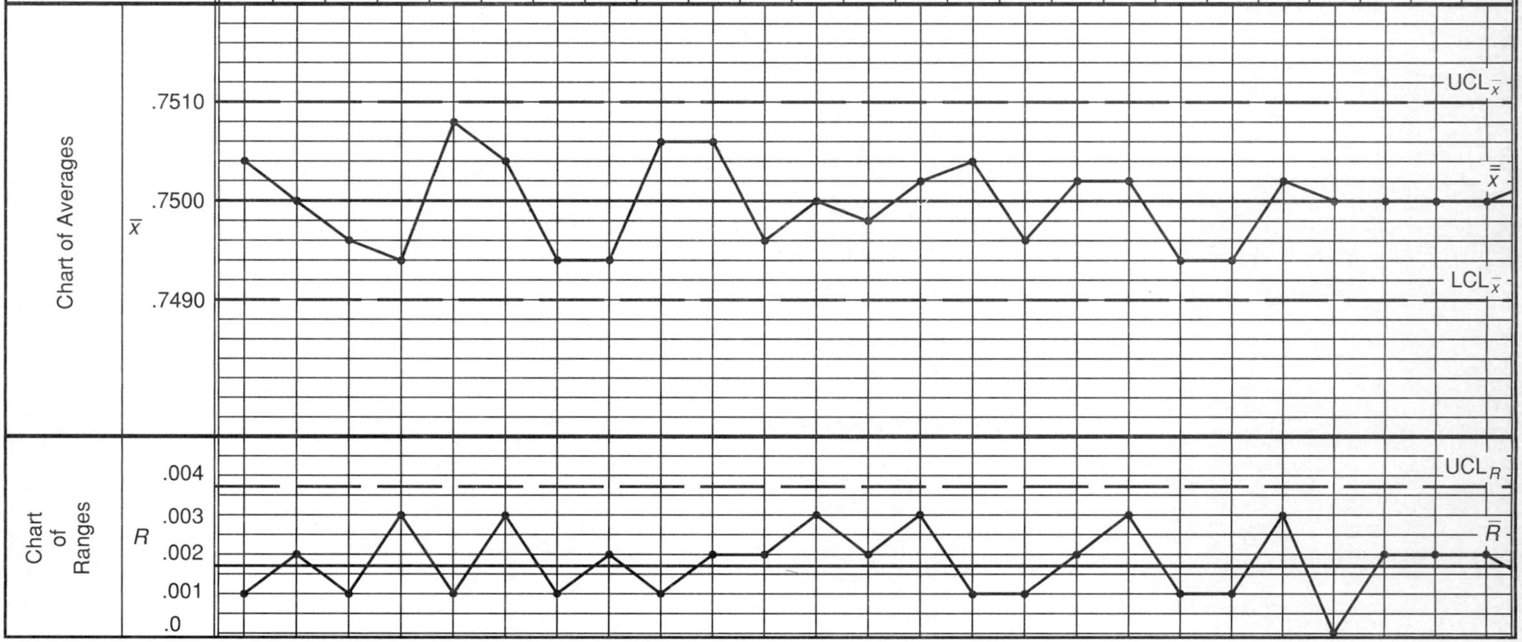

Chart of Averages

$UCL_{\bar{x}}$

$\bar{\bar{x}}$

$LCL_{\bar{x}}$

.7510

.7500 $\bar{x}$

.7490

Chart of Ranges

UCL_R

$\bar{R}$

.004
.003
R .002
.001
0

FIGURE 10.18
Vendor's control chart for Example 10.8.

296

**EXAMPLE
10.8**

A vendor supplies parts to a manufacturer, whose specifications of a critical measurement are .750 ± .0025 with a process capability, PCR, of .8. The vendor claims that the parts satisfy the requirements and submits a control chart as representative of those available. A copy of the control chart is given in Figure 10.18 on page 296.

1. Does the control chart support the vendor's claim? Create a histogram of the control chart data and calculate the mean, standard deviation, and process capability from the control chart information.
2. A sample of 200 pieces is randomly chosen from the lot with the control chart. The measurements are recorded in Table 10.1. What conclusions can be made regarding the quality of the incoming pieces? Draw a histogram using sample data and compare it to the vendor histogram formed with control chart data. Also, calculate the mean, standard deviation, and process capability from the sample data.

TABLE 10.1
Measurements for the random sample of 200 pieces

Measurement	Number of Pieces	Measurement	Number of Pieces
.7524	1	.7498	20
.7522	0	.7496	19
.7520	1	.7494	12
.7518	0	.7492	12
.7516	2	.7490	13
.7514	2	.7488	9
.7512	6	.7486	5
.7510	8	.7484	2
.7508	10	.7482	1
.7506	13	.7480	0
.7504	15	.7478	2
.7502	20	.7476	1
.7500	25	.7474	1

3. Compare the results for consistency.

Solution

The two histograms shown in Figures 10.19 on page 298 and 10.20 on page 299 (the vendor histogram and sample data histogram) match very closely. The normal shape of the distributions and the fact that they are centered at the target measurement indicate that the PCR will give a realistic picture of the process capability. They also indicate that the vendor is honestly reporting the facts about the product's quality.

FIGURE 10.19
Control chart data for Example 10.8.

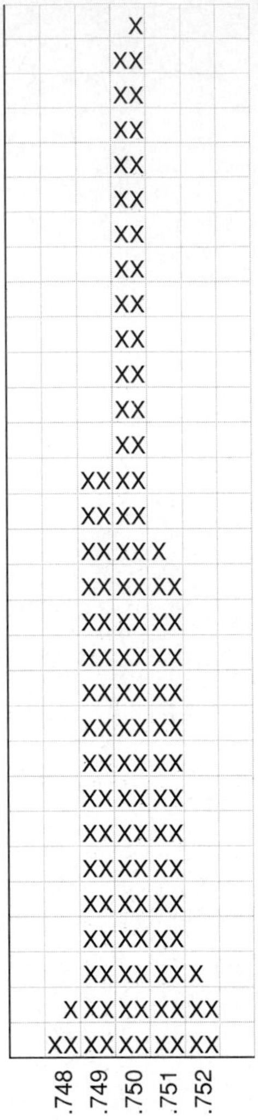

```
                    X
                   XX
                   XX
                   XX
                   XX
                   XX
                   XX
                   XX
                   XX
                   XX
                   XX
                   XX
                   XX
                XX XX
                XX XX
                XX XX X
                XX XX XX
                XX XX XX
                XX XX XX
                XX XX XX
                XX XX XX
                XX XX XX
                XX XX XX
                XX XX XX
                XX XX XX
                XX XX XX
                XX XX XX
                XX XX XX X
             X XX XX XX XX
                XX XX XX XX XX
              .748 .749 .750 .751 .752
```

1. Control chart calculations The following calculations investigate the vendor's claims.

$$\bar{\bar{x}} = \frac{\sum \bar{x}}{N}$$

$$= \frac{19.4998}{26} = .74999$$

$$\bar{R} = \frac{\sum R}{N}$$

$$= \frac{.046}{26} = .001769$$

FIGURE 10.20
Random sample data for Example 10.8.

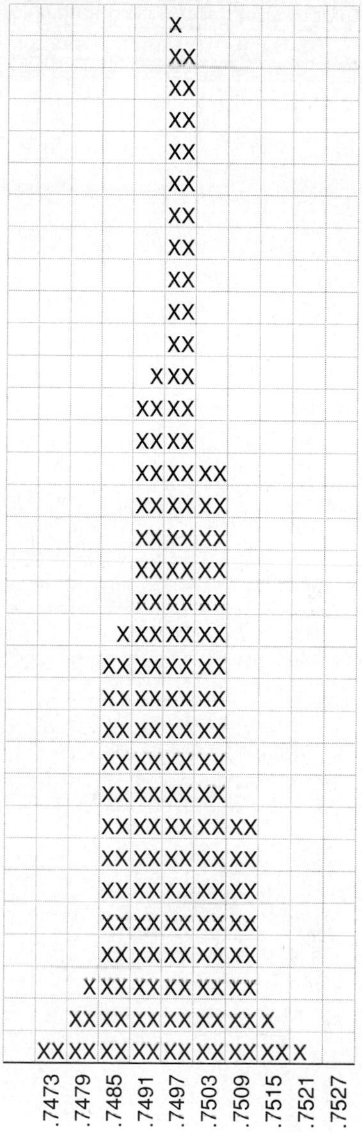

```
                        X
                       XX
                       XX
                       XX
                       XX
                       XX
                       XX
                       XX
                       XX
                       XX
                       XX
                      X XX
                     XX XX
                     XX XX
                     XX XX XX
                     XX XX XX
                     XX XX XX
                     XX XX XX
                     XX XX XX
                    X XX XX XX
                  XX XX XX XX
                  XX XX XX XX
                  XX XX XX XX
                  XX XX XX XX
                  XX XX XX XX
                  XX XX XX XX XX
                  XX XX XX XX XX
                  XX XX XX XX XX
                  XX XX XX XX XX
                  XX XX XX XX XX
                 X XX XX XX XX XX
              XX XX XX XX XX XX X
           XX XX XX XX XX XX XX XX X
         .7473 .7479 .7485 .7491 .7497 .7503 .7509 .7515 .7521 .7527
```

$$\mathrm{UCL}_R = D_4 \overline{R}$$
$$= 2.114 \times .001769$$
$$= .0037$$

$$\mathrm{UCL}_{\overline{x}} = \overline{\overline{x}} + A_z \overline{R}$$
$$= .74999 + (.577 \times .001769)$$
$$= .751$$

$$\mathrm{LCL}_{\overline{x}} = \overline{\overline{x}} - A_z \overline{R}$$
$$= .74999 - (.00102)$$
$$= .74897$$

The measurements are on target, and the control limits are acceptable. The range chart is in statistical control, but the $\bar{x}$ chart shows instability: Starting with the third point, nine consecutive points are outside the C zones. This is contributing to excessive variability.

$$\sigma = \frac{\bar{R}}{d_2}$$

$$= \frac{.001769}{2.326}$$

$$= .0007605$$

$$6\sigma = 6 \times .0007605$$

$$= .004563$$

$$PCR = \frac{6\sigma}{\text{Tolerance}}$$

$$= \frac{.004563}{.005}$$

$$= .913$$

The control chart indicates that the process uses 91.3 percent of the tolerance instead of the 80 percent that was specified. Again, too much variability.

2. Calculations from a random sample of 200 pieces   The 200 sample measurements were entered into a statistical calculator with the following results:

$$\bar{x} = .749889$$

$$\sigma = .00080643$$

$$6\sigma = .00483858$$

$$PCR = \frac{6\sigma}{\text{Tolerance}}$$

$$= \frac{.00483858}{.005}$$

$$= .968$$

The $\bar{x} = .7499$ indicates that the measurement is on target, but the standard deviation of the measurements shows that the measurements use about 97 percent of the tolerance in the PCR calculation. This is slightly worse than the control chart figure, but not different enough to suspect dishonest charting.

Recommendations   The calculations of the control chart and sample data lead to the following recommendations.

1. The measurements on the control chart are not accurate enough. The measurements should be accurate to at least .0002. The vendor should use a more accurate gauge.

2. Neither the operator nor the supervisor recognized the out-of-control situation on the control chart. Check with the vendor on the extent of their SPC training.
3. Either work with the vendor on reducing variability or monitor the vendor's efforts with continued sample checks.

In this instance, the sample calculations were consistent with the vendor information. If the vendor had tried to submit charts that overrated the quality of the product, the analyzed sample would have shown the discrepancy immediately.

Scatterplots

The *scatterplot* is a graph of measurement pairs that shows whether there is correlation between the measurements. When correlation exists, changes in one measurement will be accompanied by proportionate changes in the other. If there is *positive* correlation, the changes will be in the *same direction*. When the first measurement increases, the second increases, and when the first measurement decreases, the second decreases. When the correlation is *negative*, the two measurements move in *opposite directions*. If the first measurement increases, the second decreases, and vice versa.

Scatterplots can be useful in problem solving. When a correlation is known to exist between two measurements, cause and effect on the first can have a ripple effect on the second. The scatterplot can be a time saver in the quality effort. When correlation exists between two measurements, statistical control of the first can signal control of the second. Also, if improvements on the process of the first measurement result in decreased variability, the second measurement will often undergo a similar improvement. When process changes are made, however, the correlation factor should be verified.

Table 10.2 gives pairs of measurements of corresponding internal and external diameter measurements. Each pair of numbers specifies a point on the graph. The measurement pairs are graphed on Figure 10.21 (page 302).

TABLE 10.2
Measurements for Figure 10.21

Internal Diameter	External Diameter
.212	.512
.210	.510
.213	.513
.215	.515
.209	.509

Figure 10.21 illustrates perfect positive correlation. All points are on a straight line and the measurements increase and decrease proportionately.

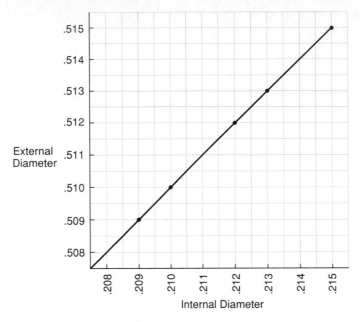

FIGURE 10.21
Perfect positive correlation.

Perfect negative correlation is illustrated in Figure 10.22. The points on the graph, given in Table 10.3 on page 303, are on a straight line. One measurement increases as the other decreases.

FIGURE 10.22
Perfect negative correlation.

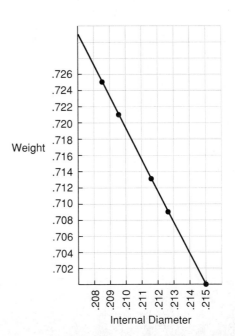

TABLE 10.3
Measurements for Figure 10.22

Internal Diameter	Weight
.212	.713
.210	.721
.213	.709
.215	.701
.209	.725

The scatterplot is more commonly used to calculate process cause and effect on a specific measurement. Variables such as RPM, temperature, pressure, spindle speeds, and voltage can influence process measurements dramatically. Figure 10.23 shows that RPMs have a direct effect on measurement A, so control of the measurement requires control of the RPMs. There is very good negative correlation in the scatterplot in this figure. The points, which are listed in Table 10.4, lie very close to a straight line.

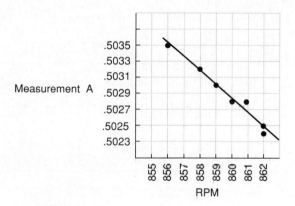

FIGURE 10.23
Very good negative correlation.

TABLE 10.4
Measurements for Figure 10.23

RPM	Measurement A
862	.5025
856	.5035
860	.5028
862	.5024
858	.5032
861	.5028
859	.5030

Figure 10.24 shows that there may be some correlation between measurement C and temperature but that other factors must be affecting the pair of measurements as well. See Table 10.5 for the measurements. Here the scatterplot shows poor positive correlation. The points do not lie close to a straight line.

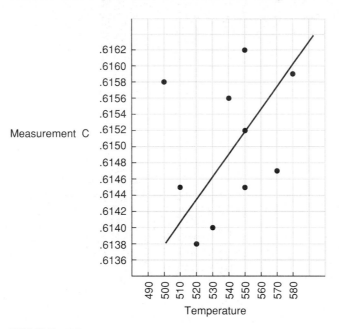

FIGURE 10.24
Poor positive correlation.

TABLE 10.5
Measurements for Figure 10.24

Temperature	Measurement C
550	.6152
580	.6159
510	.6145
530	.6140
540	.6156
520	.6138
570	.6147
550	.6145
500	.6158
550	.6162

EXAMPLE 10.9

The top adapter measurements from Example 10.7 were matched to a second top adapter measurement taken at the same time. The pairs of measurements are listed in Table 10.6 on page 305. Is there any correlation between the measurements?

TABLE 10.6
Measurements for Example 10.9

Date/Time	.215 Measurement	.503 Measurement
7/29 0745	.2134	.5025
	.2136	.5025
	.2138	.5025
	.2136	.5020
	.2147	.5025
1120	.2140	.5034
	.2138	.5037
	.2136	.5040
	.2140	.5033
	.2140	.5035
1305	.2138	.5030
	.2143	.5032
	.2143	.5025
	.2142	.5035
	.2136	.5035

Solution

The scatterplot in Figure 10.25 shows that there is *no correlation* between the two measurements, so each will have to be controlled separately. There is no line that the points approach: This set of points has no linear trend.

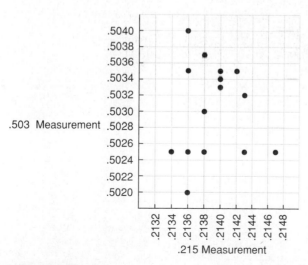

FIGURE 10.25
No correlation.

EXERCISES

1. What are the six basic steps in problem solving?
2. Why is the team approach so important in problem solving?
3. What are the basic rules for brainstorming?
4. Why is brainstorming such an effective tool in problem solving?
5. Make a flow chart for getting up in the morning and going to work or school.
   (a) without symbols
   (b) with symbols
6. Make a flowchart for buying a week's supply of groceries.
   (a) without symbols
   (b) with symbols
7. Make a cause and effect diagram for the following problem: Monthly expenses exceed monthly income.
8. Make two Pareto charts for the data in the list, one for the number of defectives and one for dollar loss. In each case, include a cumulative percent graph.

Department	Defectives	Dollar Loss
A	20	100
B	120	60
C	80	800
D	100	500
E	50	200
F	30	90

9. A vendor claims that a specific critical measurement has a mean of .600 with a standard deviation of .0013. The product specifications are .600 ± .005. A random sample is taken from the incoming parts, and following measurements are recorded.

.596	.598	.600	.602	.599	.598	.599	.601	.600	.600	.602
.603	.601	.604	.598	.598	.599	.597	.596	.599	.598	.601
.604	.600	.600	.602	.601	.601	.602	.599	.600	.600	.598
.597	.598	.598	.600	.602	.597	.599	.600	.601	.600	.598
.599	.594	.598	.595	.596	.600	.600	.602	.598	.599	.599
.598	.602	.605	.601	.600	.596	.601	.600	.600	.599	.600
.599	.601	.600	.598	.600	.598	.600	.602	.600	.598	.600
.599	.599	.600	.600	.598	.599	.597	.598	.601	.602	.601
.597	.598	.600	.600	.601	.600	.598	.600	.601	.600	.601
.599										

   (a) What is the PCR, according to the vendor's information?
   (b) What are the mean and standard deviation from the random sample?
   (c) What is the PCR from the sample information?
   (d) Does the histogram of the sample indicate that the product is normally distributed?
   (e) Does the sample information indicate that the vendor is supplying honest information?

10. **(a)** For each process make a scatterplot for the following pairs of values. Put the RPM values on the horizontal axis.

    (b) Classify each scatterplot as

        1. very good correlation

        2. good correlation

        3. poor correlation

        4. no correlation

Process I		Process II	
RPM	Measurement	RPM	Measurement
650	.906	620	1.420
675	.909	660	1.430
640	.905	680	1.425
660	.907	700	1.432
700	.908	600	1.424
600	.902	720	1.431

11

GAUGE CAPABILITY

OBJECTIVES

- Know the effect of accuracy, repeatability, reproducibility, and stability on gauge readings.
- Determine the extent of repeatability and reproducibility variation with a gauge capability study.
- Define maximum deflection and explain the ways accuracy and stability contribute to it.
- Reassess process capability by eliminating the effect of gauge variability.
- Understand the concept of indecisive zones in gauge readings.

Every measuring instrument is subject to variation. In order to use SPC effectively, gauges must be analyzed to determine the extent of gauge variability. The variation that occurs on a control chart is actually a combination of product variation and gauge variation. Hopefully, the gauge variation is minimized so that the control chart interpretation will reflect primarily process variation.

One descriptive approach to gauge capability involves accuracy and precision. A target analogy best illustrates the two. The measurements shown in Figure 11.1(a) on page 310 (shots on the target) are precise, but not accurate. The measurements shown in Figure 11.1(b) are neither accurate nor precise. Figure 11.1(c) shows measurements that are accurate, but not precise. Finally, the measurements in Figure 11.1(d) are both accurate and precise.

A lack of precision reflects an excessive amount of variation in the measurements. A lack of accuracy indicates that the average measurement is off target. The appropriate corrective steps to either problem can be determined with a gauge capability analysis. A

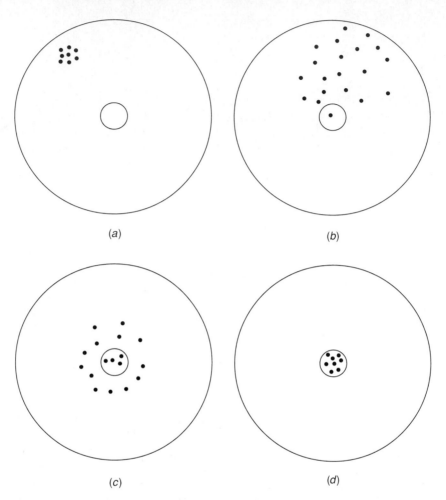

FIGURE 11.1
(eit a) Measurements are precise but not accurate. (*b*) Measurements are neither accurate nor precise. (*c*) Measurements are accurate but not precise. (*d*) Measurements are both accurate and precise.

test of gauge capability can measure four individual characteristics and their combined effect.[1]

1. Accuracy

The gauge can be calibrated to make the readings more accurate. Accuracy measures the difference between the observed average measurement and the "true" value, although

---

[1] Robert W. Traver, "Measuring Equipment Repeatability—The Rubber Ruler," *American Society for Quality Control Annual Convention Transactions* (1962). Reprinted with the permission of the American Society for Quality Control.

the true value may be unknown in many cases. There is usually some acceptable standard of comparison to determine accuracy of measurements.

2. Repeatability

This measures the consistency of readings of the same item by one person. Poor repeatability usually reflects internal gauge problems. Repeatability analysis can be used for training purposes as well. Given a gauge with very little repeatability variation, a trainee is finished with instruction on gauge use when she or he can match the repeatability standard for the gauge.

3. Reproducibility

This shows the variation in average measurement when different people use the same gauge. An excessive reproducibility value reflects a training problem.

4. Stability

This assesses the difference in average measurement over a long period of time. Gauge wear, upkeep, and periodic calibration are all factors of gauge stability.

The overall accuracy of a gauge is the combined effect of its accuracy, repeatability, reproducibility, and stability.

11.1   PREPARATIONS FOR A GAUGE CAPABILITY STUDY

Before collecting any data, complete the planning. Use the following questions to evaluate the need for the study.

- Is individual gauge capability assessment needed?
- Is training in gauge use in question?
- Is there a gauge problem in some phase of the operation?
- Is this study a preparation for control charting?

Also consider the details of the study procedure.

- How many people will be involved in taking the readings?
- How many like pieces are to be measured?
- How many repeat readings will be made by each individual?

Be sure the gauge is potentially able to do the job. The rule of 10 states that the gauge should be at least one tenth as accurate as the tolerance of the characteristic that is being measured. If the tolerance is set to the nearest .001, the gauge should read to the nearest .0001. When working with A processes, in which the 6σ spread of the measurements uses less than half of the tolerance, the rule of 10 is amended. In that case more precision is needed and the gauge should be read to one-tenth of the 6σ value.

11.2 THE GAUGE CAPABILITY PROCEDURE

The following directions refer to the gauge capability worksheet. There are 15 steps listed in the procedure, and Figure 11.2 indicates the section on the gauge capability worksheet that corresponds to each step (see page 313). Example 11.1 works along with the directions. As each step is presented, do the appropriate work on the worksheet in Figure 11.3 (page 315). Check your results with the completed worksheet in Figure 11.6 (page 320). You can also use the worksheet in Figure 11.2 as a "roadmap" because it matches the worksheet section with the procedure step.

Step 1   The pieces being measured should be numbered. The worksheet shows room for 10 different pieces.

Step 2   The measurements should be taken in random order.

Step 3   A set of "blind" measurements is best: The individual taking a measurement does not know which piece is being measured, what the previous measurements were on that piece, or what measurements other employees found on that piece.

Step 4   Record all the measurements on the worksheet. There is room on the chart for three sets of measurements by three different operators.

Step 5   After all the measurements are taken, calculate the trial range for each piece for each operator and record the values in columns 4, 8, and 12.

Step 6   Calculate all column totals and record the values in the totals row.

Step 7   Calculate the averages $\bar{x}_A, \bar{x}_B,$ and $\bar{x}_C$. Transfer the nine trial column totals to the directed boxes at the extension of columns 2, 6, and 10 (follow the arrows). Add the three column totals of each operator for the sum, then divide the sum by 30 for each $\bar{x}$ value. Each operator has taken 30 measurements, so the average measurement is the sum divided by 30.

Step 8   Calculate $\bar{R}$. As directed in the previous step, an average measurement is needed for each operator. The average range, however, is determined from *all* the measurements. The basic calculation is to add all 30 range values and then divide by 30. The worksheet does this a little differently by using the column totals.

Calculate the range column averages by dividing the column total by 10. Do this for columns 4, 8, and 12. Transfer the averages to the box for step 8 (see Figure 11.2), add the three column averages, and divide by 3.

Step 9   Calculate the control limit for the ranges in the box below columns 6, 7, and 8. The box to the left gives the values of the constant D_4.

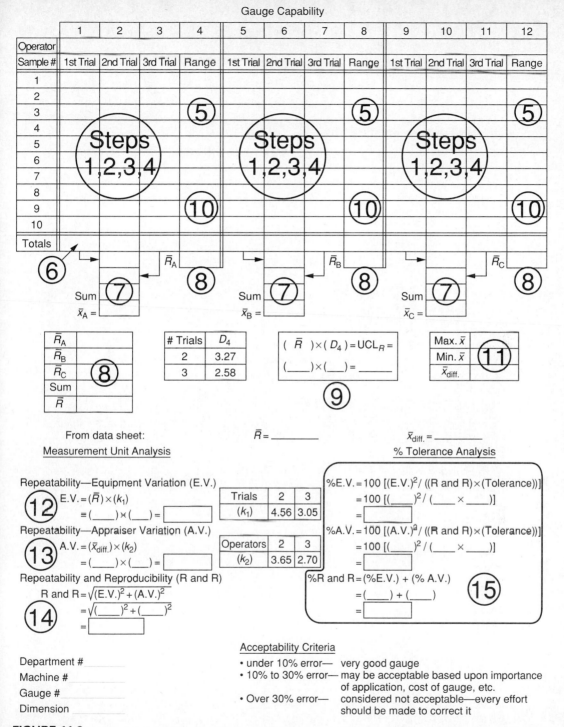

FIGURE 11.2
Sections of the gauge capability worksheet are marked to correspond to the steps of the procedure.
*Gauge capability analysis form courtesy of Saginaw Division of General Motors Corporation.

313

Step 10   Scan the range values in columns 4, 8, and 12 for points out-of-control. If any out of control values occur, take one of these two options:

1. Eliminate the out-of-control points from the set of data and recalculate the $\bar{x}$'s, $\bar{R}$, and UCL_R. Be sure to change the calculation divisors as necessary. Remember, every average is the sum divided by the number of values.
2. Have the operator measure that particular item again if only one value is clearly in error. If a few errors have been made, replace all three measurements by that particular operator in each error row. Mix in a few other measurements to keep the test blind (unbiased). Recalculate the necessary $\bar{x}$'s, $\bar{R}$'s, and UCL_R. The calculation divisors will remain the same because the number of data values has not changed with the replacement(s).

Step 11   Calculate the $\bar{x}$ range. Substract the smallest $\bar{x}$ value from the largest. This is labeled $\bar{x}_{\text{diff.}}$ on the calculation sheet.

Step 12   Complete a repeatability analysis. On the caluclation sheet, repeatability is given the symbol E.V. (for equipment variation, the main cause for repeatability errors).

Step 13   Do a reproducibility analysis. Reproducibility is represented on the calculation sheet by A.V. (for appraisor variation, the main cause for reproducibility errors). The k_2 constant is given in the box on the calculation sheet next to the A.V. calculation section.

Step 14   The combined effect of repeatability and reproducibility, called R and R on the calculation sheet, is found by adding their squared values and taking the square root of that sum. The $(\text{E.V.})^2$ and $(\text{A.V.})^2$ represent variability measures called the *variance*. When two or more sources of variability are present, the combined effect is found by adding their variances. The square root of the variance is the standard deviation, so the last step, the square root, gives the R and R as a standard deviation measure of variability. The constant factor present in the E.V. and A.V. calculation, k, makes the R and R a measurement value.

Step 15   Compare R and R with the tolerance to determine the percent error relative to the tolerance.

EXAMPLE 11.1

Figure 11.3 is a gauge capability worksheet. Steps 1 through 4 have been completed. Three operators have measured 10 different pieces three times each in the manner described in steps 2 and 3. Do the calculations on Figure 11.3 as the following steps direct. Check your results with Figure 11.6.

Solution

Begin at step 5, because steps 1 through 4 have been done. Calculate the range: On Chart 1, Operator A, Piece 1 has a high of 2.102 and a low of 2.101. Subtract for a range of .001. Piece 2 has a high of 2.107 and a low of 2.104. Subtract for a range of .003. Continue this process for the rest of the range values.

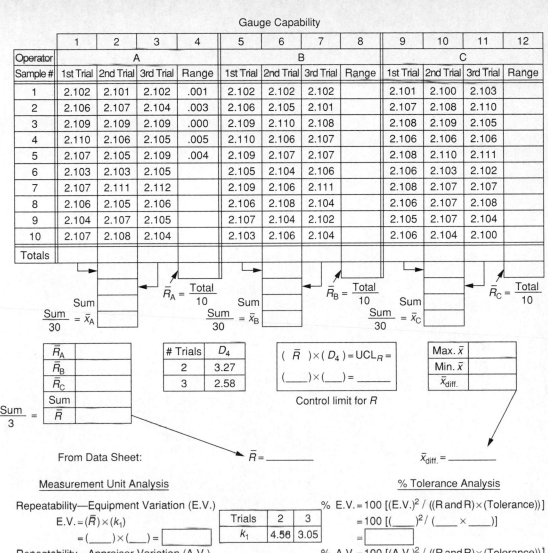
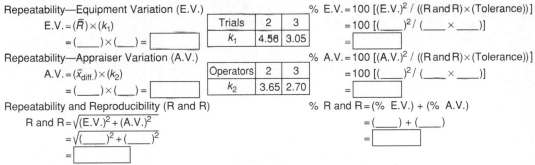

FIGURE 11.3

Gauge capability worksheet. *Gauge capability analysis form courtesy of Saginaw Division of General Motors Corporation.

Record the totals for step 6 and do the calculations for step 7.

Calculations for Operator A

21.061	Column 1 total
21.062	Column 2 total
+ 21.061	Column 3 total
63.184	Sum

$$\overline{x}_A = \frac{\text{sum}}{30}$$

$$= \frac{63.184}{30} = 2.1061$$

Calculations for Operator B

21.066	Column 5 total
21.058	Column 6 total
+ 21.052	Column 7 total
63.176	Sum

$$\overline{x}_B = \frac{\text{sum}}{30}$$

$$= \frac{63.176}{30} = 2.1059$$

Calculations for Operator C

21.061	Column 9 total
21.061	Column 10 total
+ 21.056	Column 11 total
63.178	Sum

$$\overline{x}_C = \frac{\text{sum}}{30}$$

$$= \frac{63.178}{30} = 2.1059$$

For step 8, calculate the average range.

$$\overline{R} = \frac{\overline{R}_A + \overline{R}_B + \overline{R}_C}{3}$$

$$= \frac{.0028 + .0032 + .0029}{3}$$

$$= \frac{.0089}{3}$$

$$= .00297$$

Calculate the control limit for step 9. In this case, with three trials, $D_4 = 2.58$.

$$\begin{aligned} UCL_R &= D_4 \cdot \overline{R} \\ &= 2.58 \times .00297 \\ &= .00766 \end{aligned}$$

Look for out-of-control points (range values larger than .00766) and follow the procedure for step 10. For step 11, calculate the $\overline{x}$ range:

$$\begin{array}{rl} 2.1061 & \text{Largest } \overline{x} \\ -2.1059 & \text{Smallest } \overline{x} \\ \hline .0002 & \overline{x}_{\text{diff.}} \end{array}$$

At this point, all the boxes on the upper half of Figure 11.3 should be filled.

The repeated measurements for each piece will be normally distributed. To find the repeatability spread for 99 percent of the measurements on a piece, use a z value of 2.575. This is the z value from the normal curve table that corresponds to an area of .005 in each tail, which results in a middle area of .99, or 99 percent. This is shown in Figure 11.4. That z value of 2.575 is combined with a few other necessary numerical constants

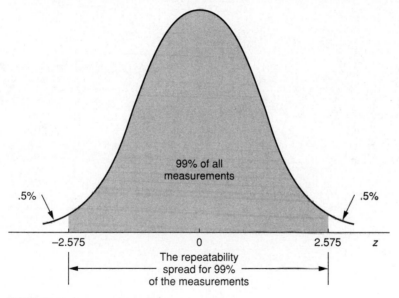

FIGURE 11.4
The distribution of measurements is normal in Example 11.1

and is represented by the k_1 on the calculation sheet. The k_1 constants are given in a box to the right of the E.V. calculation section.

$$\begin{aligned} E.V. &= \overline{R} \cdot k_1 \\ &= .00297 \times 3.05 \\ &= .00906 \end{aligned}$$

The variation caused by repeatability errors uses .00906 measurement units. Each individual piece has its average measurement, $\bar{x}$. Dividing the .00906 in half gives .0045, so 99 percent of the time the gauge will measure the piece between $\bar{x} - .0045$ and $\bar{x} + .0045$. This is illustrated in Figure 11.5.

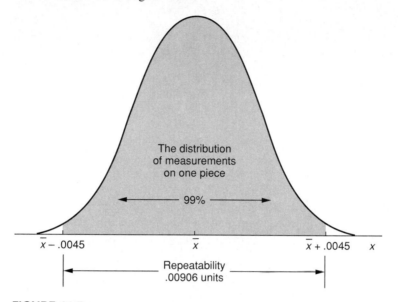

The distribution of measurements on one piece

99%

$\bar{x} - .0045$ $\bar{x}$ $\bar{x} + .0045$ x

Repeatability
.00906 units

FIGURE 11.5

The range of measurements on one piece caused by repeatability variation.

Complete the reproducibility analysis for step 13 as follows:

$$
\begin{aligned}
\text{A.V.} &= \bar{x}_{\text{diff.}} \cdot k_2 \\
&= .0002 \times 2.70 \\
&= .00054
\end{aligned}
$$

The variance must be calculated for step 14.

$$
\begin{aligned}
\text{R and R} &= \sqrt{(\text{E.V.})^2 + (\text{A.V.})^2} \\
&= \sqrt{(.00906)^2 + (.00054)^2} \\
&= \sqrt{.0000824} \\
&= .00908 \text{ measurement units (See Figure 11.7 on page 321.)}
\end{aligned}
$$

The following is the calculator sequence for R and R:

Enter .00906.

Square it. Either press the x^2 button or do the multiplication: .00906 $\times$ .00906 .0000818.

Store it in the memory: press M.

Enter .00054.

Square it.

Add it to the memory: press M+.

Recall the sum: press MR.

Square root it: press $\sqrt{\ }$.

To determine the percent error relative to the tolerance, first calculate the repeatability percent error.

$$\% \text{ E.V.} = \frac{100(\text{E.V.})^2}{(\text{R and R}) \times \text{Tolerance}}$$

$$= \frac{100(.00906)^2}{.00908 \times .1}$$

$$= \frac{100(.0000821)}{.000908}$$

$$= \frac{.00821}{.000908}$$

$$= 9.04\%$$

The calculator sequence for this process is shown here:

Press .00908, $\times$ .1, $=$.

Store the answer in the memory by pressing the M key.

Enter .00906.

Square it with the x^2 key or by multiplying.

Press $\times$, 100, $=$.

Divide by MR (the denominator, which was put in memory).

Press $=$.

Calculate the reproducibility percent error.

$$\% \text{ A.V.} = \frac{100(\text{A.V.})^2}{(\text{R and R}) \times \text{Tolerance}}$$

$$= \frac{100(.00054)^2}{.00908 \times .1}$$

$$= \frac{100(.000000292)}{.000908}$$

$$= \frac{.0000292}{.000908}$$

$$= .03\%$$

The same calculator sequence can be used here. Simply use .00054 in place of .00906.

Gauge Capability

	1	2	3	4	5	6	7	8	9	10	11	12
Operator	A				B				C			
Sample #	1st Trial	2nd Trial	3rd Trial	Range	1st Trial	2nd Trial	3rd Trial	Range	1st Trial	2nd Trial	3rd Trial	Range
1	2.102	2.101	2.102	.001	2.102	2.102	2.102	.000	2.101	2.100	2.103	.003
2	2.106	2.107	2.104	.003	2.106	2.105	2.101	.005	2.107	2.108	2.110	.003
3	2.109	2.109	2.109	.000	2.109	2.110	2.108	.002	2.108	2.109	2.105	.004
4	2.110	2.106	2.105	.005	2.110	2.106	2.107	.004	2.106	2.106	2.106	.000
5	2.107	2.105	2.109	.004	2.109	2.107	2.107	.002	2.108	2.110	2.111	.003
6	2.103	2.103	2.105	.002	2.105	2.104	2.106	.002	2.106	2.103	2.102	.004
7	2.107	2.111	2.112	.005	2.109	2.106	2.111	.005	2.108	2.107	2.107	.001
8	2.106	2.105	2.106	.001	2.106	2.108	2.104	.004	2.106	2.107	2.108	.002
9	2.104	2.107	2.105	.003	2.107	2.104	2.102	.005	2.105	2.107	2.104	.003
10	2.107	2.108	2.104	.004	2.103	2.106	2.104	.003	2.106	2.104	2.100	.006
Totals	21.061	21.062	21.061	.028	21.066	21.058	21.052	.032	21.061	21.061	21.056	.029

$$\bar{R}_A = \frac{\text{Total}}{10}$$
21.061, 21.061, 21.061 → .0028
Sum 63.184
$$\frac{\text{Sum}}{30} = \bar{x}_A \quad 2.1061$$

$$\bar{R}_B = \frac{\text{Total}}{10}$$
21.066, 21.052 → .0032
Sum 63.176
$$\frac{\text{Sum}}{30} = \bar{x}_B \quad 2.1059$$

$$\bar{R}_C = \frac{\text{Total}}{10}$$
21.061, 21.056 → .0029
Sum 63.178
$$\frac{\text{Sum}}{30} = \bar{x}_C \quad 2.1059$$

$\bar{R}_A$	.0028
$\bar{R}_B$	.0032
$\bar{R}_C$	.0029
Sum	.0089

$$\frac{\text{Sum}}{3} = \bar{R} \quad .00297$$

# Trials	D_4
2	3.27
3	2.58

$$(\ \bar{R}\ ) \times (D_4) = UCL_R =$$
$$(.00297) \times (2.58) = .0077$$

Max. $\bar{x}$	2.1061
Min. $\bar{x}$	2.1059
$\bar{x}_{\text{diff.}}$	.0002

From Data Sheet:

$$\bar{R} = \underline{.00297}$$

$$\bar{x}_{\text{diff.}} = \underline{.0002}$$

Measurement Unit Analysis

Repeatability—Equipment Variation (E.V.)

$$E.V. = (\bar{R}) \times (k_1)$$
$$= (.00297) \times (3.05) = \boxed{.00906}$$

Trials	2	3
k_1	4.56	3.05

Repeatability—Appraiser Variation (A.V.)

$$A.V. = (\bar{x}_{\text{diff.}}) \times (k_2)$$
$$= (.0002) \times (2.70) = \boxed{.00054}$$

Operators	2	3
k_2	3.65	2.70

Repeatability and Reproducibility (R and R)

$$R \text{ and } R = \sqrt{(E.V.)^2 + (A.V.)^2}$$
$$= \sqrt{(00906)^2 + (.00054)^2}$$
$$= \boxed{.00908}$$

% Tolerance Analysis

$$\% \ E.V. = 100\,[(E.V.)^2 / ((R \text{ and } R) \times (\text{Tolerance}))]$$
$$= 100\,[(00906)^2 / (.00908 \times .1)]$$
$$= \boxed{9.04\%}$$

$$\% \ A.V. = 100\,[(A.V.)^2 / ((R \text{ and } R) \times (\text{Tolerance}))]$$
$$= 100\,[(.00054)^2 / (.00908 \times .1)]$$
$$= \boxed{.03\%}$$

$$\% \ R \text{ and } R = (\% \ E.V.) + (\% \ A.V.)$$
$$= (9.04\%) + (.03\%)$$
$$= \boxed{9.07\%}$$

Acceptability Criteria
- under 10% error— very good gauge
- 10% to 30% error— may be acceptable based upon importance of application, cost of gauge, etc.
- Over 30% error— considered not acceptable—every effort should be made to correct it

Department #_____

Machine #_____

Gauge #_____

Dimension 2.10 to 2.20

FIGURE 11.6

Gauge capability answer sheet for Example 11.1. *Gauge capability analysis form courtesy of Saginaw Division of General Motors Corporation.

The total percent error can be found by adding the individual percent errors.

$$\% \text{ R and R} = \%\text{E.V.} + \%\text{A.V.}$$
$$= 9.04\% + .03\%$$
$$= 9.07\%$$

The criteria listed on the calculation sheet classify this gauge as very good (with less than 10 percent error).

The R and R figure calculated at step 14 represents the number of measurement units that account for 99 percent of the gauge variation of R and R. If the gauge is accurate and the average reading for a piece equals the true reading, then 99 percent of the readings on that piece will be between

$$\bar{x} - .00454 \text{ and } \bar{x} + .00454$$

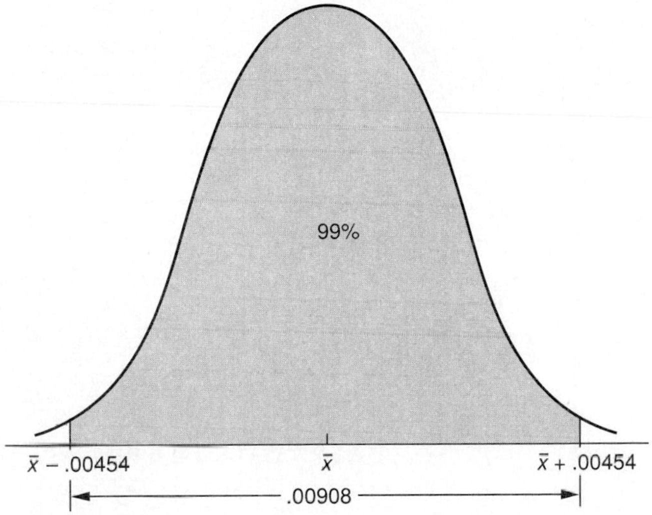

FIGURE 11.7
Measurement units that account for 99 percent of the repeatability and reproducibility variation.

EXAMPLE 11.2

Do a gauge capability study with the data in Figure 11.8 (page 322). Follow steps 1 through 15; the actual work in this example starts at step 5. The chart in Figure 11.2 again shows the section of the chart that corresponds to each step in the procedure. Check your calculations with the completed work in Figures 11.9 (page 323) and 11.10 (page 324).

Solution
Complete steps 5, 6, and 7 (steps 1 through 4 have been completed). Check your results with the partially completed chart in Figure 11.9. Do the calculations for steps 8 and 9. Check for out-of-control points in step 10 using the result of step 9 (UCL$_R$ = .0061). Complete the rest of the steps of the procedure.

	1	2	3	4	5	6	7	8	9	10	11	12
Operator	A				B				C			
Sample #	1st Trial	2nd Trial	3rd Trial	Range	1st Trial	2nd Trial	3rd Trial	Range	1st Trial	2nd Trial	3rd Trial	Range
1	.723	.723	.725		.721	.724	.725		.722	.723	.723	
2	.725	.727	.724		.726	.723	.725		.726	.726	.723	
3	.728	.725	.724		.727	.725	.728		.729	.727	.726	
4	.724	.728	.725		.726	.728	.729		.728	.727	.729	
5	.723	.725	.723		.724	.726	.724		.727	.725	.724	
6	.728	.728	.728		.726	.727	.725		.725	.724	.728	
7	.723	.724	.722		.723	.721	.721		.722	.724	.725	
8	.727	.729	.727		.725	.729	.727		.728	.728	.728	
9	.724	.725	.725		.726	.724	.726		.727	.725	.726	
10	.728	.729	.726		.727	.727	.727		.727	.729	.729	
Totals												

$\bar{R}_A$ $\bar{R}_B$ $\bar{R}_C$

Sum ____   Sum ____   Sum ____

$\bar{x}_A =$ $\bar{x}_B =$ $\bar{x}_C =$

$\bar{R}_A$	
$\bar{R}_B$	
$\bar{R}_C$	
Sum	
$\bar{R}$	

# Trials	D_4
2	3.27
3	2.58

$(\ \bar{R}\ ) \times (\ D_4\ ) = UCL_R =$

$(\underline{\quad}) \times (\underline{\quad}) = \underline{\quad\quad}$

Max. $\bar{x}$	
Min. $\bar{x}$	
$\bar{x}_{diff.}$	

From data sheet: $\bar{R} = \underline{\quad\quad}$ $\bar{x}_{diff.} = \underline{\quad\quad}$

Measurement Unit Analysis   % Tolerance Analysis

Repeatability—Equipment Variation (E.V.)

$E.V. = (\bar{R}) \times (k_1)$

$= (\underline{\quad}) \times (\underline{\quad}) = \boxed{\quad}$

Trials	2	3
k_1	4.56	3.05

% E.V. $= 100\ [(E.V.)^2\ /\ ((R\ and\ R) \times (Tolerance))]$

$= 100\ [(\underline{\quad})^2\ /\ (\underline{\quad} \times \underline{\quad})]$

$= \boxed{\quad}$

Repeatability—Appraiser Variation (A.V.)

$E.V. = (\bar{x}_{diff.}) \times (k_2)$

$= (\underline{\quad}) \times (\underline{\quad}) = \boxed{\quad}$

Operators	2	3
k_2	3.65	2.70

% A.V. $= 100\ [(A.V.)^2\ /\ ((R\ and\ R) \times (Tolerance))]$

$= 100\ [(\underline{\quad})^2\ /\ (\underline{\quad} \times \underline{\quad})]$

$= \boxed{\quad}$

Repeatability and Reproducibility (R and R)

$R\ and\ R = \sqrt{(E.V.)^2 + (A.V.)^2}$

$= \sqrt{(\underline{\quad})^2 + (\underline{\quad})^2}$

$= \boxed{\quad}$

% R and R $= (\%\ E.V.) + (\%\ A.V.)$

$= (\underline{\quad}) + (\underline{\quad})$

$= \boxed{\quad}$

Department # _____

Machine # _____

Gauge # _____

Dimension .725 ± .005

Acceptability Criteria

• under 10% error— very good gauge
• 10% to 30% error— may be acceptable based upon importance of application, cost of gauge, etc.
• Over 30% error— considered not acceptable—every effort should be made to correct it

FIGURE 11.8

Gauge capability worksheet. *Gauge capability analysis form courtesy of Saginaw Division of General Motors Corporation.

	1	2	3	4	5	6	7	8	9	10	11	12
Operator	A				B				C			
Sample #	1st Trial	2nd Trial	3rd Trial	Range	1st Trial	2nd Trial	3rd Trial	Range	1st Trial	2nd Trial	3rd Trial	Range
1	.723	.723	.725	.002	.721	.724	.725	.004	.722	.723	.723	.001
2	.725	.727	.724	.003	.726	.723	.725	.003	.726	.726	.723	.003
3	.728	.725	.724	.004	.727	.725	.728	.003	.729	.727	.726	.003
4	.724	.728	.725	.004	.726	.728	.729	.003	.728	.727	.729	.002
5	.723	.725	.723	.002	.724	.726	.724	.002	.727	.725	.724	.003
6	.728	.728	.728	.000	.726	.727	.725	.002	.725	.724	.728	.004
7	.723	.724	.722	.002	.723	.721	.721	.002	.722	.724	.725	.003
8	.727	.729	.727	.002	.725	.729	.727	.004	.728	.728	.728	.000
9	.724	.725	.725	.001	.726	.724	.726	.002	.727	.725	.726	.002
10	.728	.729	.726	.003	.727	.727	.727	.000	.727	.729	.729	.002
Totals	7.253	7.263	7.249	.023	7.251	7.254	7.257	.025	7.261	7.258	7.261	.023

$\bar{R}_A$ .0023   7.253   7.249

$\bar{R}_B$ .0025   7.251   7.257

$\bar{R}_C$ .0023   7.261   7.261

Sum 21.765 $\bar{x}_A$ = .7255

Sum 21.762 $\bar{x}_B$ = .7254

Sum 21.780 $\bar{x}_C$ = .726

$\bar{R}_A$	
$\bar{R}_A$	
$\bar{R}_A$	
Sum	
$\bar{R}$	

# Trials	D_4
2	3.27
3	2.58

$(\bar{R}) \times (D_4) = UCL_R =$

$(\_\_\_) \times (\_\_\_) = _____$

Max. $\bar{x}$	
Min. $\bar{x}$	
$\bar{x}_{diff.}$	

From Data Sheet:

$\bar{R} = _____$

$\bar{x}_{diff.} = _____$

Measurement Unit Analysis

% Tolerance Analysis

Repeatability—Equipment Variation (E.V.)

$E.V. = (\bar{R}) \times (k_1)$

$= (\_\_\_) \times (\_\_\_) = \boxed{}$

Trials	2	3
k_1	4.56	3.05

% E.V. $= 100 \, [(E.V.)^2 / ((R \text{ and } R) \times (Tolerance))]$

$= 100 \, [(\_\_\_)^2 / (\_\_\_ \times \_\_\_)]$

$= \boxed{}$

Repeatability—Appraiser Variation (A.V.)

$A.V. = (\bar{x}_{diff.}) \times (k_2)$

$= (\_\_\_) \times (\_\_\_) = \boxed{}$

Operators	2	3
k_2	3.65	2.70

% A.V. $= 100 \, [(A.V.)^2 / ((R \text{ and } R) \times (Tolerance))]$

$= 100 \, [(\_\_\_)^2 / (\_\_\_ \times \_\_\_)]$

$= \boxed{}$

Repeatability and Reproducibility (R and R)

$R \text{ and } R = \sqrt{(E.V.)^2 + (A.V.)^2}$

$= \sqrt{(\_\_\_)^2 + (\_\_\_)^2}$

$= \boxed{}$

% R and R = (% E.V.) + (% A.V.)

$= (\_\_\_) + (\_\_\_)$

$= \boxed{}$

Acceptability Criteria

- under 10% error— very good gauge
- 10% to 30% error— may be acceptable based upon importance of application, cost of gauge, etc.
- Over 30% error— considered not acceptable—every effort should be made to correct it

Department #_____

Machine #_____

Gauge #_____

Dimension .725 ± .005

FIGURE 11.9

Partially completed worksheet for Example 11.2. *Gauge capability analysis form courtesy of Saginaw Division of General Motors Corporation.

Gauge Capability

	1	2	3	4	5	6	7	8	9	10	11	12
Operator		A				B				C		
Sample #	1st Trial	2nd Trial	3rd Trial	Range	1st Trial	2nd Trial	3rd Trial	Range	1st Trial	2nd Trial	3rd Trial	Range
1	.723	.723	.725	.002	.721	.724	.725	.004	.722	.723	.723	.001
2	.725	.727	.724	.003	.726	.723	.725	.003	.726	.726	.723	.003
3	.728	.725	.724	.004	.727	.725	.728	.003	.729	.727	.726	.003
4	.724	.728	.725	.004	.726	.728	.729	.003	.728	.727	.729	.002
5	.723	.725	.723	.002	.724	.726	.724	.002	.727	.725	.724	.003
6	.728	.728	.728	.000	.726	.727	.725	.002	.725	.724	.728	.004
7	.723	.724	.722	.002	.723	.721	.721	.002	.722	.724	.725	.003
8	.727	.729	.727	.002	.725	.729	.727	.004	.728	.728	.728	.000
9	.724	.725	.725	.001	.726	.724	.726	.002	.727	.725	.726	.002
10	.728	.729	.726	.003	.727	.727	.727	.000	.727	.729	.729	.002
Totals	7.253	7.263	7.249	.023	7.251	7.254	7.257	.025	7.261	7.258	7.261	.023

$$\begin{array}{ll} 7.253 & .0023 \\ 7.249 & \bar{R}_A = \dfrac{\Sigma R}{10} \end{array}$$

Sum 21.765 $\bar{x}_A = .7255$

$$\begin{array}{ll} 7.251 & .0025 \\ 7.257 & \bar{R}_B = \dfrac{\Sigma R}{10} \end{array}$$

Sum 21.762 $\bar{x}_B = .7254$

$$\begin{array}{ll} 7.261 & .0023 \\ 7.261 & \bar{R}_C = \dfrac{\Sigma R}{10} \end{array}$$

Sum 21.780 $\bar{x}_C = .7260$

$\bar{R}_A$	.0023
$\bar{R}_B$	.0025
$\bar{R}_C$	.0023
Sum	.0071
$\bar{\bar{R}}$	.00237

# Trials	D_4
2	3.27
③	2.58

$(\bar{\bar{R}}) \times (D_4) = UCL_R =$
$(.00237) \times (2.58) = .0061$

Max. $\bar{x}$	.7260
Min. $\bar{x}$	.7254
$\bar{x}_{diff.}$	.0006

$\bar{\bar{R}} = \dfrac{\Sigma \bar{R}}{3}$

From data sheet: $\bar{\bar{R}} = .00237$ $\bar{x}_{diff.} = .0006$

Measurement Unit Analysis

% Tolerance Analysis

Repeatability—Equipment Variation (E.V.)

$E.V. = (\bar{\bar{R}}) \times (k_1)$

$= (.00237) \times (3.05) = \boxed{.0072}$

Trials	2	③
k_1	4.56	3.05

% E.V. = 100 [(E.V.)² / ((R and R) × (Tolerance))]
$= 100 [(.0072)^2 / (.0074 \times .01)]$
$= \boxed{70\%}$

Repeatability—Appraiser Variation (A.V.)

$A.V. = (\bar{x}_{diff.}) \times (k_2)$

$= (.0006) \times (2.70) = \boxed{.0016}$

Operators	2	③
k_2	3.65	2.70

% A.V. = 100 [(A.V.)² / ((R and R) × (Tolerance))]
$= 100 [(.0016)^2 / (.0074 \times .01)]$
$= \boxed{3.5\%}$

Repeatability and Reproducibility (R and R)

$R \text{ and } R = \sqrt{(E.V.)^2 + (A.V.)^2}$

$= \sqrt{(.0072)^2 + (.0016)^2}$

$= \boxed{.0074}$

% R and R = (% E.V.) + (% A.V.)
$= (70\%) + (3.5\%)$
$= \boxed{73.5\%}$

Acceptability Criteria

- under 10% error— very good gauge
- 10% to 30% error— may be acceptable based upon importance of application, cost of gauge, etc.
- Over 30% error— considered not acceptable—every effort should be made to correct it

Department # _____

Machine # _____

Gauge # _____

Dimension .725 ± .005

FIGURE 11.10

Gauge capability answer sheet for Example 11.2. *Gauge capability analysis form courtesy of Saginaw Division of General Motors Corporation.

In Example 11.2, the percent of the tolerance involved in R and R variation is 73.5 percent, a very high value. This indicates that the gauge is inadequate for the job. Compared with Example 11.1, the big difference is the tolerance demand. The gauge in Example 11.1 varies in thousandths, but the tolerance is one-tenth. In Example 11.2, the variation is also in thousandths, but the tolerance is one-hundredth.

11.3   ANALYSIS OF R AND R WITH ACCURACY AND STABILITY: MAXIMUM POSSIBLE DEFLECTION

If a gauge is not accurate, a linear shift occurs either right or left. Figure 11.11 shows a shift to the right in the gauge readings. The *maximum deflection* from the true reading on a piece, illustrated on page 326 in Figure 11.12, is calculated by

$$\frac{R \text{ and } R}{2} + \text{accuracy shift}$$

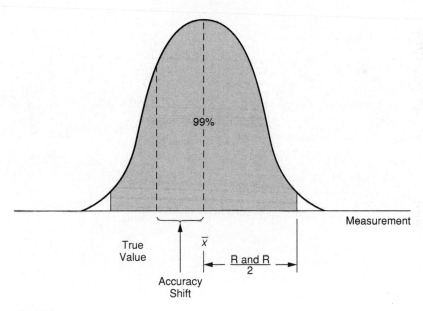

FIGURE 11.11
A shift in the distribution of gauge readings caused by an inaccurate gauge.

The (R and R)/2 corresponds to the maximum possible one-way deflection caused by repeatability and reproducibility variation. The range of possible error in measurement units from the true value is determined from the following algebraic sums:

$$-\frac{(R \text{ and } R)}{2} + \text{accuracy shift} \quad \text{to} \quad \frac{(R \text{ and } R)}{2} + \text{accuracy shift}$$

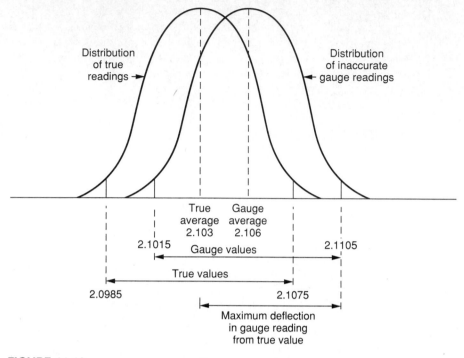

FIGURE 11.12
R and R variation: the gauge range for 99 percent of all measurements versus the true range for 99 percent of all measurements.

The accuracy shift is a positive number if the gauge is measuring high or a negative number when the gauge is measuring low.

EXAMPLE 11.3

Given that the true reading on piece 2 used in Example 11.1 is 2.103, find

1. The accuracy shift
2. The maximum possible deflection
3. The 99 percent range of gauge readings
4. The 99 percent range of true readings

Solution

There are nine measurements of each piece (three measurements by each person), so the sum of the nine readings of piece 2 divided by 9 gives the average measurement.

$$\bar{x} = \frac{\sum x}{N}$$

$$= \frac{18.954}{9}$$

$$= 2.106$$

2.106   Average reading on the piece
$\underline{-\ 2.103}$ True measurement
.003   Accuracy shift

The gauge variability caused by R and R is .00908. Half is .0045, so 99 percent of the gauge readings on piece 2 will be in the interval 2.106 ± .0045, or 2.1015 to 2.1105.

The maximum possible deflection from the true measurement is the sum of $\frac{1}{2}$(R and R) and the accuracy shift:

$$.0045 + .003 = .0075$$

The gauge is measuring high because of the accuracy shift, so a deduction of .003 from the gauge reading interval will give the interval in which the true measurement will be 99 percent of the time. This new interval is 2.0985 to 2.1075. The calculations are illustrated in Figure 11.12.

Stability also represents a shift either left or right. The stability shift is added algebraically to the accuracy shift and then combined with R and R, as before, to determine the maximum possible deflection in measurement and the possible range in measurement.

EXAMPLE 11.4

Illustrate the added effect of stability when piece 2 from Example 11.1 is tested two weeks later and $\bar{x} = 2.104$.

Solution
This represents a shift left from the previous readings.

2.106   Previous average value
$\underline{-\ 2.104}$ Latest average value
.002   Stability shift

The stability shift is −.002 because the measurements shifted left. This is illustrated in Figure 11.13 (see page 328).

In this case the stability shifted in the opposite direction as the accuracy and cancelled part of the accuracy shift. The combined accuracy and stability shift becomes

$$+.003 - .002 = +.001$$

The gauge is now reading .001 units high.

The maximum variation from the true value owing to gauge variability is

$$\frac{R \text{ and } R}{2} + \text{accuracy shift} + \text{stability shift}$$

Therefore, .0045 + .003 − .002 is .0055 units. The gauge readings on piece 2 vary between 2.104 + .0045 and 2.104 − .0045, or 2.0995 and 2.1085, 99 percent of the

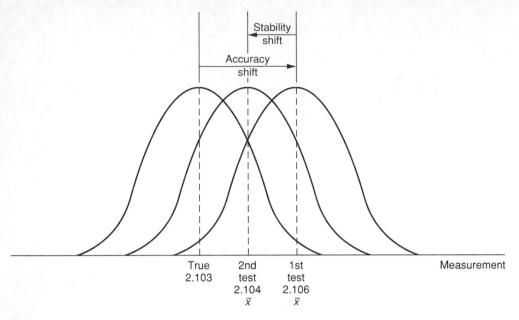

FIGURE 11.13
The distribution of measurements following an accuracy shift and a stability shift.

time. The combined effect of accuracy and stability results in the gauge reading .001 units high on any measurement.

EXAMPLE 11.5   Do an accuracy analysis on piece 2 in Figure 11.10. Given that the true measurement of the piece is .727, complete these five steps.

1. Find the average measurement.
2. Find the accuracy shift.
3. Find the 99 percent range in gauge readings.
4. Find the 99 percent range in true readings.
5. Find the maximum possible deflection.

Solution
First, find $\bar{x}$.

$$\bar{x} = \frac{\sum x}{N}$$

$$= \frac{6.525}{9}$$

$$= .725$$

Second, the accuracy shift is the difference between the average and true measurements.

$$
\begin{array}{rl}
.725 & \text{Average measurement} \\
- .727 & \text{True measurement} \\
\hline
- .002 & \text{Accuracy shift}
\end{array}
$$

The accuracy shift is a shift to the left on the measurement scale, so it is indicated by a negative number.

Third, half of R and R for the gauge is $\frac{.0074}{2} = .0037$. The 99 percent range for the gauge readings on piece 2 is $.725 \pm .0037$, or .7213 to .7287. For step 4, the 99 percent range for the true measurement of piece 2 is $.727 \pm .0037$, or .7233 to .7307.

Finally, the maximum possible deflection is

$$
\text{Accuracy shift} + \frac{\text{R and R}}{2} = .002 + .0037
$$

$$
= .0057
$$

The maximum possible deflection from the true measurement shifts left because that is the direction in which the combined effect of the two gauge variation factors is the greatest. This is illustrated in Figure 11.14.

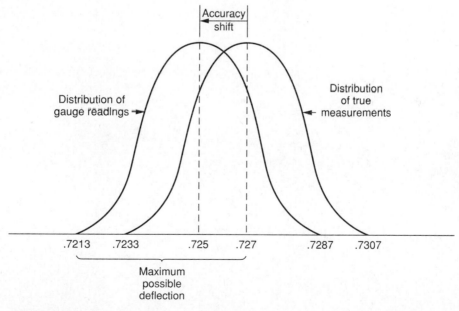

FIGURE 11.14
The accuracy shift and maximum possible deflection for Example 11.5.

11.4 THE ELIMINATION OF GAUGE VARIATION FROM PROCESS VARIATION

The measurement of process variability encompasses the accumulated effects of all sources of variation, including gauge variation, so the elimination of gauge variability allows a truer estimate of process variation. Gauge repeatability errors are generally the largest contributors to gauge variability and can be determined from the gauge capability analysis.

One concept concerning statistical variation states that if a process is in control and satisfies a normal distribution, the total variance caused by a combination of k variation sources is equal to the sum of the individual variances.

$$\sigma_{Total}^2 = \sigma_1^2 + \sigma_2^2 + \cdots + \sigma_k^2$$

Standard deviation, σ, was introduced in Chapter 3 as a statistical measure of variability. The variance, σ^2, is the square of the standard deviation value, so it is also a measure of variability. The concept that variability from several sources is additive should make sense intuitively. As a simple example, consider a lawn mower engine that is secured to a deck with four bolts. If one of the bolts becomes loose, there will be an increase in vibration with some detrimental effect on the various mower parts. If a second bolt loosens, will the vibration increase or decrease? The vibration and its effect will be worse with the two bolts loose than if either bolt were loose alone. The second source of variation causes an increase in total variability.

This concept can also be applied to process capability.[2] The total variance in the process is the sum of the process variance and the gauge variance.

$$\sigma_{Total}^2 = \sigma_{Gauge}^2 + \sigma_{Process}^2$$

By applying algebra and subtracting from both sides of the equation, the equation changes to a form in which the process variance is equal to the gauge variance subtracted from the total variance.

$$\sigma_{Process}^2 = \sigma_{Total}^2 - \sigma_{Gauge}^2$$

The process standard deviation is the square root of the process variance.

$$\sigma_{Process} = \sqrt{\sigma_{Total}^2 - \sigma_{Gauge}^2}$$

The total variability, as a standard deviation measurement, is calculated using $\overline{R}$ from the control charts.

$$\sigma_{Total} = \frac{\overline{R}}{d_2}$$

---

[2] Robert W. Traver, "Measuring Equipment Repeatability—The Rubber Ruler," *American Society for Quality Control Annual Convention Transactions* (1962). Reprinted with permission of the American Society for Quality Control.

Gauge variability is mainly caused by gauge repeatability and the standard deviation for gauge repeatability, σ_{Gauge}, is used as the estimate of gauge variability. The $\overline{R}$ from step 8 in the gauge capability study is used to determine the value of σ_{Gauge}.

$$\sigma_{Gauge} = \frac{\overline{R}}{d_2}$$

The two standard deviation formulas, σ_{Total} and σ_{Gauge}, look the same; they both equal $\overline{R}/d_2$. However, the two $\overline{R}$ and d_2 values differ. In the σ_{Total} formula, $\overline{R}$ comes from the control chart and d_2 depends on the sample size used on the control chart. For the σ_{Gauge} formula, $\overline{R}$ is the average range from step 8 in the gauge capability procedure and d_2 depends on the number of repeated measurements.

EXAMPLE 11.6

The gauge from the gauge capability study in Example 11.1 is used in a process in which the tolerance is .1. An x and $\overline{R}$ control chart from that process has samples of $n = 5$ and $\overline{R} = .0372$.

1. What is the total process capability?
2. What is the true process capability when the effect of gauge variation is removed?

Solution

For the capability calculations, the sample size on the control chart is $n = 5$. According to Table 1.1 in Appendix B, $d_2 = 2.326$.

$$\sigma_{Total} = \frac{\overline{R}}{d_2}$$

$$= \frac{.0372}{2.326}$$

$$= .016$$

$$PCR = \frac{6\sigma_{Total}}{Tolerance}$$

$$= \frac{6 \times .016}{.1}$$

$$= \frac{.096}{.1}$$

$$= .96$$

The process uses 96 percent of the tolerance.

Second, from Figure 11.6, $\overline{R} = .00297$. Each measurement was taken three times, so the sample size is $n = 3$, and $d_2 = 1.693$.

$$\sigma_{Gauge} = \frac{\overline{R}}{d_2}$$

$$= \frac{.00297}{1.693}$$

$$= .00175$$

$$\sigma_{Process} = \sqrt{\sigma_{Total}^2 - \sigma_{Gauge}^2}$$

$$= \sqrt{(.016)^2 - (.00175)^2}$$

$$= \sqrt{.000253}$$

$$= .0159$$

$$PCR = \frac{6\sigma_{Process}}{Tolerance}$$

$$= \frac{6 \times .0159}{.1}$$

$$= .95$$

The conclusion of Example 11.1 indicates that the gauge is classified as very good. The measure of process capability changed from .96 to .95 when the gauge variability was eliminated. This indicates that the gauge has very little effect on the measure of process capability.

EXAMPLE 11.7

The gauge from the capability study in Example 11.2 is used in a process in which the tolerance is .01. A control chart from that process has samples of $n = 5$ and $\overline{R} = .00442$.

1. What is the total process capability?
2. What is the true process capability when the effect of the gauge variation is removed?

Solution

The calculations from the total process capability are as follows:

$$\sigma_{Total} = \frac{\overline{R}}{d_2}$$

$$= \frac{.00442}{2.326}$$

$$= .0019$$

$$6\sigma_{Total} = 6 \times .0019$$
$$= .0114$$

$$PCR = \frac{6\sigma_{Total}}{Tolerance}$$

$$= \frac{.0114}{.01}$$

$$= 1.14$$

The process uses 114 percent of the tolerance, a poor process.

From Figure 11.10, $\overline{R}$ = .00237. Use this to calculate the second part of the problem.

$$\sigma_{\text{Gauge}} = \frac{\overline{R}}{d_2}$$

$$= \frac{.00237}{1.693}$$

$$= .0014$$

$$\sigma_{\text{Process}} = \sqrt{\sigma_{\text{Total}}^2 - \sigma_{\text{Gauge}}^2}$$

$$= \sqrt{(.0019)^2 - (.0014)^2}$$

$$= \sqrt{.00000165}$$

$$= .00128$$

$$\text{PCR} = \frac{6\sigma_{\text{Process}}}{\text{Tolerance}}$$

$$= \frac{6 \times .00128}{.01}$$

$$= \frac{.00768}{.01}$$

$$= .77$$

When gauge variability is eliminated, the process actually uses 77 percent of the tolerance.

The conclusion of Example 11.2 labels this gauge a very poor one. This example indicates that the gauge is a significant contributor to the measure of process capability. A process thought to use 114 percent of the tolerance actually uses 77 percent of the tolerance.

11.5 INDECISIVE GAUGE READINGS

The effect of gauge variability on process measurements is illustrated in Figure 11.15 (page 334). Pieces whose true measurements are in section A in this figure will always be considered good because the gauge variation is not enough to throw the reading out of specification. The maximum gauge deflection is not large enough to measure a good piece as out of specification. All pieces whose true measurements are in sections B or C will be classified as good or bad according to the effect of gauge variation on that individual measurement. If the gauge variation throws the reading toward the middle, so that it is in specification, the piece is considered good. If the gauge variation throws the reading toward the outside, it registers out of specification. Some pieces that are in specification in Sections B and C will occasionally be classified as out of specification owing to gauge variability, and some pieces that are out of specification in these areas will be considered good pieces.

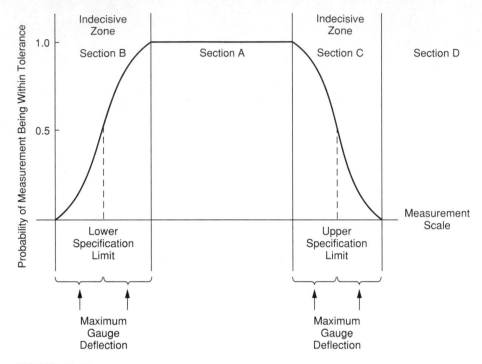

FIGURE 11.15
Indecisive zones in gauge reading. *Robert W. Traver, "Measuring Equipment Repeatability—The Rubber Ruler," *American Society for Quality Control Annual Convention Transactions* (1962). Reprinted with the permission of the American Society for Quality Control.

A piece whose true measurement falls in section D or E will always measure out of specification because the gauge variation is not large enough to throw the reading into the in-specification section.

The width of sections B and C, the indecisive zones, is determined by the amount of gauge variability. The maximum widths in each section will be twice the maximum gauge deflection.

EXERCISES

1. **(a)** Complete the gauge capability chart in Figure 11.16. (page 335).
   (b) If the gauge is accurate, what is the maximum possible deflection between the true measurement and the gauge reading?
   (c) If the gauge has an accuracy shift left of .003 (that is, if the true measurement is .546, the gauge measurement is .543), what is the maximum possible deflection between the true measurement and the gauge reading?
   (d) After a week of use, the gauge has a stability shift left of .002. Combine this information with the accuracy shift information from (c) to determine the maximum possible deflection between the true measurement and the gauge reading.

	1	2	3	4	5	6	7	8	9	10	11	12
Operator												
Sample #	1st Trial	2nd Trial	3rd Trial	Range	1st Trial	2nd Trial	3rd Trial	Range	1st Trial	2nd Trial	3rd Trial	Range
1	.542	.543	.542		.543	.545	.542		.541	.543	.544	
2	.544	.547	.545		.546	.546	.546		.544	.547	.546	
3	.544	.547	.548		.546	.544	.547		.548	.549	.545	
4	.541	.543	.544		.544	.545	.545		.542	.544	.546	
5	.546	.548	.544		.547	.546	.545		.545	.547	.547	
6	.545	.545	.546		.546	.547	.547		.544	.545	.548	
7	.547	.548	.546		.548	.546	.545		.547	.545	.548	
8	.544	.544	.547		.545	.544	.546		.543	.546	.547	
9	.542	.546	.548		.545	.547	.548		.546	.543	.547	
10	.544	.545	.547		.546	.546	.548		.549	.544	.546	
Totals												

$\bar{R}_A = \dfrac{\text{Total}}{10}$ + Sum

$\dfrac{\text{Sum}_A}{30} = \bar{x}_A$

$\bar{R}_B = \dfrac{\text{Total}}{10}$ + Sum

$\dfrac{\text{Sum}_B}{30} = \bar{x}_B$

$\bar{R}_C = \dfrac{\text{Total}}{10}$ + Sum

$\dfrac{\text{Sum}_C}{30} = \bar{x}_C$

$\bar{R}_A$	
$\bar{R}_B$	
$\bar{R}_C$	
Sum_R	
$\bar{R}$	

$\dfrac{\text{Sum}_R}{3} =$

# Trials	D_4
2	3.27
3	2.58

$(\ \bar{R}\ ) \times (D_4) = \text{UCL}_R =$

$(\underline{\quad}) \times (\underline{\quad}) = \underline{\quad}$

Control limit for R

Max. $\bar{x}$	
Min. $\bar{x}$	
$\bar{x}_{\text{diff.}}$	

From data sheet:
Measurement Unit Analysis

$\bar{R} = \underline{\qquad}$

$\bar{x}_{\text{diff.}} = \underline{\qquad}$
% Tolerance Analysis

Repeatability—Equipment Variation (E.V.)

$\text{E.V.} = (\bar{R}) \times (k_1)$

$= (\underline{\quad}) \times (\underline{\quad}) = \boxed{}$

Trials	2	3
(k_1)	4.56	3.05

% E.V. $= 100\,[(\text{E.V.})^2 / ((\text{R and R}) \times (\text{Tolerance}))\,]$

$= 100\,[(\underline{\quad})^2 / (\underline{\quad} \times \underline{\quad})\,]$

$= \boxed{}$

Repeatability—Appraiser Variation (A.V.)

$\text{A.V.} = (\bar{x}_{\text{diff.}}) \times (k_2)$

$= (\underline{\quad}) \times (\underline{\quad}) = \boxed{}$

Operators	2	3
(k_2)	3.65	2.70

% A.V. $= 100\,[(\text{A.V.})^2 / ((\text{R and R}) \times (\text{Tolerance}))\,]$

$= 100\,[(\underline{\quad})^2 / (\underline{\quad} \times \underline{\quad})\,]$

$= \boxed{}$

Repeatability and Reproducibility (R and R)

$\text{R and R} = \sqrt{(\text{E.V.})^2 + (\text{A.V.})^2}$

$= \sqrt{(\underline{\quad})^2 + (\underline{\quad})^2}$

$= \boxed{}$

% R and R $= (\%\,\text{E.V.}) + (\%\,\text{A.V.})$

$= (\underline{\quad}) + (\underline{\quad})$

$= \boxed{}$

Department #_____

Machine #_____

Gauge #_____

Dimension .540 to .550

Acceptability Criteria
- under 10% error— very good gauge
- 10% to 30% error— may be acceptable based upon importance of application, cost of gauge, etc.
- Over 30% error— considered not acceptable—every effort should be made to correct it

FIGURE 11.16
Gauge capability worksheet for Exercise 1. *Gauge capability analysis form courtesy of Saginaw Division of General Motors Corporation.

2. An $\bar{x}$ and R chart is made for samples of size $n = 5$ and $\bar{R} = .0073$. The gauge from Exercise 1 is used. Calculate the true process standard deviation by removing the effect of the gauge variation.

3. The gauge from the gauge capability study in Figure 11.10 was used on the control chart in Figure 6.4. Eliminate the effect of gauge variability, σ_{Gauge}, and calculate the process capability using $\sigma_{Process}$.

12

ACCEPTANCE SAMPLING

OBJECTIVES

- Realize the limitations associated with using OC curves and acceptance sampling by attributes.
- Plan a random sample, given the packaging information for an incoming lot.
- Construct and interpret an OC curve.
- Construct and interpret an AOC curve.
- Read and use the MLT-STD-105D tables.
- Calculate the percent of defect-free product, given the percent defective of several parts that are used to make the product.

The trend in industry has been to shift the burden of ensuring incoming quality to the vendor. Various quality assurance programs are being developed in which the vendor provides proof of product quality to the purchaser. Vendor documentation of ongoing quality improvement programs is usually required, along with access to control charts at critical process points. The receiving companies also have a vendor-rating system based on the quality history of the vendor.

Some companies, however, continue to use more traditional methods of quality assurance. With current market pressures on quality, acceptance sampling has to be considered a very temporary measure in the effort to attain top quality input. Incoming inspection is both costly and unreliable. Many different sampling plans are available, but all compromise quality to some extent. The consumer's risk is always involved. The concepts of acceptance sampling are presented here because many companies still voluntarily use it or are forced to use it by government decree (involvement in government contracts may necessitate it). However, the shortcomings of this approach to measuring incoming quality should be apparent.

12.1 THE SAMPLING DILEMMA

Sampling does a good job of accepting very good lots and rejecting very bad lots. Unfortunately, a large area of indecision lies in the middle. The sampling rules in all the formal sample plans are based on probability, but the application of probability predicts the acceptance of lots with substandard quality. This will be demonstrated in the following examples.

Suppose the "lot" is a box of 100 beads. Blue beads are desired, and red beads are considered defective. A random sample of 20 will determine if the lot is acceptable. The maximum percent defective that is allowed is 5 percent, so if the sample contains more than one defective, the lot will be rejected.

EXAMPLE 12.1

Lot A contains 95 blue beads and 5 red beads; it should be accepted. Find the probability of accepting the lot.

Solution

There are two sampling situations for which the lot will be accepted. Either zero defectives show up in the sample, *or* exactly one defective shows up. Use the "or" rule in probability and *add* the probabilities of these two situations to find the probability of acceptance.

Each of the two cases involves the "and" rule of probability because of the 20 successive events when choosing the sample: The 20 probability values are *multiplied*. By the simplest application of the random sample concept, in which each bead has an equally likely chance to be drawn, each bead will be replaced before the next one is drawn. That way each piece sampled has a probability of .95 (95 chances out of 100) of not being defective.

Case 1. No defectives are drawn.

Case 2. Exactly one defective is drawn.

For Case 1, find

P (1st not defective *and* 2nd not defective *and . . . and* 20th not defective)

$$P(\text{no defectives}) = .95 \times .95 \times .95 \times \ldots \times .95$$
$$= (.95)^{20}$$
$$= .3585$$

For Case 2, let N represent not defective and D represent defective. Drawing a sample of 20 with one defective can occur in 20 ways. For example, several possibilities are shown here:

The *first* is defective	$D\,N\,N\,N\,N\ldots N$
The *second* is defective	$N\,D\,N\,N\,N\ldots N$
The *third* is defective	$N\,N\,D\,N\,N\ldots N$
The *twentieth* is defective	$N\,N\,N\,N\,N\ldots D$

There are 20 ways of getting exactly one that is defective and 19 that are not.

$$P(N) = \frac{95}{100} \qquad P(D) = \frac{5}{100}$$
$$= .95 \qquad\qquad = .05$$

$$P(D \text{ and } N \text{ and } N \text{ and } N \text{ and } \ldots \text{ and } N) = .05 \times .95 \times .95 \times .95 \times \cdots \times .95$$
$$P(D\ N\ N\ N \ldots N) = .05 \times (.95)^{19}$$
$$= .05 \times .3774$$
$$= .01887$$

Each of the 20 ways will have this same probability because they all have one factor of .05 and 19 factors of .95. Instead of adding the 20 probability values according to the "or" rule, the repeated addition can be done by multiplication.

$$P(\text{one defective}) = 20 \times .01887 = .3774$$

There are 20 ways of getting one defective in 20, and each way has the same probability. Since the lot will be accepted if either the first case or the second case occurs, the addition rule of probability applies.

$$P(\text{accepting the lot}) = .3585 + .3774 = .7359$$

The Case 1 probability is .3585, and the Case 2 probability is .3774.

The probability of getting either one defective or no defectives in the sample is about .74, so 74 times out of 100 this lot will be accepted, and 26 times out of 100 it will be rejected. The rejected lot will then be either shipped back to the vendor or 100 percent inspected to sort out the extra defectives.

EXAMPLE 12.2

Lot B contains 97 blue beads and three red ones. What is the probability that this acceptable lot will be rejected when a sample of 20 is randomly selected?

Solution

Again, there are two cases in which the lot will be accepted.

Case 1. No defectives show up in the sample.

Case 2. Exactly one defective occurs in the sample.

The "or" rule is used to add the probabilities for each case, and the "and" rule is used to multiply the probabilities for each of the 20 selections in the sample. Each draw has $P(D) = .03$ (3 chances out of 100 for D). For Case 1:

$$P(\text{no defectives}) = (.97)^{20} = .5438$$

The exponent 20 indicates 20 successive draws. For Case 2:

$$P(\text{one defective}) = 20 \times (.03) \times (.97)^{19}$$
$$= 20 \times .03 \times .5606$$
$$= .3364$$

Twenty is the number of ways of getting one defective in 20, and each way has the same "and" probability. Add the probabilities for each case to find the probability of accepting the lot.

$$P(\text{accepting the lot}) = .5438 + .3364 = .8802$$

There is an 88 percent chance that this lot will be accepted and a 12 percent chance that it would be rejected. Twelve times out of 100 this lot will either be shipped back to the vendor as unacceptable or be 100 percent inspected.

EXAMPLE 12.3

Lot C contains 90 blue beads and 10 red ones. What is the chance that this bad lot will be accepted?

Solution
The same two cases apply for acceptance: No defectives show up in the sample of 20, or exactly one does.

$$P(N) = .9 \quad \text{90 chances out of 100 for } N$$
$$P(D) = .1 \quad \text{10 chances out of 100 for } D$$

For Case 1:

$$P(\text{no defectives}) = (.9)^{20}$$
$$= .1216$$

For Case 2:

$$P(\text{one defective}) = 20 \times (.1) \times (.9)^{19}$$
$$= 20 \times .1 \times .1351$$
$$= .2702$$

Combining both cases,

$$P(\text{accepting lot 3}) = .1216 + .2702 = .3918$$

This shows a 39 percent chance of accepting a bad lot. Thirty-nine times out of 100 the bad lot will be accepted because, by chance, not enough of the defectives will show up in the random sample.

Examples 12.1, 12.2, and 12.3 illustrate that acceptance sampling results in rejecting good lots when too many of the defects in the lot show up in the random sample. There is a nuisance factor if the rejected lot is shipped back to the vendor because the vendor will check it, see that it is acceptable and ship it back. This adds the cost of two-way shipping as well. If the rejected lot is routed to 100 percent inspection, additional cost, nuisance factor, and material delays result.

Even worse than rejecting acceptable lots, however, is taking in unacceptable lots, such as lot C. The quality program can be seriously affected by this policy.

EXAMPLE 12.4

Choice of sample size is a major factor in acceptance sampling. To demonstrate the effect of sample size, a sample of 40 will be selected in the bead problem of the first three examples. The *rejection* number will be three: The lot will be rejected if three or more defectives occur in the sample. This keeps the maximum *acceptance* ratio the same as before: Two out of 40 equals one out of 20. The lots from Examples 12.1 and 12.3 will be used.

1. Lot A contains 95 blue beads and 5 red beads. With a sample of 40, what is the chance of rejecting the lot?
2. Lot C contains 90 blue beads and 10 red ones. With a sample of 40, what is the probability of accepting lot C?

Solution

There are now three cases in which the lot will be accepted:

Case 1. No defectives are in the sample.

Case 2. Exactly one defective is in the sample.

Case 3. Exactly two defectives are in the sample.

$$P(N) = .95 \quad \text{95 chances in 100 for } N$$
$$P(D) = .05 \quad \text{5 chances in 100 for } D$$

For Case 1 for 40 successive draws:

$$P(\text{no defectives}) = (.95)^{40}$$
$$= .1285$$

For Case 2:

$$P(\text{one defective}) = 40 \times (.05) \times (.95)^{39}$$
$$= 40 \times .05 \times .1353$$
$$= .2706$$

For Case 3 the number of ways of getting two defectives in 40 pieces is illustrated as follows for several possibilities:

The first two are defective	$D\,D\,N\,N\,N\,N\ldots N$
The second and third are defective	$N\,D\,D\,N\,N\,N\ldots N$
The last two are defective	$N\,N\,N\,N\,N\ldots DD$

The two defectives can be in any other positions:

$$N\ldots D\,N\,N\ldots D\,N\ldots N$$

There are 780 ways that the two defects can show up in the sample of 40. The mathematical shortcut for calculating the 780 is called *combinations* and is discussed in Appendix A.6.2. Briefly, combinations are randomly ordered groupings that can be calculated using *factorials*. A factorial is the product of descending counting numbers (that is, 3 factorial, or 3!, is $3 \times 2 \times 1 = 6$).

$$C_{40,2} = \frac{40!}{2! \times 38!}$$
$$= 780$$

If 780 is the number of ways of getting two defectives in 40, and if each way has two .05 factors and 38 .95 factors,

$$P(\text{two defectives}) = 780 \times (.05)^2 \times (.95)^{38}$$
$$= 780 \times .0025 \times .1424$$
$$= .2777$$

The probability of accepting the lot is the sum of the probabilities of the three cases.

$$P(\text{accepting lot A}) = .1285 + .2706 + .2777$$
$$= .6768$$

There is a 68 percent chance of accepting lot A and a 32 percent chance of rejecting it. There are again three cases for the second part of Example 12.4. For Case 1:

$$P(\text{no defectives}) = (.9)^{40}$$
$$= .0148$$

For Case 2 there are 40 ways of getting one defective, and each way has one .1 factor and 39 .9 factors:

$$P(\text{one defectives}) = 40 \times (.1) \times (.9)^{39}$$
$$= .0657$$

For Case 3 there are 780 ways of getting two defectives and each way has two .1 factors and 38 .9 factors:

$$P(\text{two defectives}) = 780 \times (.1)^2 \times (.9)^{38}$$
$$= .1423$$

Combining the cases gives

$$P(\text{accepting lot C}) = .0148 + .0657 + .1423$$
$$= .2228$$

There is now a 22 percent chance of accepting the bad lot.

By juggling the sample size, the chance of making an error has been changed. The two errors that were demonstrated are called the *producer's risk* and the *consumer's risk*.

The producer's risk is the chance that a good lot will be rejected. When the sample size was 20 in Example 12.1, the producer's risk was 26 percent on lot A. However, when the sample size was increased to 40 in Example 12.4, the producer's risk increased to 32 percent.

The consumer's risk is the chance that a bad lot will be accepted. When the sample size was 20 in Example 12.1, the consumer's risk on lot C was 39 percent. When the sample size was increased to 40 in Example 12.4, the consumer's risk dropped to 22 percent.

The two examples showed that the producer's risk and the consumer's risk can be changed by changing the sample size. In general, when the sample size is increased, the consumer's risk will decrease and the producer's risk will increase. The two types of risk will also change when a different acceptance number is used for the sample.

There are three different mathematical approaches to the calculation of the probabilities associated with acceptance sampling. Each results in a different probability distribution. The first is the *hypergeometric probability distribution*, which is used to calculate the chance of getting a specific sample when there is *no replacement* of the pieces that are chosen for the sample.

EXAMPLE 12.5

A box contains 12 parts, three of which are defective. If a sample of four is taken without replacement, find the probability of getting two good parts and two defective parts in the sample.

Solution

This is an application of the hypergeometric probability distribution. The 12 parts split into two groups: the three defective parts and the nine good parts. A *success* is defined as choosing two of the three defective parts *and* two of the nine good parts. The number of successes can be calculated using mathematical combinations: The number of ways of choosing two from the three defective parts is

$$C_{3,2} = \frac{3!}{2! \times 1!}$$
$$= 3 \text{ ways}$$

The number of ways of choosing two from the nine good parts is

$$C_{9,2} = \frac{9!}{2!7!}$$
$$= 36 \text{ ways}$$

The number of successes is $3 \times 36 = 108$.

The total number of possible samples of four parts chosen from the box of 12 is

$$C_{12,4} = \frac{12!}{4! \times 8!}$$
$$= 495$$

The probability of a success is the number of successes divided by the number of possibilities.

$$P(2 \text{ good and 2 defective}) = \frac{108}{495}$$

$$= .2182$$

More details on combinations and hypergeometric probabilities can be found in Appendix A.6.

The second probability distribution that is used in sampling is the binomial distribution. The binomial distribution was used in Examples 12.1 through 12.4 and is also discussed more thoroughly in Appendix A.6.3. The binomial distribution is used for sampling *with replacement*. Example 12.5 will be repeated for the case of sampling with replacement. This will show a comparison of the hypergeometric distribution and the binomial distribution.

EXAMPLE 12.6   The same box of 12 parts with three defectives is checked by four inspectors. Each inspector checks one piece and returns it to the box. Find the probability that two inspectors will check a good part and two inspectors will find a defective part.

Solution
This is an example of sampling with replacement, and the probability is calculated with the binomial probability distribution. N is not defective; D is defective.

$$P(\text{a good part in a single draw}) = P(N)$$

$$= \frac{9}{12}$$

$$= .75$$

$$P(\text{a defective part in a single draw}) = P(D)$$

$$= \frac{3}{12}$$

$$= .25$$

$$P(2 \text{ good and 2 defective}) = C_{4,2} \times [P(N)]^2 \times [P(D)]^2$$

$$= \frac{4!}{2! \times 2!} \times (.75)^2 \times (.25)^2$$

$$= 6 \times .5625 \times .0625$$

$$= .21094$$

A comparison of the two probabilities from Examples 12.5 and 12.6 shows a small difference caused by the different sampling techniques.

The third probability distribution that is used extensively in sampling is the *Poisson distribution*. The Poisson distribution is used in acceptance sampling, and its use is illustrated in Section 12.3.

12.2 RANDOM SAMPLING

It is extremely important to have random samples in any acceptance procedure. The sampling plan must be devised to fit the packaging form for the incoming pieces. If a lot is shipped in several cartons, then a box number has to be part of the sample plan. If the pieces are carefully packed in layers, a layer number must also be included. If each layer has a set number of pieces, a piece number and a well-defined way of counting the pieces in each layer must be included. If the pieces are loose within each layer, then a wire grid should be made to fit the cartons and a piece sampled from a prescribed grid position.

Either a random number table or a random number generator on a statistical calculator can be used for selecting the pieces for the sample. If a random number comes up that is not in the proper domain for the numbers that are needed, skip it and go on to the next random number.

EXAMPLE 12.7

A lot of 4000 pieces is shipped in eight boxes. Each box contains five layers, and each layer consists of 10 rows of 10 pieces. A sample of 200 is to be taken. A three-digit random number generator on a statistical calculator is used to set up a random sample: The first random number will be used for the piece number (use the *last* two digits, 00 to 99). The second random number will specify the box number with the *first* digit and the layer number with the *last* digit. The sample will be planned as follows for all 200 pieces:

Piece Number	Random Numbers	Piece	Box	Layer
1	585, 811	85	8	1
2	358, 693	58	6	3
3	510, 946, 238, 726, 499, 293	10	2	3
4	535, 636, 457, 031, 982, 513	35	5	3

The crossed-out numbers are not in the domain for the box (1–8) or the layer (1–5). If too many unused random numbers can occur with this method, the plan can be revised to take the box number and layer number separately, if necessary. This method requires only four random numbers for piece 4:

Piece Number	Random Numbers	Piece	Box	Layer
4	535, 636, 457, 031	35	6	1

12.3 OC CURVES

OC curves (operating characteristic curves) are graphs of the probability of acceptance of a lot for all possible lot levels of percent defective. There are published OC curves for various sampling plans, but their construction is not difficult and will be presented here. The effects of changes in sample size and acceptance number will also be investigated.

The OC curve gives the probability of accepting a lot with a specific percent of defective items. The dashed line in Figure 12.1 shows that if a lot is 4 percent defective, it will pass inspection 82 percent of the time and be rejected 18 percent of the time. Every OC curve is identified by the sample size, *n*, and the maximum acceptance number, *c*. In this case, if the sample of 200 contains 10 or fewer defectives, it will be accepted. In another illustration of the OC curve in Figure 12.1, if the lot is 6 percent defective, there is a 35 percent chance that it will be accepted and a 65 percent chance that it will be rejected.

FIGURE 12.1
The ($n = 200, c = 10$) OC curve.

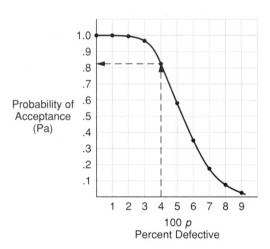

The OC curve is constructed from a Poisson probability distribution. The Poisson distribution, which is appropriate because it is skewed right to match the outcome of a random sampling situation, is preferred over the binomial distribution because it is better in a situation in which an event can occur in many ways that have low probabilities. This describes the sampling situation quite well. If a lot of 5000 items is 2 percent defective, there will be 100 defective items in the lot. How many defectives will show up in a sample of 200? The sample will most likely have between zero and eight defectives but it may have 13, 28, 54, or any other number, even 100. The chance of getting one of these higher numbers of defectives in the sample is quite low.

The construction of the OC curves is accomplished with the Poisson curves in Figure 12.2 (page 347). The curved lines on the chart correspond to specific *c* values. The first construction we will examine is the ($n = 200, c = 8$) OC curve. The horizontal axis on the Poisson chart in Figure 12.2 is labeled *pn*. The proportion of defective items in the lot is given the symbol *p*, and *n* is the sample size; *pn* is their product. The vertical scale gives the probability of acceptance, which is the probability that the sample of 200

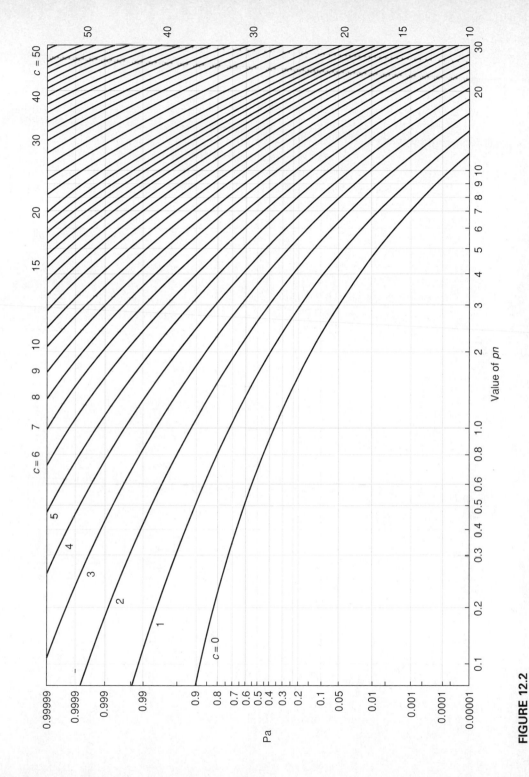

FIGURE 12.2
Poisson probabilities. Copyright 1956, Western Electric Company, reprinted by permission.

347

will have $c = 8$ or fewer defective items. The one curved line marked $c = 8$ is used for this construction. A table of values is formed from the Poisson chart in the following way:

1. The p values are chosen from 0 to .09, which will correspond to a lot that has between 0 and 9 percent defective.
2. Multiply each p value by $n = 200$ and enter it in the table.
3. Make a percent column for p and mark it $100\ p$.
4. Start at the pn value on the horizontal axis in Figure 12.2 and go straight up to the $c = 8$ curve and straight across to the vertical axis on the left. Read the Pa value on the vertical axis.
5. Record the probability of acceptance, Pa, in the table.

For example, if $p = .01$, then $200 \times .01 = 2$. Start at 2, go up to $c = 8$ and across to .9997. If $p = .02$, $200 \times .02 = 4$. Start at 4, go up to $c = 8$ and across to .975. Finally, if $p = .03$, then $200 \times .03 = 6$. Start at 6, go up to $c = 8$ and across to .855. Verify the other table values using the Poisson chart. In Table 12.1, Pa is the probability of acceptance from the vertical axis of the Poisson chart.

TABLE 12.1
Table of values for Figure 12.3

p	np	$100\ p$	Pa
0	0	0	1.0000
.01	2	1	.9997
.02	4	2	.975
.025	5	2.5	.92
.03	6	3	.855
.04	8	4	.60
.05	10	5	.34
.06	12	6	.15
.07	14	7	.06
.08	16	8	.03
.09	18	9	.006

The OC curve is constructed with the vertical scale representing the probability of acceptance, Pa. This scale is labeled from 0 through 1.0. The horizontal axis represents the percent of defective items in the lot and is labeled from 0 through 9. The horizontal scale is 100 times the p value from the table and is marked $100\ p$. To graph the values from the table and construct the OC curve, find the $100\ p$ number on the horizontal scale. Follow the grid upward from that point and mark a point on the graph that is even with the corresponding Pa value. The point should mark the intersection of a vertical line drawn from the $100\ p$ number and a horizontal line drawn from the Pa value. Do this for each pair of table values for $100\ p$ and Pa. The result is Figure 12.3(a) on page 349. Then draw a smooth curve through the points. If the shape of the curve isn't obvious or easy to draw, graph some in-between points. Choose some in-between p values, such as the

$p = .025$ in the fourth line of the table, and find the corresponding Pa values and plot the points. The in-between point plotting is helpful in the curvy sections of the graph. The curve that is drawn, Figure 12.3(b), is the OC curve.

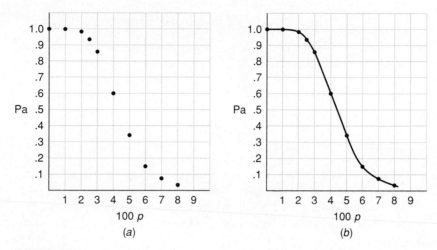

FIGURE 12.3
Construction of the ($n = 200, c = 8$) OC curve: (a) point graphed from Table 12.1; (b) a smooth curve drawn through the points.

Several more OC curves are shown with their corresponding table of values taken from the Poisson chart. Points are also given in Table 12.2 for Figure 12.1. Choose a few points from each table and verify them with the Poisson chart in Figure 12.2, following the curve for the specified c value. Then verify the graphed point on the appropriate OC curve. Remember to use the np value, not the $100\,p$ value, on Figure 12.2.

TABLE 12.2
Table of values for Figure 12.1

p	np	$100\,p$	Pa
0	0	0	1.000
.01	2	1	.9999
.02	4	2	.997
.03	6	3	.957
.04	8	4	.816
.05	10	5	.583
.06	12	6	.347
.07	14	7	.176
.08	16	8	.08
.09	18	9	.03

TABLE 12.3
Table of values for Figure 12.4

p	np	$100\ p$	Pa
0	0	0	1.000
.01	2	1	.996
.015	3	1.5	.97
.02	4	2	.88
.025	5	2.5	.78
.03	6	3	.60
.04	8	4	.30
.05	10	5	.14
.06	12	6	.048
.07	14	7	.015

Figure 12.4 shows the ($n = 200, c = 6$) OC curve (see Table 12.3 for points). Notice the dashed arrows going from Pa = .95 to the curve and from the curve down to 1.5 percent defective. These arrows define the AQL, the *acceptable quality level.*

FIGURE 12.4
The ($n = 200, c = 6$) OC curve showing the AQL.

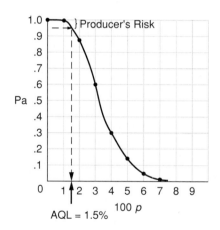

The AQL is used as a measure of quality for acceptance sampling by attributes. There are two definitions of the AQL. The first, set according to military standard MLT-STD-105D, defines the AQL as the maximum defective average allowable. The MLT-STD-105D instructions explain that when a consumer specifies an AQL value, that consumer will accept the great majority of lots with a proportion defective less than or equal to that AQL value. The *Quality Control Handbook*, 3rd edition, specifies AQL as the proportion defective that is accepted 95% of the time.[1] Example 12.14 in this chapter will show that these two definitions are compatable.

---

[1] Joseph M. Juran, ed., *Quality Contro Handbook*, 3rd ed., (New York: McGraw Hill, 1974).

Definition 1: The AQL is the maximum percent defective that is allowed as a process average.

Definition 2: The AQL is the level of quality of a submitted lot that has a 95 percent chance of being accepted.

The AQL is *not* necessarily the quality level being produced or the quality level being accepted. It is *not* always the quality goal. At the AQL, the producer's risk, or the probability of rejecting the acceptable, is 5 percent. In Figure 12.4, the AQL is slightly better than the average quality level that is allowed by that particular sample plan.

TABLE 12.4
Table of values for Figure 12.5

p	np	$100\,p$	Pa
0	0	0	1.000
.005	1	.5	.996
.01	2	1	.94
.015	3	1.5	.82
.02	4	2	.62
.03	6	3	.30
.04	8	4	.10

Figure 12.5 is the $(n = 200, c = 4)$ OC curve. Its values are given in Table 12.4. The dashed arrows define the IQL, the *indifference quality level.*

FIGURE 12.5
The $(n = 200, c = 4)$ OC curve showing the IQL.

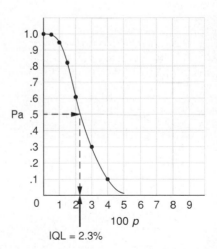

Definition: The IQL is the quality level that will be accepted 50 percent of the time.

TABLE 12.5
Table of values for Figure 12.6

p	np	$100\,p$	Pa
0	0	0	1.000
.001	.1	.1	.91
.002	.2	.2	.82
.003	.3	.3	.74
.005	.5	.5	.62
.01	1	1	.35
.02	2	2	.13
.03	3	3	.04

FIGURE 12.6
The $(n = 100, c = 0)$ OC curve showing the RQL.

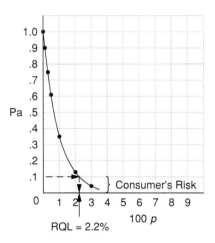

Figure 12.6 is the $(n = 100, c = 0)$ OC curve (see Table 12.5). The dashed lines define the RQL, the *rejectable quality level*.

Definition: The RQL is the level of quality that will be accepted only 10 percent of the time.

At the RQL, the consumer's risk, or the probability of accepting the unacceptable, is 10 percent.

TABLE 12.6
Table of values for Figure 12.7

	$n = 100, c = 6$				$n = 300, c = 6$		
p	np	$100\,p$	Pa	p	np	$100\,p$	Pa
0	0	0	1.000	0	0	0	1.000
.01	1	1	.9999	.01	3	1	.965
.02	2	2	.999	.015	4.5	1.5	.82
.03	3	3	.96	.02	6	2	.60
.04	4	4	.88	.03	9	3	.20
.05	5	5	.75	.04	12	4	.045
.06	6	6	.60				
.07	7	7	.45				
.08	8	8	.32				
.09	9	9	.20				
.10	10	10	.13				
.12	12	12	.05				

The interaction of the sample sizes is shown in Figure 12.7 on page 354 (see Tables 12.3 and 12.6). The acceptance level is kept constant at $c = 6$, and three OC curves are shown together for comparison. The curves show that with increasing the sample size, both the AQL and the RQL values decrease substantially. Furthermore, the steeper curve associated with the larger n value has a greater discriminatory power: It can better discriminate between good and bad lots. The indecisive zone between the AQL and the RQL is only 2.3 percentage units wide.

$$
\begin{array}{rl}
3.5\% & \text{RQL} \\
-1.2\% & \text{AQL} \\
\hline
2.3\% &
\end{array}
$$

This is the area in which acceptable lots have a good chance of being rejected and unacceptable lots have a good chance of being accepted. Compare this zone with the indecisive zone for the less steep ($n = 100, c = 6$) OC curve.

$$
\begin{array}{rl}
10.5\% & \text{RQL} \\
-\ 3.0\% & \text{AQL} \\
\hline
7.5\% &
\end{array}
$$

This one is much wider, which makes it more difficult to discriminate between acceptable and unacceptable lots.

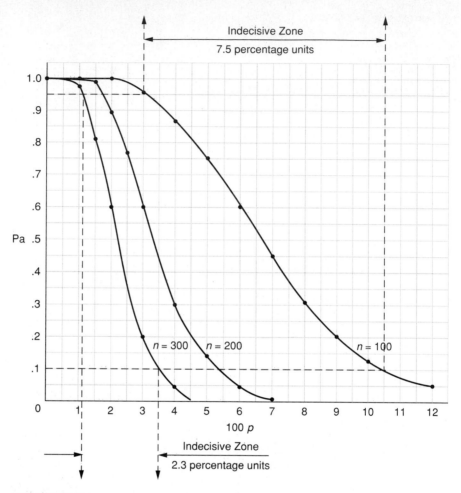

FIGURE 12.7
Three OC curves with a constant $c = 6$ and a varying n values. Larger n values create steeper curves, and steeper curves have greater discriminatory power.

TABLE 12.7
Table of values for the $n = 200$, $c = 0$ curve in Figure12.8

p	np	$100\,p$	Pa
0	0	0	1.000
.0005	.1	.05	.9
.001	.2	.1	.82
.005	1	.5	.36
.01	2	1	.12

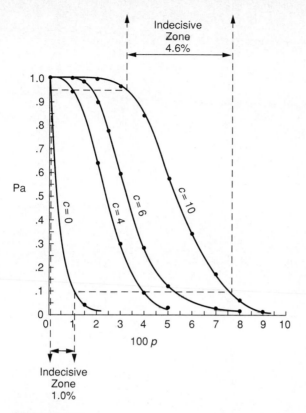

FIGURE 12.8
Four OC curves with a constant $n = 200$ and varying c values.

The values for the points on the four curves in Figure 12.8 are given in Tables 12.2, 12.3, 12.4, and 12.7 (page 355). Figure 12.8 shows that changing c while keeping n fixed can have a dramatic effect on the OC curve. The relationship of the grouped curves is quite similar to the effect shown in Figure 12.7. Figure 12.8 shows that the smaller c values decrease both AQL and RQL. Also, the smaller the c value, the steeper the curve, which means that the discriminatory power of the curve is improved. The indecisive zone for $c = 0$ is about 1 percent, and for $c = 10$ it is about 4.6 percent.

$$
\begin{array}{rl}
1.1\% & \text{RQL} \\
-\ .1\% & \text{AQL} \\
\hline
1.0\% &
\end{array}
\qquad
\begin{array}{rl}
7.8\% & \text{RQL} \\
-3.2\% & \text{AQL} \\
\hline
4.6\% &
\end{array}
$$

The illustrations show that a change in just one variable can lower the AQL and the RQL and increase the discriminatory power as the indecisive zone between AQL and RQL decreases. This can be done either by increasing the sample size, n, or by decreasing the acceptance number, c. What happens when both change?

Figure 12.9 on page 356 shows the relationship between three curves that have the same c/n ratio (see Table 12.8 on page 356). The curves are quite similar in

TABLE 12.8
Table of values for Figure 12.9

$n = 100$, $c = 4$				$n = 300$, $c = 12$			
p	np	$100\,p$	Pa	p	np	$100\,p$	Pa
0	0	0	1.000	0	0	0	1.000
.01	1	1	.996	.01	3	1	.9999
.02	2	2	.94	.02	6	2	.991
.03	3	3	.81	.025	7.5	2.5	.955
.04	4	4	.62	.03	9	3	.88
.05	5	5	.42	.04	12	4	.60
.06	6	6	.26	.05	15	5	.26
.07	7	7	.16	.06	18	6	.10
.08	8	8	.10	.08	24	8	.006
.09	9	9	.06				

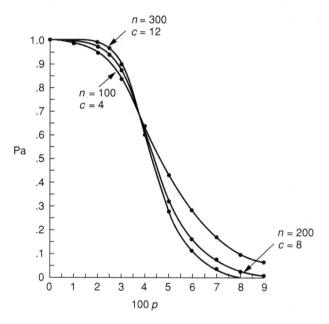

FIGURE 12.9
Three curves with a constant c/n ratio of .04.

shape, although there is a small differential of about .7 percent in the AQLs and 2 percent in the RQLs. The greater discriminatory power goes to the curve with the larger n value because it is the steepest and has the shortest percentage span between the AQL and RQL. Maximizing the discriminatory power is one of the considerations in choosing an acceptance procedure, so the use of the c/n ratio can be helpful. Reviewing the other OC curves in Figures 12.6, 12.7, and 12.8 illustrates that smaller c/n ratios correspond to greater discriminatory power of the curve. In Figure 12.7 the $(n = 300, c = 6)$ OC curve has the greatest discriminatory power, and it has a c/n ratio of .02, compared to ratios of .03 and .06 for the other two curves. In Figure 12.8 the $(n = 200, c = 0)$ OC curve has the best discriminatory power. It has a c/n ratio of 0, compared to .02, .03, and .05 for the others. Both figures show the increase in the c/n value as the discriminatory power decreases from curve to curve. Figures 12.6 and 12.8 both have the same c/n ratio of 0. This again illustrates that when the c/n ratio is the same, the higher discriminatory power is in the curve with the larger n value.

Companies establish quality standards for incoming parts and materials, and their acceptance procedures must protect that quality level by ensuring that substandard shipments are not accepted. A combination of issues is involved in considerations of acceptance procedures, but quality protection is always a major factor. One rough way to specify that protection is to state the maximum RQL value that can be used. Some companies dodge this issue, however, by specifying a constant percentage of each lot that will be inspected. This is a major error in acceptance procedures because it does not specify a bottom line of quality. Figure 12.10 shows a 10 percent sampling situation, and a comparison of the RQL values shows that the variation in incoming quality can be extensive when a constant percentage approach is used.

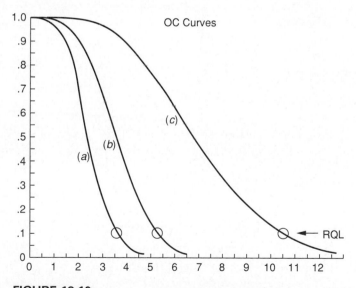

FIGURE 12.10
Three OC curves illustrate the problem with constant percent sampling (a) Lot size = 3000, $n = 300$, $c = 6$; (b) lot size = 2000, $n = 200$, $c = 6$; (c) lot size = 1000, $n = 100$, $c = 6$. These three OC curves illustrate the problem with constant percent sampling: They provide no consistent quality estimate.

Selecting the Best OC Curve

The ideal OC curve, shown in Figure 12.11, is one in which lots within the acceptable quality level are accepted with a probability of 1 and lots that are not within that standard are rejected with a probability of 1.

FIGURE 12.11
The ideal OC curve.

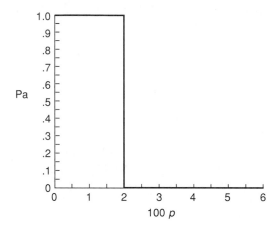

Figure 12.9 illustrates what happens if the c/n ratio is kept constant. If more curves are drawn with the same c/n ratio, such as 24/600 or 40/1000, the sequence of curves will approach the ideal with a vertical line at 100 p = 4.

Given a choice of OC curves, choose the one with the smallest c/n ratio and the smallest RQL-AQL difference. That combination gives the best average quality level and a sampling plan with the highest discriminatory power.

Selecting the AQL

Many sampling plans begin with the selection of the AQL. In some cases the AQL is chosen arbitrarily. The AQL should represent the maximum percent defective that can be tolerated for the entire population of parts being received. It may be designated by bargaining with the vendor and reflect a compromise between vendor capability and purchaser requirements.

When an assembly operation demands 100 percent final inspection, the AQL may also be determined on the basis of cost. Let

p = proportion of incoming parts that are defective

C_i = the cost of inspecting one incoming piece

C_r = the cost of dismantling, repairing, reassembling
    and testing a unit that failed because of a defective part.

The ratio C_i/C_r is the break even point. Theoretically, if the worst lot has $p < C_i/C_r$, no inspection of incoming materials is necessary. If the best lot has $p > C_i/C_r$, 100 percent inspection of incoming materials is required.

EXAMPLE 12.8 T_i is the time required to inspect a part and T_r is the time required for repair.

$T_i = \frac{1}{2}$ minute to inspect each incoming part

$T_r = 3$ minutes to dismantle and repair a unit with a defective part

Solution

In each case, the times relate directly to cost. R is the rate. For simplicity, assume equal hourly rates:

$$\text{Time} \times \text{Rate} = \text{Cost}$$

$$T_i \times R = C_i$$

$$T_r \times R = C_r$$

$$\frac{C_i}{C_r} = \frac{T_i \times R}{T_r \times R}$$

$$= \frac{T_i}{T_r}$$

$$= \frac{.5}{3}$$

$$= .17$$

If $p < .17$ on the worst lot, no incoming inspection is required. It will be less expensive to repair the defective items when they are found during the final inspection.

Suppose a lot contains $N = 1000$ pieces. At $\frac{1}{2}$ minute per piece for inspection, $(\frac{1}{2}) \times 1000 = 500$ minutes to inspect the lot. If $p < .17$, say $p = .09$, then there will be $.09 \times 1000 = 90$ defective pieces in the lot. If there is no inspection, there will be 90 repairs to do on the assembled units. At 3 minutes each, $3 \times 90 = 270$ minutes. This shows that when $p < C_i/C_r$, the cost for repairs is less than the cost of 100 percent initial incoming inspection.

EXAMPLE 12.9 Suppose T_i is $\frac{1}{2}$ minute to inspect an incoming part and T_r is 20 minutes to dismantle and repair a unit with a defective part. Is inspection or repair more cost-efficient?

Solution

$$\frac{C_i}{C_r} = \frac{T_i \times R}{T_r \times R}$$

$$= \frac{.5}{20}$$

$$= .025$$

If $p > .025$ on the best lot, then 100 percent incoming inspection is necessary. A lot of 1000 parts takes 500 minutes ($\frac{1}{2} \times 1000$) to inspect. If $p > .025$, say $p = .04$, then 40 units (.04 × 1000) will have to be dismantled and repaired if no incoming inspection is done. Twenty minutes are needed for each repair, so $40 \times 20 = 800$ minutes to complete the repairs. In this case, when $p > C_i/C_r$, it is cheaper to complete a 100 percent incoming inspection and eliminate the defectives before assembly.

Examples 12.8 and 12.9 assume that there is a 100 percent final inspection, which is contrary to the prevention system of manufacturing. Both examples suggest that some serious work should be done either to improve the vendor's product or to find a better vendor. When incoming quality is at neither of the two extremes illustrated, then sampling will be a cost-effective way to eliminate the poorer quality lots. The AQL of the sampling plan should be less than the break even ratio C_i/C_r.

12.4 THE AOQ CURVE

The AOQ (*average outgoing quality*) curve, shows the result of the incoming inspection and sorting of rejected lots. Outgoing quality, in this case, refers to the quality of the parts and materials that go from incoming inspection to manufacturing and assembly. Three assumptions are made for the inspection process:

1. All lots that pass inspection enter production as they are.
2. All lots that are rejected are inspected 100 percent, and all the nonconforming pieces are removed.
3. All pieces that are removed are replaced by conforming pieces.

Each OC curve has a corresponding AOQ curve. The points on the AOQ curve are determined as follows. For each incoming percent defective, the OC curve indicates what part is accepted for production and what part is rejected for 100 percent inspection. Only a fraction of the original number of defects makes it to production because of the sorting that occurs with the rejected lots.

EXAMPLE 12.10

Construct an AOQ curve to accompany an ($n = 200, c = 4$) OC curve.

Solution

If lots of 3000 are 3 percent defective, then each time a lot passes inspection, 90 defective pieces (.03 × 3000) go into production. But the OC curve indicates that this happens for only 30 percent of the defective lots that are submitted. The other 70 percent of the lots are fully sorted so that *no* defects go into production. If all the lots are considered, an average of 30 percent of the 90 defective pieces per lot will make it into production.

Therefore, $.3 \times 90 = 27$ defectives per lot, on the average, make it into production. This is done with the percentages in the following table: 30 percent of the 3 percent defective ($.3 \times .03 = .009$) go into production. Applying this to the lot size of 3000, 27 defectives ($.009 \times 3000$) per lot, on the average, go into production. The average outgoing percent, $\frac{27}{3000}$, is .9%.

TABLE 12.9
Values for the AOQ curve

Incoming percent defective	Percent accepted from OC curve	Percent rejected and fully sorted	Percent defects outgoing
0%	100%	0%	0%
1.0%	94%	6%	$.94 \times .01 = .0094 = .94\%$
1.5%	82%	18%	$.82 \times .015 = .0123 = 1.23\%$
2%	62%	38%	$.62 \times .02 = .0124 = 1.34\%$
3%	30%	70%	$.30 \times .03 = .009 = .9\%$
4%	10%	90%	$.10 \times .04 = .004 = .4\%$
5%	3%	97%	$.03 \times .05 = .0015 = .15\%$

The AOQ curve is constructed in the same way as the OC curves. Label the horizontal axis as incoming percent defective; the table values go from 0 percent to 5 percent (see Table 12.9), so set the horizontal scale in units (0, 1, 2, 3, 4, 5). Label the vertical axis as outgoing percent defective. The table values go from 0 percent to 1.24 percent, so set the vertical scale in tenths (0, .1, .2, ..., 1.4). Plot the points from the paired values. The horizontal value is given first.

0, 0 Mark the corner point.

1, .94 Start at 1 on the horizontal axis, go up to .94, and mark a point.

1.5, 1.23 Start at 1.5 on the horizontal axis, go up to 1.23, and mark a point.

The graphing sequence is illustrated in Figure 12.12 on page 362, and the final result is shown in Figure 12.13 (page 363). When all the points are graphed, draw a smooth curve through them. The result is the AOQ curve. The highest point on the curve is the maximum percent defective that will go into production, on the average, by this sampling plan. That point is called the AOQL, the *average outgoing quality limit*.

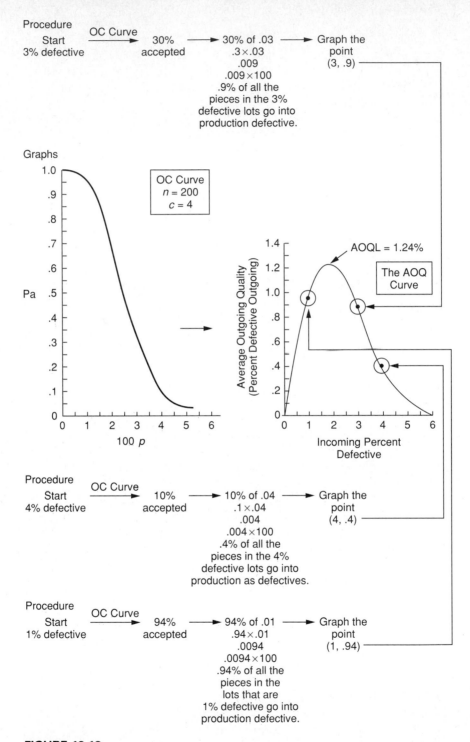

Procedure
Start
3% defective → OC Curve → 30% accepted → 30% of .03
.3×.03
.009
.009×100
.9% of all the pieces in the 3% defective lots go into production defective. → Graph the point (3, .9)

Graphs

OC Curve
n = 200
c = 4

Pa

100 p

Average Outgoing Quality (Percent Defective Outgoing)

AOQL = 1.24%

The AOQ Curve

Incoming Percent Defective

Procedure
Start
4% defective → OC Curve → 10% accepted → 10% of .04
.1×.04
.004
.004×100
.4% of all the pieces in the 4% defective lots go into production as defectives. → Graph the point (4, .4)

Procedure
Start
1% defective → OC Curve → 94% accepted → 94% of .01
.94×.01
.0094
.0094×100
.94% of all the pieces in the lots that are 1% defective go into production defective. → Graph the point (1, .94)

FIGURE 12.12
The graphing sequence for the AOQ curve.

362

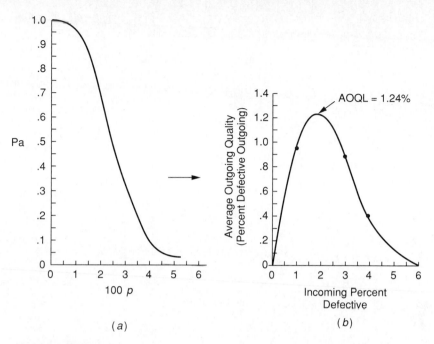

FIGURE 12.13
(a) The ($n = 200, c = 4$) OC curve; (b) the ($n = 200, c = 4$) AOQ curve.

12.5   MLT-STD-105D FOR INSPECTION BY ATTRIBUTES[2]

There are many published sampling plans that can be followed for incoming inspection. Many companies still use these plans because they believe that they are the best available; other companies use them because they are tied into regulations that accompany government contracts. The MLT-STD-105D is presented here in brief form as an example of a standard sampling plan. The complete package of charts and directions can be obtained by writing to the U. S. Government Printing Office.

Some of the variations within the sampling procedure include the classification of defects: critical defects, major defects, and minor defects. Also, inspection is subclassified as normal, tightened, and reduced, and rules dictate when to switch from one classification to another. This inspection-level classification is determined by the relationship between the lot size and the sample size. Three inspection levels are usually shown—I, II, and III—and level II is used unless otherwise specified. Four additional levels, s-1, s-2, s-3, and s-4, are used when small samples are necessary or when large sampling risks may be taken.

There are three different types of sampling plans: single, double, and multiple, which are illustrated in Figures 12.14 (page 364), 12.15 (page 364), and 12.16 (page 365). The choice of sampling plan depends on the sample size and the administrative diffi-

---

[2]Naval Publications and Forms Center, 5801 Tabor Avenue, Philadelphia, PA, 19120–5099.

culty. Usually the sample size of multiple plans is less than that of double plans. The sample size for double sampling is usually less than for single sampling plans.

d the number of defective pieces in the sample, d_1 for sample 1 and d_2 for sample 2

$\leq$ less than or equal to

$\geq$ greater than or equal to

$c < d < r$ the value for d lies between the values for c and r

FIGURE 12.14
Single sampling.

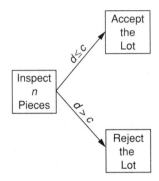

The single sampling diagram in Figure 12.14 demonstrates the sampling decision process that was used with the OC curves. Values for sample size, n, and acceptance number, c, are needed for the single sampling scheme.

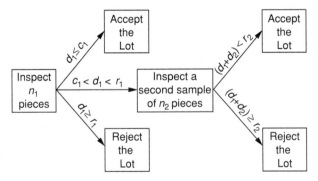

FIGURE 12.15
Double sampling.

The double sampling scheme shown in Figure 12.15 requires two sets of numbers: n_1, c_1, and r_1 for the first sample and n_2 and r_2 for the second. If d_1 is less than or equal to c_1 in the first sample, accept the lot. If d_1 is greater than or equal to the rejection number, r_1, reject the lot. If d_1 is between c_1 and r_1, take a second sample of size n_2. If the total number of defects is less than the rejection number, r_2, accept the lot; otherwise, reject it.

Double sampling is preferred sometimes because it appears to give a lot a second chance before rejecting it. Its main attribute, however, is the fact that in some situations it can lead to fewer pieces being sampled overall.

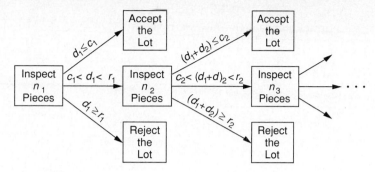

FIGURE 12.16
Multiple sampling.

Multiple sampling, as illustrated in Figure 12.16, extends the double-sampling concept to triple sampling and sometimes beyond. Each sampling step except the last involves three numbers: sample size, n, acceptance number, c, and a rejection number, r. The last step has just the sample size, n, and the rejection number, r: If the total number of defectives is less than the final rejection number, the lot is accepted.

The various sample sizes are designated by MLT-STD-105D code letters, which are listed in Table 12.10. The code letter and sample size are then used with a master table such as Table 12.11 (page 366) to determine the acceptance and rejection numbers. Three other master tables are included for comparison: Table 12.12 for tightened inspection (page 368), Table 12.13 for reduced inspection (page 370), and Table 12.14 for double sampling (page 372).

TABLE 12.10
Sample size code letters

Lot or Batch Size			Special Inspection Levels				General Inspection Levels		
			S-1	S-2	S-3	S-4	I	II	III
2	to	8	A	A	A	A	A	A	B
9	to	15	A	A	A	A	A	B	C
16	to	25	A	A	B	B	B	C	D
26	to	50	A	B	B	C	C	D	E
51	to	90	B	B	C	C	C	E	F
91	to	150	B	B	C	D	D	F	G
151	to	280	B	C	D	E	E	G	H
281	to	500	B	C	D	E	F	H	J
501	to	1200	C	C	E	F	G	J	K
1201	to	3200	C	D	E	G	H	K	L
3201	to	10000	C	D	F	G	J	L	M
10001	to	35000	C	D	F	H	K	M	N
35001	to	150000	D	E	G	J	L	N	P
150001	to	500000	D	E	G	J	M	P	Q
500001	and over		D	E	H	K	N	Q	R

TABLE 12.11
Single sampling plans for normal inspections (master table)

Sample Size Code Letter	Sample Size	0.010 Ac	0.010 Re	0.015 Ac	0.015 Re	0.025 Ac	0.025 Re	0.040 Ac	0.040 Re	0.065 Ac	0.065 Re	0.10 Ac	0.10 Re	0.15 Ac	0.15 Re	0.25 Ac	0.25 Re	0.40 Ac	0.40 Re	0.65 Ac	0.65 Re	1.0 Ac	1.0 Re	1.5 Ac	1.5 Re
A	2																								
B	3																								
C	5																								
D	8																							0 ↓	1
E	13																						↑	0 ↓	1
F	20																			0 ↓	1	↑		↓	
G	32																	0 ↓	1	↑		↓		1	2
H	50															0 ↓	1	↑		↓		1	2	2	3
J	80													0 ↓	1	↑		↓		1	2	2	3	3	4
K	125											0 ↓	1	↑		↓		1	2	2	3	3	4	5	6
L	200									0 ↓	1	↑		↓		1	2	2	3	3	4	5	6	7	8
M	315							0 ↓	1	↑		↓		1	2	2	3	3	4	5	6	7	8	10	11
N	500					0 ↓	1	↑		↓		1	2	2	3	3	4	5	6	7	8	10	11	14	15
P	800			0 ↓	1	↑		↓		1	2	2	3	3	4	5	6	7	8	10	11	14	15	21	22
Q	1250	0 ↓	1	↑		↓		1	2	2	3	3	4	5	6	7	8	10	11	14	15	21	22	↑	
R	2000	↑		↑		1	2	2	3	3	4	5	6	7	8	10	11	14	15	21	22	↑		↑	

↓ = Use first sampling plan below. If sample size equals or exceeds lot or batch size, do 100 percent inspection.

↑ = Use first sampling plan above arrow.

Ac = Acceptance number.

Re = Rejection number.

Levels (Normal Inspection)

2.5	4.0	6.5	10	15	25	40	65	100	150	250	400	650	1000
Ac Re	Ac Re	Ac Re	Ac Re	Ac Re	Ac Re	Ac Re	Ac Re	Ac Re	Ac Re	Ac Re	Ac Re	Ac Re	Ac Re
	↓	0 1		↓	1 2	2 3	3 4	5 6	7 8	10 11	14 15	21 22	30 31
	0 1	↑		1 2	2 3	3 4	5 6	7 8	10 11	14 15	21 22	30 31	44 45
0 1	↑	↓	1 2	2 3	3 4	5 6	7 8	10 11	14 15	21 22	30 31	44 45	↑
↑	↓	1 2	2 3	3 4	5 6	7 8	10 11	14 15	21 22	30 31	44 45	↑	↑
↓	1 2	2 3	3 4	5 6	7 8	10 11	14 15	21 22	30 31	44 45	↑	↑	↑
1 2	2 3	3 4	5 6	7 8	10 11	14 15	21 22	↑					
2 3	3 4	5 6	7 8	10 11	14 15	21 22	↑						
3 4	5 6	7 8	10 11	14 15	21 22	↑							
5 6	7 8	10 11	14 15	21 22	↑								
7 8	10 11	14 15	21 22	↑									
10 11	14 15	21 22	↑										
14 15	21 22	↑											
21 22	↑												

↓ = Use first sampling plan below the arrow.
↑ = Use first sampling plan above the arrow.

TABLE 12.12

Single sampling plans for tightened inspections (master table)

In the table below, each data cell gives the acceptance (Ac) and rejection (Re) numbers as the pair "Ac Re". ↓ = use first sampling plan below; ↑ = use first sampling plan above.

Sample Size Code Letter	Sample Size	0.010	0.015	0.025	0.040	0.065	0.10	0.15	0.25	0.40	0.65	1.0	1.5
		Ac Re	Ac Re	Ac Re	Ac Re	Ac Re	Ac Re	Ac Re	Ac Re	Ac Re	Ac Re	Ac Re	Ac Re
A	2	↓	↓	↓	↓	↓	↓	↓	↓	↓	↓	↓	↓
B	3	↓	↓	↓	↓	↓	↓	↓	↓	↓	↓	↓	↓
C	5	↓	↓	↓	↓	↓	↓	↓	↓	↓	↓	↓	↓
D	8	↓	↓	↓	↓	↓	↓	↓	↓	↓	↓	↓	↓
E	13	↓	↓	↓	↓	↓	↓	↓	↓	↓	↓	↓	0 1
F	20	↓	↓	↓	↓	↓	↓	↓	↓	↓	↓	0 1	↓
G	32	↓	↓	↓	↓	↓	↓	↓	↓	↓	0 1	↓	↓
H	50	↓	↓	↓	↓	↓	↓	↓	↓	0 1	↓	↓	1 2
J	80	↓	↓	↓	↓	↓	↓	↓	0 1	↓	↓	1 2	2 3
K	125	↓	↓	↓	↓	↓	↓	0 1	↓	↓	1 2	2 3	3 4
L	200	↓	↓	↓	↓	↓	0 1	↓	↓	1 2	2 3	3 4	5 6
M	315	↓	↓	↓	↓	0 1	↓	↓	1 2	2 3	3 4	5 6	8 9
N	500	↓	↓	↓	0 1	↓	↓	1 2	2 3	3 4	5 6	8 9	12 13
P	800	↓	↓	0 1	↓	↓	1 2	2 3	3 4	5 6	8 9	12 13	18 19
Q	1250	↓	0 1	↓	↓	1 2	2 3	3 4	5 6	8 9	12 13	18 19	↑
R	2000	0 1	↑	↓	1 2	2 3	3 4	5 6	8 9	12 13	18 19	↑	↑
S	3150	↑	↑	1 2	2 3	3 4	5 6	8 9	12 13	18 19	↑	↑	↑

↓ = Use first sampling plan below. If sample size equals or exceeds lot or batch size, do 100 percent inspection.

↑ = Use first sampling plan above arrow.

Ac = Acceptance number.

Re = Rejection number.

Levels (Reduced Inspection)

2.5	4.0	6.5	10	15	25	40	65	100	150	250	400	650	1000
Ac Re	Ac Re	Ac Re	Ac Re	Ac Re	Ac Re	Ac Re	Ac Re	Ac Re	Ac Re	Ac Re	Ac Re	Ac Re	Ac Re
↓		↓			↓	1 2	2 3	3 4	5 6	8 9	12 13	18 19	27 28
		0 1			1 2	2 3	3 4	5 6	8 9	12 13	18 19	27 28	41 42
	0 ↓ 1			1 ↓ 2	2 3	3 4	5 6	8 9	12 13	18 19	27 28	41 42	
0 ↓ 1			1 ↓ 2	2 3	3 4	5 6	8 9	12 13	18 19	27 28	41 42		
	1 ↓ 2	1 ↓ 2	2 3	3 4	5 6	8 9	12 13	18 19					
1 2	2 3	3 4	5 6	8 9	12 13	18 19							
2 3	3 4	5 6	8 9	12 13	18 19								
3 4	5 6	8 9	12 13	18 19									
5 6	8 9	12 13	18 19										
8 9	12 13	18 19											
12 13	18 19												
18 19													
↑	↑	↑	↑	↑	↑	↑	↑	↑	↑	↑	↑	↑	↑

TABLE 12.13
Single sampling plans for reduced inspections (master table)

Sample Size Code Letter	Sample Size	Acceptable Quality 0.010	0.015	0.025	0.040	0.065	0.10	0.15	0.25	0.40	0.65	1.0	1.5
		Ac Re	Ac Re	Ac Re	Ac Re	Ac Re	Ac Re	Ac Re	Ac Re	Ac Re	Ac Re	Ac Re	Ac Re
A	2												
B	2	↓	↓	↓	↓	↓	↓	↓	↓	↓	↓	↓	↓
C	2	↓	↓	↓	↓	↓	↓	↓	↓	↓	↓	↓	↓
D	3	↓	↓	↓	↓	↓	↓	↓	↓	↓	↓	↓	0 ↓ 1
E	5	↓	↓	↓	↓	↓	↓	↓	↓	↓	↓	0 ↓ 1	↑
F	8	↓	↓	↓	↓	↓	↓	↓	↓	↓	0 ↓ 1	↑	↓
G	13	↓	↓	↓	↓	↓	↓	↓	↓	0 ↓ 1	↑	↓	0 2
H	20	↓	↓	↓	↓	↓	↓	↓	0 ↓ 1	↑	↓	0 2	1 3
J	32	↓	↓	↓	↓	↓	↓	0 ↓ 1	↑	↓	0 2	1 3	1 4
K	50	↓	↓	↓	↓	↓	0 ↓ 1	↑	↓	0 2	1 3	1 4	2 5
L	80	↓	↓	↓	↓	0 ↓ 1	↑	↓	0 2	1 3	1 4	2 5	3 6
M	125	↓	↓	↓	0 ↓ 1	↑	↓	0 2	1 3	1 4	2 5	3 6	5 8
N	200	↓	↓	0 ↓ 1	↑	↓	0 2	1 3	1 4	2 5	3 6	5 8	7 10
P	315	↓	0 ↓ 1	↑	↓	0 2	1 3	1 4	2 5	3 6	5 8	7 10	10 13
Q	500	0 ↓ 1	↑	↓	0 2	1 3	1 4	2 5	3 6	5 8	7 10	10 13	↑
R	800	↑	↑	0 2	1 3	1 4	2 5	3 6	5 8	7 10	10 13	↑	↑

↓ = Use first sampling plan below. If sample size equals or exceeds lot or batch size, do 100 percent inspection.
↑ = Use first sampling plan above arrow.
Ac = Acceptance number.
Re = Rejection number.
* = If the acceptance number has been exceeded but the rejection number has not been reached, accept the lot, but reinstate normal inspection.

Levels (Reduced Inspection)*

2.5		4.0		6.5		10		15		25		40		65		100		150		250		400		650		1000	
Ac	Re	Ac	Re	Ac	Re	Ac	Re	Ac	Re	Ac	Re	Ac	Re	Ac	Re	Ac	Re	Ac	Re	Ac	Re	Ac	Re	Ac	Re	Ac	Re
		↓		0	1			↓		1	2	2	3	3	4	5	6	7	8	10	11	14	15	21	22	30	31
↓		0	1	↑		↓		0	2	1	3	2	4	3	5	5	6	7	8	10	11	14	15	21	22	30	31
0	↓ 1	↑		↓		0	↓ 2	1	3	1	4	2	5	3	6	5	8	7	10	10	13	14	17	21	24		
↑		↓		0	2	1	3	1	4	2	5	3	6	5	8	7	10	10	13	14	17	21	24			↑	
↓		0	2	1	3	1	4	2	5	3	6	5	8	7	10	10	13	14	17	21	24			↑			
0	2	1	3	1	4	2	5	3	6	5	8	7	10	10	13							↑					
1	3	1	4	2	5	3	6	5	8	7	10	10	13							↑							
1	4	2	5	3	6	5	8	7	10	10	13							↑									
2	5	3	6	5	8	7	10	10	13							↑											
3	6	5	8	7	10	10	13							↑													
5	8	7	10	10	13							↑															
7	10	10	13					↑																			
10	13			↑																							
↑		↑		↑		↑																					

TABLE 12.14
Double sampling plans for normal inspection (master table)

Acceptable Quality — each AQL column shows Ac (Acceptance number) and Re (Rejection number).

Sample Size Code Letter	Sample	Sample Size	Cumulative Sample Size	0.010	0.015	0.025	0.040	0.065	0.10	0.15	0.25	0.40	0.65	1.0
				Ac Re	Ac Re	Ac Re	Ac Re	Ac Re	Ac Re	Ac Re	Ac Re	Ac Re	Ac Re	Ac Re
A														
B	First	2	2											
	Second	2	4											
C	First	3	3											
	Second	3	6											
D	First	5	5											
	Second	5	10											
E	First	8	8											↓
	Second	8	16											
F	First	13	13										↓	
	Second	13	26											↑
G	First	20	20									↓		
	Second	20	40											
H	First	32	32								↓			0 ↓ 2
	Second	32	64									↑		1 2
J	First	50	50							↓			0 ↓ 2	0 3
	Second	50	100								↑		1 2	3 4
K	First	80	80						↓			0 ↓ 2	0 3	1 4
	Second	80	160							↑		1 2	3 4	4 5
L	First	125	125					↓			0 ↓ 2	0 3	1 4	2 5
	Second	125	250						↑		1 2	3 4	4 5	6 7
M	First	200	200				↓			0 ↓ 2	0 3	1 4	2 5	3 7
	Second	200	400					↑		1 2	3 4	4 5	6 7	8 9
N	First	315	315			↓			0 ↓ 2	0 3	1 4	2 5	3 7	5 9
	Second	315	630				↑		1 2	3 4	4 5	6 7	8 9	12 13
P	First	500	500		↓			0 ↓ 2	0 3	1 4	2 5	3 7	5 9	7 11
	Second	500	1000			↑		1 2	3 4	4 5	6 7	8 9	12 13	18 19
Q	First	800	800	↓			0 ↓ 2	0 3	1 4	2 5	3 7	5 9	7 11	11 16
	Second	800	1600		↑		1 2	3 4	4 5	6 7	8 9	12 13	18 19	26 27
R	First	1250	1250			0 ↓ 2	0 3	1 4	2 5	3 7	5 9	7 11	11 16	
	Second	1250	2500	↑		1 2	3 4	4 5	6 7	8 9	12 13	18 19	26 27	↑

↓ = Use first sampling plan below. If sample size equals or exceeds lot or batch size, do 100 percent inspection.
↑ = Use first sampling plan above arrow.
Ac = Acceptance number.
Re = Rejection number.
* = Use corresponding single sampling plan (or alternatively, use double sampling plan where available).

Levels (Normal Inspection)

1.5		2.5		4.0		6.5		10		15		25		40		65		100		150		250		400		650		1000	
Ac	Re	Ac	Re	Ac	Re	Ac	Re	Ac	Re	Ac	Re	Ac	Re	Ac	Re	Ac	Re	Ac	Re	Ac	Re	Ac	Re	Ac	Re	Ac	Re	Ac	Re
										0	2	0	3	1	4	2	5	3	7	5	9	7	11	11	16	17	22	25	11
										1	2	3	4	4	5	6	7	8	9	12	13	18	19	26	27	17	38	56	57
								0	2	0	3	1	4	2	5	3	7	5	9	7	11	11	16	17	22	25	11		
								1	2	3	4	4	5	6	7	8	9	12	13	18	19	26	27	17	38	56	57		
						0	2	0	3	1	4	2	5	3	7	5	9	7	11	11	16	17	22	25	11				
						1	2	3	4	4	5	6	7	8	9	12	13	18	19	26	27	17	38	56	57				
				0	2	0	3	1	4	2	5	3	7	5	9	7	11	11	16	17	22	25	11						
				1	2	3	4	4	5	6	7	8	9	12	13	18	19	26	27	17	38	56	57						
		0	2	0	3	1	4	2	5	3	7	5	9	7	11	11	16												
		1	2	3	4	4	5	6	7	8	9	12	13	18	19	26	27												
0	2	0	3	1	4	2	5	3	7	5	9	7	11	11	16														
1	2	3	4	4	5	6	7	8	9	12	13	18	19	26	27														
0	3	1	4	2	5	3	7	5	9	7	11	11	16																
3	4	4	5	6	7	8	9	12	13	18	19	26	27																
1	4	2	5	3	7	5	9	7	11	11	16																		
4	5	6	7	8	9	12	13	18	19	26	27																		
2	5	3	7	5	9	7	11	11	16																				
6	7	8	9	12	13	18	19	26	27																				
3	7	5	9	7	11	11	16																						
8	9	12	13	18	19	26	27																						
5	9	7	11	11	16																								
12	13	18	19	26	27																								
7	11	11	16																										
18	19	26	27																										
11	16																												
26	27																												

EXAMPLE 12.11

Use MLT-STD-105D to determine the sample size and the acceptance number for the following criteria:

- Single sampling
- Tightened inspection
- Inspection level II
- Lot size 6500
- AQL 1.5 percent

Solution

The code letter is taken from Table 12.10. Find the row that has the lot size 3201 to 10000. Follow it across to the inspection level II column and read the code letter, L. Single sampling with tightened inspection is shown in Table 12.12. Find the row that corresponds to the code letter L in the left column and follow it across to find the sample size, $n = 200$, and then to the column that corresponds to an AQL value of 1.5. At the intersection of the row and column are two numbers, 5 and 6. Five is the maximum acceptance number, and 6 is the minimum rejection number.

This lot is acceptable if five or fewer defective pieces are found in the sample size of 200. It should be rejected if six or more defective pieces are found in the sample.

EXAMPLE 12.12

Use MLT-STD-105D to determine the sample size and the acceptance number for the following criteria:

- Double sampling
- Normal inspection
- Inspection level II
- Lot size 6500
- AQL 1.5 percent

Solution

The code letter, L, is found in Table 12.10 as in the previous example. Table 12.14 is used for double sampling and normal inspection. The code letter L in the left column gives the appropriate row. The sample size column indicates that the first sample should be 125 pieces. If a second sample is needed, it should also be 125 pieces. Go across to the column corresponding to an AQL of 1.5. There are four numbers at the intersection of the row and column: 3, 7, 8, and 9. The 3 and 7 in the top row indicate that the acceptance number is 3 and the rejection number is 7. If the number of defectives in the first sample of 125 pieces is between 3 and 7, then a second sample of 125 pieces is taken. The acceptance total becomes 8 and the rejection total becomes 9.

This lot is accepted if three or fewer defective pieces are found in the first sample of 125. It is rejected if seven or more defective pieces are found in the first sample. A second sample of 125 is taken if the first sample has four, five, or six defective pieces. This lot is accepted if the total number of defective pieces for both samples is eight or less. If the total number of defective pieces for both samples is nine or more, the lot is rejected.

EXAMPLE 12.13

Use MLT-STD-105D to determine the sample size and acceptance number for the following criteria. Then analyze the quality protection.

- Single sampling
- Normal inspection
- Inspection level II
- Lot size 6500
- AQL 1.5 percent

Solution

The code letter L is again obtained from Table 12.10. Single sampling for normal inspection is found in Table 12.11. The row corresponding to the code letter L shows that a sample of 200 is to be taken. Follow the row across to the AQL = 1.5 column. The numbers at the intersection of the row and column are 7 and 8.

If seven or fewer defective pieces are found in the sample of 200, the lot is accepted. If eight or more defective pieces are found, the lot is rejected.

The quality protection must be determined from the OC curve (see Table 12.15 on page 376). The OC curve (Figure 12.17) shows that the actual AQL value is 2 percent instead of the planned 1.5 percent. The average proportion defective allowed by this sampling plan is slightly less than 2 percent. The RQL, rejectable quality level, is 6 percent.

FIGURE 12.17
The ($n = 200, c = 7$) OC curve.

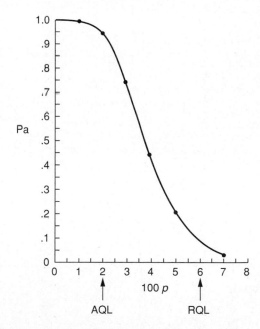

TABLE 12.15
Table of values for Figure 12.17

p	np	$100\,p$	Pa
.01	2	1	.999
.02	4	2	.95
.03	6	3	.74
.04	8	4	.46
.05	10	5	.22
.06	12	6	.09
.07	14	7	.03

12.6 THE AVERAGE PROPORTION DEFECTIVE

One of the problems with the AQL and OC curves is the apparent discrepancy between the quality goal and quality obtained. The indecisive zone on the OC curve implies that lots with higher proportions defective can be accepted far too often. The following analysis will show that the overall average proportion defective received from a vendor is slightly less than the AQL value on the appropriate OC curve.

EXAMPLE 12.14

For the past year a company received six lots from the vendor whose lot was inspected in Example 12.13, and the incoming inspection records show the following:

Lot 1	**Lot 2**	**Lot 3**	**Lot 4**	**Lot 5**	**Lot 6**
$n = 200$	$n = 200$	$n = 200$	$n = 200$	$n = 200$	$n = 200$
$d = 4$	$d = 6$	$d = 2$	$d = 4$	$d = 5$	$d = 3$

Calculate the true incoming quality that is going into production.

Solution

Total number of defects $(p) = 4 + 6 + 2 + 4 + 5 + 3 = 24$

Total number sampled $(N) = 6 \times 200 = 1200$

$$\bar{p} = \frac{24}{1200}$$

$$= .02 \quad \text{average proportion defective in the samples}$$

$$\sigma = \sqrt{\frac{\bar{p}(1 - \bar{p})}{N}}$$

$$= \sqrt{\frac{.02(.98)}{1200}}$$

$$= .004$$

The lot proportion defective, p, is normally distributed. A variation of the z formula that was introduced in Chapter 5 is used to apply the normal curve to proportions.

$$z = \frac{p - \bar{p}}{\sigma}$$

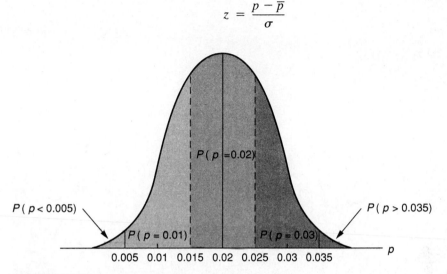

FIGURE 12.18
The normal distribution for p in Example 12.14.

The horizontal axis of the normal curve is in p units (instead of x, as in Chapter 5), with the average, $\bar{p}$, at the center. Calculate the probability that the vendor will ship a lot with 1 percent defective, $p = .01$, by finding the area under the curve from $p = .005$ to $p = .015$. This actually gives the probability that p lies between .005 and .015, but all of those p values will round off to $p = .01$. Similarly, find the probability that the vendor will send a lot with $p = .02$ ($.015 < p < .025$), $p = .03$ ($.025 < p < .035$), $p < .005$, and $p > .035$. Figure 12.18 illustrates these sections under the normal curve. These probabilities can then be combined with the information from the OC curve to give a realistic picture of the true incoming quality that makes it to production.
Find the area in the tail of the curve to the left of .005.

$$P(p = 0) = P(p < .005)$$

$$z = \frac{p - \bar{p}}{\sigma}$$

$$= \frac{.005 - .02}{.004}$$

$$= -3.75$$

From Table 3 in Appendix B, $z = 3.75$ (row 3.7, column 5) gives a tail area of .00009. This is area 1 in Figure 12.19 (page 378).

$$\text{Area } 1 = P(p = 0) = .00009$$

Next, find the area between $p = .005$ and $p = .015$.

$$P(p = .01) = P(.005 < p < .015)$$

FIGURE 12.19
The probability that $p = .01$.

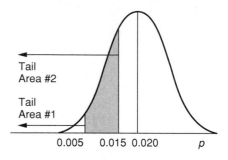

$$z = \frac{p - \bar{p}}{\sigma}$$

$$= \frac{.015 - .02}{.004}$$

$$= -1.25$$

A z value of 1.25 has a tail area of .1056, so tail area 2 in Figure 12.19 is .1056.

$$\text{Area 2} - \text{Area 1} = P(p = .01)$$
$$= 1.056 - .00009$$
$$= .1055$$

Find the area between $p = .015$ and $p = .025$.

$$P(p = .02) = P(.015 < p < .025)$$

FIGURE 12.20
The probability that $p = .02$.

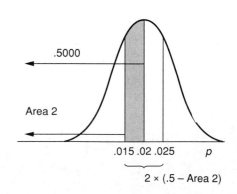

Because of the symmetry of the normal curve, the area from the center value of $p = .02$ to $p = .015$ is equal to the area from the center to $p = .025$. Remember that the area under one half of the curve is .5.

$$P(p = .02) = 2 \times (.5000 - \text{Area 2})$$
$$= 2 \times (.5000 - .1056)$$
$$= 2 \times (.3944)$$
$$= .7888$$

This is illustrated in Figure 12.20 (page 378).

The symmetry in Figure 12.18 shows that the area from $p = .025$ to $p = .035$ is equal to the area from $p = .015$ to $p = .005$. Therefore, the probability that $p = .03$ is the same as the probability that $p = .01$. Likewise, the probability that $p = 0$ is the same as the probability that $p > .035$.

$$P(p = .03) = .1055$$
$$P(p > 3.5) = .00009$$

The probability of receiving a lot with a specific proportion defective can be combined with the probability of acceptance of each of those lots from the OC curve to give the true proportion of defectives going into production.

TABLE 12.16
Proportion of incoming lots accepted for each p value

p	$P(p)$	$\times$	P(lot is accepted)	$=$	Proportion of Incoming Lots Accepted
0	.0001	$\times$	1.0	$=$	.0001
.01	.1055	$\times$	.999	$=$	.1054
.02	.7888	$\times$	.95	$=$	.7494
.03	.1055	$\times$	.74	$=$	.0781
.04	.0001	$\times$	.46	$=$	.000046
					.9330

The sum of the products in Table 12.16, .9330, is the proportion of the incoming lots that is accepted.

If the rejected lots are 100 percent sorted, then the products shown in Table 12.16 are the proportions of the incoming lots within each category that are going into production. For example, 7.81 percent of all the lots going into production are 3 percent defective.

If the rejected lots are returned to the vendor instead of being sorted, then the products have to be divided by the total, .933, to find the true proportion in each category that is going into production.

$$\frac{.0001}{.933} = .0001 \qquad 0.0\% \text{ of the lots going into production have } p = 0$$

$$\frac{.1054}{.933} = .113 \qquad 11.3\% \text{ of the lots going into production have } p = .01$$

$$\frac{.7494}{.933} = .803 \qquad 80.3\% \text{ of the lots going into production have } p = .02$$

$$\frac{.0781}{.933} = .084 \qquad 8.4\% \text{ of the lots going into production have } p = .03$$

$$\frac{.000046}{.933} = .000 \qquad 0.0\% \text{ of the lots going into production have } p = .04 \text{ or larger}$$

Determine the overall percent defective by combining the percent of the lots going into production with their proportion defective (see Table 12.17).

TABLE 12.17
Overall proportion defective

With rejected lots returned:	With rejected lots sorted:
.113 × .01 = .00113	.1054 × .01 = .001054
.803 × .02 = .01606	.7494 × .02 = .014988
.084 × .03 = .00254	.0781 × .03 = .002343
.0197	.0184

In the first case 1.97 percent of all the incoming material going into production is defective; in the second case, 1.84 percent is defective.

This analysis gives a more realistic picture of what production is facing in terms of incoming quality. It also provides data for a cost analysis regarding rejected lots. Is it cheaper to just ship the rejects back to the vendor? Does the fraction defective going into production change enough (.13 percent in this case) to make the cost and bother of 100 percent sorting worthwhile?

If the piece in the incoming lot studied in Example 12.14 combines with several different pieces feeding into production, each different piece will have to undergo a similar analysis. Then the "and" rule of probability, applied to the different defect-free proportions, will give the fraction of final product that is defect-free (as long as production does not produce any more defects).

EXAMPLE 12.15　Nine different parts received from vendors are assembled in one product. Four of the vendors are submitting parts that are 2 percent defective, and the other five vendors are producing parts that are 1 percent defective. If the incoming parts go directly into production, what percent of the final assembled product is defect free?

Solution

If the parts are 2 percent defective, they are 98 percent good. Likewise, the 1 percent defective parts are 99 percent good. The "and" rule from probability applies:

$$P(\text{good product}) = P(\text{1st part is good } and \text{ 2nd part is good}$$
$$and \ \dots \ and \text{ 9th part is good})$$
$$= (.99)^5 \times (.98)^4$$
$$= .951 \times .922$$
$$= .877$$

If no further mistakes are made in the assembly operation, 87.7 percent of the final product will be defect-free.

___

This concept may be extended: Suppose an assembled product consists of 50 parts and each of the 50 parts is 99 percent defect-free. What percent of the final product will be free of defects?

$$P(\text{defect-free product}) = (.99)^{50}$$
$$= .605$$

Only 60.5 percent of the final assembled product will be good. On an even larger scale, consider the automotive industry or another industry in which the final product consists of thousands of parts. Even 99.99 percent defect-free parts can lead to an excessive number of final products that are defective in one way or another.

12.7 VENDOR CERTIFICATION
AND CONTROL CHART MONITORING

In the quest for higher quality, accepting lots that are even 1 percent defective is becoming unreasonable. As the percent defective is forced down to levels such as .01 percent, acceptance sampling will become unrealistic owing to the large samples that will be necessary. Even now acceptance sampling is being phased out in favor of vendor certification plans. Each receiving company has its own certification plan, but in general, vendors are being asked for proof of quality: They have to provide evidence of a prevention, not detection, quality control program and of their use of SPC. Some large companies have a vendor rating system for their suppliers. Receiving companies, aiming for higher quality and cost reductions, want to be able to rely on vendor quality assurance and to move the incoming materials directly into production without incoming inspection.

    One basic method that can be used by incoming inspection in place of the inappropriate acceptance sampling features chart analysis. Certified vendors are vendors whose previous shipments were honestly and reliably quantified. Receiving companies have to determine the critical measurements on incoming materials. When those materials are purchased from a certified vendor, copies of the vendor's control charts for the critical measurements should be requested. Analysis of the charts can replace incoming inspection. Means, standard deviations, analysis for statistical control, histograms of the data on the charts, and process capability can all be determined. If any of the material is out of specification, it should show up on the control charts for that lot.

For new vendors and vendors that have not been certified and classified, large random samples (n = 100 or more) of incoming materials should be taken and the critical measurements recorded. A histogram of those measurements can give an estimate of the shape of the distribution, the mean, the standard deviation, and the process capability. These estimates can then be compared with the vendor data and the analysis of those data. When the two analyses are compatible, the frequency of checks on that vendor can be reduced until reliability and confidence have been established. Then, as with other certified vendors, there should be just an occasional audit inspection.

If discrepancies do occur between the inspection data and the vendor-submitted control chart data, each lot should be sampled so that an estimate of means, standard deviation, and distribution shape is determined. If differences continue to occur in the two sets of data, on-site inspection and discussion of procedures should take place. If a vendor is not cooperative, a search for a new supplier is in order.

EXERCISES

1. A box contains 20 parts, and four of the parts are defective. If a sample of five parts is randomly chosen without replacement, find the probability of getting three good parts and two defectives. Use the hypergeometric probability distribution.

2. The box of 20 parts from Exercise 1 is used again. A sample of five parts if chosen *with* replacement. Find the probability of getting three good parts and two defectives. Use the binomial probability distribution.

3. A lot of 2000 pieces arrives in 10 boxes that are uniformly packaged with five layers and 40 pieces per layer. Plan a random sample of 100 using a three-digit random number generator.

4. (a) Use the Poisson curves in Figure 12.2 to make an (n = 200, c = 3) OC curve.
   (b) Use the (n = 200, c = 3) OC curve to determine the percent of lots that will be accepted when the true lot proportion defective is 1 percent, 2 percent, and 4 percent.
   (c) What is the AQL?
   (d) What is the RQL?
   (e) What is the IQL?

5. Repeat Exercise 4 for an (n = 200, c = 1) OC curve.

6. Construct the AOQ curve to accompany the (n = 200, c = 3) OC curve from Exercise 4. What is the AOQL?

7. Construct the AOQ curve to accompany the (n = 200, c = 1) OC curve from Exercise 5. What is the AOQL?

8. Use the MLT-STD-105D sampling plan to determine the sample size and acceptance number for the following criteria.

   ■ Single sampling
   ■ Normal inspection
   ■ Inspection level II
   ■ Lot size 2000
   ■ The AQL 1 percent

9. Make an appropriate OC curve for the recommended sample size and acceptance number from Exercise 8. Use the OC curve to determine the actual AQL.

10. The product being produced contains 12 parts from vendors. Two of the vendors submit parts that are .5 percent defective, six vendors submit parts that are 1.5 percent defective, and the other four submit parts that are 2 percent defective. If no incoming inspection is used to weed out the defective parts and no further faulty work is done, what percent of the final product will be defect-free?

13

CASE
STUDIES

The following case studies cite various industry success stories. The changes that the companies made led to cost savings, higher quality, and higher productivity. Each report credits specific changes that the companies made that can be traced to the concepts and recommendations of the two consultants featured in Chapter 2, Deming and Crosby.

Various trade magazines have been carrying articles on the importance of the use of statistical techniques on all phases of a manufacturing process. Some companies try SPC because they have a very specific problem that they are trying ro resolve. Their results are good and the time it takes to achieve these results is relatively short: in some cases, just a few months. The application of basic statistical concepts with run charts, histograms, and control charts can provide a great deal of information about a process or about a specific point in a process.

One of the problems facing companies that want to begin using SPC is how to get started. The first case study deals with this dilemma.

CASE 13.1

Consultant Ray Milton[1] reports how EIS Brake Parts, a division of Standard Motor Parts Incorporated of Middletown, Connecticut, introduced SPC to its operation.

The key to management's application of SPC was starting small. When the first results showed positive, it was easy to expand the program a step at a time to other areas. The first application of SPC took place in the wheel cylinder department. The scrap rate of one of the parts, a master cylinder, was reduced from 30 percent defective to zero defects in 10,000 pieces inspected. The overall scrap rate for the department was reduced from a high of 1.1 percent to .3 percent over a seven-month span.

The application of SPC helped to identify faulty parts, processes, and machines. In one case it revealed that a turning machine required a new set of jaws. SPC slowly

---

[1] Ray Milton, "SPC: A Search for Zero Defects," *Modern Machine Shop* (May 1988): 60–67.

began to improve the individual products and the manufacturing process itself. It resulted in reduced scrap, higher quality, increased productivity, and lower costs.

In the second case, a process problem was solved with the help of a run chart. Various changes were tried on the process, and the effects of the changes were noted on a run chart.

CASE 13.2

Richard Stanula,[2] statistical process engineer at Mercury Marine, Brunswick Company, and Robert Hart of the University of Wisconsin report on the use of the run chart to bring a process into control.

A run chart is like a control chart, but without the controls; it simply specifies a target area. The chart is used to provide communication from the process to the operator. In this case, it was used in a cause-and-effect relationship.

Two close-tolerance dowel holes and a water passage hole were being machined in a cast drive-shaft plate. Problems with the operation were caused by out-of-tolerance dowel holes and excessive downtime for tool changes.

The initial chart showed a large percent of oversized holes that were being produced intermittently. The first step was the change from hand feed to automatic feed. This brought about some decrease in variability on the chart, but the holes were still too large and too variable. A second change featured the installation of an undersized drill reamer. The holes were nearer the target size, but variability was still excessive. Two changes were tried next: New bushings were installed on the drill reamers, and the precision hole boring operation was separated from the less critical water passage hole boring. Standard tooling was reinstalled. The charts showed that variations were reduced again but that the dowel holes were still too large. A change to undersized tooling brought the measurements into the target area, and the variation was more reasonable.

At each change the effect was noted on the run chart. The process was brought under control so that assignable causes of variation could be detected. The step-by-step improvements were the result of cooperation between the operator, inspector, engineer, and control statistician, with the run chart providing the main communication link to the process.

The authors cited the following benefits from the experience:

- Increased operator involvement
- Worker satisfaction and pride of workmanship
- Elimination of scrap and rework
- Lower costs
- Higher productivity
- A quality product
- Customer satisfaction
- A model of success for the company
- Possible early problem detection with continued use of the run chart

---

[2] Richard Stanula and Robert Hart, "A Process Improvement Tool," *Quality* (September 1987): 59.

Quality consultants generally predict that limited use of SPC will lead to disappointing results. Initial successes can be achieved, however, especially when the problem area has been fairly well defined. SPC should be one of the first steps in the total quality process. The next case features a broader approach to the application of SPC. A plantwide implementation of SPC was used to pinpoint trouble areas, and SPC techniques were then used to help solve the problems that were uncovered.

**CASE
13.3**

Quality manager James Smith and machine shop supervisor Michael Clark,[3] at Ingersoll-Rand's Von Duprin Incorporated, report that finished product rejections were reduced by 77 percent over a five-month period when SPC techniques were used.

After employees were trained in its use, SPC was implemented on a plant-wide basis to assess each department's quality performance, to determine causes for defects, and to target the corrective action needed. A quick analysis indicated that the defect rate was higher than anticipated and the capability of the machining operations was better than their performance. A major problem identified was a lack of feedback to operators regarding their individual performance. Further analysis showed a problem with the setup operation.

Corrective action was taken. A better setup was instituted, and operator control charts were started. The charts indicated that the defective pieces came from just five of the 70 operators. Over a 90-day period the first-piece defect level dropped from 42.9 percent to 14.7 percent. It has since dropped further to 4.8 percent and the entire machine shop's reject rate has decreased from 16.3 percent to 3.7 percent. Chart visibility turned out to be a strong motivating factor for the operators; they became more alert and took pride in their performance. Responsibility for quality was transferred from the inspectors to the shop floor. Operators began to consider themselves to be team members participating in problem solving.

The emphasis on control of a process through the use of control charts is an important feature of SPC. When changes have to be made within a process, such as tools sharpened and dies rebuilt, the control chart indicates when the change should be made. The control chart optimizes the use of anything that is subject to wear. A change will not be needed as long as the chart is in control, and as soon as the chart indicates that the wear is leading to a problem, the change can be made before any defective items are made. An article in the *Quality Control Supervisor's Bulletin*[4] stresses that the use of control charts on the line leads to logical decisions regarding the process. Problems such as tool wear are discovered and acted on right away before defectives are made.

Quality consultants insist that in order for a company to produce top quality products, a total commitment to quality is needed. That commitment has to start at the top management level. Management must maintain a constant pressure to ensure that everyone stays committed to the quality effort. Previous sporadic efforts for improvement may have caused a jaded outlook and that attitude must be overcome.

---

[3] James Smith and Michael Clark, "SPC Sharply Drops Rejects," *Modern Machine Shop* (May 1986): 66–69.
[4] "Statistical Methods Slam the Door on Defects," *Quality Control Supervisor's Bulletin*, 24 Rope Ferry Road, Waterford, CT, 06386.

The Ford Motor Company was one of the first American companies to change to a quality-first system of manufacturing. In the following case study, Donald Katz[5] reports on W. Edwards Deming and his efforts to arouse American industry to the need for competitive quality.

CASE 13.4

Faced with drastic losses, Ford Motor Company became one of Deming's first U.S. customers in 1980, according to Katz. Deming helped to reorganize the entire process that Ford used to make cars. Senior managers attended Deming's seminars, and statistical control methods were used in every department. Deming broke through departmental barriers and had machinists and assemblers work together to determine critical measurements. When the machinists made the parts, the assemblers were then better able to install them. Quality drastically improved.

Team members responsible for building the $3.25 billion production lines for the Taurus and Sable held seminars with suppliers regarding the necessary quality of the incoming parts. They collected 1400 suggestions from line workers and used 550 of them. When the two cars hit the market in December 1985, they were instantly successful. They became an integral part of Ford's remarkable comeback. The company's profits shot way up, to $4.6 billion in 1987.

Motor Trend's 1988 Special Issue[6] is devoted to Ford's big turnaround. In three previous years to 1987, Ford lost $1 to $1.5 billion per year. One of the major contributors to Ford's new success is reported to be teamwork. The old sequence of design to engineering to manufacturing to assembly, in which each phase is primarily finished before the next begins, has been changed. Now there is teamwork and consultation between the various divisions. The result is fewer surprises and impossible situations planned by one division for another to accomplish. The new procedure eliminates many problems and has effected a big improvement in quality.

CASE 13.5

Another case featuring a company-wide, total involvement in the quality effort occurred at Velcro and was reported in the *Harvard Business Review*. The author of the report, Theodor Krantz,[7] has been the president of Velcro USA since 1984. He states that the company received a shock in 1985 when General Motors, one of Velcro's important customers, dropped the company's rating as a supplier from the highest level to next to the lowest level. The main problem, according to GM, was that Velcro was inspecting quality into its product instead of manufacturing quality into it. The waste that accompanied Velcro's detection method kept its prices high in an industry in which continual improvement in quality and productivity is needed for cost effectiveness. Velcro was throwing away 5 to 8 percent of its tape, and that much waste had to be reflected in the cost of its product.

---

[5] Donald R. Katz, "Coming Home," *Business Month* (October 1988): 57–62.

[6] *Motor Trend Magazine*, Special Issue, 1988.

[7] K. Theodor Krantz, "How Velcro Got Hooked on Quality," *Harvard Business Review* (September-October 1989): 34–40.

Velcro's initial response to the deadline imposed by GM was to hire a local group of consultants for training and guidance. The training involved teaching SPC and problem-solving techniques to about 500 hourly and salaried personnel. The consultants were helpful because they worked across the traditional hierarchal lines of management and could effectively expose some of the company's problems.

The usual disbelief among both hourly and salaried personnel had to be overcome. Total management commitment was a necessity to convince the rest of the company that high quality and continual improvement was the new, unrevokable policy. Factors obstructing the interaction between supervision and production workers had to be eliminated. Some workers did not want the responsibility for quality placed on their shoulders; it was always easier when the quality control division had that responsibility (detection) further down the line. Some supervisors did not like the change in their job structure; they became defensive and resisted the full utilization of the production workers.

New lines of communication had to be formed. Data from the application of SPC were used by ad hoc teams organized to develop process improvements. Velcro has had about 120 teams over the first three years, and at the time the article was written, about 50 teams were functioning. The teams were initially only in production, but now some of the teams are in the administrative area, too; quality consciousness is spreading.

The results of Velcro's quality effort initially showed up in waste reduction. Waste in 1987 decreased 50 percent from 1986, and waste in 1988 was down 45 percent from 1987. The results in 1989 are not as dramatic because the company is at the little-by-little stage of progression. The management realizes, however, that there is no end to the quality process; it pervades every department and becomes a way to life.

One of the major changes that occurs in a company when SPC is used is that its quality control department changes from using detection methods to using prevention methods. In some companies that change is regarded as job threatening since a goal of the prevention method is to eliminate many inspection positions. The following case study reports that the quality department is taking an active role in the training that is needed for its new quality process.

CASE 13.6

The total commitment of the Industrial Specialities Division (ISD) of 3M to the quality process is reported in the July 1988 issue of *Quality Progress*.[8] ISD's program features a combination of outside consultants and inside champions to help implement SPC and the quality effort. The quality function at ISD plays a major role in quality training. Quality is becoming everyone's responsibility; its is not just the job of the quality control department.

When the quality training process began, outside consultants were used to train the management team and to help the quality function put together a training program. Top management then helped train others in the division. The managers became better quality coaches after their participation in the training program, and they also understood the concepts more thoroughly because they had to explain them to others. A strong sense

---

[8] Michael J. Bulduc and Kimberly S. DeGolier, "The Expanding Role of Quality in Specialized Training," *Quality Progress* (July 1988): 34–38.

of internal control and direction was maintained by adapting the materials to the unique division's operations.

ISD's quality training was implemented in five phases that featured the teachings of some of the top quality consultants. Philip B. Crosby's explanation of quality was used, and everyone in the division received a copy of this book *Quality Is Free*. Joseph Juran's set of 16 video tapes was used to teach corrective and preventive action techniques. W. Edwards Deming's book *Quality, Productivity and Competitive Position* was used extensively to present his principles. The company is developing designed experiments materials based on the work of Genichi Taguchi. Designed experiments features an analysis of planned changes in a process for the optimum path to process improvement. The last phase in the present quality plans is development of advanced designed experiments using reference materials by George E. P. Box.

The move toward making quality a primary concern demands that all employees become totally involved. Decisions on corrective action for process problems are being pushed down to the lowest level to eliminate bureaucratic delays and inefficiencies and to tap the wealth of knowledge that the hourly workers have concerning their particular phase in the process. Giving hourly workers more responsibility in the quality process has led to various ventures into participative management.

Another road to participative management occurs when a company finds its back to the wall in the developing global marketplace and looks for help internally as a last resort. Several success stories were reported in articles in the October 17, 1988, issue of *Industry Week*. "Competitive Again"[9] reports the dramatic turn-around of A. M. Castle & Company, whose metal processor/distributor business changed from a large inventory, customer search procedure to a customer-driven business that demanded a quality product. Part of its quality program involved participative management. "Partnership in the Trenches"[10] mentions successful participative ventures at Xerox, GM's Packard Electric Division, New United Motors Manufacturing Incorporated (NUMMI), and others. "Tackling Sacred Cows"[11] details Amot Control's change from an adversarial relationship between management and labor to one of participative management. In all cases, participative management contributed to product improvements and cost savings.

Another change that is developing in the effort to improve incoming quality is single sourcing. In his book *Quality, Productivity and Competitive Position*, Deming promotes this concept in his 14 points for management. He stresses that a single source reduces variability in the incoming parts and that cooperation between the vendor and the receiving company will develop economies. Two of the major economies result from the single production setup and the cost savings from the purchase of materials in larger quantities. "Betting on a Single Source"[12] in the February 1, 1988, issue of *Industry Week* outlines the pros and cons of single source purchasing.

---

[9] Michael Verespej, "Competitive Again," *Industry Week* (October 17, 1988).
[10] Michael Verespej, "Partnership in the Trenches," *Industry Week* (October 17, 1988).
[11] William Patterson, "Tackling Sacred Cows," *Industry Week* (October 17, 1988).
[12] John Sheridan, "Betting on a Single Source," *Industry Week* (February 1, 1988).

One concept that has developed in the quality effort is *just in time* (JIT) manufacturing in which production is so efficient that each piece arrives at its next process step just in time, so that no inventories develop. There are two important reasons for JIT manufacturing. First, cutting inventories brings a big cost savings. Second, quality improves because troubles cannot hide in inventory. A defective part taken from a large inventory leaves no trace of the cause of the defect, and the prevention method cannot be applied. This problem is eliminated in JIT manufacturing. When a company wants to adopt JIT manufacturing, inventories should be reduced gradually. In the process of gradual reduction, troubles will arise. Inventory reductions should be stopped until the trouble is resolved, and then further reductions can be made. The logical end to that procedure is zero inventory and single piece production in which each part arrives at the right place at exactly the right time. There are reports of some manufacturing processes that are choreographed to that extent. One major problem that can develop from JIT manufacturing, however, is an increase in stress when zero inventory is achieved and no leeway exists in product flow.[13] The ideal method is to maintain a small inventory buffer, which will allow some fluctuation in worker rates.

---

[13] Janice M. Klein, "The Human Cost of Manufacturing Reform," *Harvard Business Review* (March-April 1989).

A

MATHEMATICS
AND
STATISTICS

The individual mathematics topics needed for the applications of mathematics and statistics in SPC are introduced throughout the text. This chapter combines all the mathematics topics together in a logical sequence for a more systematic development and provides more depth on some of the topics. The following table of contents is provided for easy reference to specific topics.

CONTENTS

A.1 SIGNED NUMBERS

Signed numbers are necessary when dealing with a numerical scale. A common example of a signed number scale is a thermometer. It has a reference point of 0 with warmer temperatures indicated by positive numbers and colder temperatures indicated by negative numbers. Similarly, when a scale of numbers is put on a line or gauge, a reference point, 0, is centered between positive numbers to the right (or up) and negative numbers to the left (or down). Signed numbers are occasionally needed in SPC for some gauges and for coding data.

Operations With Signed Numbers

A signed number can be thought of as a combination of direction and a distance.

4 or +4 means 4 units to the right

−5 means 5 units to the left

When signed numbers are on a number line, the distance is the number of units from 0 (Figure A.1).

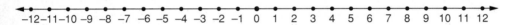

FIGURE A.1
A number line.

The absolute value of a number strips away the sign and results in a positive number or zero. The symbol for absolute value is a pair of vertical bars, one on each side of the number.

$|3| = 3$ Read, "The absolute value of 3 is 3."

$|-4| = 4$ Read, "The absolute value of negative 4 is 4."

$|0| = 0$ Read, "The absolute value of zero is zero."

Absolute value terminology is used to describe the rules for operating with signed numbers.

Addition Rules

There are two rules for addition.

Rule 1: If the signs of the two numbers are the same,
(a) add their absolute values
(b) keep their sign

This is the addition of two numbers that have the same sign (negative).

$$-5 + (-2)$$

$|5 + 2|$ (a) add their absolute values

-7 (b) keep the negative sign

This is the addition of two positive numbers.

$$4 + 3$$

$$|4 + 3| \quad \text{(a) add their absolute values}$$
$$7 \quad \text{(b) keep the positive sign}$$

This rule is consistent with regular arithmetic addition, so when adding positive numbers, just add them as usual.

> *Rule 2*: If the signs of the two numbers are different (one positive and one negative),
> (a) subtract their absolute values
> (b) keep the sign of the one that has the largest absolute value

This is the addition of two numbers with opposite signs.

$$-9 + 3$$

$$|9 - 3| \quad \text{(a) subtract their absolute values}$$
$$-6 \quad \text{(b) keep the sign of the one with the largest absolute value (the negative sign)}$$

This is the addition of two numbers with opposite signs.

$$12 + (-4)$$

$$|12 - 4| \quad \text{(a) subtract their absolute values}$$
$$8 \quad \text{(b) keep the sign of the largest in absolute value (the positive sign)}$$

The addition of signed numbers is always a three-step process:

1. Classify the problem as an addition or subtraction problem.
2. Do the appropriate addition or subtraction of absolute values.
3. Affix the proper sign (positive or negative).

EXAMPLE A.1 Do the following additions by the three step process.

Solution

$$-12 + 3 \quad \text{Classify as addition with opposite signs.}$$
$$|12 - 3| \quad \text{Subtract the absolute values.}$$
$$-9 \quad \text{Keep the negative sign.}$$

$$-8 + (-7) \quad \text{Classify as addition with the same signs.}$$
$$|8 + 7| \quad \text{Add the absolute values.}$$
$$-15 \quad \text{Keep the minus sign.}$$

$4 + (-9)$ Classify as addition with opposite signs.
$|9 - 4|$ Subtract the absolute values.
-5 Keep the negative sign.

$-6 + 13$ Classify as addition with opposite signs.
$|13 - 6|$ Subtract the absolute values.
7 Keep the positive sign.

$-4 + (-8)$ Classify as addition with the same signs.
$|4 + 8|$ Add their absolute values.
-12 Keep the negative sign.

$12 + 8$ Just add. There is no need to follow the signed number
20 rule when its a familiar problem from arithmetic.

Subtraction

The addition rules are also used for subtraction.

Rule: (a) Change the subtraction sign to addition.
        (b) Change the sign of the number on the right.
        (c) Use the appropriate addition rule.

Here the subtraction is changed to addition and the 5 is changed to -5.

$$-8 - 5$$
$$-8 + (-5)$$

$|8 + 5|$ The signs are the same, so add the absolute
-13 values and keep the negative sign.

$9 - (-4)$ The subtraction is changed to addition, and
$9 + 4$ the -4 is changed to 4.
13 Just add.

$-5 - (-8)$ The subtraction is changed to addition, and
$-5 + 8$ the -8 is changed to 8.
$|8 - 5|$ For addition with opposite signs, subtract the
3 absolute values and keep the positive sign.

When a mixture of addition and subtraction of signed numbers is encountered, the classification step of the three-step addition process is very important. If the operation is subtraction, it is changed to addition by the two-step process shown above. Then the addition has to be classified and the appropriate rule applied.

EXAMPLE A.2   Follow the addition and subtraction procedures for the following problems.

Solution

$4 - (-7)$	Classify as subtraction of signed numbers.
$4 + 7$	Change the problem to addition and change the -7 to 7.
11	Add.

$-5 + 3$	Classify as addition with opposite signs.
$\mid 5 - 3 \mid$	Subtract their absolute values.
-2	Keep the negative sign.

$-8 - (-2)$	Classify as subtraction of signed numbers.
$-8 + 2$	Change the problem to addition and change the -2 to 2.
$\mid 8 - 2 \mid$	For addition with opposite signs, subtract the absolute
-6	values and keep the negative sign.

$-9 - 4$	Classify as subtraction of signed numbers.
$-9 + (-4)$	Change the problem to addition and change the 4 to -4.
$\mid 9 + 4 \mid$	For addition with the same signs, add the absolute
-13	values and keep the negative sign.

$8 + (-13)$	Classify as addition with opposite signs.
$\mid 13 - 8 \mid$	Subtract the absolute values
-5	keep the negative sign.

$12 - 5$	Just subtract. Again, if a familiar arithmetic operation
7	is encountered, just do it as usual.

Multiplication and Division

The sign rules are the same for both multiplication and division.

Rule 1: If one of the two numbers is negative, the answer is negative.

These all have negative answers.

$$8 \times (-3) = -24 \qquad -9 \times 6 = -54$$

$$\frac{50}{-5} = -10 \qquad \frac{-32}{16} = -2$$

Rule 2: If both of the numbers are negative, the answer is positive.

These have positive products or quotients.

$$-7 \times (-4) = 28$$

$$\frac{-48}{-8} = 6$$

EXAMPLE A.3 Classify the following operations and apply the appropriate rule.

Solution

-9×3	Classify as multiplication with one negative number.
-27	The product is negative.

$-8 + 17$	Classify as addition with opposite signs.
$\lvert 17 - 8 \rvert$	Subtract the absolute values.
9	Keep the positive sign.

$$\frac{24}{3}$$ Just divide. Another familiar problem from arithmetic.

$$8$$

$-7 \times (-6)$	Classify as multiplication; both values are negative.
42	The product is positive.

$-9 - 15$	Classify as subtraction.
$-9 + (-15)$	Change the operator to addition, and change the 15 to -15.
$\lvert 9 + 15 \rvert$	For addition with the same signs, add the absolute values
-24	and keep the negative sign.

$$\frac{-36}{-12}$$ Classify as division; both values are negative.

$$3$$ The quotient is positive.

$$\frac{55}{-5}$$ Classify as division with one negative value.

$$-11$$ The quotient is negative.

A.2 VARIABLES

A variable is a symbol that represents some number. Variables are often used in formulas that determine a specific value of interest. Perhaps a familiar example is the formula for the area of a rectangle.

$$\text{Area} = \text{length} \times \text{width}$$

That formula can be written in a shorter form using variables.

$$\text{Area} = LW$$

In the short form, the variable L stands for the length of the rectangle and W represents the width of the rectangle. When two variables are placed next to each other, their values are to be multiplied.

   The symbols that are used in statistics for variables are primarily letters, but sometimes letters with subscripts are used. For example, x is often used to represent a measurement. When there is more than one measurement, they can be represented by different letters such as x, y, and z or by letters with subscripts such as x_1, x_2, and x_3.

   One of the most commonly used formulas in statistics is the average value formula: Add all the values, then divide the sum by the number of values added. In variable form, the formula can be written in different ways.

$$\bar{x} = \frac{x + y + z}{3}$$
$\bar{x}$, read "x bar," is the symbol for the average. The formula is specific for three different measurements represented by x, y, and z.

$$\bar{x} = \frac{x_1 + x_2 + \cdots + x_n}{n}$$
This formula is more general because it applies to any number of values, n.

The second formula uses subscripted variables where x_1, read "x one," represents the first measurement, x_2, read "x two," represents the second measurement, and x_n, read "x sub n" or just "x, n," stands for the nth, or last, measurement. If there were 30 measurements to average, the n value would be 30; if there were four measurements, the n value would be 4. The three dots mean to keep adding all the other measurements that lie between the x_2 and the x_n values, specifically, x_3, x_4, and all others up to x_{n-1}.

   Another formula, equivalent to the previous one, uses the Greek letter $\sum$ (capital sigma) as an addition indicator.

$$\bar{x} = \frac{\sum x}{n}$$

The formula is read, "x bar equals summation x divided by n." $\sum x$, summation x, means to add all the x measurements, and the denominator in the formula indicates that there are n measurements to average. This is the preferred formula because it is short and concise.

Operations

The formulas in statistics, as well as in other applications, contain precise directions for handling the numerical values represented by the variables. The operations are indicated by both symbol and position, and the order in which the operations are to be performed follows a strict algebraic hierarchy.

Addition

Addition is indicated by either a "+" or a "$\sum$" symbol.

$$x + y + z \quad \text{Add the three values.}$$
$$\sum x \quad \text{Add all the } x \text{ values.}$$
$$x_1 + x_2 + x_3 + \cdots + x_{15} \quad \text{Add the 15 } x \text{ values.}$$

Subtraction

Subtraction uses the "−" symbol.

$$c - b \quad \text{Subtract the } b \text{ value from the } c \text{ value.}$$

Multiplication

Multiplication has many indicators. When variables are not used, the ×, adjacent parentheses, a number next to a parentheses, and a raised dot all mean multiplication.

$$4 \times 5 = 20 \qquad (8)(5) = 40$$
$$7(9) = 63 \qquad 6 \cdot 5 = 30$$

When variables are used, the × may be confusing as a multiplication indicator because it is often used as a variable. Adjacent positions, raised dots, and parentheses are all alternative multiplication indicators.

xy	Multiply the x value by the y value.
$5x$	Multiply the x value by 5.
$(3)(x)$	Multiply the x value by 3.
$7 \cdot c$	Multiply the c value by 7.
$b(8)$	Multiply the b value by 8.

Division

Division is sometimes indicated by the "÷" symbol, but more often by the fraction bar.

$x \div y$	Divide the x value by the y value.
$\dfrac{c}{d}$	Divide the c value by the d value.

Powers

Powers are indicated by a raised number on the right side of the base value. A power indicates a repeated multiplication of the base value, and the exponent, or raised number, indicates how many factors are multiplied.

3^4, read "three to the fourth power," means $3 \cdot 3 \cdot 3 \cdot 3$

$$3^4 = 3 \cdot 3 \cdot 3 \cdot 3 = 81$$

Second and third powers have the special names of square and cube.

5^2, read "five squared," means $5 \cdot 5$

$$5^2 = 5 \cdot 5 = 25$$

6^3, read "six cubed," means $6 \cdot 6 \cdot 6$

$$6^3 = 6 \cdot 6 \cdot 6 = 216$$

x^2, read "x squared," means $x \cdot x$

There are several algebraic properties associated with powers, but the only ones needed at this time are:

Rule 1: For multiplication of powers with the same base, keep the base the same and add the exponents.

$$x^2 \cdot x^3 = x^5$$
$$2^4 \cdot 2^3 = 2^7$$
$$5^2 \cdot 5 = 5^3 \quad \text{(5 is the same as } 5^1\text{)}$$

Writing 5 is the same as writing 5^1. Also, $x^3 \cdot x^5$ means $xxx \cdot xxxxx$, but that can be written as x^8. Similarly, $2^4 \cdot 2^3$ means $(2 \cdot 2 \cdot 2 \cdot 2) \cdot (2 \cdot 2 \cdot 2)$, and that can be written as 2^7.

The cancellation rule from fractions leads to the division rule for powers.

$$\frac{6}{8} = \frac{2 \cdot 3}{2 \cdot 4} = \frac{3}{4}$$

Although the middle step is usually omitted, it is the "official" concept: Cancel common factors. Applied to powers,

$$\frac{x^3}{x^5} = \frac{1 \cdot x^3}{x^2 \cdot x^3} = \frac{1}{x^2} \qquad \frac{x^8}{x^5} = \frac{x^3 \cdot x^5}{1 \cdot x^5} = \frac{x^3}{1} = x^3$$

Rule 2: For division of powers with the same base, keep the base the same and subtract the exponents. If the larger power is in the numerator, the resulting power is is in the numerator. If the larger power is in the denominator, the resulting power is in the denominator (retain a 1 in the numerator).

The following examples illustrate this rule.

$$\frac{x^6}{x^2} = x^4 \qquad \frac{3^2}{3^5} = \frac{1}{3^3} = \frac{1}{27}$$

$$\frac{y^4}{y^5} = \frac{1}{y} \qquad \frac{2^7}{2^2} = 2^5 = 32$$

Rule 3: When a product or quotient is raised to a power, the exponent applies to each factor within the parentheses.

See the following examples

$$(ab)^3 \qquad (4x)^2 \qquad \left(\frac{2}{3}\right)^4 \qquad \left(\frac{2x}{5}\right)^3$$

$$= a^3 b^3 \qquad = 4^2 \cdot x^2 \qquad \qquad$$

$$= 16x^2 \qquad = \frac{2^4}{3^4} \qquad = \frac{2^3 \cdot x^3}{5^3}$$

$$= \frac{16}{81} \qquad = \frac{8x^3}{125}$$

Roots

Roots are the opposite of powers. The symbol for a root is called a radical sign, $\sqrt{}$. A square root is indicated by the $\sqrt{}$ alone. Any other root has a root index: $\sqrt[3]{}$ indicates a cube root, and $\sqrt[4]{}$ signals a fourth root. The square root of 16, $\sqrt{16}$, means the number whose square is 16. Because $4^2 = 16$, $\sqrt{16} = 4$.

The root and power have a cancelling effect when they match.

$$\sqrt{4^2} = 4$$

$$\sqrt{x^2} = x \quad \text{for positive values of } x$$

$$\sqrt[3]{y^3} = y$$

Square roots of numbers that are not perfect squares can be done with a calculator. Virtually all calculators have a $\sqrt{}$ key. If some other root is needed, such as cube root, a scientific calculator is needed.

$$\sqrt{49} \qquad \sqrt[3]{8} \qquad \sqrt{12}$$

$$= \sqrt{7^2} \qquad = \sqrt[3]{2^3} \qquad \text{Press 12 } \sqrt{} \text{ on the calculator}$$

$$= 7 \qquad = 2 \qquad = 3.46410$$

As with powers, there are several algebraic properties of radicals, but just the multiplication and division properties are needed here.

$$\sqrt{a} \cdot \sqrt{b} = \sqrt{ab} \qquad \frac{\sqrt{a}}{\sqrt{b}} = \sqrt{\frac{a}{b}}$$

$$\sqrt{4} \cdot \sqrt{9} = \sqrt{36} \qquad \frac{\sqrt{144}}{\sqrt{9}} = \sqrt{\frac{144}{9}} = \sqrt{16}$$

The two rules can be verified by evaluating the roots on the numerical examples.

$$\sqrt{4} \cdot \sqrt{9} = \sqrt{4 \cdot 9} = \sqrt{36} = 6$$

or

$$\sqrt{4} \cdot \sqrt{9} = 2 \cdot 3 = 6$$

$$\frac{\sqrt{144}}{\sqrt{9}} = \sqrt{\frac{144}{9}} = \sqrt{16} = 4$$

or

$$\frac{\sqrt{144}}{\sqrt{9}} = \frac{12}{3} = 4$$

The radical rules can be used to simplify algebraic expressions containing radicals.

$$\sqrt{2} \cdot \sqrt{x} = \sqrt{2x}$$

$$\frac{\sqrt{15x}}{\sqrt{3}} = \sqrt{\frac{15x}{3}} = \sqrt{5x}$$

$$\sqrt{\frac{6x}{25}} = \frac{\sqrt{6x}}{\sqrt{25}} = \frac{\sqrt{6x}}{5}$$

A.3 ORDER OF OPERATIONS

When more than one operation has to be performed, it is necessary to know the correct sequence. For example, the calculation $4 + 3 \cdot 2$ equals 14 if the addition is done first or 10 if the multiplication is done first. The calculation should have just one answer, so the proper sequence must be followed.

The order of operations sequence has four steps.

1. If there are any grouping symbols, do the operations within the grouping symbols.
2. Evaluate all powers and roots
3. Do the multiplication and division as they occur in order, left to right.
4. Do the addition and subtraction in order from left to right.

Order of operations with special statistical quantities involves $\sum x^2$, $(\sum x)^2$, and expressions such as $\sum (x - 5)^2$.

$\sum x^2$ Square all the x values, then add all the squared values.

$(\sum x)^2$ Add all the x values first, then square the sum.

$\sum (x - 5)^2$ Subtract 5 from all the x values first, square each difference, then add all the squared values.

In each of the preceding statistical quantities, the $\sum$ sign acts as a grouping symbol around the sum of the quantities to its right.

EXAMPLE A.4   Use the order of operations to evaluate the following:

$$4 + 3 \cdot 2, \quad (5 + 4) - \frac{15 + 6}{3}, \quad \frac{3 + 18 - 2 \cdot 3}{3 + 2}, \quad \text{and} \quad \sqrt{3^2 + 4^2}$$

Solution

$4 + 3 \cdot 2$ Do the multiplication first, then add.
$= 4 + 6$
$= 10$

$(5 + 4)^2 - \dfrac{15 + 6}{3}$ Add inside the grouping symbols (both the parentheses and the fraction line).

$= 9^2 - \dfrac{21}{3}$ Square the 9.

$= 81 - \dfrac{21}{3}$ Divide by 3.

$= 81 - 7$ Subtract.

$= 74$

$\dfrac{3 + 18 - 2 \cdot 3}{3 + 2}$ The division line is a grouping symbol, so all the operations in both the numerator and denominator must be done first before the division can be performed. The multiplication in the numerator and the addition in the denominator are done first. The addition and subtraction are done as they occur, left to right.

$= \dfrac{3 + 18 - 6}{5}$

$= \dfrac{21 - 6}{5}$

$= \dfrac{15}{5}$ Divide.

$= 3$

$\sqrt{3^2 + 4^2}$ The $\sqrt{}$ is a grouping symbol, so all the operations must be completed inside before the square root step. Square first.

$= \sqrt{9 + 16}$ Add.

$= \sqrt{25}$ Take the square root.

$= 5$

EXAMPLE A.5   Given the measurements 4, 2, 7, and 3, calculate $\sqrt{4 \sum x^2 - (\sum x)^2}$.

Solution
There are actually four grouping symbols: the $\sqrt{}$, the parentheses, and the two $\sum$ signs. Calculate the summation first.

$$\sum x = 4 + 2 + 7 + 3$$
$$= 16$$
$$(\sum x)^2 = (16)^2$$
$$= 256$$
$$\sum x^2 = 16 + 4 + 49 + 9$$
$$= 78$$

Substitute the values into the original expression. Multiply first, then subtract. The square root is done with a calculator: Press 56 $\sqrt{}$.

$$\sqrt{4 \cdot 78 - 256}$$
$$= \sqrt{312 - 256}$$
$$= \sqrt{56}$$
$$= 7.48333$$

EXAMPLE A.6 Given the measurements 2, 4, 5, and 9, find $\sum(x - 5)^2$.

Solution

The subtraction in the parentheses is done first (second column). The differences are then squared (third column).

x	$x - 5$	$(x - 5)^2$
2	-3	9
4	-1	1
5	0	0
9	4	16
		26

The last step is to find the sum of the squared values (add the third column).

$$\sum(x - 5)^2 = 26$$

A.4 INEQUALITIES

The algebraic properties of inequalities are not needed for the work in this text, but the language of inequalities is used. When quantities are not equal, a statement indicating which is larger or smaller can be made using an inequality sign.

> The symbol ">" is read "greater than."
> The symbol "<" is read "less than."

Both symbols will always point to the smaller number.

$$4 > -1 \quad \text{Read, "Four is greater than negative one."}$$
$$7 < 12 \quad \text{Read, "Seven is less than 12."}$$

Two less than statements or two greater than statements can be combined for a "between" statement.

$$-6 < 4 < 10 \quad \text{Read, "Four is between negative six and 10."}$$
$$8 > 5 > 2 \quad \text{Read, "Five is between eight and two."}$$

When a variable is used with an inequality, a set of numbers is described and a picture of that set of numbers can be drawn using a number line. For example, $x > 4$ is illustrated by a line that extends infinitely to the right. There is no "next number" after 4 because of the infinitely many decimal values (4.1, 4.01, 4.0001, and so on), so the graph, or picture, illustrates this with an open circle. This is shown in Figure A.2.

FIGURE A.2
The graph of $x > 4$ and $x \leq 3$.

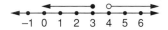

When a set of numbers has a definite beginning, a different symbol is used: $\geq$, read "greater than or equal to," and $\leq$, read "less than or equal to." A solid endpoint is used when graphing the "or equal to" inequalities.

$$x \leq 3 \quad \text{Read, "x is less than or equal to 3."}$$

This is also illustrated in Figure A.2.

$$0 \leq p \leq 1 \quad \text{Read, "p lies between 0 and 1, inclusive" (including the 0 and the 1).}$$

See Figure A.3.

FIGURE A.3
The graph of $0 \leq p \leq 1$.

EXAMPLE A.7

Interpret the following with a statement and a graph: $x > 2.5$, $8.3 < x < 12.2$, $x < 3.25$, and $6 \geq x \geq 1.7$.

Solution

	Statement	Figure
$x > 2.5$	x is greater than 2.5	Figure A.4
$8.3 < x < 12.2$	x is between 8.3 and 12.2	Figure A.5
$x < 3.25$	x is less than 3.25	Figure A.6
$6 \geq x \geq 1.7$	x is between 6 and 1.7, inclusive	Figure A.7

See page 407 for Figures A.4 through A.7.

FIGURE A.4
The graph of $x > 2.5$.

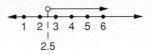

FIGURE A.5
The graph of $8.3 < x < 12.2$.

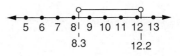

FIGURE A.6
The graph of $x < 3.25$.

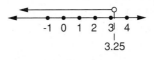

FIGURE A.7
The graph of $1.7 \leq x \leq 6$.

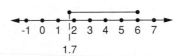

A.5 STATISTICS

Statistics is the science of data handling. The application of the statistical concepts normally involves using sample information to make decisions about a population of measurements.

A *population* is the set of all possible data values of interest

A *sample* is a subset, or part, of the population.

There are four phases involved in the application of statistics.

1. Collection of data

The data collected can be all the data in the population or, as is usually the case, a sample of the data in a population. When a sample is used, the sample must fairly represent the population because conclusions about the population depend on the information from the sample.

2. Organization of data

The data collected must be organized so that the information they contain can be understood. Tables, charts, graphs, and other pictures are used for the organization.

3. Analysis of data

The analysis of data involves concise numerical measures of the data. The measures fall into two main classifications: a middle value, called a measure of central tendency, and a data spread indicator, called a measure of dispersion.

4. Interpretation of the data

Conclusions are made about the population of measurements based on the charts, graphs, and statistical calculations that are applied to the samples taken.

Data Collection

Data collection can sometimes be the most difficult part of a statistical application. The sample chosen must be random, so the sample requires careful planning. In a *random* sample, each data value in the population has an equal chance of being used in the sample. All the formulas in statistics that relate to samples assume the use of random samples. If the sample is not random, then it is *biased* and some elements of the population are more likely to be chosen for the sample than others. *Biased samples lead to false conclusions regarding the population.*

A haphazard sample is often thought to be random, but unexpected biases may sneak in. For example, pieces chosen haphazardly on an incoming inspection may have a large proportion of the "easy to get at" pieces, and they can be carefully checked and placed by the vendor. The resulting inspection will imply that the quality of the incoming shipment is higher than it actually is. For another example, an operator given some leeway in taking production samples may subconsciously wait until things seem to be going well before taking the sample. Again, the biased sample may imply that the pieces produced are better than they actually are. Use of random numbers in planning a sample can be the best defense against a haphazard bias.

EXAMPLE A.8

Use a random number generator on a statistical calculator to plan the random times for six samples during an 8-hour shift that begins at 7:00 A.M. Plan how the random number digits will be used before starting. The calculator generator has three-digit numbers.

Solution
Let the digits represent hour:minutes from 0:00 to 7:59, and add the hour digit to the 7:00 A.M. beginning of the shift. Omit any random numbers that don't apply.

Random Digits	Sample Time	
3<u>70</u>	—	(doesn't apply, 70 > 59)
2<u>97</u>	—	(doesn't apply, 97 > 59)
0<u>78</u>	—	(doesn't apply, 78 > 59)
6<u>79</u>	—	(doesn't apply, 79 > 59)
644	1:44 P.M.	(7:00 + 6:44)
541	12:41 P.M.	(7:00 + 5:41)
<u>8</u>25	—	(doesn't apply, 8 > 7)
115	8:15 A.M.	(7:00 + 1:15)
046	7:46 A.M.	(7:00 + 0:46)
343	10:43 A.M	(7:00 + 3:43)
1<u>93</u>	—	(doesn't apply, 93 > 59)
538	12:38 P.M	(7:00 + 5:38)

If the time that it takes to gather the sample pieces exceeds three minutes (if, for example, the sample times at 12:38 P.M. and 12:41 P.M. overlap), take two consecutive samples starting at the earlier time (12:38 P.M.). This procedure is quick and should be done for each shift taking samples each day.

Data Organization

In tables, data can be listed in order from smallest to largest. It can also be condensed into a frequency distribution. Data can be shown in charts, graphs, pictures, and diagrams. Individual data values can be charted on a run chart as they are produced. Either individual values or sample averages can be charted on a control chart. If the data occur in pairs of measurements, the paired values can be graphed on a scattergram. A bar graph or histogram can be used to picture the distribution of the data or the frequency distribution.

A.5.1   THE FREQUENCY DISTRIBUTION

1. Calculate the range of the data.

$$\text{Range} = \text{largest data value} - \text{smallest data value}$$

If the range does not exceed approximately 10 measurement values (hundredths, thousandths, or whichever value is used), the frequency distribution can be made using the individual measurements on the horizontal scale and the frequency of the measurements on the vertical scale. Otherwise, proceed with the grouped values method.

2. Use the G chart in Appendix B, Table 2, to determine the optimum number of classes for the given number of data values.
3. Divide the range by the number of classes indicated from the G chart. Round the quotient *up*. The resulting number is the class range.
4. Set the class boundaries. If the data values can coincide with a class boundary, use either of the following options.

   - Use the rule that if the data value equals a class boundary, it is put in the higher class.
   - Change the boundaries so they use half of the next place value (i.e., if the measurement is in thousandths, make the boundaries in 5 ten-thousandths).

5. Use the class boundaries for the horizontal scale of the tally histogram and the frequency (number of data values in each class) on the vertical scale.
6. Tally the data with X's in the appropriate column.
7. Count the X's in each class and make the frequency distribution table.

EXAMPLE A.9   For the set of data in Table A.1 (page 410) make a frequency distribution and the accompanying tally histogram.

TABLE A.1

.912	.910	.911	.904	.905	.910	.910
.914	.912	.914	.910	.913	.908	.909
.907	.909	.913	.913	.912	.909	.908
.902	.906	.908	.909	.907	.906	.910
.915	.909	.909	.910	.911	.912	.909

Solution
1. The range $= .915 - .902 = .013$.
2. Thirteen units is too many for chart of individual values. The G chart recommends 7 classes.
3. Divide.

$$7 \overline{) .013} = .001+$$

Round up to .002 units per class.

The class boundaries are set on the horizontal scale in two ways: one for the "higher class" rule and one using 5 ten-thousandths. Use graph paper for consistent frequency representation.

TABLE A.2
Frequency distribution
using the higher class rule

Class	Frequency
.902 to .904	1
.904 to .906	2
.906 to .908	4
.908 to .910	10
.910 to .912	8
.912 to .914	7
.914 to .916	3

TABLE A.3
Frequency distribution
using 5 ten-thousandths

Class	Frequency
.9015 to .9035	1
.9035 to .9055	2
.9055 to .9075	4
.9075 to .9095	10
.9095 to .9115	8
.9115 to .9135	7
.9135 to .9155	3

The two set-up procedures (see Tables A.2 and A.3 on page 410) result in the same tally histogram and the same distrubition of frequencies (see Figures A.8 and A.9). Use whichever method seems easier.

FIGURE A.8
The tally histogram (higher class rule) for Example A.9.

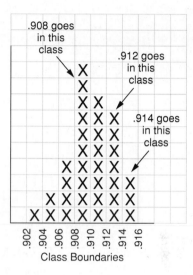

FIGURE A.9
The tally histogram (5 ten-thousandths rule) for Example A.9.

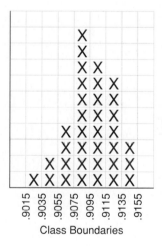

The Histogram

The histogram is a bar graph with the adjacent sides touching (no space between bars). It is used to illustrate the shape of the distribution of measurements. The histogram for

Example A.9 could be made by just drawing the vertical bars over the X's or redrawn using the information from the tally histogram (Figures A.10 and A.11).

FIGURE A.10
The tally histogram.

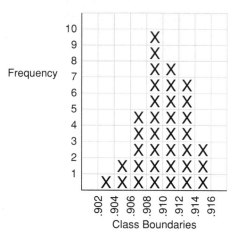

FIGURE A.11
The histogram.

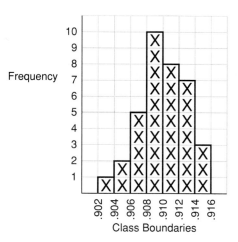

It is assumed that there is a definite shape of the population histogram at any one time and that the shape of the sample histogram will be quite similar to that of the population histogram, just smaller. It is important realize that a tally histogram grows in jumps and spurts. For example, Figure A.12 on page 413 shows what the tally histogram from Example A.9 looks like after 10 entries, 15 entries, 20 entries, and 30 entries. Compare this with the final histogram shown in Figures A.8 and A.9.

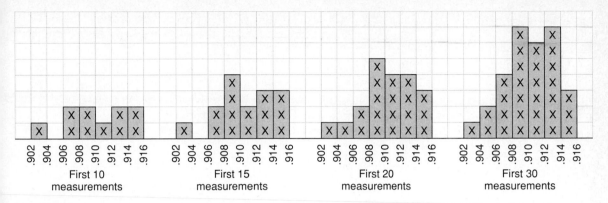

FIGURE A.12
The growing tally histogram.

As the sample size increases, the shape of the histogram becomes stable and the assumption is made that it looks more and more like the true population histogram. In application, a sample size of $n = 100$ is usually relied on to set the pattern.

FIGURE A.13
The normal pattern.

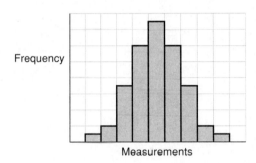

A histogram is usually expected to have a normal pattern as shown in Figure A.13 with the highest frequency in the center and the frequencies decreasing symmetrically on the sides as the distance from the center increases. When a data histogram does not have that pattern, something has probably affected the process. The shape of the data histogram, along with other pertinent information, is used to analyze the process and to find the cause of the process problem(s). The histogram is one of the simplest statistical concepts, but it is a very powerful tool in process analysis.

A.5.2 CONTROL CHARTS AND RUN CHARTS

Making control charts and run charts involves interpreting a numerical scale and graphing a point. Figure A.14 (page 414) features a vertical scale marked off in five-thousandths from .700 to .715. Four data values are given in their production sequence and are marked at the bottom of the chart. Graph the four points and connect them with a broken-line graph.

To graph three of the four numbers in Figure A.14, the position of the point must be estimated. The value .713 lies between .710 and .715. Imagine that the space between each line is divided into five equal spaces (four imaginary dividing lines) to estimate the position of the point more easily. Connect the points with line segments.

FIGURE A.14
Charting points on a control chart or run chart.

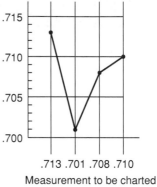

Measurement to be charted

Visualizing four units between the lines in Figure A.15 will make the estimation of point position easier. Imagine that the space between the lines is divided in half and that the two smaller spaces are divided in half again. Then estimate the position of the measurements and connect the points with straight line segments.

FIGURE A.15
Charting points on a control chart or run chart.

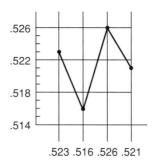

Measurement to be charted

The Run Chart

A run chart can be made for tracking the measurements of consecutively produced pieces. A target line is shown on the chart, and the relationship between the charted points and the target line, as well as the relationship between the points themselves, is continually analyzed as the pieces are being produced. The two initial considerations are the closeness of the points to the target line and the extent of the variation in the measurements.

The run chart can be used for process diagnosis and also for process improvement, in which case it is used in a cause and effect fashion. The effect of each process change is analyzed on the run chart.

In some situations, a high and low warning line is included on the run chart. The relation of points to the warning line is then watched as well as the previously mentioned relationships.

The set-up and charting procedure will follow that of the x and MR charts discussed in Chapter 7. The run chart does not include the moving range analysis.

EXAMPLE A.10   Use the data from Table A.1 to make a run chart. Assume that the order of production is by column, and that the target measurement is .910.

Solution
The data range is .013, so a scale of .001 units per line will be used (Figure A.16). It is important not to make the scale too large. The height of the chart should be between 1 and 2 inches for easier interpretation.

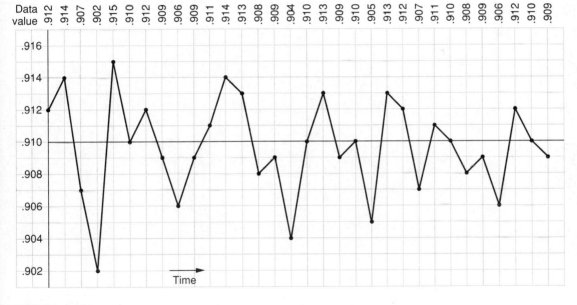

FIGURE A.16
The run chart for Table A.1 (target = .910).

A.5.3   THE SCATTERGRAM

A scattergram is used to determine whether a relationship exists between two measurements. The measurements may have a cause and effect relationship, in which a change in one measurement causes a specific change in another, or they may change simultaneously because they are mutually affected by some other variable(s). Both types of relationships are important to know. If there is an optimum measure of one variable, it may be controlled at that value with the help of another when a cause and effect relationship exists. In the other situation, if two variables are known to be closely related in value, control of one implies control of the other. Fewer control charts have to be maintained.

The scattergram is a graph of ordered pairs of numbers (x, y). The first number in the ordered pair, represented by x, is located on the horizontal scale. The second number, represented by y, is located on the vertical scale. A point that aligns with both values is graphed for the ordered pair. This is shown in Figure A.17.

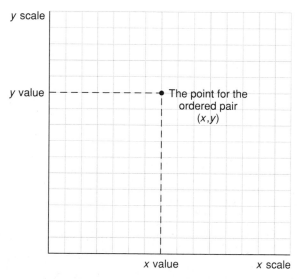

FIGURE A.17
An ordered pair on a scattergram.

EXAMPLE A.11 Graph the following ordered pairs: (2,12), (5,14), (7,15), (10,16), (12,18).

Solution
The horizontal scale extends as far as 12 and the vertical scale goes up to 18. The points, plotted in Figure A.18, on page 417, are almost in a straight line. That indicates that there is a strong linear correlation between the measurements x and y.

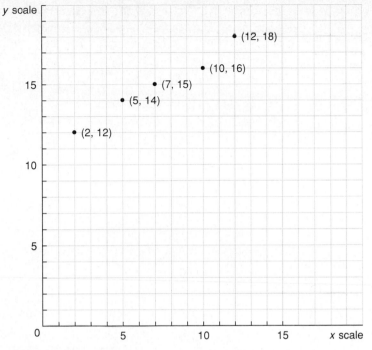

FIGURE A.18
Ordered pairs on a scattergram.

If it is suspected that a cause and effect relationship exists between the two measurements, it is important to associate the independent variable or measurement with x and the horizontal axis. The dependent value, associated with y and the vertical scale, is the measurement of interest that is to be controlled. When the cause and effect relationship is verified, the independent variable, x, will be held at the optimum value predicted by the graph that will keep the measurement of interest, y, at the desired value. A *line of best fit* is drawn through the points to balance the points above the line and the points below the line. There are statistical equations that will define the line precisely, but for now just an estimated line of best fit will be used to discuss the concepts involved.

In a cause and effect relationship, the desired y value is associated with a specific x value using the line of best fit. That x value will then be maintained in the process in an effort to keep y, the measurement of interest, at the desired level. This is shown in Figure A.19 (page 418).

If the two measurements are thought to have a common cause relationship instead of a cause and effect relationship, the specific choice of which variable to graph on the horizontal scale and which on the vertical scale is arbitrary.

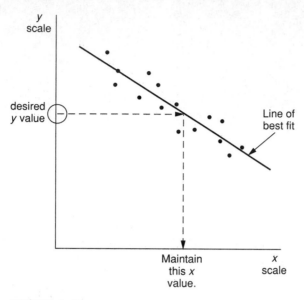
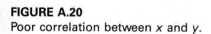

FIGURE A.19

The line of best fit on a scattergram with a cause and effect relationship.

FIGURE A.20

Poor correlation between x and y.

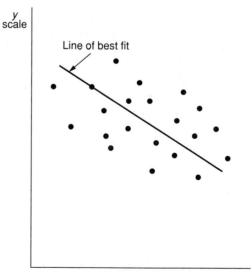

A graph that has all the points close to the line of best fit is said to have a strong linear trend and good correlation between the variables. Figures A.20 (page 418) and A.21 show examples of poor correlation between x and y and no correlation between x and y. In the latter, there is no line of best fit.

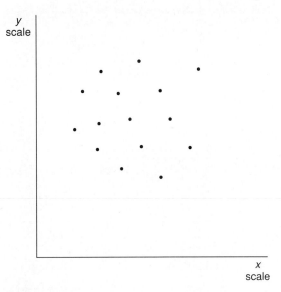

FIGURE A.21
No correlation between x and y.

EXAMPLE A.12

Draw the scattergram for the following pairs.

Temperature	Measurement
158	.625
164	.631
147	.617
152	.623
161	.629
142	.613
169	.633

Solution
In this case, if there is cause and effect, the temperature will be the cause and the measurement the effect. This makes the temperature the independent variable (on the horizontal scale) and the measurement the dependent variable (on the vertical scale). See Figure A.22 on page 420 for the drawing.

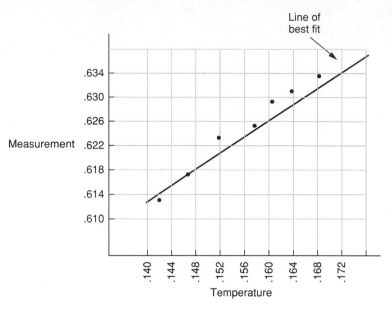

FIGURE A.22
The scattergram for Example A.12.

A.5.4 ANALYSIS OF DATA

The most often used measure of the middle of a set of data is the mean. The mean is the average of the data values, and it is calculated by dividing the sum of all the data values by the number of data values.

$$\overline{x} = \frac{\sum x}{n}$$

Given a set of measurements (x values), add the values ($\sum x$ means to add all the x's) and then divide by the number of values that were added (n).

EXAMPLE A.13 Find the mean for the set of measurements in Table A.4.

TABLE A.4

2.340	2.339	2.352	2.348	2.344
2.342	2.342	2.337	2.343	2.346
2.351	2.345	2.350	2.344	2.345

Solution

$$\overline{x} = \frac{\sum x}{15}$$

$$= \frac{35.168}{15}$$

$$= 2.3445$$

One disadvantage of using the mean as a measure of the center of a set of data is that if extreme data values are present, the average is no longer in the middle. Extreme values adversely affect the mean. To illustrate this effect, suppose there is one more data value in Table A.4 that has the value 2.460. The mean is now

$$\overline{x} = \frac{\sum x}{n}$$

$$= \frac{35.168 + 2.460}{16}$$

$$= 2.35175$$

This number is larger than all but one of the original 15 values. The 2.35175 is the mean, but it is no longer in the center of the data.

The Median

The median represents the data value that is physically in the middle when the set of data is organized from smallest to largest. The symbol for the median is $\tilde{x}$. The median can occur in two possible ways:

1. If there is an *odd* number of data values, there will be just one value in the middle when the data are ordered, and that value is the median.
2. If there is an *even* number of values, order the values and average the two values that occur in the middle.

EXAMPLE A.14

Find the median for the set of data in Table A.5.

TABLE A.5

4.231	4.238	4.234	4.227	4.225	4.230	4.225

Solution
Order the data values:

4.225, 4.255, 4.227, 4.230, 4.231, 4.234, 4.238

There are seven values (an odd number), so the median is the one in the middle when they are ordered. The median, $\tilde{x}$, is 4.230.

EXAMPLE A.15

Suppose one additional data value, 4.150, is included in the data of Table A.5. Find the median.

Solution
Order the data values.

4.150, 4.225, 4.225, 4.227, 4.230, 4.231, 4.234, 4.238

Average the two in the middle

$$\tilde{x} = \frac{4.227 + 4.230}{2}$$

$$= \frac{8.457}{2}$$

$$= 4.2285$$

Even though an extremely small data value was included, the value of the median was not adversely affected; it's still a measure of the middle.

Mode

The mode is usually included in a discussion of measures of central tendency, but it is not necessarily a measure of the center. The mode represents the data value that occurs the most or the class that has the highest frequency in a frequency distribution. It is often used in a descriptive manner with distributions. The distribution in Example A.7 was unimodal (one mode) because there was one class with the largest frequency.

EXAMPLE A.16

Find the mode for the set of data in Table A.6.

TABLE A.6

2.9	2.5	2.8	2.5	2.9	2.8
2.7	2.1	2.9	2.9	2.4	2.9
2.5	2.6	2.9	2.2	2.5	2.7
2.5	3.0	3.1	2.5	2.9	3.0

Solution
Order the data

2.1, 2.2, 2.4, 2.5, 2.5, 2.5, 2.5, 2.5, 2.5, 2.6, 2.7, 2.7, 2.8, 2.8, 2.9, 2.9, 2.9, 2.9, 2.9, 2.9, 2.9, 3.0, 3.0, 3.1

The mode is 2.9 (the measurement that occurs the most). The distribution is bimodal because it has two distinct high frequencies at 2.5 and 2.9.

Measures of Dispersion

Range The range shows the entire spread of the measurements. It is the difference between the largest and smallest measurements:

$$\text{Range} = \text{largest measurement} = \text{smallest measurement}$$

Variance The variance is an average squared difference between the individual measurements and the mean. There are statistical techniques that use variance directly, but for the usual use in statistical process control, the variance is one step away from the standard deviation: The square root of the variance gives the standard deviation. The symbol for variance is σ^2 (read, "sigma squared").

There are two basic formulas for calculating the variance.

$$\sigma^2 = \frac{\sum(x - \bar{x})^2}{n - 1}$$

This is the instructive form that shows that variance is an average squared difference between the measurements, x, and the average value, $\bar{x}$. Follow the order of operations for the equation:

1. Calculate $x - \bar{x}$ for all x values.
2. Square each difference.
3. Add the squared values.
4. Divide by $n - 1$. (This makes it an "almost" average.)

The calculation works best in a table format.

EXAMPLE A.17 Find the variance for the values 8, 10, 11, 15, 16, and 18. (Complete Table A.7.)

Solution

TABLE A.7

x	$x - \bar{x}$	$(x - \bar{x})^2$
8	$8 - 13 = -5$	25
10	$10 - 13 = -3$	9
11	$11 - 13 = -2$	4
15	$15 - 13 = 2$	4
16	$16 - 13 = 3$	9
18	$18 - 13 = 5$	25
$\sum x = 78$		$76 = \sum(x - \bar{x})^2$

$$\bar{x} = \frac{\sum x}{n} \qquad \sigma^2 = \frac{\sum (x - \bar{x})^2}{n - 1}$$

$$= \frac{78}{6} \qquad = \frac{76}{5}$$

$$= 13 \qquad = 15.2$$

The second formula for calculating variance is

$$\sigma^2 = \frac{n \sum x^2 - (\sum x)^2}{n(n - 1)}$$

The formula looks worse than the first one, but it is actually easier to use. Two sums are needed: $\sum x$ and $\sum x^2$. It is important to recognize the difference in the order of operations in the two expressions $\sum x^2$ and $(\sum x)^2$.

$\sum x^2$ Square the x values first, then add the squared values.

$(\sum x)^2$ Add the x values first, then square the sum.

EXAMPLE A.18 Use the same set of data from Table A.7 and calculate the variance with the second variance formula.

Solution

TABLE A.8

x	x^2
8	64
10	100
11	121
15	225
16	256
18	324
$\sum x = 78$	$1090 = \sum x^2$

Use the data from Table A.8 for the formula.

$$\sum x = 78$$

$$\sum x^2 = 1090$$

$$(\sum x)^2 = 6084$$

$$\sigma^2 = \frac{n \sum x^2 - (\sum x)^2}{n(n-1)}$$

$$= \frac{6(1090) - 6084}{6(5)}$$

$$= \frac{6540 - 6084}{30}$$

$$= \frac{456}{30}$$

$$= 15.2$$

The two values for variance will come out exactly the same because the formulas are algebraically equivalent. However, if the mean is rounded off before the subtraction in Example A.17, there will be a slight difference because of the rounding error.

Standard Deviation

The standard deviation is a measure of dispersion that is used extensively in statistical process control. Every time a control limit is calculated or the process capability is determined, the standard deviation is involved. Standard deviation is the square root of the variance. The symbol for the standard deviation is the Greek letter, σ, sigma (lowercase).

The variance was described as an average squared difference between the individual measurements and the mean. Similarly, the standard deviation is an average difference between the individual measurements and the mean. The standard deviation can be calculated directly using either of the formulas:

$$\sigma = \sqrt{\frac{\sum (x - \bar{x})^2}{n-1}} \qquad \sigma = \sqrt{\frac{n \sum x^2 - (\sum x)^2}{n(n-1)}}$$

Or, because the quantity under the radical sign is the same as the variance, the standard deviation can be calculated by taking the square root of the variance. The standard deviation for the set of values in Example A.18 is

$$\sigma^2 = 15.2$$
$$\sigma = \sqrt{15.2}$$
$$= 3.899$$

Using the Statistical Calculator

When a calculator is put in the statistics mode, data are usually entered with the $\sum$ key. Some calculators use a different data entry key such as the M+ key.

After all the data have been entered, the values of the mean and standard deviation can be found by pressing the appropriate keys. Usually there are two standard deviation keys: σ_n and σ_{n-1}. The two versions refer to the divisors in the formula.

The first formula is used for the population standard deviation, when all the measurements in the population are used in the calculation.

$$\sigma_n = \sqrt{\frac{\sum (x - \bar{x})^2}{n}}$$

The second formula is used to find the sample standard deviation and is the formula used in SPC. It is technically the best estimate of the population standard deviation, based on sample information.

$$\sigma_{n-1} = \sqrt{\frac{\sum (x - \bar{x})^2}{n - 1}}$$

Other calculator key variations include

$$\sigma_n \qquad \sigma_{n-1}$$
$$\sigma \qquad s$$
$$s_n \qquad s_{n-1}$$

EXAMPLE A.19 Use a statistical calculator to find the standard deviation for the set of data 8, 10, 11, 15, 16, 18.

Solution
1. Put the calculator in statistical mode.
2. Enter the data: $8\sum$, $10\sum$, $11\sum$, ..., $18\sum$. In some calculators, the number of data entries will show on the display when the $\sum$ key is pressed.
3. When all the data are entered, press $\bar{x}$ for the mean, $\bar{x} = 13$, and S for the standard deviation, $S = 3.899$. These may be second function keys for which the 2nd key or the INV key must be pressed first.
4. Many statistical calculators will also give the sums used in the calculation formulas, $\sum x$ and $\sum x^2$. Check the calculation sums in Example A.18 by pressing the $\sum x$ and $\sum x^2$ keys. $\sum x^2 = 1090$ and $\sum x = 78$.

The Standard Deviation from Control Charts

An estimate of the population standard deviation is used in control chart calculations. When small samples are taken (sample size is usually four or five) and the sample means are charted, the sample ranges are also charted to show the variability within the samples. The average of the sample ranges for k samples, $\bar{R} = (\sum R)/k$, is used to establish control limits for the chart. When the chart is in statisitical control, $\bar{R}$ is again used to estimate the standard deviation of all the measurements in the population.

$$\sigma = \frac{\bar{R}}{d_2}$$

Here d_2 is a constant that depends on the sample size, n. A chart of the d_2 constant values for different sample sizes is given in Appendix B, Table 1.1.

A.5.5 CODING DATA

Coding measurements is a method used to simplify the arithmetic associated with averaging and finding the ranges and standard deviations for measurements. Instead of dealing with measurements, coding uses a base value and translates each measurement to a coded number that reflects its positive or negative distance from the base value.

> *Coding Rule 1:* The measurement unit is the base factor and the coded value for a measurement is the number of measurement units from the base value.

If the measurements differ by thousandths, then the coded numbers represent thousandths and the base factor is .001. If the measurements differ by hundredths, then the coded numbers represent hundredths and the base factor is .01. Often the target value is used for the base value. This keeps the coded numbers small in absolute value, but the arithmetic for signed numbers must be used. Another choice for a base value is a number smaller than all the measurements. The coded numbers are then larger, but they are all positive and the more familiar arithmetic of whole numbers applies.

In the following illustration, the base value 2.315 is used. The coded numbers represent thousandths, and the base factor is .001. See Table A.9.

- The coded value 1 corresponds to .001 units above the base, so 2.316 codes to 1.
- The coded value 2 corresponds to .002 units above the base, so 2.317 codes to 2.
- The coded value −4 corresponds to .004 units below the base, so 2.311 codes to −4.
- The coded value .23 corresponds to .00023 units above the base, so 2.31523 codes to .23.

> *Coding Rule 2:* To change the coded number back to measurement units, multiply by the base factor.

TABLE A.9

Measurement	Coded Value	Base = 2.315
2.314	−1	1 coded unit below base
2.321	6	6 coded units above base
2.316	1	1 coded unit above base
2.310	−5	5 coded units below base
2.315	0	the base codes as 0
2.319	4	4 coded units above base
2.309	−6	6 coded units below base
2.313	−2	2 coded units below base

The concepts regarding the transformation from measurement to coded value, the calculations with the coded values, and the transformation back to measurement values can best be illustrated with an example.

If the preceding measurements are averaged directly, their average value will be the sum divided by 8. The sum of the eight measurements is 18.517.

$$\frac{18.517}{8} = 2.314625$$

The average of the coded values is the sum divided by 8. The coded sum is -3.

$$\frac{-3}{8} = -.375$$

The coded average gives the number of coded units from the base measurement to the average measurement. When the coded average is multiplied by the base factor, the result is the measurement change from the base measurement to the average measurement.

$$-.375 \times .001 = -.000375 \quad \text{measurement change}$$

Coding Rule 3: When the measurement change is added to the measurement base, the measurement value results.

To continue the example, add the measurement change and the measurement base.

$$- .000375 + 2.315$$
$$= | 2.315 - .000375 |$$
$$= 2.314625$$

Subtract their absolute values and keep the positive sign. This is the same as the average calculated directly from the measurements.

To simulate the range of samples and the calculation of the standard deviation from a control chart, pair the values from Table A.9 for samples of size 2. Calculate the sample range by subtracting the smaller value from the larger, and then calculate the average range value. For the illustration, this is done for both the measurements and the coded values. See Table A.10 on page 429.

The average range for the measurements is the sum, .021, divided by 4:

$$\frac{.021}{4} = .00525$$

The average range for coded values is again the sum divided by 4:

$$\frac{21}{4} = 5.25$$

Notice that the product of the coded range and the base factor is the measurement range.

TABLE A.10

		Base = 2.315		
Range	Measurement	Sample Number	Coded Value	Range
.007	2.314 2.321	1	−1 6	7
.006	2.316 2.310	2	1 −5	6
.004	2.315 2.319	3	0 4	4
.004	2.309 2.313	4	−6 −2	4

The standard deviation for a set of measurements is determined by dividing the average range by a numerical constant that is determined from the sample size, (constant d_2, found in Appendix B, Table 1.1). The constant for a sample of size 2 is 1.128. The standard deviation for the measurements is $\overline{R}/d_2$.

$$\frac{.00525}{1.128} = .004654$$

The coded standard deviation is

$$\frac{5.25}{1.128} = 4.654$$

To change the coded value back to the measurement value, apply rule 2 and multiply by the base factor.

$$4.654 \times .001 = .004654$$

This is the same as the direct calculation using the measurements.

EXAMPLE A.20   Six samples of size 3 are given in Table A.11 (page 430). Code the measurements and calculate the average and the standard deviation. For samples of this size, divide the average range by 1.693 (d_2 for samples of size 3) to calculate the standard deviation. A table containing these numerical constants is shown in Appendix B, Table 1.1.

Solution

To get only positive coded numbers this time, a base value of 23.50 will be used (a number smaller than all the measurements). The measurements differ by hundredths, so the base factor is .01.

TABLE A.11

Sample	1	Code	2	Code	3	Code	4	Code	5	Code	6	
					Base = 23.50							
	23.59	9	23.57	7	23.58	8	23.55	5	23.58	8	23.54	4
	23.62	12	23.54	4	23.51	1	23.54	4	23.62	12	23.57	7
	23.61	11	23.63	13	23.62	12	23.59	9	23.57	7	23.61	11
Range		3		9		11		5		5		7

For 18 coded values,

$$\text{Average coded value} = \frac{\text{sum}}{18}$$

$$= \frac{144}{18}$$

$$= 8$$

$$\text{Measurement change} = \text{coded average} \times \text{base factor}$$
$$= 8 \times .01$$
$$= .08$$

$$\text{Average} = \text{base} + \text{measurement change}$$
$$= 23.50 + .08$$
$$= 23.58$$

For six sample ranges,

$$\text{Average coded range} = \frac{\text{sum}}{6}$$

$$= \frac{40}{6}$$

$$= 6.66667$$

$$\sigma = \frac{\overline{R}}{d_2} \qquad d_2 = 1.693$$

$$\text{Coded } \sigma = \frac{6.6667}{1.693}$$

$$= 3.938$$

$$\text{Measurement standard deviation} = \text{coded } \sigma \times \text{base factor}$$
$$= 3.938 \times .01$$
$$= .03938$$

A.6 PROBABILITY

When a set of counts or measurements can be separated into two distinct groups, the concepts of probability can be applied. Let one group be classifed as the successes and the other as failures.

$$P(\text{success}) = \frac{\text{number of successes}}{\text{number of successes } + \text{ failures}} = \frac{\# \text{ successes}}{\# \text{ possibilities}}$$

The following are some applications of probability. First, a coin is tossed. Let a head be a success and a tail be a failure.

$$P(\text{success}) = \frac{1 \text{ success}}{2 \text{ possibilities}}$$

$$= \frac{1}{2}$$

Second, if a bag contains three red beads, four white beads, and five blue beads, and one bead is drawn from the bag, find the probability that it is a red bead. Let a red bead be a success and the white and blue beads be failures.

$$P(\text{red}) = \frac{3 \text{ reds}}{12 \text{ beads}}$$

$$= \frac{3}{12}$$

$$= \frac{1}{4}$$

Finally, a routing tray contains 88 good parts and 12 defective parts. One part is chosen from the tray. Find the probability that it is a good part. Let a good part be a success and a bad part be a failure.

$$P(\text{good}) = \frac{88 \text{ good parts}}{100 \text{ parts}}$$

$$= \frac{88}{100}$$

$$= \frac{22}{25}$$

In each case, the probability represents the chance or likelihood of a success. Probability is defined as a fraction, but as with any other fraction, it can also be expressed as a decimal or a percent. In the preceding example, the language of probability indicates that the probability of drawing a red bead is $\frac{1}{4}$, or .25, or that there is a 25 percent chance of drawing a red bead.

Probability values are restricted to number between 0 and 1, inclusive.

$$0 \leq P(\text{success}) \leq 1$$

This restriction is easily demonstrated. In a bag of 12 red, white, and blue beads, find the $P(\text{green})$. There are no green beads, so

$$P(\text{green}) = \frac{0 \text{ successes}}{12 \text{ possible beads}}$$

$$= \frac{0}{12}$$

$$= 0$$

This is an impossible situation; there are no successes in the set of possibilities. When one bead is drawn from this same bag, find the probability that it is not orange.

$$P(\text{not orange}) = \frac{12 \text{ successes}}{12 \text{ possible beads}}$$

$$= \frac{12}{12}$$

$$= 1$$

This is a sure thing because every element in the set of possibilities is a success.

A.6.1 COMPOUND PROBABILITY

The "Or" Probability

When more than one possible success can occur in a probability calculation, it is described using the word "or." The probability that either event A or event B occurs, $P(A \text{ or } B)$, is equal to the sum of the individual probabilities.

$$P(A \text{ or } B) = P(A) + P(B)$$

EXAMPLE A.21 A bag contains beads of several colors: four red, two white, five black, one green, and three blue beads.

1. If one bead is drawn from the bag, what is the probability that it is either red or white?
2. If one bead is drawn from the bag, what is the probability that it is either a black, green, or blue bead.

Solution
For the first problem,

$$P(\text{red or white}) = P(\text{red}) + P(\text{white})$$

$$= \frac{4}{15} + \frac{2}{15}$$

$$= \frac{6}{15}$$

$$= \frac{2}{5}$$

Second

$$P(\text{black or green or blue}) = P(\text{black}) + P(\text{green}) + P(\text{blue})$$

$$= \frac{5}{15} + \frac{1}{15} + \frac{3}{15}$$

$$= \frac{9}{15}$$

$$= \frac{3}{5}$$

The one necessary condition for the "or" rule is that the events are *mutually exclusive*; that is, no two events can occur simultaneously. For example, when one bead is drawn, it can not be both green and blue; it must be one or the other.

There are situations in which different events can occur simultaneously. When that happens, simply adjust the additional probabilities to exclude the simultaneous occurrences. Make sure that no event is counted more than once.

$$P(A \text{ or } B) = P(A) + \text{adjusted } P(B)$$

EXAMPLE A.22 Draw one card from a standard deck of 52 cards. Find the probability of getting either a 9 or a heart.

Solution
The two events could occur simultaneously because a 9 of hearts could be drawn. The adjusted or rule must be used. Adj P signifies adjusted probability.

$$P(9 \text{ or heart}) = P(9) + \text{adj } P(\text{heart})$$

$$= \frac{4}{52} + \frac{12}{52}$$

The numerator 4 is the 4 nines and the numerator 12 is the remaining 12 hearts. The 9 of hearts was counted in the first term.

$$P(9 \text{ or heart}) = \frac{16}{52} = \frac{4}{13}$$

The terms could be written in either order, but the second term must always be adjusted accordingly. The main idea is to make sure that none of the successful events are counted more than once. If the hearts are taken first, there are 13 successes; the nines would then be adjusted to three additional successes because the 9 of hearts was already counted among the 13 hearts of the first term.

EXAMPLE A.23

Find the probability of drawing either a face card or a seven.

Solution

These events are mutually exclusive; none of the success cards occur simultaneously. No adjustment is needed, so the first version of the "or" rule is used. There are 12 face cards: the Jack, Queen and King of each suit.

$$P(\text{face card or } 7) = P(\text{face card}) + P(7)$$
$$= \frac{12}{52} + \frac{4}{52}$$
$$= \frac{16}{52}$$
$$= \frac{4}{13}$$

EXAMPLE A.24

Find the probability of getting an 8 or a diamond or a 10.

Solution

These events can occur simultaneously, so the adjusted probability rule must be used.

$$P(8 \text{ or diamond or } 10) = P(8) + \text{ adj } P(\text{diamond}) + \text{ adj } P(10)$$
$$= \frac{4}{52} + \frac{12}{52} + \frac{3}{52}$$

The numerators signify the 4 eights, the remaining 12 diamonds (8 of diamonds is in the first term) and the remaining 3 tens. The 10 of diamonds is in the second term.

$$P(8 \text{ or diamond or } 10) = \frac{19}{52}$$

If the order of the terms is changed, the adjustments change accordingly.

$$P(8 \text{ or } 10 \text{ or diamond}) = P(8) + P(10) + \text{adj } P(\text{diamond})$$
$$= \frac{4}{52} + \frac{4}{52} + \frac{11}{52}$$

The last term is adjusted to eliminate the 8 and 10 of diamonds, which were counted in the first two terms.

$$P(8 \text{ or } 10 \text{ or diamond}) = \frac{19}{52}$$

The result is the same.

"And" Probabilities

When succesive events are described, the "and" is used in the probability description. The probability of an "and" situation is found by multiplying the individual probabilities.

$$P(A \text{ and } B) = P(A) \times P(B)$$

EXAMPLE A.25   A coin is tossed three times. Find the probability of getting three heads.

Solution
The three tosses of the coin are three successive events, so the "and" rule applies. A success consists of getting a head on the first toss *and* a head on the second toss *and* a head on the third toss. Let H represent a head.

$$P(H \text{ and } H \text{ and } H) = P(H) \times P(H) \times P(H)$$
$$= \frac{1}{2} \times \frac{1}{2} \times \frac{1}{2}$$
$$= \frac{1}{8}$$

The "and" rule can be verified by using the basic definition of probability on the set of all possible outcomes. Let H represent a head, T represent a tail, and adjacent letters represent "and" (*HT* means a head *and* then a tail). The following are the possible outcomes of tossing a coin 3 times:

HHH HHT HTH THH TTH THT HTT TTT

The probability is

$$P(3\ H) = \frac{1}{8}$$

This result agrees with the solution in Example A.25.

The "and" rule applies when there is only one way for a success to occur. When a success can happen in more ways than one, a combination of "and" and "or" rules applies.

EXAMPLE A.26

A coin is tossed three times. Find the probability of getting two heads and one tail.

Solution

The basic probability rule is the "and" rule because of the three successive events. The "or" rule is used to add the probabilities of all the different ways the success can occur. The event ($2H$ and $1T$) can occur three ways: The tail could be on the first toss *or* the second toss *or* the third toss.

$$P(2H \text{ and } 1T) = P(THH) \text{ or } P(HTH) \text{ or } P(HHT)$$

$$= \left(\frac{1}{2} \times \frac{1}{2} \times \frac{1}{2} \right) + \left(\frac{1}{2} \times \frac{1}{2} \times \frac{1}{2} \right) + \left(\frac{1}{2} \times \frac{1}{2} \times \frac{1}{2} \right)$$

$$= 3 \left(\frac{1}{2} \times \frac{1}{2} \times \frac{1}{2} \right)$$

Each way has the same "and" probability. Multiply by 3, the number of ways, instead of the repeated addition.

$$P(2H \text{ and } 1T) = \frac{3}{8}$$

This combination of "and" and "or" rules can be verified by applying the basic definition of probability to the set of possible outcomes. There are eight possible outcomes (*HHH, HHT,* and so on.) and three of them have two heads and one tail.

$$P(2H \text{ and } 1T) = \frac{3}{8}$$

EXAMPLE A.27

A tray contains eight good parts and two defective parts. A part is chosen at random, inspected, and replaced by four different inspectors. Find the probability that two of the inspectors found a defective part.

Solution

On each single inspection the probability of getting a good part is $P(G) = \frac{8}{10} = .8$. The probability of getting a defective part is $P(D) = \frac{2}{10} = .2$.

There are four successive events, so the basic probability rule that applies is the "and" rule. A success can occur in several ways, so the "or" rule applies, too. The probabilities for each different success must be added, but because each of the different successes has the same probability, multiplication by the number of ways can be used instead of the repeated addition. Two good parts and two defective parts can be chosen in the following ways: *GGDD* or *GDGD* or *DGGD* or *DGDG* or *DDGG* or *GDDG*.

$$P(2G \text{ and } 2D) = P(G \text{ and } G \text{ and } D \text{ and } D) \times 6 \text{ ways}$$
$$= .8 \times .8 \times .2 \times .2 \times 6$$
$$= .1536$$

Adjusting the "And" Rule

When the "and" rule is used, the successive events must be *independent*: The probability of each successive event is not affected by the preceding events. When tossing a coin, each toss is independent of all the previous tosses. When sampling with replacement, each selection is independent of the previous selections. However, if the successive sampling is done without replacement, the probability of successive events is affected by what happened in the previous events. In this case, adjust the probabilities accordingly. When successive events are not independent,

$$P(A \text{ and } B) = P(A) \times \text{ adj } P(B)$$

EXAMPLE A.28 If two successive cards are drawn from a standard deck (no replacement), find the probability of drawing two kings.

Solution
Use an adjusted probability.

$$P(\text{king and king}) = P(\text{king}) \times \text{adj } P(\text{king})$$

$$= \frac{4}{52} \times \frac{3}{51}$$

The second factor is adjusted because three kings remain, with 51 cards from which to choose.

$$P(2 \text{ kings}) = \frac{12}{2652}$$

$$= \frac{1}{221}$$

Another variation of the "and" rule includes both adjusting factors and determining the number of ways that a success can occur. This is the most inclusive form because all possible variations are shown. The overall version of the "and" rule is

$$P(A \text{ and } B) = P(A) \times \text{ adj } P(B) \times \# \text{ ways}$$

The thought sequence is as follows:

1. These are successive events, so the "and" rule applies.
2. Is adjustment needed?
3. Can a success occur in more than one way?
   a. If all the probabilities are the same, multiply by the number of ways.
   b. If the probabilities are different, add all the different products.

EXAMPLE A.29

Draw three cards from a standard deck of cards without replacement. Find the probability of getting two aces and one face card.

Solution

1. There are three successive events, so the "and" rule applies.
2. Is adjustment needed? Yes, it is, because the cards are not replaced.
3. Is there more than one success? Yes, the face card may be drawn either first or second or third (*FAA* or *AFA* or *AAF*). The probabilities are all the same, so multiply by the number of ways.

$$P(2 \text{ aces and 1 face card}) = P(A) \times \text{ adj } P(A) \times \text{ adj } P(F) \times \# \text{ ways}$$

$$= \frac{4}{52} \times \frac{3}{51} \times \frac{12}{50} \times 3$$

The numerators represent 4 aces on the first draw, 3 aces in the remaining 51 cards, and 12 face cards in the remaining 50 cards. The 3 signifies the three ways this can happen.

$$P(2 \text{ aces and 1 face card}) = \frac{1}{13} \times \frac{1}{17} \times \frac{6}{25} \times 3$$

$$= \frac{18}{5525}$$

The adjustments will be different if the factors are rearranged, but the product of the three fractions will remain the same. The only change is that the numerator factors would occur in a different order. This is why the "$\times$ 3 ways" shortcut can be used. For example, the *FAA* product is $\frac{12}{52} \times \frac{4}{51} \times \frac{3}{50}$. Both the numerator product, $12 \times 4 \times 3$, and the denominator product, $52 \times 51 \times 50$, are the same as before.

A.6.2 COUNTING WITH PERMUTATIONS AND COMBINATIONS

The Number of Ways

In the previous examples, the number of ways that a success could occur was determined by listing all the possibilities. A more efficient method is needed for complicated situations.

Permutations, $P_{N,n}$

The number of *permutations* refers to the number of arrangements of N objects when n of them are used. As a numerical example, $P_{7,3}$ is the number of arrangements of seven objects when three of them are used. If the objects are letters, $P_{7,3}$ gives the number of different three-letter "words" that can be formed when no letter occurs more than once in any word.

EXAMPLE A.30 How many three-letter words can be formed from the seven letters (A,B,C,D,E,F,G) if no letter occurs more than once in any word?

Solution
There are three decisions to make when forming a word:

_____	and	_____	and	_____
Choose the first letter (7 choices)		Choose the second letter (6 choices)		Choose the third letter (5 choices)

When the letters are chosen to form a word, there are seven choices for the first letter *and* six choices for the second letter *and* five choices for the third letter.

$$P_{7,3} = 7 \times 6 \times 5$$
$$= 210 \text{ words}$$

EXAMPLE A.31 How many seven letter words can be formed from the seven letters if the letters can not be repeated in any word?

Solution
There are seven decisions to make when forming a word.

_____	and	_____	and	_____	and	_____	and	_____	and	_____	and	_____
First letter		Second letter		Third letter		Fourth letter		Fifth letter		Sixth letter		Seventh letter

When filling in the blanks to form a word, there are seven choices for the first letter, six choices for the second letter, and so on.

$$P_{7,7} = 7 \times 6 \times 5 \times 4 \times 3 \times 2 \times 1$$
$$= 5040 \text{ words}$$

Factorials

A *factorial* is the product of a number and all the counting numbers descending from it to 1. The product of the descending counting numbers from 7 to 1 is 7!, read "7 factorial,"

$$7! = 7 \times 6 \times 5 \times 4 \times 3 \times 2 \times 1 = 5040$$

The factorial can be thought of as a mathematical shorthand.

$$4! = 4 \times 3 \times 2 \times 1 = 24$$
$$12! = 12 \times 11 \times 10 \times 9 \times \cdots \times 1 = 479,001,600$$

There is one special definition of convenience:

$$0! = 1$$

This definition allows the general use of factorials in mathematical formulas without the need for special exceptions.

The formula for the permutations of n things taken from a population of N things is

$$P_{N,n} = \frac{N!}{(N - n)!}$$

The denominator, $(N - n)!$, eliminates the lower factors by cancellation when only part of the population, N, is used. If the formula is applied to Example A.30.

$$P_{7,3} = \frac{7!}{(7 - 3)!} = \frac{7!}{4!} = \frac{7 \times 6 \times 5 \times 4 \times 3 \times 2 \times 1}{4 \times 3 \times 2 \times 1}$$

$$= 7 \times 6 \times 5 = 210$$

For simpler writing, factorials can be cancelled in total.

$$P_{7,3} = \frac{7 \times 6 \times 5 \times 4!}{4!} = 7 \times 6 \times 5 = 210$$

For Example A.31, the $0! = 1$ definition is needed.

$$P_{7,7} = \frac{7!}{(7 - 7)!} = \frac{7!}{0!} = \frac{5040}{1} = 5040$$

Many scientific and statistical calculators have a factorial key, $x!$, for easy calculations of factorials. All the factorial calculations can be calculated by one of two procedures:

1. Repeatedly multiply the descending factors.
2. Use the factorial key, $x!$, on the calculator. On some calculators, $x!$ is a second function and the 2nd or INV key has to be pressed first.

For 6!, the calculator sequence is

        6 $x!$ The display shows 720.

or,   6 2nd $x!$ The result is 720.

Use whichever of these two sequences is appropriate on your calculator.

For the permutation

$$P_{8,2} = \frac{8!}{(8 - 2)!} = \frac{8!}{6!} = \frac{8 \cdot 7 \cdot 6!}{6!} = 8 \cdot 7 = 56$$

the calculator sequence is 8 $x!$ $\div$ 6 $x!$ = for 56.

The *Mississippi* Problem

Another variation of the arrangement problem involves repeated letters. For an easy first example, how many different "words" could be formed by rearranging the six letters in the word *kisses*? There are six letters, so 6! gives the total number of rearrangements. However, some of the rearrangements do not form a new word. In fact, any rearrangement of the three *s*'s in the word kisses does not give a new word. There are 3! ways of rearranging the three *s*'s in every different word, and that has to be eliminated from the 6! total. It is eliminated by division.

$$\frac{6!}{3!} = \frac{6 \times 5 \times 4 \times 3!}{3!}$$
$$= 6 \times 5 \times 4$$
$$= 120 \text{ words}$$

On the calculator $6\ x!\ \div\ 3\ x!\ =$ gives the answer.

How many "words" can be formed by rearranging the letters in *ABBBBCC*?

$$\frac{7!}{4! \times 2!}$$

There are seven letters. The 4! eliminates the arrangements of the four *B*'s, and the 2! eliminates the arrangements of the two *C*'s.

$$\frac{7!}{4! \times 2!} = \frac{7 \times 6 \times 5 \times 4!}{4! \times 2 \times 1}$$
$$= \frac{7 \times (3 \times 2) \times 5}{2 \times 1}$$
$$= 7 \times 3 \times 5$$
$$= 105$$

On the calculator: $7\ \times\ x!\ \div\ 4\ x!\ \div\ 2\ x!\ =$ is 105.

Now solve the *Mississippi* problem. How many different words can be formed by rearranging the letters?

$$\frac{11!}{4! \cdot 4! \cdot 2!} = \frac{11 \times 10 \times 9 \times 8 \times 7 \times 6 \times 5 \times 4!}{4! \times 4 \times 3 \times 2 \times 1 \times 2 \times 1}$$
$$= 34{,}650$$

There are four *s*'s, four *i*'s, and two *p*'s in the 11-letter word. 11! gives the total number of rearrangements of the eleven letters and the two 4!'s and the 2! eliminate repeated words. On the calculator: $11\ x!\ \div\ 4\ x!\ \div\ 4\ x!\ \div\ 2\ x!\ =$ gives 34,650.

The Two-Letter Word Problem

Determining the number of words that can be formed by rearranging the letters of a set that contains repetitions of just two different letters is an applications of the *Mississippi* problem.

How many words can be formed by rearranging *ssssff*? With two *f*'s and four *s*'s,

$$\frac{6!}{2! \times 4!} = \frac{6 \times 5 \times 4!}{2 \times 1 \times 4!}$$
$$= 3 \times 5$$
$$= 15$$

On the calculator, $6\ x! \div 4\ x! \div 2\ x! =$ gives 15.

The choice of letters in this problem may have given you a hint at the eventual usefulness of all these "word games." The two-letter word problem applies directly to the probability calculations illustrated in Example A.27 and to probabilities associated with random sampling. In Example A.27, the number of ways that two good parts and two defective parts can occur was determined by listing all the possibilities. Using the two-letter word approach,

$$\frac{4!}{2! \times 2!} = \frac{4 \times 3 \times 2 \times 1}{2 \times 1 \times 2 \times 1} = 6$$

Now the more complicated "number of ways" can be easily calculated using the word game concepts.

EXAMPLE A.32   A box of parts contains 40 good parts and 10 bad parts. If eight parts are randomly removed from the box, find the probability of getting five good parts and three bad ones.

Solution
1. This is an "and" problem because of the eight successive events. The probabilities are multiplied.
2. Adjustments must be made because the parts are not replaced.
3. There is more than one way to draw five good parts and three bad parts from the box, so the number of ways must be calculated.

The number of ways of drawing 5 good parts and 3 bad parts, *GGGGGBBB*, can be determined by using the two-letter word problem.

$$\frac{8!}{3! \times 5!} = \frac{8 \times 7 \times 6 \times 5!}{3 \times 2 \times 1 \times 5!}$$
$$= 8 \times 7$$
$$= 56$$

On the calculator, $8\ x! \div 5\ x! \div 3\ x! =$ gives 56.

$$P(5G \text{ and } 3B) = \frac{40}{50} \times \frac{39}{49} \times \frac{38}{48} \times \frac{37}{47} \times \frac{36}{46} \times \frac{10}{45} \times \frac{9}{44} \times \frac{8}{43} \times 56$$

Adjust the "and" probabilities for the 5 G's. Adjust for the 3 B's, too.

$$P(5 \text{ good and } 3 \text{ bad}) = .147$$

If a set of objects is a withdrawn from a population in an *ordered* fashion, the number of ways that it can be done is found by using *permutations*. Orderly withdrawal without replacement, a sampling concept, is closely associated to the word games. The number of ways the sample can be drawn from the population and the number of words that can be made by choosing and rearranging letters is the same; both are calculated by permutations.

EXAMPLE A.33

Given the population (A, B, C, D, E, F, G, H),

1. How many three-letter words can be formed by choosing and rearranging three letters at a time?
2. Eight parts are in a bin with letter tags on them. How many ways can three parts be removed from the bin for inspection?

Solution

For the first problem, to form a word, there are eight choices for the first letter, seven choices for the second letter, and six choices for the third letter of the word (8 *and* 7 *and* 6).

$$P_{8,3} = 8 \times 7 \times 6$$
$$= \frac{8!}{(8-3)!}$$
$$= \frac{8!}{5!}$$
$$= 336 \text{ words}$$

For the second problem, to form the sample, there are eight choices for the first part, seven choices for the second part, and six choices for the third part (8 *and* 7 *and* 6).

$$8 \times 7 \times 6 = P_{8,3} \dots$$

This uses exactly the same analysis for 336 ways.

Combinations

When objects are withdrawn from a population *without regard to order*, the number of possible groups that can be formed is calculated by *combinations*. In Example A.33, part 2, the order in which the parts were chosen really wasn't important from a sampling point of view. Whether parts A, C, and G or parts C, G, and A were sampled did not matter because they formed the same sample.

Another everyday example that illustrates the difference between permutations and combinations occurs with clubs or organizations. Electing three officers from the group—president, vice president, and secretary—is a *permutation* because the order in which the three are chosen is important: who is elected President, and so on. Choosing a committee of three from the group to work on a project, on the other hand, is a *combination* because the order in which the three are chosen is not important. The committee consisting of Jack, Jane, and Phyllis is the same as the committee of Jane, Phyllis, and Jack.

The formula for calculating combinations starts with the permutation formula and eliminates the rearrangements by division. This is the same concept that was used in the *Mississippi* problem. The formula for permutations,

$$P_{N,n} = \frac{N!}{(N-n)!}$$

includes all the rearrangements of the n objects in the sample. In the formula for combinations, however, the $n!$ eliminates the rearrangements of the n objects in the sample.

$$C_{N,n} = \frac{N!}{(N-n)! \cdot n!}$$

EXAMPLE A.34

A club consists of 12 members.

1. How many slates of officers could be formed if the offices of president, vice president, and secretary are to be filled?
2. How many committees of three could be formed to plan the Christmas party?
3. If the club consists of nine women and three men, how many ways could the men and women be seated in a row of 12 chairs (for example, M, W, W, W, M, M, W, W, W, W, W, W)

Solution

Problem 1 is a permutation because the order of the three people on the slate is important.

$$P_{12,3} = \frac{12!}{(12-3)!}$$

$$= \frac{12!}{9!}$$

$$= \frac{12 \times 11 \times 10 \times 9!}{9!}$$

$$= 1320$$

On the calculator, the sequence 12 $x!$ ÷ 9 $x!$ = gives 1320.

Problem 2 is a combination because the order in which the committee is chosen is not important.

$$C_{12,3} = \frac{12!}{(12 - 3)! \cdot 3!}$$

$$= \frac{12!}{9! \cdot 3!}$$

$$= \frac{12 \times 11 \times 10 \times 9!}{3 \times 2 \times 1 \times 9!}$$

$$= 220$$

On the calculator, $12 \; x! \; \div \; 9 \; x! \; \div \; 3 \; x! \; = \;$ is 220.

The third problem is a two-letter word problem.

$$\frac{12!}{3! \cdot 9!} = \frac{12 \times 11 \times 10 \times 9!}{3 \times 2 \times 1 \times 9!}$$

$$= 220$$

The two-letter word problem has the same calculation as a combination.

A.6.3   THE BINOMIAL PROBABILITY DISTRIBUTION

Binomial probability refers to the possible ways two specific events can occur and the probabilities associated with those ways. The two events will be classified as *s*, success, and *f*, failure. Any binomial outcome can be categorized in this general fashion. A systematic look at the binomial distribution of successes and failures involves the number of repeated trials, the possible outcomes from the repreated trials, and a simplified algebraic form to represent each outcome. See Table A.12.

Letters placed together represent an "and" situation: *sf* means a success followed by a failure. Similarly, *fss* means a failure on the first trial *and* a success on the second trial *and* a success on the third trial.

TABLE A.12
Binomial outcomes for repeated trials

Number of Trials	Possible Outcomes
1	*s* or *f*
2	*ss* or *sf* or *fs* or *ff*
3	*sss* or *ssf* or *sfs* or *fss* or *ffs* or *fsf* or *sff* or *fff*
4	*ssss* or *sssf* or *ssfs* or *sfss* or *fsss* or *ssff* or *sffs* or *ffss* or *sfsf* or *fsfs* or *fssf* or *fffs* or *ffsf* or *fsff* or *sfff* or *ffff*

The algebraic form simplifies the situation. In the case of four trials, *ssss* can be written in exponent form as s^4. Several ideas that were discussed previously come together here.

Repeated trials form an "and" situation.

- "And" leads to a multiplication
- A repeated multiplication is a power.
- The number of ways of getting a particular number of successes and failures is the two-letter word problem.
- The two-letter word problem is solved by combinations.

Three successes and one failure can occur in four ways.

Algebraic form: $4s^3f$

Two successes and two failures can occur in six ways.

Algebraic form: $6s^2f^2$

The "or" situation leads to addition. See Table A.13.

TABLE A.13

The binomial expansion

Number of Trials	Algebraic Form for the Possible Outcomes
1	$s + f$
2	$s^2 + 2sf + f^2$
3	$s^3 + 3s^2f + 3sf^2 + f^3$
4	$s^4 + 4s^3f + 6s^2f^2 + 4sf^3 + f^4$
5	$s^5 + 5s^4f + 10s^3f^2 + 10s^2f^3 + 5sf^4 + f^5$
6	$s^6 + 6s^5f + 15s^4f^2 + 20s^3f^3 + 15s^2f^4 + 6sf^5 + f^6$
7	$s^7 + 7s^6f + 21s^5f^2 + 35s^4f^3 + 35s^3f^4 + 21s^2f^5 + 7sf^6 + f^7$

The algebraic form shows all possible outcomes in a condensed form. In the seven trials case, $21s^5f^2$ indicates that five successes and two failures can occur in 21 different ways. If the seven trials case were written in the long form shown in Table A.12,, there would be 21 "words" with 5 *s*'s and 2 *f*'s.

If *s* represents the probability of a success in a single trial and *f* represents the probability of a failure, the probability of any repreated trial event can be calculated by chosing the appropriate term from the algebraic form. The algebraic form is referred to as the *binomial expansion*. When probabilities are substituted for the variables *s* and *f*, the result is a *binomial probability distribution*.

EXAMPLE A.35

If a single die is tossed four times, find the probability of getting a 3 twice (two 3s and two other numbers).

Solution

- There are four trials because the die is tossed four times.
- A success is getting a 3 when the die is rolled.
- A failure is getting a 1, 2, 4, 5, or 6 when the die is rolled.
- $s = P(\text{success}) = \frac{1}{6}$
- $f = P(\text{failure}) = \frac{5}{6}$
- The binomial distribution term for getting two successes is $6s^2f^2$. Calculation of the combination gives six ways, and the s and f are squared to signify two successes and two failures.

$$C_{4,2} = \frac{4!}{2!2!}$$
$$= 6 \text{ ways}$$
$$= 6s^2f^2$$

$$6\left(\frac{1}{6}\right)^2\left(\frac{5}{6}\right)^2 = \frac{6 \times 1 \times 25}{36 \times 36}$$
$$= .1157$$
$$P(2 \text{ threes in 4 tosses}) = .1157$$

EXAMPLE A.36

A box contains 48 good parts and 12 defective parts. If 10 parts are inspected and returned at different times, find the probability that four of the inspected parts were defective.

Solution

There are 10 repeated trials because 10 parts are inspected. A success is getting a defective part because the problem is set up in terms of defective parts.

$$s = P(\text{success}) = P(\text{defective})$$
$$= \frac{12}{60}$$
$$= .2$$

A failure is getting a good part.

$$f = P(\text{failure}) = P(\text{good})$$
$$= \frac{48}{60}$$
$$= .8$$

The binomial distribution term that represents four successes and six failures is determined by matching the exponents to the number of successes and failures. The coefficient (number of ways) is determined by a combinations calculation. The formula

$C_{10,4}s^4f^6$ indicates a combination for 10 trials with four successes, times two power factors that represent four successes and six failures.

$$C_{10,4} = \frac{10!}{(10-4)!4!}$$

$$= \frac{10!}{6! \cdot 4!}$$

$$= \frac{10 \times 9 \times 8 \times 7 \times 6!}{4 \times 3 \times 2 \times 1 \times 6!}$$

$$= 210$$

The calculator sequence: $10 \; x! \; \div \; 6 \; x! \; \div \; 4 \; x! \; = \;$ gives 210.

$$P(4 \text{ defectives}) = 210 \times (.2)^4 \times (.8)^6$$

On the calculator use the following sequence: $.2 \; x^y \; 4 \; = \; \times \; .8 \; x^y \; 6 \; = \; \times \; 210 \; =$ to get the answer.

$$P(4 \text{ defectives}) = .088$$

The Simple Random Sample

Drawing a random sample is not really simple at all. It has to be carefully planned. There are two basic procedures that can be considered.

1. When a single element is chosen for a sample, every element in the population must have an equal chance of being chosen. This concept, used in the introductory samples of Chapter 11, allows the possibility that an individual item will be chosen more than once for a particular sample because each item is returned to the population before the next is drawn. The probability model for this is the binomial probability distribution.

2. When a sample of size n is chosen from a population, every possible sample of that size must have an equal chance of begin chosen. Choosing a set of items from a population, without regard to order, is related to the concept of combinations; the combinations formula gives the number of different sets or samples of size n that could be drawn from a population of size N. The probability model that was previously used for this case was the "and" situation with adjusted probabilities (no replacement), and the number of ways was determined by combinations.

A.6.4   THE HYPERGEOMETRIC PROBABILITY DISTRIBUTION

The probability model that can be used for no-replacement sampling involves the use of combinations within the basic probability formula:

$$P(\text{success}) = \frac{\#\ \text{successes}}{\#\ \text{possibilities}}$$

The number of successes and the number of possibilities are calculated using combinations.

EXAMPLE A.37

From a bag that contains five red and four blue marbles, find the probability of drawing a sample that contains three red marbles and one blue marble (no replacement).

Solution

A success consists of getting three reds from the available five red marbles *and* getting one blue from the available four blue marbles. The number of possible successes is $C_{5,3} \times C_{4,1}$. The total number of possibilities consists of choosing any four marbles from the available nine, which is $C_{9,4}$.

$$P(\text{success}) = \frac{C_{5,3} \times C_{4,1}}{C_{9,4}}$$

$$C_{5,3} = \frac{5!}{3!2!} = \frac{5 \times 4 \times 3!}{3! \times 2 \times 1} = 10$$

$$C_{4,1} = \frac{4!}{1!3!} = \frac{4 \times 3!}{1 \times 3!} = 4$$

$$C_{9,4} = \frac{9!}{4!5!} = \frac{9 \times 8 \times 7 \times 6 \times 5!}{4 \times 3 \times 2 \times 1 \times 5!} = 126$$

$$P(\text{success}) = \frac{10 \times 4}{126}$$

$$= \frac{40}{126}$$

$$= .317$$

This is an illustration of the use of the hypergeometric probability distribution. The hypergeometric distribution is used for sampling *without replacement*.

Example A.37 can also be solved using the adjusted "and" probabilities.

$$P(3 \text{ red and } 1 \text{ blue}) = \frac{5}{9} \times \frac{4}{8} \times \frac{3}{7} \times \frac{4}{6} \times 4 \text{ ways} = .317$$

EXAMPLE A.38

A box contains 40 good parts and 10 bad ones. If a sample of eight parts is taken, find the probability that the sample contains five good parts and three bad ones. This is sampling without replacement, so use the hypergeometric distribution.

Solution

A success is choosing five good parts from the available 40 good parts ($C_{40,5}$) *and* three bad parts from the available 10 bad parts ($C_{10,3}$). The total number of successes is

$$C_{40,5} \times C_{10,3}$$

The "and" signifies multiplication. The total number of possibilities involves choosing any eight parts from the available 50, which is $C_{50,8}$.

$$P(5 \text{ good and 3 bad parts}) = \frac{C_{40,5} \times C_{10,3}}{C_{50,8}}$$

Calculate each combination:

$$C_{50,8} = \frac{50!}{8!42!} = 536,878,650$$

$$C_{40,5} = \frac{40!}{5!35!} = 658,008$$

$$C_{10,3} = \frac{10!}{3!7!} = 120$$

$$P(5 \text{ good and 3 bad}) = \frac{658,008 \times 120}{536,878,650}$$

$$= .147$$

Compare this result with that of Example A.32. The same problem is done by the two different methods, and the same probability results.

Factorial numbers increase in size rapidly and extend beyond the whole number display capability of calculators at about 14!. When that happens, the calculator automatically changes into scientific notation, and a split number format shows up in the calculator display.

14! shows 8.7178291 10	This means that the decimal point is really 10 places to the right, which would give approximately 87,178,291,000.
50! shows 3.0414093 64	The decimal point is 64 places to the right, which would give a 65-digit number.
70!	This extends beyond the calculator capability and shows an error message, E.

The preceding calculation can be done entirely within the calculator without having to write down the intermediate results. Do the combination in the denominator first and store it in the memory. Then do one of the combinations from the numerator, divide it by the quantity in the memory, and place the result back in the memory. Do the last combination in the numerator and multiply it by the quantity in the memory. That completes the calculation. This procedure is shown here for calculators.

$$50\ x!\ \div\ 8\ x!\ \div\ 42\ x!\ =\ M$$
$$40\ x!\ \div\ 5\ x!\ \div\ 35\ x!\ =\ \div\ MR\ =\ M$$
$$10\ x!\ \div\ 3\ x!\ \div\ 7\ x!\ =\ \times\ MR\ =\ (\ \text{display will show .147})$$

EXAMPLE A.39   A lot of 60 pieces is 5 percent defective. If a sample of six pieces is drawn, find the probability of getting one defective piece in the sample. This is sampling without replacement, so use the hypergeometric distribution.

Solution
If 5 percent of the 60 pieces are defective, there are three $(.05 \times 60)$ defective pieces in the lot. A success is choosing five good pieces from the 57 good ones $(C_{57,5})$ *and* choosing one bad piece from the three bad ones $(C_{3,1})$. The "and" signifies multiplication.

$$C_{57,5} \times C_{3,1}$$

The total number of possibilities involves choosing any six from the 60 pieces, $C_{60,6}$.

$$P(1\ \text{defective}) = \frac{C_{57,5} \times C_{3,1}}{C_{60,6}}$$

Calculate each part of the formula. The calculator sequence is shown on the right.

$$C_{60,6} = \frac{60!}{6! \cdot 54!} = \qquad 60\ x!\ \div\ 54\ x!\ \div\ 6\ x!\ =\ M$$

$$C_{57,5} = \frac{57!}{5! \cdot 52!} = \qquad 57\ x!\ \div\ 5\ x!\ \div\ 52\ x!\ =\ \div\ MR\ =\ M$$

$$C_{3,1} = \frac{3!}{1! \cdot 2!} = \qquad 3\ x!\ \div\ 2\ x!\ \div\ 1\ x!\ =\ \times\ MR\ =$$

$$P(1\ \text{defective}) = .251$$

A.7 DISTRIBUTIONS

The concept of distributions is one of the basic building blocks of statistics. The first distribution that is usually encountered in the study of statistics is the frequency distribution. When a sample is taken, the measurements are distributed among the classes of the frequency distribution in a specific pattern with a set number in each class. Figure A.12 illustrated how the frequency distribution takes on a specific shape as the number of data items increases. Eventually the sample size gets large enough to establish the pattern and any further data additions result in just minor fluctuations within the set pattern.

Once the frequency distribution pattern is set, it can be changed to a probability distribution. The sum of the frequency column gives the total number of measurements in the table. When each frequency is divided by the number of measurements, n, the result is the probability associated with that class. This forms a probability distribution: The probabilities are distributed to each class.

EXAMPLE A.40

Make a probability distribution for the given frequency distribution.

Frequency Distribution

Class	Frequency
.618–.622	2
.622–.626	5
.626–.630	10
.630–.634	16
.634–.638	10
.638–.642	6
.642–.646	1
	$n = 50$

Solution

Probability Distribution

Class	f/n = Probability
.618–.622	2/50 = .04
.622–.626	5/50 = .10
.626–.630	10/50 = .20
.630–.634	16/50 = .32
.634–.638	10/50 = .20
.638–.642	6/50 = .12
.642–.646	1/50 = .02

Referring to the above probability distribution, the probability that a measurement is in the .626 to .630 class is .20, or 20 percent. The $P(x \geq .638) = .12 + .02 = .14$, or 14 percent. The $P(.626 \leq x < .638) = .20 + .32 + .20 = .72$, or 72 percent.

The above probability distribution is specific to the set of data from which it was formed. The above probabilities refer specifically to the sample data.

Statisticians assume that once the sample distribution stabilizes, it looks like the population histogram. This means that the population *probability* distribution must look like the sample *probability* distribution. The histogram for the sample is used to find a standard probability distribution with the same shape or pattern, and that pattern is used to calculate probabilities concerning the population. Those probabilities are then used to make predictions or decisions concerning the population. The most often used standard probability distribution is the normal probability distribution. This procedure is illustrated as follows.

1. The data from a sample form a sample histogram. See Figure A.23.

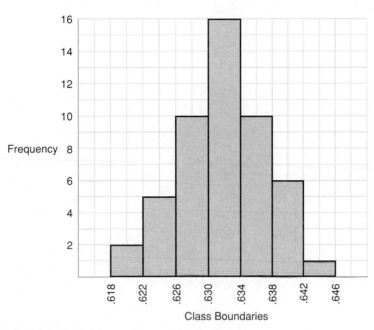

FIGURE A.23
The frequency distribution (histogram).

2. The sample histogram has a probability distribution with the same shape. See Figure A.24 on page 454.
3. The histogram and probability distribution of the population have the same shape as that of the sample. See Figure A.25 (page 454).
4. There is a standard probability distribution that has approximately the same shape as the sample distribution and therefore the same shape as the population distribution. In this case, the normal probability distribution matches. See Figure A.26 on page 455.
5. The normal distribution is used to calculate probabilities for the population. Those probabilities are used in decision making for action on the process.

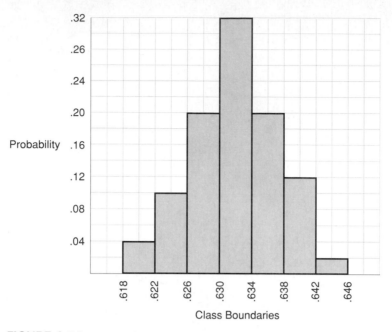

FIGURE A.24
The probability distribution.

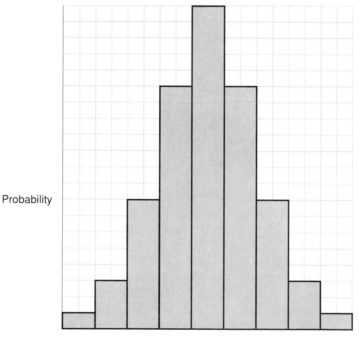

FIGURE A.25
The population probability distribution.

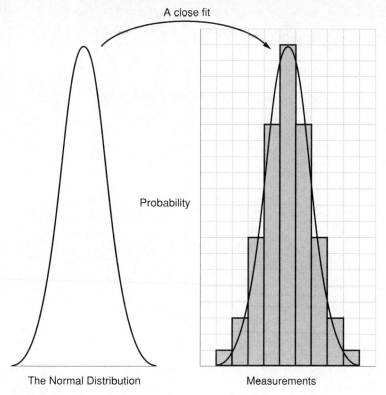

FIGURE A.26
The normal distribution fits the measurement distribution.

A.8   THE NORMAL PROBABILITY DISTRIBUTION

There is no single normal curve, but a whole family of normal curves that are specified by a mean, $\bar{x}$, and a standard deviation, σ.

The mean, $\bar{x}$, is at the center of the curve, and its position is located on the measurement scale. The standard deviation, σ, determines the specific spread of the curve. The normal curve has a single mode at the center and is symmetric about the center value. The ends of the curve flatten out and extend indefinitely, always getting closer to the horizontal axis, but never touching it.

The *area under the curve corresponds to probability*. For example, the area under the curve to the right of a measurement x is equal to the probability that a measurement in the population has a value larger than that x value.

The curve may have different shapes, tall and thin or short and wide (depending on σ), but the total area under the curve is always 1. The normal probability table is used to find specific areas under the normal curve, and those areas translate to probability, or percent of product.

Two related scales are used with the normal curve. The problem is analyzed using a sketch of the curve; the value in the middle, $\bar{x}$; a specific measurement of interest, x; and an area under the curve adjacent to the x value. The x value is transformed to a z value with the equation

$$z = \frac{x - \bar{x}}{\sigma}$$

The resulting z value is actually the distance from the center in standard deviation units. Figure A.27 shows the double scale on the horizontal axis.

FIGURE A.27
Each measurement x matches a z value.

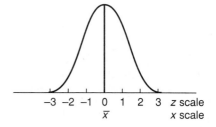

A normal curve table translates the z value to the area of a section under the curve, and *area equals probability*. The calculated z value may be positive or negative, depending on which is larger, x or $\bar{x}$. A positive z value indicates that the measurement is right of the center. A negative z value indicates that the measurement is left of the center. Because the curve is symmetrical, positive and negative z values are associated with the same areas. Most normal tables list only the positive z values, and the user applies the symmetry concepts when finding areas associated with negative z values.

EXAMPLE A.41 A population has a mean, $\bar{x}$, of 44.3 and a standard deviation, σ, of 2.1. What percent of the measurements is larger than 46?

Solution
1. Analyze the problem with a sketch of the normal curve.
   a. Sketch the normal curve. See Figure A.28.
   b. Locate $\bar{x} = 44.3$ at the center.

FIGURE A.28
Analyze the problem with a sketch of the normal curve.

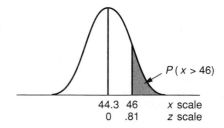

c. Locate $x = 46$ as a point to the right of center.
d. Shade the area of interest. Measurements larger than 46 corresponds to the area to the right of 46.
2. Calculate z.

$$z = \frac{x - \bar{x}}{\sigma}$$

$$= \frac{46 - 44.3}{2.1}$$

$$= \frac{1.7}{2.1}$$

$$= .81$$

3. Find the area in the normal curve table that corresponds to $z = 0.81$.
   a. Use Table 3 in Appendix B.
   b. The drawing at the top of Table 3 shows that the table gives the tail area under the curve.
   c. This is a three-digit table: The first two digits are located in the left column under $|z|$, (0.8), and the third digit corresponds to the appropriate column to the right (column marked 1). According to the table, the area is .2090.
4. Translate the table area to the desired probability. In this case, the table area equals the desired probability (both are tail areas). $P(x > 46)$ is .2090, so 20.9 percent of the measurements are larger than 46.

EXAMPLE A.42   The average measurement is $\bar{x} = .954$, and the standard deviation is $\sigma = .007$. Find the percent of measurements less than .960. Next, find the percent of measurements between .940 and .960.

Solution
1. Sketch the curve. This is shown in Figure A.29.
   a. Locate $\bar{x} = .954$ at the center.
   b. Locate $x = .960$ to the right.
   c. Shade the area of interest: All the area to the left of the .960 corresponds to measurements less than .960.

FIGURE A.29
Analyze Example A.42 with a sketch of the normal curve.

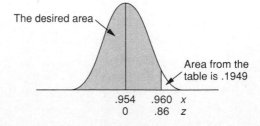

The desired area

Area from the table is .1949

| .954 | .960 | x |
| 0 | .86 | z |

2. Calculate z.

$$z = \frac{x - \bar{x}}{\sigma}$$

$$= \frac{.960 - .954}{.007}$$

$$= \frac{.006}{.007}$$

$$= 0.86$$

3. In Table 3, Appendix B, find 0.8 in the $|z|$ column, then go across to the column marked 6. Read the area. Area = .1949.
4. The area in the table corresponds to the area in the clear section of the sketch (the right tail area). The total area under the curve is 1, so $1 - .1949$ will give the desired area.

$$P(x < .960) = 1 - .1949$$
$$= .8051$$

This means that 80.51 percent of all the measurements in the population are less than .960.

For the second part of the question, find the percent of measurements between .940 and .960.

1. Sketch the curve. The sketch is shown in Figure A.30 (page 459).
   a. Locate $\bar{x} = .954$ at the center.
   b. Locate .960 to the right of center and .940 to the left of center.
   c. Shade the area between .960 and .940. This represents the probability that measurements will be between the two values.
2. Calculate the two z values (one for each measurement). Use subscripts when dealing with more than one measurement. We have calculated x_1, z_1 and Area$_1$ in the first part of the example: $x_1 = .960$, $z_1 = .86$, and Area$_1 = .1949$.

$$z = \frac{x - \bar{x}}{\sigma}$$

$$z_2 = \frac{.940 - .954}{.007}$$

$$= \frac{-.014}{.007}$$

$$= -2$$

The negative z value just means that the x value and the area lie to the left of the center.

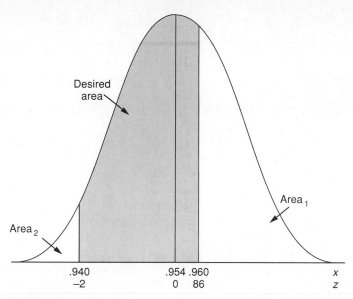

FIGURE A.30
Analyze Example A.42 with a sketch of the normal curve.

3. In Table 3, Appendix B, find 2.0 in the $|z|$ column, go across to the column marked 0, and read the area. Area$_2$ = .0228.
4. The Area$_1$ value is the area of the clear tail section on the right of the sketch in Figure A.30. The Area$_2$ value is the area of the clear section on the left of the sketch. Add the two tail areas .1949 + .0228 = .2177 to get the area under the curve that is *not* wanted.

   The total area under the curve is 1. Subtract the area that is not wanted from 1 to get the desired area (1.0000 − .2177 = .7823). $P(.940 < x < .960)$ = .7823, so 78.23 percent of the measurements in the population are between .940 and .960.

Other Normal Curve Tables

Calculations of probability that involve area under the normal curve rely on a few basic concepts that apply to any normal curve table. Other versions of the normal curve table are occasionally encountered, and the areas have to be juggled around to transform the table area to the shaded area in the sketch.

All the work in this text uses the "tail area" table, Table 3 in Appendix B. Other versions of the normal curve table are available and will be discussed briefly for the sake of completeness. There are three different versions of normal curve tables. Each is identified by a drawing that shows the area given in the table. With all versions, the basic concepts to keep in mind are the following:

- Areas of sections can be added or subtracted.
- The total area under the curve is 1.000.
- The mid-line, at the $\bar{x}$ value, divides the curve in half so that the areas to the right and left of the middle are .500.

The version of normal curve table used in the previous examples gave the area in the "tail."

The drawing in Table 3 of Appendix B indicates that the table values give the area in the tail. A second version measures the area from the center to the calculated z value. The drawing in Table 4 of Appendix B indicates that the area in the table spans from the center to the calculated z value. The third version measures the total area to the left of the calculated z value. The drawing in Table 5 of Appendix B indicates that the total area to the left of the z value is given in the table.

An example to illustrate the use of the three tables follows.

EXAMPLE A.43

A population of measurements has a mean and standard deviation of $\bar{x} = 70$ and $\sigma = 6$. Find the percent of measurements greater than $x = 75$. Then find the percent of measurements between $x = 60$ and $x = 75$.

Solution

The first step, no matter which table is used, is to calculate the z values for each x value. There are two different x values and two different z values to work with, so use subscripts.

$$x_1 = 75 \qquad\qquad x_2 = 60$$

$$z_1 = \frac{x_1 - \bar{x}}{\sigma} \qquad\qquad z_2 = \frac{x_2 - \bar{x}}{\sigma}$$

$$= \frac{75 - 70}{6} \qquad\qquad = \frac{60 - 70}{6}$$

$$= \frac{5}{6} \qquad\qquad = \frac{-10}{6}$$

$$= .83 \qquad\qquad = -1.67$$

The sketch for the first part of Example A.43 is shown in Figure A.31 (page 461). Here $x = 75$, $z = .83$, and the table area, found in Table 3 in Appendix B, is .2033. This means that 20.33 percent of the measurements are greater than 75.

From Table 4 in Appendix B with the same values of x and z, the table area is .2967. The area spans from the center to the z value, as shown in Figure A.32 on page 461. The total area to the right of the center is .50. Notice that it is in two sections: the desired area and the area from the table. Subtraction will provide the desired area.

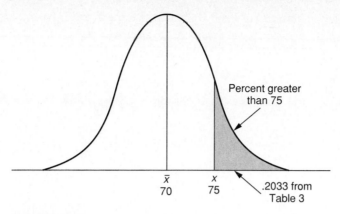

FIGURE A.31
Tail area with Table 3 from Appendix B.

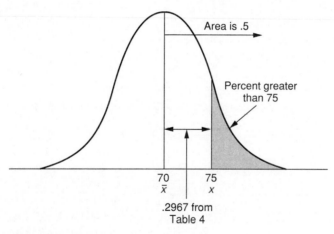

FIGURE A.32
Tail area with Table 4 from Appendix B.

$$
\begin{array}{ll}
.5000 & \text{Area of the right half} \\
-\;.2967 & \text{Table area} \\
\hline
.2033 & \text{Tail area}
\end{array}
$$

The results using Table 4 also indicate that 20.33 percent of the measurements are greater than 75.

Table 5 in Appendix B gives a table area of .7967 for $x = 75$ and $z = .83$. The total area under the curve, illustrated in Figure A.33 (page 462), is partitioned into two sections: the table area and the tail area. Subtraction will give the tail area.

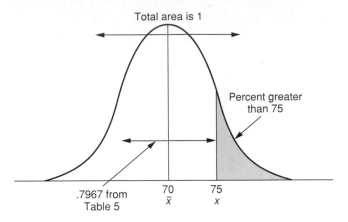

FIGURE A.33
Tail area with Table 5 from Appendix B.

$$
\begin{array}{rl}
1.0000 & \text{Total area under the curve} \\
-\ .7967 & \text{Table area} \\
\hline
.2033 & \text{Tail area}
\end{array}
$$

Again, 20.33 percent of the measurements are greater than 75.

For the second part of the example, find the percent of measurements between 60 and 75.

$$
\begin{array}{ll}
x_1 = 75 & x_2 = 60 \\
z_1 = .83 & z_2 = -1.67
\end{array}
$$

The total area under the curve in Figure A.34 (page 463) is divided into three sections, table area 1, table area 2, and the section in between, which is the desired area. From Table 3 from Appendix B, $Area_1 = .2033$ and $Area_2 = .0475$. Add the two tail areas and subtract the sum from 1.

$$
\begin{array}{rl}
.2033 & \text{Right tail area} \\
+\ .0475 & \text{Left tail area} \\
\hline
.2508 & \text{Tail area sum}
\end{array}
$$

$$
\begin{array}{rl}
1.0000 & \text{Total area under the curve} \\
-\ .2508 & \text{Tail area sum} \\
\hline
.7492 & \text{Area between 60 and 75}
\end{array}
$$

Therefore, 74.92% of the measurements are between 60 and 75.

Table 4 in Appendix B gives a table $area_1$ of .2967 and table $area_2$ of .4525. Both areas are measured from the center: one to the right and the other to the left. The sum of the two areas will give the area between 60 and 75.

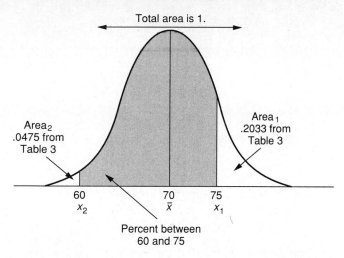

FIGURE A.34
Area between $x_1 = 75$ and $x_2 = 60$ using Table 3 from Appendix B.

$$
\begin{array}{rl}
.2967 & \text{Area from the center to 75} \\
+\ .4525 & \text{Area from the center to 60} \\
\hline
.7492 & \text{Area between 60 and 75}
\end{array}
$$

Again, 74.92 percent of the measurements are between 60 and 75. See Figure A.35.

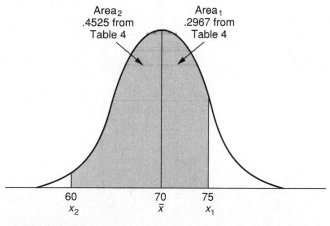

FIGURE A.35
Area between the values using Appendix B, Table 4.

According to Table 5 in Appendix B, table area$_1$ = .7967 and table area$_2$ = .0475. The area between 60 and 75 is overlapped by area 1, as shown in Figure A.36. Subtraction will give the area between these values.

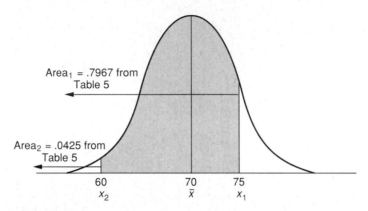

FIGURE A.36
Area between the values of *x* using Table 5 from Appendix B.

$$
\begin{array}{rl}
.7967 & \text{Total area to the left of 75} \\
-\ .0475 & \text{Area to the left of 60} \\
\hline
.7492 & \text{Area between 60 and 75}
\end{array}
$$

74.92 percent of the measurements lie between 60 and 75.

EXERCISES

1. Evaluate

(a) $-12 + 7$

(b) $-8 - 5$

(c) $9 - 17$

(d) $7 - (-11)$

(e) $\dfrac{-32}{4}$

(f) $\sqrt{36}$

(g) $-16 + (-3)$

(h) $-8 - (-6)$

(i) $\sqrt{\dfrac{100}{9}}$

(j) $17 + (-9)$

(k) $-\dfrac{40}{-10}$

(l) $4 + 3 \times 5$

(m) $(-12)(-3)$

(n) $5(-9)$

(o) $(5 + 2 + 3)^2 + \dfrac{20 + 2}{4}$

(p) $-4(5)$

(q) $\dfrac{48}{-6}$

(r) $\sqrt{49 + 9}$

2. Use the given numerical values to evaluate the algebraic expressions.

$$x_1 = 4 \qquad y = 12$$
$$x_2 = 9 \qquad w = 3$$
$$x_3 = 2 \qquad z = 5$$
$$x_4 = 7$$

(a) $\sum x$ (b) $z^2 w$ (c) $\dfrac{y + w}{w}$

(d) wy (e) $4w^2$ (f) $(w + z)^2$

(g) $\sqrt{yw}$ (h) $\sqrt{x_1} \times \sqrt{x_2}$ (i) $3z$

(j) $\dfrac{w^2}{y}$ (k) w^4 (l) $\dfrac{\sqrt{y}}{\sqrt{w}}$

(m) $\sum x^2$ (n) $\left(\sum x\right)^2$ (o) $\sum(x - 2)^2$

3. Use a random number generator on a calculator to plan random sample times for 10 samples that are to be taken during an eight-hour shift that begins at 7:00 A.M..

4. Make a run chart with the following measurements on each of the given charts: 4.21, 4.19, 4.18, 4.26, 4.22, 4.24, 4.29.

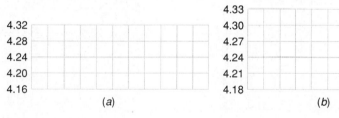

5. (a) Make a histogram for the given data. Find the recommended number of groups from the G chart in Appendix B.

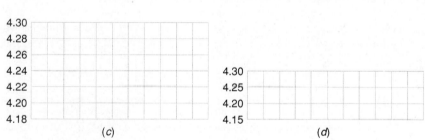

.726	.744	.725	.738	.727	.726
.714	.725	.730	.732	.736	.723
.715	.728	.731	.727	.719	.727
.742	.719	.724	.719	.740	.727
.735	.727	.726	.721	.728	.739

(b) If each column forms a sample of five measurements, find the median for each sample.

(c) What is the mode for all the measurements?

6. Given the x values 12, 8, 11, 15, 9, and 11,

  (a) Calculate the mean using

$$\bar{x} = \frac{\sum x}{n}$$

  (b) Calculate the median.

  (c) Calculate the variance using

$$\sigma^2 = \frac{n \sum x^2 - (\sum x)^2}{n(n-1)}$$

  (d) Calculate the standard deviation using

$$\sigma = \sqrt{\sigma^2}$$

  (e) Check your results by entering data on a statistical calculator. To check σ, press σ_{n-1}. To check σ^2, press σ_{n-1} and then x^2.

7. Given the measurements .812, .824, .817, .820, .815, .813, and .817,

  (a) Code the measurements using the base .810.

  (b) Find the average measurement using the coded values.

  (c) Check your results in part **(b)** by calculating the mean using the measurement values.

8. Samples of size 4 are given.

.314	.312	.316	.317	.313
.318	.315	.315	.314	.315
.312	.314	.315	.316	.315
.315	.314	.316	.314	.312

  (a) Code the measurements using the base .315.

  (b) Find the average measurement using the coded values.

  (c) Check the answer to part **(b)** by averaging the measurements.

  (d) Find the five range values, R, from the coded values and then from the measurements.

  (e) Using

$$\sigma = \frac{\bar{R}}{2.059}$$

find σ from the coded values and then from the measurements.

  (f) Code the measurements using the base .310 and repeat **(b)**, **(d)**, and **(e)** for the new coded values.

9. (a) Make a scattergram from the ordered pairs (T, m).

(120, 2.581)	(118,2.580)	(134, 2.595)
(125, 2.592)	(130,2.594)	(118, 2.578)
(110, 2.575)	(123,2.590)	(132, 2.594)

  (b) Draw the line of best fit.

  (c) What m value corresponds to $T = 115$, according to your line of best fit?

  (d) How would you describe the scattergram: good correlation, poor correlation, or no correlation?

10. Seven percent of a line's output must be reworked, and 2 percent of the output must be scrapped.

(a) If one piece is randomly chosen from the line, what is the probability that it is a good piece?

(b) If one piece is chosen, what is the chance that it must be either scrapped or reworked?

(c) If two pieces are chosen, what is the probability that the first must be reworked and the second is acceptable?

(d) If three pieces are taken from the line, what is the chance of getting one in each category (good, scrap, rework)?

11. Evaluate:

(a) $6!$ (b) $P_{8,3}$ (c) $0!$ (d) $\dfrac{10!}{6!4!}$

(e) $C_{9,4}$ (f) $C_{5,5}$ (g) $\dfrac{12!}{7!}$ (h) $C_{11,3}$ (i) $P_{4,4}$

12. A bin contains 50 good pieces and 10 defective pieces. If a sample of four is taken, what is the probability that three out of the four are good pieces?

13. A line is producing 5 percent defectives. If 10 pieces are randomly chosen with replacement, what is the probability that two are defective? Use the appropriate binomial distribution term.

14. A box contains 30 good parts and 10 bad parts. If a sample of nine parts is taken, find the probability of getting

(a) Nine good parts.

(b) Six good parts and three bad parts.

15. The average measurement on a control chart is $\bar{x} = 3.514$, and the standard deviation of the measurements is $\sigma = .009$.

(a) Find the percent of measurements that are larger than 3.525.

(b) Find the percent of measurements that are less than 3.500.

(c) What percent of the measurements are between 3.510 and 3.520?

B

CHARTS AND TABLES

B.1 FORMULAS AND CONSTANTS FOR CONTROL CHARTS

Average and Range Charts: $\bar{x}$ and R

The sample size, n, is less than or equal to 10; n is usually three to five consecutive pieces.

The $\bar{x}$ chart:

Center line: $\bar{\bar{x}} = \dfrac{\sum \bar{x}}{k}$ for k samples.

Upper control limit: $\text{UCL}_{\bar{x}} = \bar{\bar{x}} + (A_2 \times \bar{R})$

Lower control limit: $\text{LCL}_{\bar{x}} = \bar{\bar{x}} - (A_2 \times \bar{R})$

The R chart:

Center line: $\bar{R} = \dfrac{\sum R}{k}$

Upper control limit: $\text{UCL}_R = D_4 \times \bar{R}$

Lower control limit: $\text{LCL}_R = D_3 \times \bar{R}$

The standard deviation for all measurements: $\sigma = \dfrac{\bar{R}}{d_2}$

TABLE 1.1
Constants for an $\overline{x}$ and R chart

Sample size n	A_2	D_3	D_4	d_2
2	1.880	0	3.267	1.128
3	1.023	0	2.574	1.693
4	0.729	0	2.282	2.059
5	0.577	0	2.114	2.326
6	0.483	0	2.004	2.536
7	0.419	0.076	1.924	2.704
8	0.373	0.136	1.864	2.847
9	0.337	0.184	1.816	2.970
10	0.308	0.223	1.777	3.078

Median and Range Charts: $\tilde{x}$ and R

The sample size, n is most often an odd number less than 10, usually three or five consecutive pieces.

The $\tilde{x}$ chart:

Center line: $\overline{\overline{x}} = \dfrac{\sum \tilde{x}}{k}$ for k samples

Upper control limit: $\text{UCL}_{\tilde{x}} = \overline{\overline{x}} + (\tilde{A}_2 \times \overline{R})$

Lower control limit: $\text{LCL}_{\tilde{x}} = \overline{\overline{x}} - (\tilde{A}_2 \times \overline{R})$

The R chart:

Center line: $\overline{R} = \dfrac{\sum R}{k}$

Upper control limit: $\text{UCL}_R = D_4 \times \overline{R}$

Lower control limit: $\text{LCL}_R = D_3 \times \overline{R}$

The standard deviation for all measurements: $\sigma = \dfrac{\overline{R}}{d_2}$

TABLE 1.2
Constants for an $\tilde{x}$ and R chart

Sample size n	$\tilde{A}_2$	D_3	D_4	d_2
3	1.187	0	2.574	1.693
5	0.691	0	2.114	2.326
7	0.509	0.076	1.924	2.704
9	0.412	0.184	1.816	2.970

Average and Standard Deviation: $\bar{x}$ and s

The sample size, n, is usually three or more.

The $\bar{x}$ chart:

Center line: $\bar{\bar{x}} = \dfrac{\sum \bar{x}}{k}$ for k samples

Upper control limit: $\text{UCL}_{\bar{x}} = \bar{\bar{x}} + (A_3 \times \bar{s})$

Lower control limit: $\text{LCL}_{\bar{x}} = \bar{\bar{x}} - (A_3 \times \bar{s})$

The s chart:

Center line: $\bar{s} = \dfrac{\sum s}{k}$

Upper control limit: $\text{UCL}_s = B_4 \times \bar{s}$

Lower control limit: $\text{LCL}_s = B_3 \times \bar{s}$

The standard deviation for all measurements: $\sigma = \dfrac{\bar{s}}{C_4}$

TABLE 1.3
Constants for an $\bar{x}$ and s chart

Sample size n	A_3	B_3	B_4	C_4
2	2.659	0	3.267	.7979
3	1.954	0	2.568	.8862
4	1.628	0	2.266	.9213
5	1.427	0	2.089	.9400
6	1.287	0.030	1.970	.9515
7	1.182	0.118	1.882	.9594
8	1.099	0.185	1.815	.9650
9	1.032	0.239	1.761	.9693
10	0.975	0.284	1.716	.9727

Individual Measurement and Moving Range: x and MR

Chart consecutive pieces.

Center line: $\bar{x} = \dfrac{\sum x}{N}$ for N consecutive pieces

Upper control limit: $\text{UCL}_x = \bar{x} + 2.659\overline{MR}$

Lower control limit: $\text{LCL}_x = \bar{x} - 2.659\overline{MR}$

$$MR = |x_{N-1} - X_N|$$

$$\overline{MR} = \frac{\sum MR}{N - 1}$$

Attributes Charts

A p chart works for large samples, $n > 20$. The number of nonconforming pieces, np, should be approximately 5.

$$p = \frac{np}{n} = \frac{\text{number nonconforming}}{\text{total number in sample}}$$

Center line: $\bar{p} = \dfrac{\sum np}{\sum n}$.

Upper control limit: $UCL_p = \bar{p} + 3 \times \sqrt{\dfrac{\bar{p}(1 - \bar{p})}{n}}$

Lower control limit: $LCL_p = \bar{p} - 3 \times \sqrt{\dfrac{\bar{p}(1 - \bar{p})}{n}}$

When sample sizes differ: $\bar{n} = \dfrac{\sum n}{k}$ for k samples

Use an np chart: with a constant sample size of 20 or more when np is approximately 5.

Center line: $\overline{np} = \dfrac{\sum np}{k}$ for k samples

Upper control limit: $UCL_{np} = \overline{np} + 3 \times \sqrt{\overline{np}(1 - \bar{p})}$

Lower control limit: $LCL_{np} = \overline{np} - 3 \times \sqrt{\overline{np}(1 - \bar{p})}$

For a c chart, the inspection unit should be large enough that $\bar{c} \geq 5$ where c is the number of non-conformities per inspection unit. Inspection units should be of constant size.

Center line: $\bar{c} = \dfrac{\sum c}{k}$ for k units

Upper control limit: $UCL_c = \bar{c} + 3 \times \sqrt{\bar{c}}$

Lower control limit: $LCL_c = \bar{c} - 3 \times \sqrt{\bar{c}}$

With a u chart, n should be large enough that $\bar{u} \geq 5$ where

$$u = \frac{c}{n} = \frac{\text{number of nonconformities}}{\text{sample size}}$$

Use with a sample size of $n > 20$; n may vary.

Center line: $\bar{u} = \dfrac{\sum c}{\sum n}$

Upper control limit: $\text{UCL}_u = \bar{u} + 3 \times \sqrt{\dfrac{\bar{u}}{\bar{n}}}$ $\quad \bar{n} = $ average sample size

Lower control limit: $\text{LCL}_u = \bar{u} - 3 \times \sqrt{\dfrac{\bar{u}}{\bar{n}}}$

B.2 THE _G_ CHART

TABLE 2
The _G_ chart

Number of Measurements	Recommended Number of Groups
10	4
20	5
30	6
40	7
50	8
70	9
100	10
130	11
180	12
230	13
300	14
350	15
430	16
520	17
640	18
750	19
900	20

For any other number of measurements, choose the closest table value and use the corresponding recommended number of groups.

B.3 THE NORMAL DISTRIBUTION TABLE (TAIL AREA)

TABLE 3
The normal distribution table

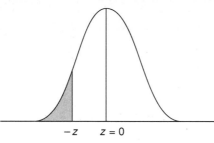

A negative z gives the left tail area.
Area = Probability that a measurement is less than x.

A positive z gives the right tail area.
Area = Probability that a measurement is greater than x.

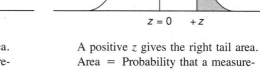

$$z = \frac{x - \bar{\bar{x}}}{\sigma}$$

$|z|$	0	1	2	3	4	5	6	7	8	9
0.0	.5000	.4960	.4920	.4880	.4840	.4801	.4761	.4721	.4681	.4641
0.1	.4602	.4562	.4522	.4483	.4443	.4404	.4364	.4325	.4286	.4247
0.2	.4207	.4168	.4129	.4090	.4052	.4013	.3974	.3936	.3897	.3859
0.3	.3821	.3783	.3745	.3707	.3669	.3632	.3594	.3557	.3520	.3483
0.4	.3446	.3409	.3372	.3336	.3300	.3264	.3228	.3192	.3156	.3121
0.5	.3085	.3050	.3015	.2981	.2946	.2912	.2877	.2843	.2810	.2776
0.6	.2743	.2709	.2676	.2643	.2611	.2578	.2546	.2514	.2483	.2451
0.7	.2420	.2389	.2358	.2327	.2297	.2266	.2236	.2206	.2177	.2148
0.8	.2119	.2090	.2061	.2033	.2005	.1977	.1949	.1922	.1894	.1867
0.9	.1841	.1814	.1788	.1762	.1736	.1711	.1685	.1660	.1635	.1611
1.0	.1587	.1562	.1539	.1515	.1492	.1469	.1446	.1423	.1401	.1379
1.1	.1357	.1335	.1314	.1292	.1271	.1251	.1230	.1210	.1190	.1170
1.2	.1151	.1131	.1112	.1093	.1075	.1056	.1038	.1020	.1003	.0985
1.3	.0968	.0951	.0934	.0918	.0901	.0885	.0869	.0853	.0838	.0823
1.4	.0808	.0793	.0778	.0764	.0749	.0735	.0721	.0708	.0694	.0681
1.5	.0668	.0655	.0643	.0630	.0618	.0606	.0594	.0582	.0571	.0559
1.6	.0548	.0537	.0526	.0516	.0505	.0495	.0485	.0475	.0465	.0455
1.7	.0446	.0436	.0427	.0418	.0409	.0401	.0392	.0384	.0375	.0367
1.8	.0359	.0351	.0344	.0336	.0329	.0322	.0314	.0307	.0301	.0294
1.9	.0287	.0281	.0274	.0268	.0262	.0256	.0250	.0244	.0239	.0233
2.0	.0228	.0222	.0217	.0212	.0207	.0202	.0197	.0192	.0188	.0183
2.1	.0179	.0174	.0170	.0166	.0162	.0158	.0154	.0150	.0146	.0143
2.2	.0139	.0136	.0132	.0129	.0125	.0122	.0119	.0116	.0113	.0110
2.3	.0107	.0104	.0102	.0099	.0096	.0094	.0091	.0089	.0087	.0084
2.4	.0082	.0080	.0078	.0075	.0073	.0071	.0069	.0068	.0066	.0064

TABLE 3 *(continued)*

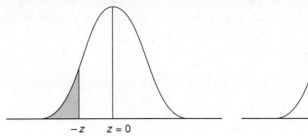

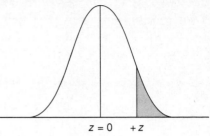

A negative z gives the left tail area. Area = Probability that a measurement is less than x.

A positive z gives the right tail area. Area = Probability that a measurement is greater than x.

$$z = \frac{x - \bar{\bar{x}}}{\sigma}$$

$|z|$	0	1	2	3	4	5	6	7	8	9
2.5	.0062	.0060	.0059	.0057	.0055	.0054	.0052	.0051	.0049	.0048
2.6	.0047	.0045	.0044	.0043	.0041	.0040	.0039	.0038	.0037	.0036
2.7	.0035	.0034	.0033	.0032	.0031	.0030	.0029	.0028	.0027	.0026
2.8	.0026	.0025	.0024	.0023	.0023	.0022	.0021	.0021	.0020	.0019
2.9	.0019	.0018	.0018	.0017	.0016	.0016	.0015	.0015	.0014	.0014
3.0	.00135	.00131	.00126	.00122	.00118	.00114	.00111	.00107	.00104	.00100
3.1	.00097	.00094	.00090	.00087	.00084	.00082	.00079	.00076	.00074	.00071
3.2	.00069	.00066	.00064	.00062	.00060	.00058	.00056	.00054	.00052	.00050
3.3	.00048	.00047	.00045	.00043	.00042	.00040	.00039	.00038	.00036	.00035
3.4	.00034	.00032	.00031	.00030	.00029	.00028	.00027	.00026	.00025	.00024
3.5	.00023	.00022	.00022	.00021	.00020	.00019	.00019	.00018	.00017	.00017
3.6	.00016	.00015	.00015	.00014	.00014	.00013	.00013	.00012	.00012	.00011
3.7	.00011	.00010	.00010	.00010	.00009	.00009	.00008	.00008	.00008	.00008
3.8	.00007	.00007	.00007	.00006	.00006	.00006	.00006	.00005	.00005	.00005
3.9	.00005	.00005	.00004	.00004	.00004	.00004	.00004	.00004	.00003	.00003
4.0	.00003									

B.4 THE NORMAL DISTRIBUTION TABLE (CENTER AREA)

TABLE 4
Normal probability distribution: area from the center

$|z|$	0	1	2	3	4	5	6	7	8	9
0.0	.0000	.0040	.0080	.0120	.0150	.0199	.0239	.0279	.0319	.0357
0.1	.0398	.0439	.0479	.0519	.0558	.0598	.0638	.0678	.0718	.0758
0.2	.0793	.0832	.0871	.0910	.0948	.0987	.1026	.1064	.1103	.1141
0.3	.1179	.1217	.1255	.1293	.1331	.1368	.1406	.1443	.1480	.1517
0.4	.1554	.1591	.1628	.1664	.1700	.1736	.1772	.1808	.1844	.1879
0.5	.1915	.1950	.1985	.2019	.2054	.2088	.2123	.2157	.2190	.2224
0.6	.2258	.2291	.2324	.2357	.2389	.2422	.2454	.2486	.2518	.2549
0.7	.2580	.2612	.2642	.2673	.2704	.2734	.2764	.2794	.2823	.2852
0.8	.2881	.2910	.2939	.2967	.2996	.3023	.3051	.3079	.3106	.3133
0.9	.3159	.3186	.3212	.3238	.3264	.3289	.3315	.3340	.3365	.3389
1.0	.3413	.3438	.3461	.3485	.3508	.3531	.3554	.3577	.3599	.3621
1.1	.3643	.3665	.3686	.3708	.3729	.3749	.3770	.3790	.3810	.3830
1.2	.3849	.3869	.3888	.3907	.3925	.3944	.3962	.3980	.3997	.4015
1.3	.4032	.4049	.4066	.4082	.4099	.4115	.4131	.4147	.4162	.4177
1.4	.4192	.4207	.4222	.4236	.4251	.4265	.4279	.4292	.4306	.4319
1.5	.4332	.4345	.4357	.4370	.4382	.4394	.4406	.4418	.4430	.4441
1.6	.4452	.4463	.4474	.4485	.4495	.4505	.4515	.4525	.4535	.4545
1.7	.4554	.4564	.4573	.4582	.4591	.4599	.4608	.4616	.4625	.4633
1.8	.4641	.4649	.4656	.4664	.4671	.4678	.4686	.4693	.4700	.4706
1.9	.4713	.4719	.4726	.4732	.4738	.4744	.4750	.4756	.4762	.4767
2.0	.4773	.4778	.4783	.4788	.4793	.4798	.4803	.4808	.4812	.4817
2.1	.4821	.4826	.4830	.4834	.4838	.4842	.4846	.4850	.4854	.4857
2.2	.4861	.4865	.4868	.4871	.4875	.4878	.4881	.4884	.4887	.4890
2.3	.4893	.4896	.4898	.4901	.4904	.4906	.4909	.4911	.4913	.4916
2.4	.4918	.4920	.4922	.4925	.4927	.4929	.4931	.4932	.4934	.4936
2.5	.4938	.4940	.4941	.4943	.4945	.4946	.4948	.4949	.4951	.4952
2.6	.4953	.4955	.4956	.4957	.4959	.4960	.4961	.4962	.4963	.4964
2.7	.4965	.4966	.4967	.4968	.4969	.4970	.4971	.4972	.4973	.4974
2.8	.4974	.4975	.4976	.4977	.4977	.4978	.4979	.4980	.4980	.4981
2.9	.4981	.4982	.4983	.4983	.4984	.4984	.4985	.4985	.4986	.4986

TABLE 4 *(continued)*

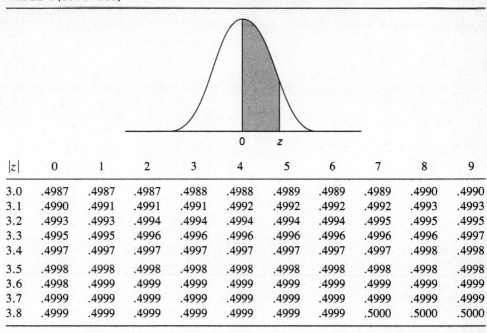

$|z|$	0	1	2	3	4	5	6	7	8	9
3.0	.4987	.4987	.4987	.4988	.4988	.4989	.4989	.4989	.4990	.4990
3.1	.4990	.4991	.4991	.4991	.4992	.4992	.4992	.4992	.4993	.4993
3.2	.4993	.4993	.4994	.4994	.4994	.4994	.4994	.4995	.4995	.4995
3.3	.4995	.4995	.4996	.4996	.4996	.4996	.4996	.4996	.4996	.4997
3.4	.4997	.4997	.4997	.4997	.4997	.4997	.4997	.4997	.4998	.4998
3.5	.4998	.4998	.4998	.4998	.4998	.4998	.4998	.4998	.4998	.4998
3.6	.4998	.4999	.4999	.4999	.4999	.4999	.4999	.4999	.4999	.4999
3.7	.4999	.4999	.4999	.4999	.4999	.4999	.4999	.4999	.4999	.4999
3.8	.4999	.4999	.4999	.4999	.4999	.4999	.4999	.5000	.5000	.5000

B.5 THE NORMAL DISTRIBUTION TABLE (LEFT AREA)

TABLE 5
Normal probability distribution: total area to the left

$|z|$	0	1	2	3	4	5	6	7	8	9
0.0	.5000	.5040	.5080	.5120	.5150	.5199	.5239	.5279	.5319	.5357
0.1	.5398	.5439	.5479	.5519	.5558	.5598	.5638	.5678	.5718	.5758
0.2	.5793	.5832	.5871	.5910	.5948	.5987	.6026	.6064	.6103	.6141
0.3	.6179	.6217	.6255	.6293	.6331	.6368	.6406	.6443	.6480	.6517
0.4	.6554	.6591	.6628	.6664	.6700	.6736	.6772	.6808	.6844	.6879
0.5	.6915	.6950	.6985	.7019	.7054	.7088	.7123	.7157	.7190	.7224
0.6	.7258	.7291	.7324	.7357	.7389	.7422	.7454	.7486	.7518	.7549
0.7	.7580	.7612	.7642	.7673	.7704	.7734	.7764	.7794	.7823	.7852
0.8	.7881	.7910	.7939	.7967	.7996	.8023	.8051	.8079	.8106	.8133
0.9	.8159	.8186	.8212	.8238	.8264	.8289	.8315	.8340	.8365	.8389
1.0	.8413	.8438	.8461	.8485	.8508	.8531	.8554	.8577	.8599	.8621
1.1	.8643	.8665	.8686	.8708	.8729	.8749	.8770	.8790	.8810	.8830
1.2	.8849	.8869	.8888	.8907	.8925	.8944	.8962	.8980	.8997	.9015
1.3	.9032	.9049	.9066	.9082	.9099	.9155	.9131	.9147	.9162	.9177
1.4	.9192	.9207	.9222	.9236	.9251	.9265	.9279	.9292	.9306	.9319
1.5	.9332	.9345	.9357	.9370	.9382	.9394	.9406	.9418	.9430	.9441
1.6	.9452	.9463	.9474	.9485	.9495	.9505	.9515	.9525	.9535	.9545
1.7	.9554	.9564	.9573	.9582	.9591	.9599	.9608	.9616	.9625	.9633
1.8	.9641	.9649	.9656	.9664	.9671	.9678	.9686	.9693	.9700	.9706
1.9	.9713	.9719	.9726	.9732	.9738	.9744	.9750	.9756	.9762	.9767
2.0	.9773	.9778	.9783	.9788	.9793	.9798	.9803	.9808	.9812	.9817
2.1	.9821	.9826	.9830	.9834	.9838	.9842	.9846	.9850	.9854	.9857
2.2	.9861	.9865	.9868	.9871	.9875	.9878	.9881	.9884	.9887	.9890
2.3	.9893	.9896	.9898	.9901	.9904	.9906	.9909	.9911	.9913	.9916
2.4	.9918	.9920	.9922	.9925	.9927	.9929	.9931	.9932	.9934	.9936
2.5	.9938	.9940	.9941	.9943	.9945	.9946	.9948	.9949	.9951	.9952
2.6	.9953	.9955	.9956	.9957	.9959	.9960	.9961	.9962	.9963	.9964
2.7	.9965	.9966	.9967	.9968	.9969	.9970	.9971	.9972	.9973	.9974
2.8	.9974	.9975	.9976	.9977	.9977	.9978	.9979	.9980	.9980	.9981
2.9	.9981	.9982	.9983	.9983	.9984	.9984	.9985	.9985	.9986	.9986

TABLE 5 *(continued)*

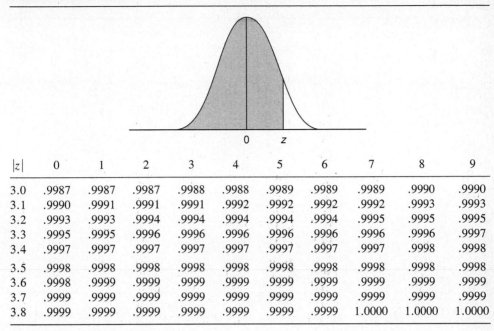

$|z|$	0	1	2	3	4	5	6	7	8	9
3.0	.9987	.9987	.9987	.9988	.9988	.9989	.9989	.9989	.9990	.9990
3.1	.9990	.9991	.9991	.9991	.9992	.9992	.9992	.9992	.9993	.9993
3.2	.9993	.9993	.9994	.9994	.9994	.9994	.9994	.9995	.9995	.9995
3.3	.9995	.9995	.9996	.9996	.9996	.9996	.9996	.9996	.9996	.9997
3.4	.9997	.9997	.9997	.9997	.9997	.9997	.9997	.9997	.9998	.9998
3.5	.9998	.9998	.9998	.9998	.9998	.9998	.9998	.9998	.9998	.9998
3.6	.9998	.9999	.9999	.9999	.9999	.9999	.9999	.9999	.9999	.9999
3.7	.9999	.9999	.9999	.9999	.9999	.9999	.9999	.9999	.9999	.9999
3.8	.9999	.9999	.9999	.9999	.9999	.9999	.9999	1.0000	1.0000	1.0000

B.6 PROCESS CAPABILITY

$$PCR = \frac{6\sigma}{\text{Tolerance}}$$

$$Cpk = \frac{|\text{ Nearest specification limit} - \bar{x}|}{3\sigma}$$

TABLE 6
The process capability grid

Process Classification	Process Capability	Control Chart
A	$PCR \leq .5$ $Cpk \geq 2$	Recommended
B	$.51 \leq PCR \leq .7$ $1.42 \leq Cpk \leq 1.99$	Recommended
C	$.71 \leq PCR \leq .9$ $1.11 \leq Cpk \leq 1.41$	Required
D	$PCR \geq .91$ $Cpk \leq 1.1$	Required

C

GLOSSARY OF SYMBOLS

$A_2, \tilde{A}_2$	Control chart factors
AOQ	Average outgoing quality
AOQL	Average outgoing quality limit
AQL	Acceptable quality level
A.V.	Appraiser variation (reproducibility)
c	The number of defects for control charting; the acceptance number in sampling
$\overline{c}$	The average number of defects
$C_{n,r}$	Combinations of n objects using r of them
Cpk	A process capability measure
d_2, D_3, D_4	Control chart factors
E.V.	Equipment variation (reproducibility)
f	frequency
G chart	A chart for determining the optimum group size for frequency distributions or histograms
LCL	Lower control limit
LSL	Lower specification limit
MR	Moving range
$\overline{MR}$	The average moving range value
n	Sample size
N	Lot size; the number of values in a population
np	The number of defective pieces

OC	Operating characteristic
p	The proportion of defective items
$\bar{p}$	The average proportion of defective items
$100\,p$	The percent of defective items
PCR	A process capability measure
$P_{n,r}$	The permutation of n objects using r of them
$P(A)$	The probability that event A occurs
R	Range
$\bar{R}$	Average range
R & R	Repeatability and reproducibility in gauge variation
s	Sample standard deviation
s^2	Sample variance
UCL	Upper control limit
USL	Upper specification limit
u	The average number of defects per unit in a sample
$\bar{u}$	The average of the u values
x	A measurement value
$\bar{x}$	The average measurement
$\bar{\bar{x}}$	The average of the $\bar{x}$'s, or the grand average
$\tilde{x}$	The median
$\bar{\tilde{x}}$	The average of the medians
z	The scale value for the normal curve
$\sum$	The Greek letter sigma (upper case), whch indicates "the sum of." $\sum x$ is the sum of the x values
σ	The Greek letter sigma (lower case), which is the symbol for the standard deviation of a population of measurements
σ_{n-1}	The calculator key for s
σ^2	The variance of a population of values

INDEX